The Pyramid and the Common

The Pyramid and the Common

Social Reproduction, Value Praxis, and Transformation

Massimo De Angelis

BLOOMSBURY ACADEMIC
LONDON • NEW YORK • OXFORD • NEW DELHI • SYDNEY

BLOOMSBURY ACADEMIC
Bloomsbury Publishing Plc, 50 Bedford Square, London, WC1B 3DP, UK
Bloomsbury Publishing Inc, 1359 Broadway, New York, NY 10018, USA
Bloomsbury Publishing Ireland, 29 Earlsfort Terrace, Dublin 2, D02 AY28, Ireland

BLOOMSBURY, BLOOMSBURY ACADEMIC and the Diana logo are trademarks of Bloomsbury Publishing Plc

First published in Great Britain 2026

Cover design by Francis Kenney

A catalogue record for this book is available from the British Library.

Library of Congress Cataloging-in-Publication Data available

ISBN: HB: 978-1-3505-4143-6
PB: 978-1-3505-4142-9
ePDF: 978-1-3505-4145-0
eBook: 978-1-3505-4144-3

Series: In Common

Typeset by Amnet

For product safety related questions contact productsafety@bloomsbury.com.

To find out more about our authors and books visit www.bloomsbury.com and sign up for our newsletters.

The book is dedicated to Leonardo and Nicola, my two sons, with much love.

*You were always in my thoughts while I was writing it—even if, at times,
the fridge was empty because I couldn't stop to go shopping.*

*You already sense it—that something in the world is off-beat.
A feeling in the body: a tension, a dissonance, a rhythm that doesn't quite hold.
And you are already walking toward a world still in formation.*

*There will be voices promising quick answers, sharp borders, certain maps.
But between now and the not-yet, between our days together and
the life you will shape, there is you—sometimes following
what is given, sometimes staying with what calls.*

*May you be part of a social force that, through care, joy, and love,
helps shape the world anew.*

Contents

Figures

Acknowledgments

The arguments of this book come from years of study and reflection, abrupt moments of insight, and downward falls into depressive feelings of hopelessness and from self-disciplined recursions that shaped the material and gave it a coherent form, in what may generally be conceived as a kind of self-imposed solitary confinement. Yet one must do what one must do, and in the end, even in the solitude of writing, an author is never alone. Not only does one share time with the ancient authors of many books. The questions I carried in my mind and the attitudes I took to address them are echoes of half a century of unfinished conversations with many people from many walks of life, who, like me, do not feel this is the best of all possible worlds. And given my age, an increasing number of these coauthors are far gone into another dimension. Yet, without their passions and insights, I would not be here writing this introduction, this book. So it is not only a performative gesture but a deeply felt resonance with Indigenous sensibilities that leads me to acknowledge the multitude of ancestors whose voices have left a trace through me, as through everybody, if one cares to pause and notice.

But an author has a body, and the body needs to be nourished not only with food but with warmth, love, and presence—a relational nourishment that we always seek, despite capitalism. And so I must thank Dagmar Diesner, my *compagna* and wife, and our two sons, Leonardo and Nicola, for their loving efforts to attune to my idiosyncrasies. Dagmar has also read large portions of the book, providing many encouraging comments and clearly marking where I was failing to make sense.

Maurizio Pentenero held the secret keys to Romano Alquati's most impenetrable texts. Beyond offering generous feedback on an earlier version of Chapter 9, Maurizio helped me navigate the dense jungle of Alquati's writings from the 1980s and 1990s and kindly shared access to crucial out-of-print material. I owe him not only insights but also orientation. Federico Battistutta and Sandro Mezzadra gave important feedback on early drafts of major sections of the book, and Emanuele Leonardi offered encouraging comments on the final version of the Gaia chapter. To all three, my sincere thanks—for the critiques, the nudges, and the comradeship.

As I was writing the numerous drafts of this book, I had several opportunities to test some of the material in public—particularly around the architecture of the pyramid and the thorny question of organization. On these occasions, I often discovered just how much work was still needed to make the pyramid not only analytically sound but also intelligible. Critical, encouraging, and even silent responses (sometimes the most honest kind!) helped me recalibrate and keep going. I want to send a hug to David Harvie, Amber Huff, Nic Beuret, and all the other wonderful people I met at the taster weekend of the "Master in Commons Administration" at the University of Essex in June 2022. The warm response I received from them after presenting an awkward drawing heartened me to persevere.

Thanks to the organizers and participants of the Commoning Beyond Growth seminar in Nottingham (June 2024), especially Andreas Wittel, for the warm welcome and engaged discussion. I also thank Stevphen Shukaitis and his merry crew at the Centre for Commons Organising, Values, Equalities and Resilience at the University of Essex for inviting me to present an early version of the pyramid back in February 2023.

There is material that didn't make it into this already too-long book, but that nonetheless shaped my thinking and continues to do so. One such thread is the question of transversal organization on the terrain of social reproduction, only briefly touched on here but, for a while, deeply resonant with my reading of Stafford Beer and the broader legacy of cybernetic thinking. A word of thanks, therefore, goes to Stavros Stavrides, who gave me the opportunity to present and receive feedback on an early formulation of the cybernetics of organization for social reproduction—in the context of the pyramid—during the two-day symposium on Spatial Justice and Urban Commons: Contemporary Policy Dilemmas and Potentialities for Praxis in Athens (April 2023). I'm also grateful to Angela Espinosa and Jon Walker for clarifying aspects of the cybernetic tradition and for their generous engagement with my earlier work—both in private conversations and during a Metaphorum seminar, where they kindly invited me to present. Their contributions helped deepen my reflection on how systemic design might meet lived struggle.

Finally, my gratitude goes to Katja Schubel, David Bollier, and all the participants in the Infrastructure of Commoning workshop at the New Institute in Hamburg (May 2024), where I had the chance to catch up and engage with the kaleidoscope of commoning approaches.

Introduction

Immanence and ambivalence

We live in an epoch and coproduce a world. The epoch does not bode well. Those who can read trend graphs see this clearly. Those who cannot read them, however, feel that the seasons are no longer the same. The stark images of violence, death, and destruction flow from mobile phones to the rhythm of our thumbs, creeping into the interstices of everyday life consumed by coproducing a world that relentlessly accelerates. Even the opposable thumb, the enabling tool of human creative manipulation of objects, now becomes a tool for getting used to the wickedness of the world. The rich get richer and richer. The poor get poorer and poorer. Those in the middle gasp to keep themselves there: The rat race never seems fast enough. We feel mesmerized and helpless before the spectacle of chaos, war, and ecological collapse, while we continue to coproduce the world in the same way out of necessity or habit. "It's capitalism, baby!" Fine, we agree. But what are we to make of the rationalization of this refrain? Should we take it as cynical resignation? Ideological cover? Affective coping? Ironic distance? Or as critical diagnosis? Each mode carries a different posture toward the world and our role in coproducing it. This book does not rest in resignation, nor does it indulge in distant critique. It takes the rationalization seriously enough to unpack it, trace its systemic roots, and ask what it would mean to engage not only analytically but also existentially and politically with its implications.

This book develops a systemic critique of capitalism as a hierarchical organization of social cooperation, driven by the reproduction of capital and structured through a pyramid of command and domination that permeates every aspect of life—from the intimate rhythms of the everyday to planetary governance. Rather than viewing the common merely as a resource or space outside capital, the book conceptualizes it as both the ontological condition of social life and the terrain of its possible transformation. Through an exploration of value praxis, autopoiesis, and the interplay between different levels of social cooperation, the book traces how the capitalist system captures cooperation while also generating the conditions for its recomposition. Engaging with cybernetics, political economy, and emancipatory movements, the book argues for a politics of commoning grounded in care, reciprocity, and the poiesis of freedom.

A method compatible with this approach must be both analytical and enactmental, able to traverse systemic layers without flattening difference, and sensitive to the rhythms through which life reproduces itself, even amid domination. This book starts with contemporary capitalism as the common condition of our coproducing the world and ends with the making and acting in common that produces another world out of this world. In between are many distinctions and disquisitions that, at least in their intentions, seek to recognize the complexity of the conditions within which we seem to be trapped, without, however, abandoning the search for a way out—or, rather, through the conviction that it is only through the recognition of this complexity that we can hope to find our way out.

The world we inhabit—the order of things within which our lives unfold and are reproduced—is called capitalism. The concern that underlies this book is disarmingly simple and perhaps even naive to those disenchanted with the present: How do we change the world? How do we lift ourselves from a common condition that binds us into a social cooperation which, in increasingly unequal and evident ways, exhausts, stresses, humiliates, destroys, kills, pollutes, seduces with false myths, and reproduces injustice, domination, and ecological catastrophe? How do we act in the face of a system that manufactures endless "blah blah blah"—to borrow Greta Thunberg's apt phrase—from ever more powerful governments and economic-financial complexes that repaint their facades while leaving the foundations intact? And above all, how do we transform a world that lives through us—through our affective attachments, our daily routines, our participation in its flows of goods, desires, promises, and its commodified imaginations—when adapting to its logics is the price of survival and when the cost of such adaptation is increasingly paid in neurosis, burnout, and collective psychosis?

I do not claim—nor could I—to offer practical answers. What I can do is name the deeper questions that have animated this research: questions born of a spirit of defection from this world yet tempered by the recognition of my daily entanglement in it. Like the vast majority, I am an ambivalent being. Still, I am convinced that something other-than-capitalism endures in the world—within the sensibilities, consciences, and practices of those who coproduce it. But this other-than-capitalism is so deeply entangled with capitalist forms that it often becomes difficult to draw clear distinctions, locate footholds, or discern the fulcrums upon which we might lean and gain leverage. We live on bread and roses, and both are produced through a social cooperation that weaves our lives into complex interdependencies. From this condition arose the need for a cartographic method—a way to develop tools of orientation from within the world, a map that renders visible the systemic knots in which we are caught, while offering a broad panorama, a perspectival horizon from which to recover a sense of direction for coproducing the world otherwise.

Drawing a map of this world in order to navigate it—and ultimately to change it—has been my aim. This book is the map I have drawn, inspired by tools lent to me by thinkers of many kinds: social critics, feminists, ecologists, cyberneticians, sociologists, economists, biologists, anthropologists, philosophers, psychologists, saints, musicians, friends, neighbors, natives, revolutionaries, and poets. They came to my aid at different points in my intellectual journey, often appearing just when needed—to answer a question, to offer a nuance, or to open a new vista. The map that follows is thus a work of bricolage, stitched together across domains, disciplines, and lived concerns. I do not invoke it as a badge of methodological legitimacy but to underline its openness: This is a map drawn from a particular history of encounters, questions, intuitions, and omissions. Some elements had to be left out—by necessity, by chance, or by choice. Yet the bricolage is not arbitrary. Its construction has been animated by a processual tension: to articulate the fragments in ways that return a sense of orientation, a provisional coherence amid the diversity of our predicaments. In this sense, the map may itself become a building block for someone else's bricolage. But as we all know, a map is not the territory. And a territory as entangled and dynamic as the world we coproduce—and need to transform—cannot be mapped by a single cartographer. It requires a multitude.

The map I offer in this book bears, I believe, an original and necessary feature—especially if we begin from the naive but vital question of how to change the world. It attempts to hold together dimensions that are too often separated in contemporary theorizations of capitalism. First, the real as systemic power: a totalizing machinery that, as Marx and Foucault show in different ways, orders, excludes, subsumes, disciplines, exploits, controls, and encompasses. Second, the real as a site of rupture and constitution: a field of radical imagination—à la Castoriadis—or desiring-production, as Deleuze and Guattari would say, where alternative forms of social cooperation emerge and overflow capture.

To these, I add a third concern: the relation between the totality of the system—capitalism as a global, recursive structure—and the singularities, both individual and collective, that strain toward the not-yet. Here, systems theory and cybernetics (Bateson, Maturana, and Varela) offer tools to think through the co-emergence of parts and wholes, the tension between autonomy and constraint, and the operational closure through which each system makes sense of its world. And following Heinz von Foerster, and later Niklas Luhmann, I am aware that any act of mapping—this one included—is also an act of second-order observation: observing not only systems but the ways in which we observe them, the distinctions we draw, and the blind spots we generate in the very act of making sense. As von Foerster insisted, the observer is not outside the system but a participant in its construction; objectivity is not neutrality but responsibility for one's observations. Luhmann extended this insight into a theory of social systems as operationally closed yet cognitively open, in which each observation is shaped by the systemic distinctions that make it possible. This reflexive tension is not a limitation but a generative condition for the work—one that invites us to think of theory not as a mirror of reality but as a form of enactive engagement, borrowing from Francisco Varela. Knowing is doing; cognition arises through embodied interaction with the world. In this sense, the cartography offered here is not merely descriptive but performative: It enacts a way of seeing and orienting, even as it remains aware of its own partiality. It is a map drawn from within the territory by a subject entangled in its contours, seeking to recover a perspective without claiming transcendence.

It is from this vantage that my own orientation emerges. I am driven by a double disposition. On the one hand, I view the world through a kind of psychedelic consciousness: not in the pharmacological sense but as an expanded relational awareness in which boundaries blur, thresholds shift, and new ecologies of meaning become visible. This resonates with Guattari's ecosophy, Lefebvre's rhythmanalysis, or the enactive turn in cognitive science. On the other hand, I am also a materialist: I trace concrete dynamics and observe how embodied actions reproduce systems structured by capitalist logics—norms, values, and power hierarchies—through circuits of cooperation, domination, and adaptation. The map that follows unfolds within this tension—between enchantment and disenchantment, rupture and reproduction, and first- and second-order perspectives. Yin and Yang, not as opposites to be reconciled but as polarities to be inhabited: a rhythm through which to think, to feel, and perhaps to act otherwise.

Finally, the map I offer of the world—and of the horizons of its possible transformation—is necessarily synchronic. It captures a constellation of relationships and systemic entanglements as they appear in a given time frame, even though in life these relations are always in motion, enmeshed in dynamic processes. The systems thinking with which I flirt does allow for glimpses into some of these dynamics, but this map cannot fully reflect the long diachronic trajectories of history—the very processes that have produced the territory I attempt to map, the world we seek to change.

To account for history would require not a map but a series of maps, layered or sequenced like an atlas: a cartographic composition that reveals how, for over three centuries, the fundamental relations of capitalism have continued to reproduce themselves—even as their forms, faces, and functions have mutated. Such an atlas remains to be drawn. But perhaps this map, in its partiality, may still help shift the contours of the territory of social cooperation we inhabit.

Intermezzo I—autopoiesis, negentropy, and the reproduction of capital

This book is grounded in a hybrid theoretical terrain that weaves together feminist insights on social reproduction, ecological and thermodynamic perspectives on social metabolism, and systemic critiques of capitalist power. Its approach draws from Marx, Federici, Guattari, Bateson, Maturana, Varela, Alquati, and others to develop a systemic model of contemporary capitalism that I call the "pyramid of capital." This is more than a metaphor: It is an analytical tool for understanding how capitalist society reproduces itself as a hierarchical, dynamic system—a machine that changes in order to remain fundamentally the same. At the heart of this model is the concept of autopoiesis: the capacity of a system to regenerate and maintain itself over time, adapting to perturbations without losing its systemic identity. Originally formulated by Maturana and Varela to describe living organisms as self-producing systems—organizationally closed but structurally open—autopoiesis helps us think about how social systems like capitalism sustain themselves through recursive feedback and internal regeneration. In this view, change is not necessarily transformation; it is often the adjustment of form to preserve function.

Closely linked to autopoiesis is the thermodynamic notion of negentropy—the capacity of a system to locally reduce entropy (disorder) by organizing flows of energy and matter. As Ilya Prigogine (1997) showed, complex systems far from equilibrium do not collapse into chaos but may develop new forms of order—*dissipative structures*—through processes of self-organization and energy exchange. While this concept is rooted in physics and biology, it also applies to social systems, which must continually reorganize energy, meaning, and cooperation to persist. Drawing from Lovelock's Gaia hypothesis, we might say that life—at all scales—is a negentropic phenomenon: not a denial of entropy but a constant dance with it, resisting dissipation through organization.

When applied to capitalism, this framework reveals a powerful mechanism of reproduction. Capitalism is an autopoietic mega-system that must continuously regenerate its components—labor, nature, and social meaning—by subordinating them to its organizing principle: the accumulation of value. To do so, it must transform not only production but also everyday practices of consumption, education, care, and communication—absorbing other forms of value praxis (use, relational, symbolic) and resignifying them in the register of exchange value. In this way, capitalism produces its own internal negentropy—containing resistance, crisis, and refusal—by reorganizing and refunctionalizing life itself.

But this internal order comes at a cost. To maintain its systemic coherence, capitalism exports entropy to the domains it draws from: to the field of social reproduction; to the ecological cycles of Gaia; and to the material, affective, and relational fabric of social life. It preserves itself by displacing disorder—fragmenting communities, exhausting bodies, eroding ecosystems, and overloading care systems. As Marx puts it, *abstract* labor becomes the form through which human activity is subsumed under capital's logic, the engine of its negentropic reordering—but always through an asymmetrical exchange that undermines the very conditions of life it depends upon.

It is through this continuous autopoietic process that capitalism reveals itself as a system for the boundless imposition of work—not simply as the exploitation of labor power but as a central mechanism of social control and subject formation, as Harry Cleaver (2000) powerfully argued. This imposition is not undone by the high-tech miracles of capitalism. Each time a major technological novelty arrives—be it the personal computer in the 1980s, the internet boom, artificial intelligence (AI), or the latest green-tech promise—we are treated to the familiar ritual: pundits, executives, and futurologists assuring us that liberation is just an upgrade away. And yet the promised leisure society never boots up—while the workload and the surveillance keep auto-updating.

This, too, is the inner logic of what George Caffentzis (2008: 71; see also Caffentzis 2013) calls "the law of the increasing dispersion of the organic composition of capital"—a law whereby "every increase in the introduction of science and technology . . . in one branch of industry . . . will lead to an equivalent increase in the introduction of low organic composition production in [an]other."

Since only living labor produces value—because only living beings can infuse action with social meaning and orient it within shared worlds—machines, however efficient, remain mute in this regard. From the perspective of social cooperation as a whole, their operations are mechanical, not meaningful: They can register patterns of significance if programmed to do so, but they do not participate in the shared negotiation of needs, purposes, or values. They process distinctions but do not inhabit worlds. They do not struggle, love, or care. They do not reconfigure norms or generate meaning through lived contradictions. They execute but do not engage in the situated cocreation of the social—the kind of praxis through which value emerges not merely as signification (as in Laclau) but as the embodied, relational enactment of life together.

Thus, the autopoietic machine of capital continually recreates the conditions for the subjection of life to abstract labor by stripping away livelihoods, redistributing them along lines of inequality, externalizing the costs of social reproduction onto human bodies and the body of Gaia, or appropriating even the most ordinary digital and virtual gestures into circuits of valorization. Without this, technological development would cause the average rate of profit to plummet to zero, and the order of capital would dissolve into an entropic cloud. This has an important consequence for anti-capitalist movements: One of the most effective ways to disrupt capitalism is to block its ability to evade the consequences of the falling rate of profit—by making exploitation more difficult in those domains where capital depends on intensive inputs of living labor and unpaid ecological processes. This includes struggles in both waged and unwaged sectors, as well as ecological resistances that challenge capital's appropriation of energy, matter, and life-supporting systems. Hence, every struggle for care, land, health, education, working conditions, rights to one's own body, or migration rights becomes, in its own way, a struggle against entropy and a challenge to the autopoietic coherence of the capitalist system.

Yet capitalism is not the only autopoietic social form. Movements, commons, collectives, and even relationships of love or solidarity can also be seen as autopoietic systems—struggling to reproduce themselves under hostile conditions, with their own circuits of value, energy, and meaning. The political task, then, is not to reject the idea of systemic organization itself but to exit the dominant logic of capitalist social cooperation by reorienting which systems we cultivate, what values we enact, and whose reproduction we collectively sustain: the reproduction of capital or the reproduction of living systems and the body of Gaia.

This book proposes that the way out of the pyramid is not escape but transformation—from within. It is about cultivating and organizing other autopoietic forces, rooted in commoning, care, and the plural registers of value that capitalism subordinates but cannot fully erase. Not terraformation but regenerative transformation—a process grounded in the repair of relational conditions that sustain life, echoing what Amitav Ghosh (2021) calls for in response to the ecological and colonial devastations of our time.

Intermezzo II—Luhmann and the material limits of systems theory

Before turning to the chapters ahead, I want to clarify my critical distance from a key forerunner in the application of autopoiesis to social systems: Niklas Luhmann (1995). This distance begins with the question of the body and extends across three further dimensions: functionalism, hierarchy, and value.

1. *The Body.* Luhmann's theory is a powerful attempt to grasp the internal logic of social systems through the lens of communication. Yet, in doing so, he brackets out the very elements that ground any serious critique of capitalism: value, exploitation, alienation, and struggle. His social subjects are not embodied, ambivalent, or conflictual—they are functional placeholders, adapted to the operational codes of the systems within which they act. Even where psychic or biophysical dimensions are acknowledged, they are analytically excluded. As a result, social systems in Luhmann's view are communicatively closed worlds, relatively indifferent to bodies, histories, and antagonisms.

   Luhmann famously separates social systems, which reproduce themselves through communication, from psychic systems, which operate through consciousness. Interaction between the two occurs through structural coupling but with no serious engagement with the materiality of this mediation. Communication is treated almost as a disembodied process, severed from the ways bodies, labor, and lived experience ground and shape meaning. In contrast, Marx—and later feminist and ecological thinkers—emphasizes that mediation is not only symbolic but embodied. The body, as Silvia Federici (2004, 2012, 2020) and others show, is a battleground: disciplined, exploited, and regulated under capitalism and patriarchy but also a site of resistance. Especially for women, control over one's body has historically been central to both subjugation and struggle. In general, work is not merely a "communication" or systemic abstraction but a bodily activity that directly connects individuals to economic and social structures. Feminism reminds us that reproductive labor is not abstract communication but a material, relational infrastructure of life. Similarly, political ecology foregrounds how Gaia's body is appropriated to sustain capital's circuits.

   Luhmann's systems are not built to account for these dynamics. As such, his approach offers little for imagining a politics beyond capitalism. His theory describes the internal consistency of systemic operations but not the possibility of transformation. If one wants to understand how subjects resist, reroute, or recompose systemic logics, Luhmann leaves us empty-handed.

2. *Extreme Functionalism.* Luhmann interprets society as a constellation of functionally differentiated, self-referential systems, each governed by a

binary code: *payment/nonpayment* in economics, *legal/illegal* in law, and so on. Each system processes only what it can translate into its own code. In this model, agency and critique are displaced by operational closure and adaptive reproduction. The fundamental questions become: *Is it paid? Is it legal? Is it administratively valid?*—not *Is it just? Is it harmful? Does it nourish or exhaust?* These latter questions matter to bodies, to communities, and to ecosystems—yet they fall outside the narrow syntax of systemic code. What cannot be encoded is rendered invisible or irrelevant.

This invisibility, however, is not always a misdescription of how economic or legal systems function—it often captures their internal logic accurately. But it is not all that goes on. Social cooperation exceeds what is communicable within system codes. If we are to think systemically in relation to social change, we must account for this excess: for the embodied, affective, and relational dimensions that persist beneath, alongside, and against the dominant codifications—and that constitute not simply codes but social relations.

By contrast, the only "functionalism" underlying my approach is this: that capital *seeks* to functionalize life according to its own logic of accumulation. It reorganizes all domains—labor, care, nature, desire, law, economy, and administration—around the imperative of valorization. Even moments of rupture, such as the Kairos of creative power and insubordination described by Negri (2000) or the "lines of flight" celebrated by Deleuze and Guattari (1988), can be neutralized and reintegrated. My concern is precisely with the historical persistence of lines of landing when the creative force of the multitude is reabsorbed into capital's autopoiesis. The political question, then, is not only how capital reproduces itself but how relatively weak or intermittent the autopoiesis of alternative forces has been—those rooted in use and relational values, struggling to subvert the dominant order of value praxis.

3. *Hierarchy.* Luhmann's model is structurally polycentric: Subsystems, such as politics, law, and the economy, are relatively autonomous, differentiated not hierarchically but functionally. There is no central trunk or commanding node—only networks of structurally coupled systems.

   While I, too, view society as a dynamic coalescence of interdependent circuits, this alone does not make it capitalism. What defines capitalism is the hegemonic subordination of all value forms to the register of exchange value. Capitalism is not a flat network but a hierarchical system—a pyramid—that continually reorganizes social cooperation according to the priorities of valorization. Its autopoiesis depends on reproducing this hierarchy: extracting use and relational values and functionalizing them to the logic of capital accumulation. Without this pyramid, the complex systemic machine would not be capital but something else.

4. *Value Versus Code.* Perhaps the most fundamental difference lies in my focus on value rather than code. Luhmann's binary distinctions (*payment/nonpayment, legal/illegal*) describe how systems organize communication. But they do not grasp how meaning is produced in social life—how action becomes oriented, how bodies act with purpose, and how cooperation is shaped by relational, practical, and symbolic values. Value concerns what is considered significant or important in a social context, orienting choices and actions, relations—that is, praxis—and thus "work." The production of value thus becomes embodied in the experience of singular bodies and the social body. It is linked to dimensions such as practical utility (use value), economic importance (exchange value), or social relations (relational value), and often these dimensions are interrelated and fluid, syncopated, or the sources of friction, or placed in hierarchical order depending on contexts.

   Value, in my view, is embedded in social praxis: It is how people give significance to what they do, what they share, and what they struggle over. It is embodied, situated, and contested. Luhmann's *payment/nonpayment* code cannot distinguish between a transaction in a small, self-managed market like *Campi Aperti* in Bologna (De Angelis and Diesner 2020) and a billion-euro order from a multinational arms manufacturer. Both register as *payment.* But in the multinational case, value is realized first and foremost as profit, distributed through bonuses and shares, and embedded in a praxis of abstract labor and disenchanted contribution to the production of genocide. In the self-organized market, by contrast, while exchange value is present, it is embedded within a dense ecology of use and relational values: an alternative relationship with Gaia, a problematization of coproductive relations among subjects, and the deliberate imposition of limits on market logic itself.

This is why the real question is not *market or nonmarket* but which dimensions of value are privileged in a given configuration of social cooperation and how the order among them is structured, enacted, and contested in different contexts of life and reproduction. As Bateson might say, *a difference that makes all the difference.*

My approach and Luhmann's agree on only one thing: that social systems are autopoietic and must manage complexity—that is, capable of self-reproducing and responding to environmental perturbations while maintaining internal coherence. But beyond that, we part ways. He remains descriptively neutral, analytically disembodied, and politically closed. I treat autopoiesis as a critical and political concept: not only to understand how capital sustains itself but to imagine how it can be transformed.

Navigating the chapters

This book is structured in three interrelated parts, each engaging a distinct aspect of the relationship between the common and social cooperation. The parts are not isolated steps but phases in an unfolding argument that moves from ontological grounding to subjective constitution to systemic reproduction and transformation. If the first part is primarily concerned with the common as an ontological condition, the final part expands the horizon to think the common as a project—as a possible mode of production—against and beyond the capitalist pyramid. Between these, the middle section turns to the subject, the everyday, and the structuring of value praxis as the field in which both systemic reproduction and the potential for transformation are enacted.

Part I: The Common as Condition. This first part lays the philosophical, political, and systemic foundation of the book by presenting the common not simply as a resource to be shared but as the underlying condition of social existence. Here, I describe the general character of social cooperation in which we are all involved, albeit in different forms, places, activities, and positions within a hierarchy of remuneration and other forms of power. Yet this condition is not neutral: It is shaped, constrained, and ordered by the dominant systemic logic of capitalism. The common as a condition *is* capitalism.

Across these first three chapters, I outline the general character of social cooperation—a field in which we are all immersed. I describe capitalism as an assemblage of fundamentally different ways of cooperating, a "mixed constitution" not just of political forms of power (Hardt and Negri 2000) but also of social praxes dominated by a hegemonic force—capital—that organizes social relations into a pyramidal order of things. This pyramid is not just an economic or social hierarchy; it is a systemic hierarchy, concentrating power and normativity in ways that allow capital to pursue its own ends: the reproduction of itself and its command and domination over social cooperation.

However, this reproduction of capital is never complete or uncontested. It continually clashes with the needs of social reproduction, which seeks to reproduce life—in its broadest sense—rather than profit. The great crises of our time—and the growing sense that they will intensify, from ecological devastation and climate catastrophe to imperial wars, from rising poverty amid grotesque wealth to the resurgence of fascist revanchism—emerge from and are given form through this systemic collision: the reproduction of capital versus the reproduction of life.

These chapters establish the broad terrain upon which change must be thought, the tensions internal to social cooperation that define the field of struggle.

Chapter 1 opens with a Heraclitean provocation: The common is not something to be invented or constructed from scratch—it is already here, an ontological condition that underlies our existence and the very possibility of social cooperation. Whether or not we are conscious of it, we coproduce the world within a web of interdependencies—among ourselves, with Gaia, and through shared practices, resources, and meanings. The point is to wake up to the common: to recognize it not as a moral ideal or voluntary association but as the ground of cooperation itself, however alienated or exploited it may be—and, in this sense, to stake our collective claim to co-ownership of it.

I frame social cooperation as a dynamic and contradictory field, where the common persists as both an immanent condition and a site of struggle and alternatives. This framing opens the path to understanding capitalism as a specific, hegemonic organization of social cooperation—an organization that seeks to capture and orient the common under the imperative of accumulation. Capital seeks to organize, extract, and discipline the common, subordinating the pluriverse of commoning to the logic of its own reproduction. Yet another praxis of the common continues to pulse beneath and against the structures that seek to dominate it.

In Chapter 2, I introduce one of the book's central distinctions: the distinction between capital reproduction and social reproduction. Before drawing this distinction, however, I clarify what is meant by reproduction more generally—not in biological terms but as the renewal of the conditions of social production. Reproduction, in this expanded sense, encompasses the material, symbolic, energetic, and organizational conditions that sustain social existence over time. Social cooperation as a whole is thus understood as *societal* reproduction, always situated within and dependent on the broader metabolic processes of Gaia. The particular mode and effects of societal reproduction as a whole result from the complex intertwining of two dominant social forces—capital and social reproduction—whose logics often necessarily clash. In this sense, I distinguish societal reproduction (the overall renewal of social cooperation) from its two contending autopoietic logics: capital reproduction and social reproduction. Although both operate within the same world, they pursue different ends: Capital must grow to exist, while life must live to persist. These divergent imperatives generate competing *measures of things*, different selections within the tapestry of our social practices, and different answers to the fundamental questions of social cooperation—*Who produces? How? For whom? How much? When? Why?* These are not abstract dilemmas; they are resolved, contested, and sedimented daily in the friction of forces. Although both forces are active, they do not operate on a level playing field: Capital possesses a structural advantage. Through its quasi-monopoly over the means of existence and its cybernetic apparatuses of surveillance, control, and norm-setting, capital has succeeded in imposing a claustrophobic order of things in which its own logic of valorization is naturalized and insulated from challenge. Chapter 2 thus lays the groundwork for understanding social cooperation as a field of systemic struggle, one in which the reproduction of capital and the reproduction of life are not merely opposed in principle but interlocked in practice, continuously negotiating the terms, scale, and meaning of the world we coproduce. This chapter therefore frames the terrain on which later chapters will work: how social reproduction can accumulate coherence and variety to contest this asymmetry.

Chapter 3 deepens the theoretical architecture of the book by introducing a relational and systemic understanding of social forces. Drawing on the concept of autopoiesis, I define social forces not as externally imposed structures or effects of contingent interactions but as systems capable of reproducing their own organizational logic within the field of social cooperation. This means capital and social reproduction are treated as living systems with their own recursive organization, structural couplings, and boundary maintenance. Capital and social reproduction are approached here not as static structures but as living, self-maintaining systems, each pursuing its own purpose and logic through recursive organizational processes. Taken together, they give rise to a dynamic force field through which systemic reproduction occurs, where opposing logics bend, distort, and recompose social cooperation.

In this framework, capital does not operate purely through its own autopoiesis. Instead, it constantly integrates and reconfigures both allopoietic (externally imposed) and sympoietic (coproduced) processes to sustain its systemic reproduction. Thus, capitalism is not a system that opposes cooperation or emergence; it thrives on them but *only insofar as they are functionalized to its meta-purpose*: the reproduction of capital. This insight also opens a space for thinking about how alternative forces—those grounded in social reproduction, care, and relational value—might reorganize themselves not merely by resisting capital's logic but by cultivating their own autopoiesis, grounded in different value priorities and capable of systemic coherence.

The second major move of this chapter is a reframing of class struggle. Rather than treating it as a secondary effect of structural contradictions—as some Marxist traditions do—I argue that class struggle must be understood as the foundational antagonism between capital reproduction and social reproduction and as a conflict over the very horizon of what counts as value: the opposing measures of things that each system enacts. This antagonism plays out not only in workplaces or wage relations but also across the entire social field—in care work, migration, ecology, education, and the reproduction of subjectivities. *From this perspective, class is not a fixed sociological identity but a transversal front line—an autopoietic tension that cuts across institutions, territories, and bodies, as the measures of capital and life collide in everyday practice.* In sum, Chapter 3 establishes a conceptual matrix for understanding how systemic reproduction and conflict are interwoven. It moves beyond dualisms and determinisms to offer a nuanced view of the politics of reproduction—where the possibility of social transformation hinges not on external disruption alone but on the capacity of social reproduction to cohere into an autopoietic counterforce, capable of reshaping cooperation according to different values and purposes.

Together, these three chapters form the ontological and systemic threshold of the book. They propose that the world we inhabit is not just capitalist—it is composed of many modes of cooperation. But it is capital that has hegemonized their coordination, imposed its logic of measure, and structured reproduction through an architecture of domination. Understanding this is the first step in imagining how the common might be reclaimed.

Part II: The Making of the Common. If Part I gives voice to the uneasiness of inhabiting an interconnected world run amok, Part II (Chapters 4–8) moves from the systemic scale of reproduction to the subjective and relational field of praxis—from the common as condition to the everyday, embodied, lived, and contested terrain in which it is made, unmade, and remade.

The journey of writing these chapters began as a way to clarify a theoretical encounter with Romano Alquati's *Modellone* or "big model"—a body of work gesturing toward a meta-systemic vision of contemporary capitalism, which I discuss in the first chapter of Part III. Alquati, an Italian sociologist, political theorist, and activist, is known for his work with the Operaist journal *Quaderni Rossi* and for his Marxist analyses of labor practices at FIAT and Olivetti.

It was both surprising and affirming to discover that a major figure within the autonomist Marxist tradition I come from had turned to the same theoretical materials—particularly its engagements with cybernetics, complexity theory, and references to the work of Maturana and Varela, which had long influenced my own thinking—to interrogate the systemic reproduction of capital. However, much of what survives of Alquati's *Modellone* exists as out-of-print lecture notes—dense, circular, often fragmented, and at times dazzlingly spiraled to the point of disorientation. Yet beneath this apparent chaos lies a deep coherence: a meta-systemic effort to grasp capital not just as a structure but as an evolving, recursive totality woven through everyday life and struggle. And crucially, this totality is analyzed not from above but from the standpoint of a self-constituting part—one that seeks another way to constitute the world. Intrigued by the *Modellone*, I chose not to reconstruct Alquati's model exegetically but to pursue its core intuition along my own path. This required me to start to problematize the relation between parts and whole in the everyday.

In Chapter 4, I thus address the first major theoretical challenge that emerged from engaging Alquati's approach: How can we account for the relation between the part (the subject, the fragment, and the struggle) and the systemic totality without falling into reductionism or functionalism—both anathema to any genuine process of social change? This question is inseparable from the one Guattari identifies as central to transformation: the reorganization of the relation between the subject and their exteriority. To address this, I first needed to clarify how social relations and their multiple tensions are enacted and reproduced—not only in systemic abstractions but in the textures of everyday cognition, perception, and practice.

Enactivism here offers an essential insight: The world is not given in advance but co-constructed through embodied interaction between the subject and the environment. Applied to the social realm, enactivism allows us to see how capitalist structures depend on the patterned reproduction of enactive practices—how the pyramid of capital is built and sustained through the repeated, situated actions of subjects, and forms of consciousness somehow congruent with those contexts. But daily life is not only where domination is enacted; it is also where openings emerge. Enactive practices—mundane, repetitive, or ambivalent—can be redirected toward new forms of cooperation, value, and escape.

But does this potentiality truly exist in the subject? We live, after all, in claustrophobic times in which disenchantment, cynicism, and collective hypnosis are said to rule. Chapters 5 and 6 attempt to answer this by proposing that we are all subject-holons—relational and situated subjects, both part and whole, embedded yet capable of generating perturbations. Neither fully autonomous nor fully determined, the subject-holon challenges the dominant conceptions of subjectivity: the liberal figure of the sovereign, rational actor on one side, and the structurally overdetermined subject—shaped entirely by ideology or system—on the other. This relational, situated subject draws on long-standing insights from feminist theory, enactivist philosophy, post-structuralism, and autonomist Marxism, which all contest the fixity of the subject and foreground its embeddedness in social, material, and affective circuits. What the subject-holon offers is a way to operationalize this relationality within a systemic framework: as a node dynamically coupled to environments, systems, and other subjects, intermittently capable of reflection, rupture, and reconfiguration. This figure—the subject-holon—becomes a red thread throughout the book. It reappears in Part III (especially Chapter 16) as the experiential operator of systemic recomposition. To make sense of contemporary subjectivity—ambivalent, fractured, and deeply contextual—I draw inspiration from Alquati's classification of subjects as reproducers of dominant structures, ambivalent actors, or carriers of counter- and alter-power. I interpret these not as fixed types but as positions along a continuum. This continuum does not define a typology of subjects but rather degrees of subjectivity enacted in different contexts by everybody, depending on the relational field, the value regime, and the affective and material conditions at play. Each subject is an instantiation of a moving threshold between adaptation and transformation, between acting within the system and perturbing it from within. The subject-holon captures this dynamic: a relational node intermittently capable of rupture and reconfiguration, whose ambivalence is not a flaw but a constitutive condition—a space from which social recomposition and transformation might emerge. Because subject-holons traverse multiple domains of social cooperation, they carry diverse capacities and intentional vectors. Their consciousness is intermittent, shaped by embodied encounters and systemic pressures. Agency, in this view, is not continuous or guaranteed but emergent, unfolding in moments of resonance, rupture, or collective co-enaction. Rather than treating this intermittency as a flaw, I frame it as constitutive—an expression of the layered and nonlinear temporality of social life, through which insight and transformation can arise.

Chapter 7 turns to the interface where this subjective potential meets systemic form: the domain of praxis. This is the plane where subjects, by engaging with the world in given forms, reproduce it. It is where the reproduction of dominant orders and the possibility of their transformation are mediated—not abstractly but through concrete practices: work, care, resistance, participation, and refusal. This is not a shift away from subjectivity but a move into the relational and systemic field where subjectivity becomes socially operative—where subjects either conform to or reconfigure the circuits of social cooperation. This is where the concept of value praxis becomes crucial—a concept I develop by interrogating contemporary critical theory. It describes how subjects, through their relation to the world, actively construct it: through practices shaped by, and in turn shaping, purpose, norm, and relatedness, all of which carry some form of value. These three components form the triadic structure through which action is oriented, coordinated, and contested. But more than this, it is from these elemental processes of value praxis that the broader anatomy of social cooperation takes shape. Structures, networks, circuits, and systems are not abstract entities but emergent embodied configurations—stabilized over time through recursive patterns of value praxis that embed selections and distinctions made within specific value domains. Overtime, these configurations harden into institutions: durable forms of social organization that sediment the priorities, exclusions, and rhythms of past value praxis into the norms and structures of the present. Thus, value praxis is not simply about what people do but about how practices carry meanings, reproduce or disrupt relations, and enact or contest systemic priorities. It provides a way to understand social cooperation not as a neutral backdrop but as a normatively saturated and materially mediated terrain where every act—whether of compliance or resistance—participates in the ongoing structuration of the social. Through this lens, the world is not just experienced but enacted—not just inhabited but co-constituted. From these enactments, entire ecologies of social cooperation arise, forming the terrain of both reproduction and struggle. This prepares Chapter 8's articulation of value domains and registers—relational, use, exchange, and command—as the patterned outcomes of value praxis sedimented into institutions. Clearly, the degree to which a collective subject is perturbed or can perturb, and the extent to which it is shaped or can shape, is defined by the force field it enacts—and may in turn transform. That is, value praxis takes place within a dynamic field of power relations, material constraints, systemic thresholds, and copresent subjectivities—a field that not only conditions the subject's agency but can also be reconfigured through it, giving rise to new alignments, meanings, and institutions.

Since different configurations of purpose, norm, and relatedness organize action around different criteria of what is meaningful, necessary, or valuable, it is possible to distinguish distinct domains of value praxis orienting social cooperation. In Chapter 8, I argue that these are not static or separated spheres but intermingle in dynamic orders of value wherever value gives rise to selection, organization, and contestation. The four primary domains—relational values, use values, exchange values, and command—reflect distinct planes for coordinating social action and assigning value. Within each domain, value registers function as internal structuring principles that guide which practices, norms, and relations are considered meaningful and legitimate in given contexts. They do so by defining a range of acceptable selections and shaping the contested spectrum of what is recognized as appropriate, valuable, or possible within that domain, thereby grounding the interdependence of purpose, norm, and relatedness in specific social and cultural contexts.

It follows from this that institutions are not neatly contained within a single domain but are shaped by overlapping configurations of these value domains. It is the task of command—as both a domain and a function—to rank and order these domains in particular ways, depending on the context and the prevailing force field of social cooperation, thereby determining which values are prioritized, marginalized, or instrumentalized. A school, a family, a social center, a movement, or a corporation may draw from multiple domains simultaneously, depending on how value is enacted and stabilized within them—an ordered multiplicity, however, ranked according to the prevailing situated context and the force field of social cooperation. Social cooperation as a whole, then, emerges as a complex and layered assemblage of interwoven domains. This analysis of value domains and registers lays the groundwork for understanding how capitalism imposes a hierarchical ordering among them—subordinating relational and use-value logics to the imperatives of exchange and command—and prepares the conceptual terrain for the systemic analysis undertaken in the chapters that follow.

With these tools in hand, I could finally make Alquati's *Modellone* speak to me as a deeply generative framework for understanding how capital organizes social cooperation and how it might be reconfigured from within.

Part III: The Pyramid of Capital and Beyond. The final part of the book (Chapters 9–16) presents a systemic analysis of contemporary capitalism as an autopoietic hierarchical mega-system that captures, reorganizes, and dominates social cooperation. While not a historical account in the strict sense, this analysis is punctuated by historical references and periodizations where necessary to illuminate the evolving forms and mechanisms of capitalist command in recent decades. Yet it also opens the door to envisioning the common not only as a condition but as a mode of production—an autonomous systemic force capable of recomposing life and value on different terms.

Chapter 9 introduces the book's central systemic image: the pyramid of capital. Drawing inspiration from Alquati's Modellone—not as a rigid schema but as a meta-systemic hypothesis—it visualizes capitalism as a hierarchical and stratified macro-system composed of distinct levels of value praxis and command. Each level is not merely a functional layer but a lived domain of social cooperation, shaped by a dominant value domain and a multiplicity of corresponding value registers. Rather than a vertical succession of social classes, the pyramid represents a dynamic architecture in which each level is both a condition of existence for the one above and functionally subordinated to it. It is this systemic configuration that reproduces class and other social stratifications.

Importantly, the pyramid includes not only horizontal articulations of cooperation at each level but also vertical axes of command and exploitation that cut across levels—transforming exclusions, differences, and stratifications into mechanisms of differential subordination and control. These vertical lines help maintain the autopoietic coherence of capital by translating inequality into functionality. The order among levels is maintained through systemic constraint; higher levels set the horizon of possibility for the ones below, while lower levels provide the material and relational conditions for capital's continued reproduction.

The pyramid is thus a living diagram of domination: a machinic and autopoietic structure that reorganizes its internal components to absorb turbulence, internalize rupture, and re-functionalize even resistance. It draws contradictions, struggles, and turbulence from below into its own architecture, transforming them into new mechanisms for the continuation of capital's autopoietic reproduction. Rather than simply repressing opposition, it transforms contradictions into an adaptive force—recomposing its circuits through systemic feedback and structural coupling. This chapter therefore introduces a crucial analytic: the pyramid as the diagram of the permanent subordination of social reproduction to capital reproduction and as a heuristic device that guides the systemic mapping of value, conflict, and cooperation across the rest of Part III.

Chapters 10–14 explore each level of the pyramid in turn, moving from the bottom up—beginning with Gaia and ascending through the procommons, and the meso-, meta-, and mega-levels—hinting at historical dynamics while emphasizing their comparative composition, internal logic, and dominant value regime. Chapter 10 begins with the level of Gaia, which is not discussed in Alquati, establishing that the metabolic relation with the Earth is not an externality but the foundational ground of all social reproduction. Strictly speaking, this is not a proper level of social cooperation—nor does it operate through human ends—but it is the necessary condition for any such cooperation: the domain of ecosystemic processes, trophic chains, and biogeochemical cycles that render the planet habitable. I include it at the base of the pyramid to highlight that every level above it depends on, perturbs, and draws from this substrate. This level is where the autopoiesis of the Earth system unfolds—self-organizing, adaptive, and relational—yet increasingly strained by the metabolic rift produced by capital's logic of accumulation. Gaia, then, is both the lowest layer and the living envelope of the entire pyramid, a reminder that domination over nature ultimately declares war on the conditions of life itself. Chapter 11 turns to the level I call the procommons. This level is also not discussed in Alquati, though hints of it appear in his fragmented treatment of subsystems. For my analysis, however, it defines a dimension of social cooperation that is foundational to any politics of transformation. The procommons is the realm of relational values and of the vernacular and often informal circuits of cooperation—those beneath and beyond the reach of capital and the state—where the latent potential of the common as project begins to emerge. But this vernacular is not pure, nor should it be romanticized. Here, I emphasize how the procommons includes both care and conflict, reciprocity and exclusion—the everyday textures of solidarity but also the scars of patriarchy, racism, structural violence, extraction, and exploitation. The procommons is not an outside to the system but a relational field of life-making and of direct social relations, constantly traversed and strained by the imperatives of higher levels of valorization and command. It is a site of ongoing contestation, where relational values are both cultivated and compromised and where alternative rhythms emerge only to be threatened by compression under the abstract tempo of capital. And it is here—in the sedimentation of lived experience in relational fields—that struggles for and processes of recomposition find their emergent impetus, core motivation, and energy, and where we find the center of gravity of any possibility of systemic transformation.

Chapter 12 analyzes the meso-level of use-value production. At this level, following Alquati, I identify distinct social areas of use-value production—such as artefacture, reproductive and destructive consumption, and institutional politics—to which I also add agriculture. These areas are not fixed sectors but dynamic and conflictual zones, shaped by the contrasting value logics. The meso-level is structurally oriented toward effectiveness—the concrete organization of means to socially necessary ends—yet it is under constant pressure: from above, by the meta-level of valorization, which subordinates production to profitability; and from below, by the procommons and Gaia, where relational, ecological, and reproductive values resist subsumption. As a result, the meso-level becomes a threshold space, where the systemic ordering of value is both operationalized and contested. The same institution—a school, a hospital, a farm, a factory—can, to varying degrees, either serve the reproduction of life or be functionalized to the reproduction of capital, depending on the relative weight of the value registers at play. This makes the meso-level a strategic site of struggle, where the orientations of labor, utility, care, and governance are not neutral decisions but the outcomes of ongoing systemic conflict across the vertical and horizontal layers of the pyramid.

Chapter 13 examines the meta-level, where regimes of valorization and accumulation coordinate the reproduction of value across society. Following Alquati, I divide this level into two interrelated sublevels: valorization, where capital circuits shape social cooperation to make it produce exchange value and capital, and accumulation, which orients investment in society by selecting what counts as productive in correspondence to profitability. Together, these sublevels steer waged and unwaged labor, finance, and infrastructure under capital's expanding logic of exploitation and extraction. Here, I illustrate the working of this meta-level by sketching the arc of neoliberal globalization as a planetary reorganization of fields of social reproduction, structured through competition, relocation, and benchmarking. Social reproduction is a cost to be minimized, and capital pits territories, institutions, and subjectivities against one another in a systemic race to cheapen life. Within this meta-level, the dominant criterion is no longer effectiveness, as in the meso-level but efficiency—not the effective provisioning of care and use values to meet social needs but the maximization of returns and minimization of the costs of social reproduction borne by capital. This level is the structural source of the capitalist *measure of things*: a logic that seeks to recode any other values and naturalizes the systemic subordination of life to capital.

Chapter 14 addresses the mega-level, the apex of command and domination, where war, geopolitics, and macroeconomic governance converge to stabilize, or diverge to rupture, the system. Drawing on insights from word systems, political economy, and cybernetics, I introduce the notion of the six throbs of command—purpose, agency, crisiscraft, displacement, instrumentality, and threshold recalibration—which name the deep regulatory logics through which the pyramid absorbs turbulence and reorganizes itself. These throbs operate as systemic feedback mechanisms, enabling the mega-level to sense, process, and respond to instability in ways that reinforce capital's long-range reproduction. They work as filters and amplifiers for the whole system's signal flow—selecting purposes, agents, crisis narratives, displacements, instruments, and thresholds to keep accumulation somehow synchronized. Chapter 15 contextualizes these throbs historically across three phases—postwar consolidation, neoliberal reconfiguration, and today's conflictual multipolarism marked by waning US coordinating power and rival centers of accumulation (e.g., China/BRICS). It reads "defensive" policy arcs—trade wars, tariff regimes, and monetary diplomacy—as attempts to preserve hegemonic coordination amid chronic turbulence. Otherwise, it is a kind of retrospective X-ray of the pyramid in motion. Together, these chapters map not a static hierarchy but a living architecture of domination, in which each level interacts with the others through feedback, capture, and constraint—allowing the pyramid to adapt and recompose itself amid crisis while subordinating all value domains to the imperatives of capital reproduction. Chapter 16 then asks how this ordering can be reversed in practice—by retiming and reregulating the meso-level from the standpoint of social reproduction.

Chapter 16 closes the book by returning to the beginning—but now the common is not only the condition we inherit; it is the project we enact as a process of autopoiesis on the terrain of social reproduction. The chapter shows how systemic transformation hinges on reorienting the meso-level from within—subordinating its institutional and productive logics to the relational and reproductive values of the procommons—so that use value becomes the measure of production, rather than its residue. It develops the dual movements of counter- and alter-regulation and introduces the ecology of necessary and emergent commons: the former reclaim and redirect captured infrastructures and services; the latter create what capital has abandoned or cannot recognize. Their recursive interaction composes a living field of recomposition. The figure of the subject-holon reappears as the operator of this process—simultaneously part and whole—learning to act locally and systemically across a sympoietic ecology of organizations. Finally, the chapter names love as the organizational force of commoning: not sentiment but a plural, embodied practice that confronts hierarchy (centrally, the wage), repairs schismogenesis, and composes eurhythmia across Gaia, procommons, and the meso-level. In this light, commoning is the praxis that turns resonance into regulation and resistance into autopoietic organization—the groundwork for reversing the pyramid's ordering of value.

Part I

The common as condition

1

Changing the common

One world in common

Heraclitus, the ancient pre-Socratic Greek philosopher famous for the claim that one cannot bathe twice in the same river and that there is nothing permanent apart from change, also tells us this:

> For those who are awake, there is one world in common, but of those who are asleep, each is withdrawn into his own private world.[1]

It is also true that, many centuries later, psychoanalysis shows us that the subject's entire daytime life, memories, hopes, and fantasies converge in the dreamwork and that, therefore, the daytime world of when one is awake and the nighttime world of when one is asleep interface. We are never alone; even solitude is a social relationship. But, the sense of an awake subjectivity, as evoked in Heraclitus's fragment, I believe, must be traced back to the awareness that it is or would be necessary today to live and operate in a common world, the awareness of the need to renew one's relationship with the human and nonhuman web of life.

This one world in common is the theme from which I want to start, and by "world" here, I do not mean only the biosphere, Gaia, the Earth, and its ecosystem. I also mean the human world, which, in its more general interaction to reproduce its species on this planet, enters into certain social relationships and metabolic exchanges with nonhuman nature. It is from this human world that we have to start in its ways of doing, relating, and striving to be in the world. It is in this human world that lies the frontier between oppression and emancipation, between ecological devastation and care for the common home we inhabit. The complex web of relationships and processes that creates and recreates this world is what we call "social cooperation" in the broadest sense.

Look around you. Any object you see—whether handmade or industrially manufactured, whether donated to you or purchased, whether discarded in the rubbish or placed in plain sight in the middle of a room—or any "service" you receive—whether one you actually need such as medical care or one that is insistently offered to you by salesmen who swear they know your needs better than you do—is the manifestation of some form of social cooperation.

Today's social cooperation articulates our lives in a myriad of productive and reproductive lattices; channels our vital energies into generative circuits of things and services; subjects them to rationalities and measures of things that often clash with those with which we identify; makes use of a gigantic apparatus of energy and material extraction from the Earth, and uses the air, water, land; and subsoil to incessantly disperse its abundant and unsustainable residues. Despite all our real differences as participants in these grids that encircle the globe, and as their subjective instances, we share this social cooperation as a common condition, and this makes us part of a complex cooperating multitude, pervaded by multifarious stratifications of alienation and separation and segmented into gradations of power, exploitation, and subsumption to the currents of command and domination that shape our social cooperation. *When we do not fight, or when we do not construct alternative forms of social cooperation to these currents—that is, when we do not problematize our relationship with the network of social cooperation—then, in that automatic normality in which we reproduce our lives, we are both the victims and the accomplices of this form of social cooperation.* We are victims who receive from the social cooperation system the inescapable signals that demand our adaptation: Run away from war or environmental disaster; accept lower wages; work harder to beat the competition (i.e., other workers); look for work; become more entrepreneurial; study only what is useful to the market, not what is useful to life; obey the manager even if they are clearly incompetent and the system they run does not produce social utility; retrain yourself; align your desires with advertising imagery; adapt to hour-long queues in the emergency room; breathe the unhealthy air of the Po Valley and get by; wait a few more years for the hoped-for state aid after the last flood; and leave the organic products in the supermarket untouched because otherwise we won't make it to the end of the month. We are accomplices, that is, to the extent by reproducing our material and symbolic conditions of existence, we contribute to reproducing the material and symbolic networks of the market and domination and their rationality and measure of things. By desiring, we are in some way functional to it. Thus, not only do "we," in our everyday lives, reproduce our bodies and affective networks, but at the same time, we also pursue our desiring being by buying into this sphere the signs of distinction, uniqueness, and status—signs to be projected onto our worlds. It has never been so true, with Gilles Deleuze and Félix Guattari (1984: 30), that "desire produces reality," but given the state of the world, we have to ask ourselves which desires produce which realities.

Each of these products, each of these services provided, enters the cycle of our lives. They are the means of reproduction of our lives, of our living human capacities. At the same time, each of these objects, each of these services received, has cost effort, commitment, and physical and psychic energy. It has also cost nature materials and life-forms. In other words, it has cost the consumption of living capacities, human and nonhuman. This "we," then, is traversed by an ancient paradox: To create living capacity, one has to consume living capacity; that is, human and nonhuman beings must be drawn into processes of energy expenditure, transformation, and work in a broad sense. Seen within the complex web of social cooperation, this simple fact makes clear that contemporary cooperation is generated by an "us" that cannot fully speak its name: a fragmented collectivity of "I"s—at best small "we"s—divided by economic conditions and identity boundaries, and driven into perpetual rivalry, each urged to look only after their own small garden. Social cooperation as a whole is based on this unpronounceable "we," a "we" that exists, is real, and has material effects but cannot be identified or named as "we" because, between you and me, there is a boundary, a separation, and an alienation. And the basis of this alienation is the fact that although to varying degrees we are all consumers and reproducers of living capacity, the system in which we cooperate and articulate our lives recognizes us now as one, now as the other, never as complete subjects. Based on this lie, it divides and stratifies us.

Instead of talking about "us" and our social cooperation as a system of processes and relations in which our sensuous bodies are entangled, we talk about the economy as an external entity, with its own laws, which we must accept, thus forgetting that we ourselves are the coproducers of this "economy." Or, instead of talking about a cosmopolitan "us" projected onto the now largely globalized world about the praxis and products of social cooperation, old provincialisms are dusted off and new ones invented. Anxiety and terror are felt at the possibility of cultural cross-fertilization. National borders are reinforced with walls, watchtowers, and pacts with bloody regimes to keep at bay what is the ineluctable result of this globalization of social cooperation amid the chaos of climate change, war, and ever-changing economic fortunes: the great migratory processes of our time. Or, finally, instead of rethinking our social cooperation in order to reshape our relationship with Gaia, we continue to subordinate the needs of the web of life to those of the economy, promoting the unhealthy idea that replacing one technology with others that are "greener" as fuel for economic growth, and shifting environmental costs to other national spaces, will somehow solve the ecological problem.

Talking about a "we" always implies an interconnection of "I"s, each participating in the making of that "we." Yet this interconnection does not unfold on equal ground: It invests singular subjects—situated differently within the networks of power and possibility—with a shared, though uneven, co-responsibility. It calls into question not merely their capacity to act but the forms of implication through which they respond, comply, or resist within the situation generated by the "we." For "we" are the creators and reproducers of this social cooperation, which is not external to its making but immanent in it. "We" are immanent in the very form of our cooperation—in its organization, its pattern of relations, and the hierarchy of aims it assumes. It is these forms and this hierarchy of purposes that generate and perpetuate the vast social and environmental problems we face. Only by transforming this dominant form of cooperation at its roots can "we" begin to address the problems born of our own collective making.

The mixed constitution of social cooperation

The "we" of social cooperation is clearly differentiated, not only in its qualitative multiplicities but also, and above all, in its power relations and stratifications. Posing the question of the "we," therefore, also implies posing the question of how these stratifications of power reproduce the problematic form of social cooperation we call capitalism. But, here, I am interested in emphasizing that this social cooperation, this common condition of ours, does not present itself as a monolith in its social form. The modalities, social relations, rationalities, measures of things, and orders of purpose implemented in the circuits that give rise to social cooperation as a common condition are multiple. The social systems that emerge from it are also multiple. And it is precisely by starting from social cooperation as a common condition in its generality that we are able to distinguish, or at least glimpse, its multiform complexity. We therefore speak of a social cooperation that has a "mixed constitution." This is a concept that I borrow from Hardt and Negri (2000), although I extend it to social cooperation as a whole, and not only with regard to the forms of its governance. To speak of a mixed constitution indicates a social cooperation composed of different systems of production and social relations, articulated and intertwined at different scales of social action, and corresponding to different forms of governance and regulation of human activity and its metabolism with nonhuman nature. Hence, it follows that today's major problems (from environmental destruction to precariousness, from growing poverty in the midst of wealth to the reproduction of hierarchies of power based on racism and patriarchy) are connected to a particular configuration and *order of things* that channel their operation and assign some ends above others.

In order to appreciate this composite and mixed totality in the forms of social cooperation, let us think of any field of social cooperation—for example, education—and consider the plurality of social forms and systems involved in its reproduction as a totality. We have public systems such as schools, governed by a vertical hierarchy both within the school (headmaster, teachers, students, support staff, etc.) and outside it (educational departments and agencies, ministries, etc.). Although teachers have teaching autonomy within the classroom, their action is confined within the limits of regulations given by the upper layers of the hierarchy. Schools rely heavily on reward-and-punishment mechanisms such as grades, mechanisms that mirror those employed by the economy in general and that are based on salary rewards linked to productivity gains. A hierarchy of grades thus reproduces the idea that individual work effort, and the resulting "merit," is solely responsible for improvements in rewards, when in fact "merit" depends very much on where you were lucky enough to be born and grow up, what resources you were able to avail yourself of, personal history, and so on. Individual merit is always based on commonly created conditions of production, measured as a deviation from collective standards, and largely dependent on the financial, time, and emotional resources available. Education then continues within families, when parents or guardians interact with children and adolescents, exposing them to their images of the world, values, and judgments. Children and adolescents then assemble these images into unique selections as they grow up and seek coherence between what they observe and experience and what they have accumulated as inherited cultural residue. Education then continues within the networks of friendship they weave—in the street, in sports centers, in parks, in community centers, in dance clubs—in which experience is matured and enriched and through which they find their own unique subjective ways to process. It is nurtured within social movements of various kinds, in instances of rebellion, indignation, and collective struggle. Education now continues on social networks under the rhythms of algorithms designed to capture attention, shape desire, and channel participation into circuits of visibility, consumption, and control. It unfolds through the constant influx of promotional messages that advertise styles, products, and images of what is distinctive and desirable and through the ways adults around children and young people confront—or fail to confront—the contradictions of our time: advertising that feeds consumerist logic; ideas about the "other," the foreigner, and women's bodies as objects or threats; the marginalization of the poor; and the destruction of the ecological fabric. In a word, education today is reproduced through the interweaving of multiple systems of social cooperation, each with its own norms, relational modes, and purposes—some hierarchical and grounded in command, others competitive and exclusionary, and still others solidarity-based and horizontal. Each, in its own way, is interwoven with and shaping the others.

Or consider the lunch I prepared for my family. The pasta is produced by an agribusiness multinational organized in a hierarchical chain of command within it and in competition with others outside it. So is the water, gifted by Gaia but still supplied by a corporate multi-utility, despite the fact that a victorious referendum over a decade ago in Italy decreed water to be a not-for-profit common good. Tomato sauce is no less so, since I have finished my self-produced one, and every time I use the one purchased from the supermarket, I can't help but think of the living conditions and overexploitation of the migrants who harvest the tomatoes. If it is summer, the vegetables I use come from our home garden; otherwise, they come from the local shop or the supermarket, both tied to large agribusiness circuits. If I can reach the city, I buy them from an association of small farmers committed to fair and sustainable farming. However the ingredients are procured, when the pasta pot is ready, I put it on the table for horizontal sharing. Here, too, on the kitchen table, we see an interweaving, hybridization, and mixed constitution of different (often strongly contrasting) forms of social cooperation.

In this sense, if I may be allowed to use a broad brush, I would say that, prima facie, today there are three ideal-typical organizational principles of social cooperation and the relative rationales linking means and ends: the capitalist, statist, and communist principles. Contemporary social cooperation, in its totality, involves the mixed constitution of these three principles, giving rise to numerous hybrid forms (such as the example of education or the plate of pasta I cooked for my family). These different organizing principles, incorporated by different systems (at different scales), often have very different and often opposing purposes, and this, at the same time, structures the social norms adopted by practices and shapes social relations.

The capitalist principle is defined by self-interest and the pursuit of profit as the meta-end of social cooperation (accumulation) and by the creation of the means necessary to achieve and possibly maximize profitability. The meta-end of the statist principle is to preserve the existing configuration of power—a certain hierarchy of command—in the face of numerous recurring or new pressures and challenges or to facilitate a transformation of the power structure. The meta-end of the communist principle of social cooperation is the collective pursuit of conditions that lead to a good and just life for all based on the principle of "to each according to their needs, by each according to their abilities" and, we might add, aspirations. To each of these meta-ends correspond, of course, sets of sub-ends that are functional—that is, subordinate—to the pursuit of these meta-ends, which are to be assessed from the contexts and scales at which they arise.

Now I would like to dwell for a moment on the principle of communism, given the confusion surrounding this term. Like the statist and capitalist principles, it is implemented in multiple moments of social cooperation;

indeed, in some ways and in different forms, it is a pervasive principle in social cooperation in the broadest sense of the everyday. As David Graeber (2008: 3, my emphasis) reminds us:

> The standard line, which we accept more or less unthinkingly, is that communism means state control of the economy, and this is an impossible utopian dream because history has shown it simply "doesn't work." Capitalism, however unpleasant, is thus the only remaining option. *But in fact communism really just means any situation where people act according to the principle of "from each according to their abilities, to each according to their needs"*—which is the way pretty much everyone always act if they are working together to get something done. If two people are fixing a pipe and one says "hand me the wrench," the other doesn't say, "and what do I get for it?" (That is, if they actually want it to be fixed.) This is true even if they happen to be employed by Bechtel or Citigroup. They apply principles of communism because it's the only thing that really works. This is also the reason whole cities or countries revert to some form of rough-and-ready communism in the wake of natural disasters, or economic collapse (one might say, in those circumstances, markets and hierarchical chains of command are luxuries they can't afford).

It is obvious that just as there are different forms of capitalism and statism, there are also different forms of communism, based on the hybridization of these principles with others in given forms and contexts. For example, "the more creativity is required," Graeber (2008) continues,

> the more people have to improvise at a given task, the more egalitarian the resulting form of communism is likely to be: that's why even Republican software engineers, when trying to innovate new software ideas, tend to form small democratic collectives. It is only when work becomes standardised and boring—as on production lines—that it becomes possible to impose more authoritarian, even fascist, forms of communism. But the fact is that even private companies are, internally, organised communistically.

Communism is therefore not a future state of affairs; it already exists in the here and now, in the everyday. The point—the political horizon—is not only how to democratize it, as Graeber says, but also how to make it the hegemonic principle of social cooperation.

Let us therefore return to the idea of social cooperation and its mixed constitution of social practices and systems in society. Every social practice is always a value practice (De Angelis 2007), as both subjects and the worlds in which they operate entail selections and distinctions about what is included or excluded, considered good or bad, and pleasurable or unpleasant. These choices embody a judgment, which can only be understood within a system or register of values. Value has a *dual constitution*: It is both internal to the subject and systemic, embedded, for example, in norms (of politeness, hierarchy, and productivity) and in implicit or explicit purposes (why do we act?). If this is true, social praxis is always a value praxis (Chapter 7) but one with *multiple dimensions*, corresponding to different domains of valuation in life (Chapter 8). At different moments, we may value relationships in their own terms or an object for its usefulness or for the money we can get from it if we exchange it in the market. These are three completely different domains of valuation, although highly interrelated. These domains do not directly coincide with institutions (schools, families, corporations, governments, etc.) but are instead patterns of practices and relations that interact and interpenetrate in every dimension of our lives, although in different measures across different institutional contexts and with different rankings of importance. Thus, institutions derive their systemic identity from the specific ordered configurations of these domains expressed in diverse cultural forms. These fundamental domains shape all social praxis from everyday interactions to large-scale organizations and the system of social cooperation as a whole, and they order the dimensions of value—the meaning we assign to action, whether as individuals or within cooperative plurality. Capitalism is the totality of these domains of value praxis, *hierarchically ordered* at a meta-systemic level and organized in such a way that exchange value is maintained as dominant.

I therefore understand a "social formation" or a "mode of production" (I use the broad brush here; I am not interested in the subtle distinctions between the two) as a specific configuration of these different domains in such a way that one of these achieves hegemony over the others. Its specific meta-end and measures of things (see Chapter 2) act as a powerful organizing force of social cooperation, while the meta-ends and measures of things of the other domains are made functional in pursuit of the ends and measures of things of the dominant domain. This does not eliminate the other domains but merely subordinates them.

Thus, I can live in a community pursuing virtuous, sustainable activities by practicing a form of direct democracy in the management of things. And yet, at a different scale, the same community is faced with state constraints on its actions, or perhaps it is forced to access the capitalist market that pits its virtuous products against those of other communities around the world or against goods produced by capitalist enterprises. One can also add layers of questions. Where do I get my food or clothing? Or where do the taxes we pay go? Part of the taxes paid by members of the pacifist and ecologist community goes into armaments, and another part goes into subsidies for the oil industry. The point is that *each* principle of social cooperation in this mixed constitution is in relation to others not only horizontally (in alliance or competition with others) but also vertically (in submission or command).

Through periods of rupture and reconfiguration by means of diverse processes of expropriation of communities (the so-called primitive accumulation or simply enclosures (De Angelis 2007) and integration processes on the basis of commodification, the historical course of the last few centuries has led to the emergence of the capitalist hegemony as an organizing principle of social cooperation as a whole and its corresponding hierarchy of aims and orders of value-praxis domains. The multiplicity of modes of production is thus subsumed within a master narrative *embodied* in the mechanisms of social cooperation that articulates and hierarchizes all value domains of our lives—and therefore purposes—within a macro-finality (and its consequent social norms and relations). Ironically, despite postmodern philosophers declaring the death of master narratives, the mechanisms of social cooperation continue to articulate and hierarchize all purposes within a dominant framework and a dominant form of rationality, thereby reinforcing a structured and stratified order of goals and social relations. The mixed constitution of social cooperation in our world—our common as a condition—is called capitalism, a particular project of "civilization" that started a few centuries ago, whose aim is to set profit and accumulation as the superior purpose of social cooperation, subordinating all other purposes to this, and to keep the domain of exchange value firmly at the top, subordinating all other purposes and value domains to this. Civilization projects aim to integrate different cultures and social systems to form social macro-systems. Capitalism is a hierarchical, pyramidal social macro-system. This is the common as condition.

The subordination of all value domains to exchange value is not fixed once and for all. It is constantly contested by acts of subtraction, resistance, and struggle. To maintain its dominance, capitalism must continually reproduce itself—even in the face of these disruptions. It does so through policies and systemic mechanisms that generate dependence on the market and thus reinforce vulnerability. These include repressive filters—media manipulation, selective policing, and bureaucratic opacity—and amplifiers such as algorithmic governance, legal codification, and toxic cultural narratives (Chapters 8 and 14). Alongside these, processes of colonization extend market logic into every facet of life. Financial markets turn shelter into speculative assets; digital platforms commodify personal data; health care is transformed into a competitive service (Chapter 12). These are not anomalies but are integral to a broader dynamic that reshapes life to fit the imperatives of capital's measure of things (Chapter 2).

On a larger scale, this dynamic subverts the traditional concentric relationship between the economy, society, and nature. Karl Polanyi's (1944) idea that the economy is embedded within society, and society within nature, is turned on its head by capitalism's relentless drive for expansion. Instead, we are presented with a reversed image: Nature is subordinated to society, and society is embedded within the economy. This is, of course, a fraudulent inversion but one that effectively reflects the structure of capitalist command, where accumulation and economic growth take absolute priority over social and ecological reproduction.

Capitalism has achieved this inversion by elevating exchange value, economic growth, market relations, and self-interested behavior to the top of the social hierarchy, shaping the organization of social cooperation around these imperatives. What Polanyi depicted as an inverted pyramid, where larger spheres (nature and society) encompass smaller ones (the economy), becomes in capitalism an actual command pyramid, where economic rationality dominates and directs the other spheres toward accumulation. This reversal is not merely an ideological construct; it manifests in systemic hierarchies, shaping both our perceptions and our material conditions. It operates within our minds, framing the economy as the ultimate sphere of necessity, and through our bodies, conditioning everyday actions to conform to economic rationality. In doing so, it continuously restructures society, where cooperation and commonality would otherwise prevail, into an instrument for capitalist ends. The same logic extends to the state, which, rather than standing apart as a counterbalance, is increasingly subsumed within this systemic hierarchy, reinforcing the imperatives of accumulation.

Building on this point, the capitalist mode of production operates as a hierarchy of ends, with the relentless drive for accumulation systematically placed at the apex. As a result, state principles have been repeatedly enlisted at different stages of capitalism to establish, enforce, and maintain the power structures necessary to sustain these overarching capitalist imperatives. One of the clearest expressions of this is the state's role in facilitating successive waves of *primitive accumulation*—the violent separation of communities from their means of subsistence. This foundational process underpins a cascading series of separations: workers from the means of production and existence, labor from management, waged from unwaged labor, fellow workers from one another, communities from Gaia, citizens from citizens across borders, and identities from identities. These separations are not incidental; they are operations of displacement that fragment the field of value praxis, isolate relations, and recalibrate thresholds of solidarity. In this way, the living tissue of social cooperation is torn into governable units, rendered vulnerable to control, and subjugated to the command of accumulation.

Beyond these systemic separations, state principles—understood as the imposition of hierarchical command—are embedded deep within capitalist institutions. Corporations, driven by profit, reproduce the state's vertical logic through managerial layers that coordinate conflict and enforce control. But this architecture of command extends further: It infiltrates the sphere of everyday life where both statist and market logics reappear in disguised forms. Statist structures surface when codified hierarchies enforce the subordination of women and children to male authority, as in patriarchy; market logics emerge when households internalize exchange principles, allocating reproductive labor through transactions rather than through reciprocity and care. In this way, both the state and the market extend their reach beyond formal institutions, shaping even the most intimate textures of social cooperation.

The common as a condition and social change

As a set of social processes and relationships, social cooperation today is an immensely complex and global phenomenon. It spans the entire planet, driving extractive industries, reshaping ecologies, and altering the climate. It consists of countless interconnected circuits of social production, forming a web of interdependence that is constantly evolving. At any given moment, social cooperation is not just the sum of these interconnections but is also shaped by the specific nature of this interdependence—how it is actualized, the effects it produces, and the emotions and transformations it generates across individuals, ecologies, and societies.

Social cooperation operates at multiple spatiotemporal scales: the local, the urban, the regional, the continental, and the global. In its totality, across these different levels, social cooperation constitutes what we can call the common—the fundamental condition of our existence. The common is not only what sustains life across diverse contexts but also what generates crises, suffering, and inequalities. It is the force-field that both nurtures and destroys, commands and obeys, rewards with money, and punishes with violence. It creates dependencies while also opening paths to autonomy; it prioritizes certain needs and suppresses others.

The common as a condition is thus the web of social relations that shape our lived experiences. It is the process through which our collective actions impact the planet, reinforce or challenge hierarchies, and structure wealth and power. It is the mechanism that enriches a few while impoverishing many, assigning authority to those who can afford the price of influence. It is within this process that we, as individuals, find ourselves navigating the reproduction of our lives—either as obedient actors, confined to predefined roles; as ambivalent agents, caught between competing value systems, aware of contradictions but uncertain of alternatives; or as alter-subjects, poised to resist and collaborate in creating new forms of social cooperation (Chapter 5).

Recognizing the common as a condition means not only exposing the contradictions and destructive effects of today's dominant mode of social cooperation but also identifying openings for transformation. It means seeing the potential for the common as a project—a deliberate, collective effort to reshape cooperation beyond capitalist imperatives. This is the path toward establishing and expanding the common as a mode of production, where social relations are reconfigured to prioritize collective well-being and a new relation with Gaia over accumulation and control.

While this conception of the common shares important resonances with other contemporary contributions—such as Dardot and Laval's (2019) emphasis on the *common as a political principle* and Negri's (2023) rearticulation of the *common as constituent power* rooted in ontological productivity—my approach departs from both by grounding the common first in its systemic condition: the historically stratified, metabolically entangled, and hierarchically ordered web of social cooperation shaped by the dominance of capital. Unlike Dardot and Laval, I do not treat the common primarily as a normative alternative to state sovereignty or private property but as a conflicted field of value praxis within which capitalist command organizes life itself. It is within this field that any normative alternative must be located and calibrate its political measures. And unlike Negri, who foregrounds the constituent power of living labor as the engine of the common, I place greater emphasis on the mixed constitution of social cooperation, the stratified ordering of value domains, and the recursive dynamics that reproduce or contest the pyramid of capital. Again, it is this mixed constitution, as it is expressed in situated contexts, that the constituent power of living labor must navigate as it seeks ways to challenge recursive constraints, metabolic dependencies, and stratified hierarchies that shape the terrain on which its productivity unfolds. The crucial point is this: Political principles and constituent power are two sides of the same coin (De Angelis 2021)—praxis, a value praxis of transformation that operates within a social cooperation whose own value hierarchies are hegemonized by capital. It is only through this praxis—reflexive, situated, and materially engaged—that the common can become not only a horizon but a force of reorganization within the world as it is, a mode of production.

2

Reproductions and the measures of things

Hierarchies in the common as condition

Social cooperation as a whole emerges from countless interconnected productive circuits that operate across multiple scales and encompass diverse modes of production and social relations. Under the hegemony of capital, these interactions continuously generate and reinforce hierarchies of income and wealth.

There are several dimensions to this hierarchy. The first is a pronounced division between those who produce use values as wage earners and those who, by owning capital, benefit from the fruits of production without directly engaging in it. While waged workers create the essential goods and services that drive economic activity, capital owners and financiers extract surplus value through rents, profits, and other nonwage mechanisms (Marx 1976; Harvey 2010). This structural separation not only deepens economic inequality but also reinforces power imbalances by allowing wealth to accumulate independently of labor, thereby perpetuating disparities on a global scale.

Second, among wage earners, income hierarchies are structured along gendered and racialized lines, where systemic discrimination and historical inequities create distinct pathways to economic advantage and disadvantage. Women, undocumented migrants, and racial minorities are frequently channeled into lower-paying positions and face significant barriers to career advancement due to overt bias and the structural devaluation of work traditionally performed by these groups (England 2010; Roithmayr 2014; Hall and Greenman 2015). These hierarchical structures not only reflect social inequities but also serve capital by ensuring a segmented and inexpensive labor force that underpins continued profit maximization. The deliberate pitting of one group against another functions as a fundamental strategy to weaken collective bargaining and maintain competitive pressure among workers.

Moreover, these disparities are further deepened when we consider unwaged labor, which includes domestic care work predominantly performed by women, unpaid internships undertaken by students, and volunteer services. These forms of labor play a crucial yet often overlooked role in sustaining both social reproduction and the broader capitalist economy.

They generate essential use values that support waged production yet remain excluded from traditional economic metrics such as GDP, leading to their systematic undervaluation and invisibility in policy debates (Folbre 2001; Federici 2004). The persistent undervaluation of this labor not only reinforces entrenched gender and social inequalities but also contributes to significant time poverty and "work–life imbalances" (Gambles et al. 2006) in a context in which work has become a historically hegemonic principle of social life (Schor 1991). This undervalued labor not only sustains waged production but also absorbs the fallout from cost-cutting measures in public services. For example, when governments reduce spending on health care and other social expenditures, families and communities are compelled to compensate through increased unpaid labor, effectively bearing the hidden costs of austerity policies. Such dynamics exacerbate entrenched inequalities by shifting the burden of essential care and social support from the state to individuals, underscoring the critical need to recognize and support unwaged work in public debates.

Widening income and wealth polarization has become a defining feature of modern capitalism, as the benefits of economic growth increasingly accrue to a small, oligarchic elite segment of society. Structural changes—such as technological advancements, deregulation, and the financialization of the economy—have shifted power toward capital owners, leading to significant disparities in income distribution (Piketty 2014). This concentration of wealth undermines social mobility and exacerbates economic inequality, posing significant challenges to democratic governance and social cohesion (Stiglitz 2012; Atkinson 2015). As globalization intensifies competition and transforms labor markets, and as cuts to social services widen, the resulting imbalances call for policy responses that include progressive taxation and enhanced social safety nets. Yet neoliberal globalization has depended precisely on the dismantling of the welfare state and cuts to corporate taxes to attract foreign investment. Against the backdrop of growing wealth concentration and the dismantling of traditional welfare systems, many argue that alternative models of social protection—such as Universal Basic Income (UBI)—are essential to counter the effects of neoliberal austerity, labor-market precarity, and technological automation. UBI is increasingly proposed not only as a means of restoring economic security but also as compensation for unwaged labor, including the invisible work of feeding the data machine of platform capitalism. Advocates contend that it would establish an economic floor; reduce income insecurity; and empower individuals to invest in education, care, and community engagement without the constant pressure of precarious employment (Standing 2017; Fumagalli 2018). Decoupling income from work is thus seen as a necessary response to the pressures of contemporary capitalism and as a corrective to systemic inequalities that have long marginalized vulnerable groups. Yet the systemic logic of global capitalism seems to favor such decoupling only when it expands unwaged work, rather than redistributing power or autonomy.

As we have *broadly* mapped the hierarchies generated by the system of social cooperation, we can now return to our central theme with a more precise question: If cooperation as a whole does not serve a singular purpose but instead unfolds through intersecting circuits of production that entrench inequality—and, as we shall see, also generate crises and contradictions, including ecological breakdown—then what is its underlying function?

Reproduction

To address this question is to face the problematic of reproduction. The innumerable circuits that constitute social cooperation are highly differentiated in their specific purposes, each oriented toward the production of particular use values, whether material or immaterial. This differentiation becomes all the more pronounced as the social division of labor deepens. The vast array of use values generated by social cooperation serves an obvious function: the satisfaction of a wide range of social needs, ranging from the most basic necessities to complex and specialized demands. Screws and tanks, books and video games, vegetables and medical care—all are produced to meet distinct needs. It is unnecessary to dwell here on the profound inequalities, wastefulness, and contradictions that shape how these needs are socially composed and distributed. What is important to underline, however, is that the purpose of a given productive circuit does not coincide entirely with the satisfaction of a need, in part because, in contemporary forms of social cooperation, the process of need satisfaction is often external to the production circuit that creates the means for its fulfillment.

As soon as a productive system sets itself the task of satisfying a need not just once but continuously and in succession—producing a given use value a million and one times—the question of its reproduction necessarily arises. Reproduction entails producing again, as suggested by the prefix "re-." But in the context of social cooperation as a whole, reproduction does not simply entail making a copy of what was previously produced. Whereas production is a process that starts with given conditions and culminates in a result—a use value, whether material or immaterial—reproduction is the process through which that result is transformed back into a condition. In doing so, it closes the loop and renders visible the circular dynamic of praxis itself: the ongoing creation of the conditions of production that sustain and regenerate social cooperation over time.

Social cooperation, in its generality, demands a continuous process of reproduction. As Marx (1976: 711) reminds us, production cannot exist without reproduction; the very continuity of society depends on it:

> Whatever the social form of the production process, it has to be continuous, it must periodically repeat the same phases. A society can no more cease to produce than it can cease to consume. When viewed, therefore, as a connected whole, and in the constant flux of its incessant renewal, every social process of production is at the same time a process of reproduction.

Reproduction is not merely the reproduction of outputs but the ongoing regeneration of the enabling conditions—biological, material, social, ecological, and symbolic—that make production possible in the first place. However, what distinguishes reproduction in the context of social cooperation as a whole is not just this circularity but the orientation of its values and purposes.

Reproduction purposes

To create the conditions of production—that is, to reproduce social cooperation in general—entails two fundamental tasks. First, it requires the reproduction of the structural components necessary for production systems at different scales to function: ensuring that a labor force is available, making raw materials accessible, and maintaining infrastructures that allow for productive activity. This also includes the cultivation of subjectivities appropriate to the kinds of operations required within a given system. Second, it involves reproducing the relations among these components in a way that sustains the system's identity. If, for an individual subject, identity concerns the formation of selfhood through experience, relationships, and choices, then for a system, identity refers to the continuity of its structure and function over time. A system reproduces itself when it maintains its internal relations and operative principles in a way that preserves its coherence, even if certain components change. Maintaining functional coherence is closely related to purpose.

This continuous reproduction of conditions—of structural components and their relations—is what allows all productive systems to sustain themselves. It is not a mechanical repetition of production but a recursive, self-organizing process that ensures production continues in ways specific to the system that pursues it. Reproduction thus determines the forms through which production, organizational structures, and social relations are shaped in accordance with the systemic purposes that orient them.

While the productive purposes within social cooperation are as numerous as the range of use values produced, the reproductive purposes of productive systems are far more limited. This is because reproductive purposes function as meta-ends—orientations that unify multiple production circuits under shared systemic imperatives. A multinational agribusiness, an oil company, a pharmaceutical corporation, and a financial institution each produce vastly different use values and operate through distinct production processes. Yet their reproductive aim is fundamentally the same: to generate profit and expand their operations. Likewise, a parent cooking dinner, a teacher explaining a subject, and a nurse checking a patient's blood pressure engage in very different productive activities, yet their reproductive aim is identical: to sustain and regenerate the conditions of life, thereby ensuring the continuity of human capacities for living. For that matter, even a worker on an assembly line, once self-conscious of their own bodily needs and desires, shares the same reproductive orientation.

The number of reproductive meta-ends in social cooperation is therefore far more constrained than the immense diversity of use values produced. In fact, these meta-ends can be reduced to two fundamental orientations: social reproduction and capital reproduction. Yet they do not operate in the same way. Capital reproduction possesses an *immanent structural teleology*—a drive inscribed in its very logic. It is *immanent* because the drive arises from within the system itself, rather than from any external cause or transcendent purpose; *structural* because it is encoded in the organization of relations rather than in individual will or ideology; and *teleological* because the process has an inherent directionality—accumulation as an end in itself. Capital's reproduction is thus bound to the perpetual expansion of value, an imperative dictated by its own systemic logic. If accumulation ceases, the system enters into crisis: Growth is not merely one possible path of development but an existential necessity within the system.

Social reproduction, too, possesses an *immanent structural teleology*: It must continuously seek out and enact the conditions of living within specific and changing contexts. It is *immanent* because its drive arises from within the very processes of life and cooperation, rather than from any external command or transcendent purpose; *structural* because this drive is embedded in the relational organization of social life—the ways bodies, ecologies, and institutions interact to sustain existence; and *teleological* because it has directionality, oriented toward the sustenance and regeneration of life. Yet this teleology differs profoundly from that of capital. Both forms of reproduction are adaptive and historically situated, but their orientations diverge in their relation to value. Capital's adaptation serves the imperative of accumulation: Every transformation, innovation, or act of regulation ultimately aims to restore or expand the circuit of value. Here, value stands above life—it is the abstract measure to which human and ecological energies are subordinated. Social reproduction's adaptation, by contrast, serves the renewal of living capacities and the maintenance of shared conditions of existence. In this case, value is reabsorbed into life itself: It names what sustains, connects, and enables flourishing. The former follows a closed, self-reinforcing logic in which value dominates life; the latter remains open, contingent, and plural, where value is redefined through the collective negotiation of what it means to live well. This distinction—between a mode of reproduction ordered by accumulation and one oriented toward the regeneration of life—underlies the fundamental tension shaping social cooperation.

However, while social reproduction unfolds through a diversity of practices, it is also embedded in relatively stable institutions—such as the welfare state, public education, care infrastructures, and the family—that mediate and shape its historical trajectory. Yet these institutions remain structurally exposed to capital's imperatives and are vulnerable to reconfiguration, financialization, commodification, and enclosure. As capital expands, it disciplines and appropriates the very conditions that sustain life, restricting access to the means of existence and reshaping social reproduction to align functionally with accumulation—even when this generates crisis and contradiction.

At the same time, because social reproduction is not fully enclosed within capital's logic, it remains a contested space where struggles over care, labor, and ecological sustainability resist, negotiate, or reconfigure this subordination. This asymmetry defines a fundamental tension: Social reproduction is oriented toward sustaining life in all its dimensions—bodily, cognitive, affective, emotional, and relational—whereas capital reproduction is concerned with sustaining accumulation, instrumentalizing life-making processes to serve its own teleology.

This contradiction is not merely a matter of abstract theory; it is enacted and embodied within circuits of value praxis (Chapter 6), traversing the singular and collective bodies of those who inhabit them. It expresses itself not only in conflicts of interest but in a structural clash between a system that must accumulate and a heterogeneous domain of life reproduction that sustains existence through multiple, contingent, and relational forms of cooperation and organization.

These contradictions and entanglements do not stop at the level of institutions. They unfold within the most immediate forms of life reproduction—families, households, networks of friends, and local communities—shaped by patriarchal structures, the necessity of accessing markets for survival, and the pervasive pressures of consumerism. The entanglement runs through us: through the bodies and psyches of individual subjects, the mixed constitution of our desires, all of us navigating the tensions of social cooperation across neighborhoods, workplaces, and institutions. These tensions perturb us, demanding patterns of adaptation and transformation, and inscribe themselves in our emotional lives—in the form of anxiety, stress, and toxic ideological responses that seek to mask or manage our fears.

The dominance of capital reproduction ensures that social reproduction is frequently reorganized to maintain compatibility with accumulation, even at the cost of deepening crises and contradictions.

Social reproduction and the reproduction of capital are both social forces that permeate and, in their tension, give shape to social cooperation and the broader reproduction of society as a whole. This, in turn, occurs within the ecosystem—that is, the set of reproductive processes of nonhuman nature (Figure 2.1). By *societal* reproduction (Brenner and Laslett 1991), I, thus, mean the complex of processes, social relations, and corresponding embodied material and energy flows that take place through social

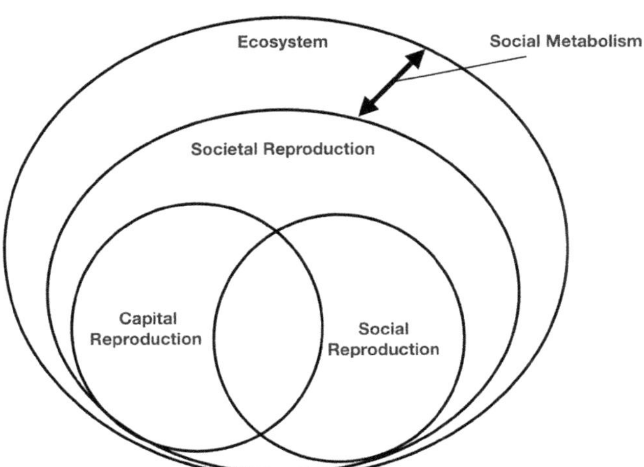

Figure 2.1 Social cooperation and the common as a condition

cooperation *in its entirety* and its various forms. This broad conception of societal reproduction implies two key aspects. First, social cooperation is presented here as the general reproduction of society, which is the *emergent* result of the interplay between the different social forces shaping social cooperation, with their contrasting purposes, organizational processes, and ways of measuring things. As discussed in Chapter 1, we can define this *emergent* form of societal reproduction with the term capitalism, insofar as societal reproduction is a mixed constitution of modes of production under the hegemony of a particular social force—capital and its meta-reproductive purpose. Second, society as a whole reproduces itself, meaning that it creates the specific conditions of its existence in historically determined forms through social interactions (internal to society) that necessarily correspond to forms of interaction with the ecosystem—that is, nonhuman nature. This means that society as a whole reproduces itself through exchange with nonhuman nature. Following Marx (1976), we refer to this exchange and the processes through which it takes place as *social metabolism*, which is the dynamic interface between the reproduction of society as a whole (common as a condition, capitalism) and the reproduction of nonhuman nature, the ecosystem. We will discuss this in more detail in Chapter 10.

Reproduction, organization, and social forces

Let us return to the crux of the matter, that is, the exploration of the two social forces we have identified as social and capital reproduction. While definitions vary depending on the theoretical framework (see Chapter 3), the concept of *social forces* is used across various disciplines to describe the structural and collective dynamics that shape social life. Social forces generally refer to designed or emergent pressures, movements, or structures that influence social cooperation, political arrangements, and economic processes. Social forces are thus emergent organizations of collective powers-to (*potentia*) oriented toward specific purposes, social praxes that seek to shape their environments. Social and capital reproduction can pursue their respective teleologies through such an articulation of collective powers across different modalities and scales of social cooperation.

This understanding of social forces as emergent from collective powers and relational modes directly ties into a broader discussion of *organization*. In a broad sense, organization is a process through which diverse elements coordinate, relate, and interact to form a somewhat coherent system, maintaining a degree of stability over time while adapting to their environment. Organization applies to biological, cognitive, social, and political systems and always implies a relation between internal structure and external dynamics. But organization is not a simple thing that maps directly onto our common understanding of what constitutes an "organization" when we refer to an institution.

Every living or social system exists and reproduces itself—regardless of its teleology—through an organization that defines its identity and conditions of persistence over time in constant interaction with its surrounding environment. Organization permeates the social field (Nunes 2021), manifesting in both decentralized and centralized systems, operating at molecular and molar levels (Deleuze and Guattari 1988), and located along a continuum between planned and emergent forms.

Organizational forms emerge both as coalescences of autonomous parts without a general coordination plan and as collective systems guided by intentional planning. We thus find organizations in the form of what Hayek (1973) distinguished between *cosmos* and *taxis*. In reality, these oppositions form part of a continuum that Nunes describes as "distributed organisation." For instance, every company operates within the market according to an internal plan, yet the interaction among competing firms generates an emergent organization—the market itself. This market, in turn, can be subjected to planning through industrial policy, fiscal and monetary policy, as well as geopolitical and geoeconomic forces that shape its contours and limits. A market can even be embedded within a grassroots commons (De Angelis and Diesner 2020).

Similarly, a neighborhood committee or a political collective acts according to a plan that structures its political interventions: demonstrations, campaigns, press releases, and the dissemination of propaganda materials. In pursuing its objectives, this organization interacts with other actors and realities, forming an ecology of relations and practices that, taken together, constitute a movement. A social movement, in this sense, is already a form of organization, though not in the traditional sense of a closed hierarchical structure. Following Nunes (2021), a movement is better understood as a political ecology: a diffuse and plural network of relations among groups, collectives, and individuals who share common orientations but operate with different levels of coordination and autonomy. This perspective challenges the idea that movements lack organization; rather, they self-organize through emergent and adaptive dynamics in response to the historical and social conditions in which they operate. But then the different elements of the movement interacting in an ecology can be brought together in assemblies that seek to define the contours of its action, thus moving it toward the planned edge of the spectrum.

The distinction between organization as a planned process and as an emergent phenomenon is essential, yet these two modes are not mutually exclusive; as we will discuss in Chapter 3 through the concepts of allopoiesis and sympoiesis, they continuously interact and shape one another. Social forces, such as social and capital reproduction, arise from specific interweavings of these modes, generating broader and more distributed forms of organization across the social field.

This dynamic positioning of any singular organization along the continuum between planned and emergent structures, and the articulation of different organizational modes in generating social forces, calls for a framework that captures how these modes interact rather than remain separate. Autopoiesis functions precisely through this interweaving, integrating externally imposed structures (*allopoietic* processes) with emergent, collectively coproduced dynamics (*sympoietic* processes) to varying degrees. This recursive integration enables the ongoing reproduction of social forces in ways that are not purely imposed or spontaneous but guided by evolving internal purposes. Autopoietic organizations thus mediate between designed and emergent orders, reconfiguring themselves in response to both imposed structures and adaptive patterns, while remaining oriented toward the continuity of their own operative logic.

I maintain that autopoietic organization is a key feature of capital and social reproduction, the organizing principle that makes them social forces. In what follows, I provide only a general sketch of this link, as I discuss it at greater length in the next chapter, where I also explore the nuanced interrelation between autopoietic, allopoietic, and sympoietic processes, and their entanglement within the broader problematic of social and ecological transformation.

Autopoiesis, reproduction, and social forces

Autopoiesis is a fundamental notion for understanding social forces. I take this concept from biology and translate it to the social with due precautions. Maturana and Varela (1987) introduced the concept of autopoiesis to define the fundamental characteristic of living systems. For them, a living organism is neither a taxonomy of characteristics nor merely a system that undergoes metabolism or responds to stimuli; rather, it is a self-producing entity that continuously regenerates and maintains its own components through recursive internal processes. Thus, by autopoietic organization, they mean a particular way of exercising autonomy, that is, *the capacity for self-assertion of systems in given contexts.*[1] An autopoietic system is a machine that produces its own components and relations and occupies a space within which it carries out its production processes *in the face of external perturbations, pursuing goals that are not set by external observers but emerge internally as the result of an evolutionary process.* They describe living systems as *operationally closed*, meaning that their organization is not determined by external inputs but is instead *self-referential*, sustaining itself through its own dynamics. Autopoiesis thus defines life as a process of self-organization and self-maintenance: A cell, for example, is autopoietic because it constantly produces the very components (membranes, enzymes, proteins) that constitute it, ensuring its structural integrity and autonomy. This operational closure does not mean that the system is isolated from its environment—living beings are structurally open; they interact with their surroundings through structural coupling, meaning that they acquire structural elements from their environment and undergo changes in response to external perturbations while maintaining their organizational coherence. From this perspective, then, life is not characterized by what a system *does* at a given moment and in a given environment but by how it sustains itself as a coherent, self-reproducing entity, regardless of external conditions. This perspective fundamentally differs from input–output models of biological organization, which see living systems as primarily responding to external stimuli. Instead, autopoietic systems determine their own internal states while remaining structurally coupled to their environment.

It is clearly necessary to translate the concept of autopoiesis into the realm of social forces and social organization, and I will do this in the next chapter. Suffice it here to anticipate that the self-produced and recursively generated components in an autopoietic *social* system are the meanings, values, and embodied relational patterns through which organizations are constituted. Autopoiesis, when applied to social subjects and social systems, is thus the *continuous self-production of components of meaning given to action, of relations between components, and of the purposes orienting them.* A subject, a collective, a coalescence, a circuit, an institution, or a social system becomes an element of a social force insofar as it is bent to its autopoiesis, enacting it through praxis, and insofar as it is part of its cybernetic circuits of energy retention that produce value(s), organizing both material and immaterial components into a coherent and self-sustaining social whole.

This is where social autopoiesis intersects with value production. The social realm is not merely a site of exchange but a space in which internally generated orders of value shape and organize life. While biological autopoiesis ensures the persistence of living systems through the continuous regeneration of biochemical components, social autopoiesis sustains collective life by reproducing social organization through specific *social* components—value praxes aligned with purpose. In biological systems, organizational patterns are maintained through self-referential biochemical processes governed by genetic and epigenetic mechanisms that regulate cellular self-maintenance and reproduction. By contrast, social organization does not rely on a fixed genetic code; instead, it emerges through the ongoing social and historical reproduction of meanings, norms, and values that orient praxis. Where living organisms sustain themselves through biochemical cycles, social systems do so through semiotic, material, and relational processes that structure collective existence. The key distinction lies in their governing constraints: Biological systems are shaped by biochemical limits, whereas social systems are structured by historically variable and contested orders of value domains that shape praxis and relational dynamics. Within these orders, value struggles are everywhere in social cooperation.

Capital, in its complex generality, is an autopoietic system. It produces its components by assigning specific value registers to all of its structural components, thus making them part of a social praxis oriented toward its own specific purpose: accumulation. This is also true of any single company operating within it and of the supply chains they give rise to. They seek to survive and prosper in an environment that is necessarily turbulent because it is the home of the social and biological living subjects (living, hence also endowed with their own socially reproductive autopoiesis) and therefore offers resistances of all kinds, as well as *opportunities* to capital for further commodification and subsumption within the boundaries of its own autopoietic system. Capital seeks to reproduce itself by ensuring the continuous accumulation of (exchange) value, shaping labor, production, and social organization in ways that sustain its cycle of accumulation. In contrast, social reproduction's ability to pursue its purposes—sustaining life through use and relational values—is asymmetrically dependent on access to exchange value, which is mediated by and largely subordinated to the imperatives of capital reproduction. This dependence reinforces structural asymmetries, as social reproduction must continuously navigate and contest the ever-shifting constraints imposed by capitalist accumulation while striving to maintain its own coherence and autonomy amid the turbulence it generates. This contestation, even if only at the levels of friction, pervades the social field at the "molecular" and "molar" level (Deleuze and Guattari 1988) but also tends to unfold in cycles of collective struggle, with different compositions, shapes, and degrees of rupture and disruption.

At various critical levels, depending on the contexts of their nucleation and geographies of diffusion, collective action and crises disrupt capital's mechanisms of reproduction, introducing perturbations that may destabilize its autopoietic organization and force structural transformations. However, while these struggles can impact the institutional and regulatory frameworks through which capital operates, they do not alter its fundamental autopoietic logic, which remains bound to the imperative of accumulation. Thus, the extent to which these struggles generate lasting shifts depends on their capacity to sustain alternative modes of reproduction, effectively challenging capital's ability to reabsorb opposition into its expansive logic. It depends therefore on the powers (*powers to* and *powers over* capital reproduction) deployed by social reproduction in giving effective organizational form to its own autopoiesis. Today, in spite of the great crises pervading the social body and the body of Gaia, the many and increasing struggles on the terrain of social reproduction remain fragmented, pointing to the need for social reproduction to find ways to cohere into a counterforce capable of asserting its own autopoiesis—its logic—against the self-perpetuating structures of capitalist accumulation. I will discuss this further in Chapters 3 and 16.

Transversality and the deal

Social and capital reproduction are *transversal* social forces, meaning that they do not operate as discrete or isolated structures but as dynamically interwoven processes that cut across multiple domains of social life, shaping and being shaped by their interactions. They are not confined to separate spheres but are entangled within every institutional, economic, and cultural configuration of society. The workplace, the home, the school, the state, and the ecological environment are all sites in which the interaction between these forces unfolds: capital's teleology attempts to reshape social cooperation according to its logic, while social reproduction struggles to assert its own priorities across different contexts.

This transversality means that no aspect of social life is immune to the pressures and tensions of this dynamic. It is not simply that capital and social reproduction interact at key points; rather, their entanglement permeates the very conditions of existence, continually redefining how work, play, care, knowledge, and resources are organized. Through this ongoing interrelation, both social forces take on their historically specific forms—not as fixed entities but as processes that evolve in response to shifting power relations, struggles, and systemic crises. The transversal nature of social and capital reproduction thus reveals not only their interdependence but also the constant contestation over the terms of their reproduction, as different institutional and social configurations mediate, reinforce, or resist capital's attempts to subordinate life to accumulation.

This transversal entanglement is not merely a structural condition; it is also the terrain on which struggles over governability are staged. It is through the governance of the contested interaction between the forces of capital accumulation and social reproduction that the overall shape of societal reproduction is determined. At certain historical moments, this interaction has been actively managed to create an apparent dynamic balance, often through institutional frameworks designed to stabilize the relationship between them. Foucault (2002) described governability as the "management of flows," which, in this context, can be understood as an attempt by power to regulate and mediate the tensions between these two forms of reproduction, preventing their contradictions from becoming ungovernable.

A striking instance of such management emerged in the postwar period, when Keynesian policies and welfare state architectures sought to contain the crises of capital accumulation while simultaneously ensuring the reproduction of labor power and social infrastructures (De Angelis 2000). This balance was not merely technical or economic; it was political. As George Caffentzis (2013) argues, this apparent balance between capital and social reproduction takes the form of a *deal*—a historically contingent arrangement that seeks to stabilize the contradictions between capital and social reproduction, the temporary regulatory strategies forged at the intersection of these transversal forces, aiming to contain crisis and maintain legitimacy through selective inclusion and deferred promises.

During the post–Second World War Keynesian era, the deal took the form of a historically specific arrangement through which capital promised social stability, rising wages, and access to goods and services in exchange for labor discipline and political acquiescence. The *Keynesian deal* was underpinned by full employment policies, welfare state architectures, and strong unions, institutionalizing a form of partial inclusion through consumption and national citizenship. Even energy itself functioned as a medium of social cooperation within this arrangement—a condition of the wage deal (Caffentzis 1992). Yet these deals were never contracts among equals. They were inherently asymmetrical instruments of command: They could be revoked unilaterally by capital, while waged and unwaged workers were held to their side of the bargain. Their inclusions were always selective, built on racialized, gendered, and geopolitical hierarchies that externalized costs onto marginalized groups and territories.

Beginning in the 1970s, with the onset of stagflation, the collapse of Bretton Woods, and successive energy crises, this Keynesian deal entered a period of crisis. What followed was not the end of deal-making but its neoliberal reconfiguration. In its place, a neoliberal deal was constructed through restructuring, debt, and financialization, each producing its own broken promises and atmospheres of disaffection. The neoliberal deal offered credit in place of wages, precarity in place of security, and global integration in place of national solidarity. This reconfiguration maintained the logic of the promise but increasingly deferred it into the future while redistributing its risks downward. The legitimacy of these new arrangements rested not on tangible delivery but on the continued belief in upward mobility, market participation, and fiscal discipline. Yet as these promises faltered—through deindustrialization, structural adjustment, financial crises, and the disintegration of public infrastructure—resentment and disillusionment proliferated. The 2007–8 financial collapse marked a decisive moment in the breakdown of the neoliberal deal, exposing the emptiness of its promises and catalyzing widespread refusal of the deal alongside heightened affective volatility (Midnight Notes Collective and Friends 2009).

In the wake of this second fracturing, right-wing populist projects have emerged as attempts to reconfigure the deal on exclusionary grounds, offering protection, identity, and partial restoration in exchange for the abandonment of universalist claims and the reinforcement of new internal and external frontiers. These are not simply ideological positions but affective and political bargains aimed at restoring governability amid promise fatigue and the structural unraveling of capital's capacity to organize social reproduction.

Crisiscraft—the throb of command that fabricates capitalist order from disorder (Chapter 14)—operates precisely through the manipulation of these promises. It extends them, defers them, resignifies them, or weaponizes their betrayal. Crisiscraft works not to restore the content of past promises but to *reconfigure expectations and allegiances*. Austerity promises stability. Green capitalism promises salvation. Authoritarian populism promises the return of dignity through exclusion. These are not merely ideological messages but affective bargains, saturated with the residue of previous betrayals.

Today, the possibility of sustaining a balance between social and capital reproduction has become increasingly tenuous. The deepening ecological and climate crisis, the financialization of everyday life, the precaritization of labor, and the war regime all point to the growing impossibility of reconciling capital's need for accumulation with the demands of social reproduction. Any attempt to take the side of social reproduction in a substantive and *radically inclusive way* would require drastically curtailing capital's capacity for accumulation, actively pursuing de-accumulation, and expanding and deepening grassroots forms of democratization of social cooperation, as emphasized, for example, in the degrowth literature (D'Alisa et al. 2015; Barca 2017; Andreucci and Engel-Di Mauro 2019; Kallis et al. 2020). Capital is systemically unable to support social reproduction within its own framework without producing deeper crises in the reproduction of life itself.

The measure of things

As social forces, capital and social reproduction orient human activity—praxis—within social cooperation. This orientation is not merely about directing action but about situating it within registers of meaning that define what praxis is and what it is for. As we will see throughout this book, and especially in Chapter 7, meaning is inseparable from value, and the way value is assigned to praxis fundamentally shapes social cooperation. In other words, in seeking to orient social cooperation through its transversal dimensions, social forces measure things, and they do so in contradictory and clashing ways.

The argument I am making about the central contradiction of our times—rooted in the tension between capital reproduction and social reproduction—is not new. It echoes the distinction between use value and exchange value in Marx's (1976) critique of political economy, which he inherited from classical political economists. Marx identifies the dominance of the commodity form in capitalism as the Gordian knot that must be untied to free use value from its subordination to exchange value (Leonardi 2026). However, I begin with the distinction between the two forms of reproduction not only to highlight their opposing systemic meta-finalities but also to show how they shape different orientations in the form of autopoietic organization of social cooperation. These social forces do not merely structure social and economic processes; they actively generate, prefigure, or determine different kinds of social relations. Thus, the contrast between social and capital reproduction cannot be reduced to a simple opposition between use value and exchange value. A third type of value must be considered: relational value, the value attributed to relationships within social cooperation. Relational values matter because they orient social cooperation toward purposes where the relationship itself is the end, not a means—making them irreducible to instrumental or economic logics. The production of use value—whether subordinated to exchange value (profit) or embedded in logics of gift and solidarity—always presupposes specific social relationships to which we ascribe meaning and assign value. Social cooperation is never merely a mechanical process of production and exchange; it is a meaning-laden activity shaped by how we evaluate, justify, and orient action across different contexts.

To fully grasp social cooperation, we must account for these three forms of value—use value, exchange value, and relational value—not as isolated categories but as elements of a broader process of valuation, one that is always bound to specific forms of measurement. I refer to this process as the *measure of things*.

The measure of things is part of a process through which value is ascribed to praxis—the activity of life, social labor, and human action. Every society, and every form of social cooperation, measures its activity in some way, whether through explicit quantification (monetary value, productivity metrics) or through implicit social and cultural standards (worth, necessity, justice, care). This measurement is never neutral; it makes distinctions and selections, defines lines of inclusion and exclusion, and thus establishes orders of relevance, and it thus structures social life by answering fundamental questions: *Who produces? What is produced? How much is produced? Where is it produced? When and for how long? Why is it produced?* These questions and their corresponding answers do not merely describe reality—they actively shape it, determining how human effort, time, and resources are allocated and valued, as well as the forms of relations among coproducers and between them and Gaia.

However, the significance of these questions is not fixed or universal. Their weight, meaning, and priority depend on the reproductive meta-ends that frame them in different contexts. Different meta-ends—whether oriented toward capital reproduction or social reproduction—assign different levels of importance to these questions, directing human activity accordingly. What counts as meaningful, necessary, or valuable in one framework may be rendered invisible or secondary in another. Different meta-finalities not only assign different levels of importance to these questions but also define how value is measured. In this sense, the process of measuring things is not simply a matter of accounting or evaluation; it is an active force that structures social cooperation itself, shaping not only what is done but also how it is perceived, justified, and sustained over time.

Can value exist beyond measure? Hardt and Negri (2000: 356) argue that, under post-Fordist conditions, value is constructed beyond measure; that is, reproductive and cooperative activity takes place autonomously from any external regime of measurement. They suggest that immaterial and affective labor, digital cooperation, and the production of the common generate forms of value that escape capital's quantification and point toward a mode of production that capital cannot fully capture.

However, while the production of an excess beyond capitalist measure at any given time is always the case, capital has never ceased in its drive to measure and quantify even the most seemingly immeasurable forms of activity (Caffentzis 2005; De Angelis and Harvie 2006). Financialization, algorithmic governance, and the integration of digital labor into capitalist accumulation all demonstrate capital's ability to impose measurement where none previously existed. The commodification of attention, the monetization of social interactions, and the expansion of data-driven value extraction suggest that no domain of social cooperation lies *inherently* beyond capitalist measure; instead, measurement itself becomes a terrain of struggle.

Social reproduction, in this sense, does not exist outside measurement but is measured differently. It is embedded in qualitative assessments of care, well-being, sustainability, and justice rather than in measures of profitability or efficiency. Yet, as capital extends its reach, these alternative measures are subsumed, eroded, or rendered invisible within capitalist valuation. The struggle over the measure of things, then, is not just a struggle over different conceptions of value but over the very mechanisms of valuation and measurement that define social cooperation itself.

Within the logic of capital reproduction, the measure of social cooperation subordinates both humans and nature to the imperatives of financial accounting. Budgets, profits, and growth dictate priorities. Social relations, ecological concerns, and human well-being are measured only in terms of their *instrumental* value for capital accumulation. By contrast, from the perspective of social reproduction, alternative "measures of things" take precedence—values tied to well-being, care, sustainability, and the flourishing of life.

This divergence in how value is measured leads to a stark difference in the role played by *limits*. Capital reproduction has no inherent limit; it is compelled to expand indefinitely, treating every material, social, and ecological constraint as an obstacle to be overcome. Social reproduction, by contrast, is inherently bounded. It is constrained by the concrete needs of living bodies engaged in praxis—needs that are socially and materially shaped. These needs are as finite as the planet itself, which provides the resources for their satisfaction; as finite as the twenty-four-hour day, which imposes the necessity of rest; as finite as the body's capacity to absorb nutrients; and as finite as the recurring need for a break. Capital, in contrast, recognizes no such constraints. This contrast results in a fundamental opposition in the very nature of praxis under these two forms of reproduction, an opposition that becomes especially clear when we examine how the same form of praxis used to produce use values—namely labor—takes on radically different meanings depending on which logic it serves.

For capital reproduction, labor is abstract labor—what Marx (1976: 128) defines as "human labour power expended without regard for the form of its expenditure." This means that the qualitative aspects of labor—its conditions, its impact on well-being, its social and ecological context—are irrelevant or secondary, as long as it contributes to the accumulation of value. The devaluation of reproductive labor—largely performed by women—further entrenches this indifference, as care work and social reproduction are rendered invisible, intensified by welfare cuts, or taken for granted within the logic of capital. Bureaucratic and algorithmic systems further entrench this abstraction, while extreme precarity pushes workers into a state of pragmatic indifference, as their life is a continuous juggle among "opportunities" for survival.

The abstraction of labor, the reduction of social relations to instrumental means to an end, and the reduction of the nonhuman world to a resource intensify as subjectivities are increasingly shaped by the imperatives of capital reproduction under the weight of material and social necessity. A process of normalization and desensitization becomes inevitable. Yet such indifference, abstraction, and reduction are never total. The body resists, exhaustion sets in, social bonds form, desires take lines of flight, and struggles emerge—reminders that labor is always an embodied, social activity, *never fully reducible* to abstract value extraction. From the standpoint of social reproduction, the opposite is true: for subjects, whether waged or unwaged, the form in which their living capacity is expended is a fundamental aspect of how they live and experience their lives.

Just as capital seeks to abstract labor from the worker's subjective experience and their social and ecological nexus, so media infrastructures transform real violence into an endless flow of content, stripping it of immediacy and ethical urgency. War atrocities and genocides streamed through digital platforms are thus normalized. Just as workers may become numb to their own exploitation, so too can spectators be conditioned to passively consume images of suffering without engagement. Algorithmic feeds, geopolitical interests, and media sensationalism shape which horrors remain visible and for how long, just as corporate balance sheets determine what forms of social labor are recognized and valued. Yet both work exploitation and the numbing effects of digital spectacle are resisted in multiple ways. And resistance poses a transformational question: How do we reclaim embodied experience and ethical responsibility in social cooperation? Not only in work—where praxis is bent to capitalist reproduction—but also in the ways we confront the broad consequences of that reproduction, including its mediated spectacle of suffering.

To reclaim embodied experience is to challenge its abstraction and fragmentation. It is to insist that the praxis of living be grounded in a sensuous, responsive, and ethically engaged inhabitation of the world. Ethical responsibility, then, is not an external moral code but a capacity to act from within relationality, acknowledging the entanglements that shape our actions and their consequences. It means recasting social praxis by challenging the dissociation fostered by capital—between the body and its worlds, social labor and its meaning, action and responsibility, subject and others, subjects and Gaia—so that life may be lived as a connected practice of being in the world. This requires and invites the constitution of a collective subject, of a transversal organization on the terrain of social reproduction in the broad sense.

Reproduction from feminist roots to the horizon of the common

As discussed in this chapter, social reproduction is a historically contingent and heterogeneous process through which human life and its capacities are sustained, renewed, and transformed within social cooperation. It encompasses bodily, cognitive, affective, emotional, and relational dimensions, unfolding through diverse practices, institutions, and struggles. Feminist theory has been foundational over the decades in conceptualizing social reproduction, particularly in highlighting the gendered, unpaid, and often rendered invisible labor required to sustain life and human capacities (Dalla Costa and James 1975; Federici 2004; Bhattacharya 2017).

Marxist feminist interventions, particularly those by Mariarosa Dalla Costa and James (1975) and Silvia Federici (2004), emphasize that capital depends on social reproduction while refusing to pay for it, treating it as an externalized, unpaid resource. The Wages for Housework movement was instrumental in showing that the reproductive labor performed by women within households was essential to capital accumulation, yet systematically devalued. This argument also reveals that capital is necessarily coupled to social reproduction, but it does not autonomously reproduce the living capacities it requires.

Feminist work on social reproduction also highlights the crises produced by capital's relentless exploitation of reproductive labor. Fraser (2016), among others, has analyzed how neoliberalism has hollowed out social infrastructures, forcing reproductive labor into crisis as states withdraw from public welfare provisions, increasing the burden on unpaid and low-paid workers. Emma Dowling (2021) extends this critique, showing how financialized care systems intensify precarity, extract unpaid emotional labor, and deplete caregivers, pushing social reproduction to a breaking point. Thus, capital's tendency to extract value from social reproduction ultimately destabilizes it, undermining the very capacities on which it depends.

The relationship between social reproduction and ecological sustainability has been a central concern of ecofeminist scholars, who have long argued that the extraction of unpaid reproductive labor and the exploitation of nature are structurally linked under capitalism. Maria Mies (1986) was among the first to systematically connect the exploitation of women's reproductive labor, the dispossession of subsistence communities, and ecological destruction, arguing that the capitalist mode of production relies on the simultaneous subordination of both women and nature. This perspective also aligns with my approach, emphasizing that social reproduction must be understood not only in relation to labor power but as the broader reproduction of human and ecological life, bringing together labor, care, and environmental struggles.

Stefania Barca (2020, 2022) expands the discussion of social reproduction to include ecological dimensions, framing it as an ongoing struggle over the conditions of life itself. She argues that environmental degradation and the climate crisis cannot be understood apart from the framework of social reproduction, linking capitalist extraction directly to the depletion of human and nonhuman life. Barca's work builds on the ecofeminist tradition while expanding its analysis into broader critiques of political economy and environmental justice. Her argument underscores that the capitalist organization of social reproduction is ecologically unsustainable, not only because it relies on unpaid labor but because it externalizes the costs of social and ecological renewal, producing systemic depletion and crisis.

Feminist theory has made important contributions by showing how women's reproductive labor is invisibilized and devalued under capitalism. But social reproduction is not only a site of capital's exploitation but also a contested terrain where alternative forms of social cooperation emerge. And at certain historical moments, struggles around its many dimensions—housing, reproductive rights, education, health care, labor and work conditions, and ecological sustainability—coalesce, transforming social reproduction into a more coherent counterforce to capital's hegemony while at the same time seeking to build nonpatriarchal and nonracist alternatives.

While my approach to social reproduction builds on feminist insights—especially the recognition that capital depends on it but does not pay for it—it extends beyond them by emphasizing three key aspects.

First, while feminist and Marxist scholars have long expanded the scope of social reproduction beyond domestic and gendered labor to include affective labor, waged care work, and the role of institutions (Federici 2012; Fraser 2016; Bhattacharya 2017), my emphasis is on understanding this expanded field as inherently *transversal*—cutting across all domains of social cooperation and value praxis. I thus wish to extend the concept of social reproduction to encompass waged life. This includes not only waged care work in households and hospitals but also the affective and relational labor involved in waged work across other sectors. It therefore concerns not only unwaged domestic labor, care work, emotional labor, and community-based survival strategies (Glenn 1992; Hochschild 2000) but also how these very forms of reproductive labor—care, emotional labor, and collective strategies of survival—operate within sites of formal employment. A waiter managing emotional tone to reassure customers; a worker maintaining calm after a manager's rebuke to preserve workflow; workers sustaining themselves, physically and emotionally, within the workplace, whether through self-care, affective regulation, or mutual support networks, adapting to or resisting the demands of capital. These practices are not residual; they are central to the ongoing regeneration of social cooperation. Yet under capitalist command, they are frequently subordinated to logics of accumulation that distort their relational and life-sustaining purposes. In this sense, I am preoccupied with the *transversal* domain of *worked* lives (Morini 2022). It goes without saying that, in all these cases, social reproduction is historically contingent, shaped by social and cultural variability rather than being a fixed or universal structure.

Second, while many feminist and Marxist theorists have powerfully demonstrated that social reproduction is structurally necessary for the reproduction of capital (Dalla Costa and James 1975; Fraser 2016; Bhattacharya 2017), my approach foregrounds the fragmented and historically contingent nature of its autopoiesis, which can rise to challenge that of capital. While capitalism relies on reproductive labor to sustain accumulation, social reproduction itself does not operate as a cohesive, self-regulating system capable of subordinating capital. Its autopoietic organization unfolds through multiple, interwoven practices dispersed across different nodes of social cooperation that do not always coalesce into a coherent force—localized alignments of care, mutual support, and knowledge-sharing that respond to immediate needs. This makes social reproduction highly vulnerable to shifting conditions of capitalist reproduction. Informal care exchanged between neighbors may fill gaps left by retreating welfare states; underfunded schools and overstretched hospitals still function but under strain; mutual aid networks create powerful moments of social coordination yet often lack long-term infrastructural support; NGO interventions may stabilize a crisis but usually within narrow scopes. These practices sustain life through fragmented, contingent configurations, shaped by necessity, solidarity, improvisation, and struggle in a context of continuous capitalist encroachment and institutional drift. Phases of threshold recalibration (Chapter 14)—when basic reproductive capacities are strained through cuts and austerity—make these limitations visible. This, in turn, raises the crucial question of how social reproduction might be effectively organized beyond its role as a subordinate function within capitalist reproduction.

Third, feminist scholars have long argued that social reproduction is not merely a site of capital's exploitation but also a terrain of struggle (Federici 2012; Fraser 2016; Bhattacharya 2017). By integrating feminist insights while expanding the concept of social reproduction—understanding it as transversal—this perspective regards it as a field of immense recompositional possibility projected on the transformation of the entirety of social cooperation hegemonized by capital. In this sense, the approach I propose moves toward a *commonist* perspective—one that foregrounds the whole of social cooperation as a site of contestation, transformation, and the potential reorganization of life on the terrain of social reproduction.

3

Reproductions as social forces

Social forces as autopoietic systems

To approach social forces through the concept of autopoiesis is to make a decisive break with conventional definitions. In the sociological tradition, social forces have typically been understood as structural constraints external to individual agency—Durkheim's (1982) social facts being the classical example—operating as objective norms that exert coercive force on the subject from without. In the Marxist lineage, social forces are often interpreted as expressions of class relations or political-economic structures, ultimately determined "in the last instance" by the economic base and the organization of production (Althusser 1971; Marx 1977). These traditions, among others, though distinct in their analytical commitments, tend to conceptualize social forces either as overarching structures or as historical mechanisms that act upon subjects through causally determinate constraints.

More recent theoretical movements, such as actor-network theory (Latour 2005) and assemblage theory (DeLanda 2006, 2016), have attempted to move away from this structural paradigm by emphasizing emergence, heterogeneity, and the fluidity of relational interactions. Here, social forces are not imposed from above or reducible to class positions but are instead understood as effects of contingent alignments among human and nonhuman actors, technologies, infrastructures, affective intensities, and institutional scripts. These approaches rightly reject determinism and offer a powerful critique of top-down accounts of social order. They help us see how constraints themselves are emergent products of distributed, often fragile, processes of alignment and feedback.

What these relational and emergentist perspectives illuminate, then, is that constraints are not necessarily prior to interaction—they can be its result. This is an important corrective. But in treating social forces primarily as emergent effects, they often neglect the recursive, self-reinforcing dynamics that allow certain configurations of power, value, and cooperation to persist, stabilize, and scale. What an autopoietic approach reveals is that these forces are shaped by the constraints of their environment, yet also reproduce and transform those constraints through the "power-to" they mobilize. In this view, emergence is not the opposite of constraint but its recursive companion:

autopoietic systems both arise from and pattern the field in which they are embedded. This dual articulation—of being shaped by and reshaping their conditions of operation—defines the systemic organization of social forces and the historical persistence of their reproductive logics.

An autopoietic approach draws on this insight into emergence but adds a critical dimension: It asks which emergent patterns become self-organizing—namely, which ones are able to recursively stabilize their own logic, reproduce their own components, and reshape the very field in which they operate. In this view, social forces are not simply temporary alignments or fluid assemblages; they are self-producing systems embedded in a relational environment that they also transform. This opens a different question—not just how social forces emerge but how they endure, and under what conditions they reconfigure the space of social cooperation in their own image.

This is where the concept of autopoiesis—developed by Maturana and Varela (1980, 1987)—becomes especially powerful: It brings constraint and emergence into the same analytic frame by asking a deeper question. It allows us to understand social forces not just as effects or positions but as self-producing systems—recursive logics that generate and regenerate the components, values, and boundaries necessary for their continued operation within a relational field they also help to shape.

This understanding is not merely theoretical. It is fundamental to framing the problematic of radical social change. For if social forces are autopoietic, then transformation cannot rely solely on disrupting surface behaviors or displacing particular actors. It must intervene in the recursive processes by which a system reproduces itself—its rhythms, its infrastructures, its forms of coordination, and sense-making. Only then does it become possible to imagine not just resistance but the emergence of alternative reproductive logics capable of reorganizing the field itself.

In their biological formulation, Maturana and Varela define autopoietic systems as self-producing, self-maintaining units. A living system, for them, is not characterized by its response to external stimuli or its metabolic exchanges alone but by its capacity to continuously regenerate the components that constitute it—its membranes, enzymes, internal processes, and relations—under the guidance of its purpose: to live and to keep living.

But where does this guidance come from?

Crucially, for Maturana and Varela, this purpose is not imposed from outside, nor is it a representational goal held by the system. It emerges immanently from the system's own organization. The living system "knows" how to live only by virtue of the fact that it continuously reproduces the organization that makes it alive. In this sense, its purpose is not declared but *enacted*. Its autonomy does not lie in separation from the environment but in the recursive logic by which it regenerates its own systemic identity through internal operations while being structurally coupled to its surroundings. The system is guided by no *external* telos; it is guided instead by the necessity of maintaining the conditions of its own continuation.

This idea of *purpose without representation*—of autonomy as an emergent property of ongoing systemic self-reproduction—is what makes autopoiesis such a powerful lens for understanding not only living beings but also social forces. For when we speak of systems such as capital or social reproduction as autopoietic, we are pointing to the way each seeks to regenerate the conditions of its own persistence—not by following a blueprint but by enacting a logic of reproduction within a structured and dynamic environment.

This is what defines the system's autonomy—not as separation from its environment but as the internal capacity to maintain its systemic identity through recursive organization, even amid ongoing interaction.

To translate this into social theory, a social force is not merely an effect of structural position or collective intention. It is a self-reproducing formation—a system that recursively regenerates its organizational logic, value regime, and operative boundaries within the broader terrain of social cooperation. From this perspective, what it "does" at any given moment matters less than how it reproduces the conditions for its own doing over time and across contexts. It is in this sense that we can speak of capital reproduction and social reproduction as social forces: each seeks to maintain coherence, project teleology, and reproduce systemic patterns—not by being externally imposed or passively emergent but by generating and regulating its own conditions of persistence.

This translation of autopoiesis into social theory, however, requires clarification. As Mingers (1995: 123–5) points out, the biological notion of component production—where a living cell literally produces the components that constitute it—cannot be directly applied to social systems. For example, an enterprise does not produce its own machinery and certainly does not reproduce the bodies of its workers or the internal operations of nature. The material components on which it depends are produced elsewhere—often at great distances and through circuits that lie beyond the enterprise's own operational boundaries.

But this does not invalidate the application of autopoietic theory to the social. Autopoietic systems are, by definition, structurally open: They engage in continuous exchanges of matter and energy with their environment. What defines them is not material self-sufficiency but operational closure—the recursive processes internal to the system that allow it to maintain its identity and coherence over time.

Thus, for example, Marx (1976) shows that the components of the means of production and labor power are produced externally to a given capital or, as in the case of the fragments of nature that enter as raw materials, and in the case of labor power, even outside the circuits of capital tout court. Yet, as soon as these elements enter into the production circuit of capital through market exchange, they do not simply act as means of production or labor power in the general sense—as use values available for productive activity. Instead, they acquire a new meaning from the perspective of the systemic logic of a specific capital: They become what Marx terms constant capital and variable capital, that is, capital invested with a specific *purpose*, whose function is entirely oriented toward the reproduction and expansion of value.

From the point of view of a particular enterprise, or of capital as an autopoietic social force more generally, this means that capital produces its own components by producing the social meaning and functional integration of otherwise heterogeneous elements. It integrates them within a relational context—defined by competition with other capitals, by the need for hierarchical control of labor, and by strategies of extraction and accumulation. The same machines or bodies, when organized within a different reproductive logic—say, that of social reproduction—would be made to function otherwise. They would become components of another system, defined by another measure of things and governed by another *purpose*.

Capital, in this sense, does not just use labor and nature—it recontextualizes them within its own reproductive logic. It transforms their role through the application of a particular systemic code: value creation and accumulation. This transformation is organizational and relational. It is enacted through the ongoing operations of capital as a collective subject—through investment decisions, logistical design, legal form, managerial control, extraction, and exploitation.

What capital produces, as capital, is not use values or material wealth per se. It produces capital—that is, it reproduces the conditions for its own expansion. This includes surplus value but also the social infrastructure of accumulation: commodified labor, compatible legal architectures, and forms of subjectivation. It produces the value regime, the measurement apparatus, and the social relations through which bodies, machines, and ecologies are mobilized in service of its self-reproduction. From this perspective, capital's primary output is not a thing—it is a systemic orientation, a logic that organizes the field of cooperation as a field of valorization. It is this capacity that makes capital an autopoietic force.

Capital does not merely respond to market signals; it produces them—organizing social cooperation, bodily time, and ecological metabolism into circuits of valorization. Its autopoiesis spans financial algorithms, legal architectures, affective conditioning, and logistical flows.

In its autopoiesis, capital is structurally coupled to systems that reproduce gendered and racialized divisions of labor, institutional norms, and symbolic orders—persisting even when individuals within them resist or subvert their logic. In this way, these systems become functional to capital while being reinforced by it in turn. Patriarchy, for example, stabilizes capital's circuits by naturalizing the gendered separation between productive and reproductive labor. It relegates the work of care, bodily maintenance, and affective support—the reproduction of labor-power—to women, typically in the private or informal sphere, and frames this labor as outside the domain of value. In doing so, it provides capital with an immense reservoir of life-making labor at minimal or no cost. Capital also reorganizes gendered roles and relations to fit the needs of accumulation—incorporating women into wage labor under precarious conditions, commodifying aspects of care (from childcare to surrogacy), and responsibilizing individuals, especially women, for the management of social reproduction amid austerity and crisis. As a result, patriarchal norms and hierarchies are not simply inherited from tradition; they are continually refashioned within capital's own reproductive logic.

In this way, patriarchy and capital maintain their own organizational coherence, yet reproduce through a relational entanglement—a structural coupling in which the stability of each depends on the adaptive reinforcement of the other. Their coupling contributes to the patterned curvature of the social field, shaping how labor, care, and social roles are distributed, devalued, or made invisible.

Patriarchy and racism, while structurally coupled with capital, also shape the very texture of social reproduction, embedding domination within the institutions, affects, and daily rhythms through which life is maintained. Yet, just as social cooperation as a whole includes forms of praxis that exceed capital, so social reproduction embeds practices that exceed and seek to counter different forms of domination. Ultimately, social reproduction names a contrasting—though far from unconflicted—mode of autopoietic organization. It is historically rooted in the collective sustenance of life: in the reproduction of bodies, relations, and ecologies across generations. But it is not a site of purity or autonomy. The autopoiesis of social reproduction unfolds through the relational labor of care and renewal, through the continuous making of life in concrete, situated terms—or collapses into exhaustion, abandonment, and violence when those conditions are undermined.

Social reproduction is a less integrated form of autopoiesis than capital reproduction. It relies on dispersed circuits—of care, community, and ecological stewardship—that are repeatedly interrupted, reorganized, or co-opted. But beyond these vernacular or procommons spaces (Chapter 11), social reproduction also unfolds through a wider reproductive sector, composed of infrastructures such as education, health systems, and welfare institutions (Chapter 12). These institutions mediate the renewal of human capacities at scale, providing the material, affective, and cognitive conditions under which life can be sustained and regenerated. Yet under capitalist conditions, this reproductive sector is increasingly shaped by the imperatives of what, in Chapters 9 and 12, we will call the meta-level of the pyramid of capital: performance metrics, fiscal constraints, accumulation logics, and extractive redesigns.

The result is a contradictory dynamic: systems meant to reproduce life are reorganized to reproduce capital, while the reproductive logic they carry is simultaneously instrumentalized and depleted. Still, these circuits persist—because they must. In the midst of Greece's devastating austerity crisis of 2007, when public health services were gutted, hundreds of self-organized doctors and nurses established autonomous clinics to care for those abandoned by the state (Sitrin 2014). During the COVID-19 pandemic, people around the world mobilized in mutual aid networks (Sitrin and Collective Sembrar 2020). In Gaza, under continuous bombardment and systematic siege, health workers keep working—under relentless exhaustion and impossible odds—because life demands it. These moments make visible the deep force of reproductive autopoiesis: not sustained by stability or resources but by the urgency of life's continuation under hostile conditions.

The asymmetry between capital and social reproduction lies in the degree of autopoietic closure, infrastructural reach, and control over the conditions of reproduction that each system possesses. This disparity is not only a question of institutional dominance; it also shapes how each force interacts with the broader field of social cooperation.

Systems with greater autopoietic closure and infrastructural integration—like capital—exert a stronger capacity to orient behaviors, values, and institutional forms. They are not only self-reproducing; *they warp the field around themselves*. They function as *attractors*: systems that not only maintain internal coherence but also draw other processes into alignment with their reproduction. Autopoietic social forces function as attractors. They do not only maintain themselves; they shape the surrounding environment, drawing in subjectivities, institutions, and value practices that begin to orbit their logic. This field effect helps to illuminate why some systems persist while others disintegrate and how counterforces might achieve coherence despite asymmetry.

From autopoiesis to attractor

In systems theory and dynamical modeling, an attractor is a configuration toward which a system tends to evolve—organizing the behavior of elements around it and drawing them into recurring patterns or stabilized forms. A whirlpool is an attractor for water flow; a magnet, for iron filings. But attractors are not necessarily physical entities. A social attractor does not merely structure behavior; it redefines the space of meaning-making through which social cooperation occurs. It shapes institutions, discourses, infrastructures, and desires in ways that sustain its internal logic. The more an autopoietic system consolidates its reproduction, the more it bends the field around it—not as a passive consequence but as an active condition of its continuation. Attractors, in this sense, are not static centers of gravity but dynamic—because they also embed conflict, tension, friction, and inertia—and generators of orientation; they reconfigure what seems natural, possible, or desirable within a given social terrain.

The concept of the attractor has been deployed across many fields to describe how order emerges from complexity without central control. A stable ecosystem may function as an attractor, drawing diverse species, feedback loops, and energy flows into a dynamic but reproducible configuration—a patterned environment within which ecological niches emerge and stabilize. In enactive cognitive science, the mind is seen as a system of attractors: patterns of perception, thought, and emotion into which the embodied subject tends to fall based on its history of interaction. In finance, speculative capital behaves like an attractor when it becomes the dominant orientation of investment, governance, and even social aspiration—regardless of its material irrationality. And in political theory, hegemony can be understood as an attractor: a gravitational force that seeks to stabilize institutions and imaginations around a normative center.

Across these domains, the attractor is not an object but a systemic tendency that shapes the terrain around it. It exerts force less through direct coercion than through orientation—redefining what seems natural, possible, or valuable, even as coercive mechanisms may intervene to stabilize that orientation when it is contested. And the stronger the autopoietic organization of a system—the more tightly it can reproduce its own logic—the greater its capacity to act as an attractor. Autopoietic social forces operate in this way. By continually reproducing their own logic, they generate structured zones of attraction, reshaping institutions, subjectivities, and infrastructures around themselves. The stronger the autopoietic loop, the greater the gravitational pull.

This is how we must understand capital and social reproduction. As autopoietic forces, they do not only persist through internal coherence. They generate zones of attraction in the social field: sites, institutions, and practices that begin to orbit their logic. Capital becomes an attractor when public services are reorganized for cost-efficiency, when education becomes job training, and when everyday time is synchronized to market rhythms. Social reproduction, too, produces attractors—when cooperative practices, care infrastructures, common-based alternatives, social movements, or the rich tapestry of the vernacular begin to sediment the spaces they inhabit and reproduce life while putting pressure on institutional politics to shift its orientation toward deeper democracy, social provision, and welfare. But as we have seen, the power of social reproduction as an attractor is deeply asymmetrical because the force field in which it operates is already bent by capital's infrastructural dominance.

Capital reproduction is a paradigmatic case. Its self-reproduction is not only internal (valorization, reinvestment, accumulation) but also externalized through the shaping of markets, urban and rural spaces, policy, subjectivity, environments, and rhythms. It manifests as an attractor when public institutions adopt cost-efficiency logics above all else, when individuals internalize productivity metrics above everything else, or when entire life plans are organized around credit, debt, and investment. Unlike periods of "primitive accumulation," these are not imposed by sheer force; they arise because capital, as an autopoietic system, modulates the field in its own favor—pulling the social world into its orbit.

Social reproduction, though less consolidated, can also function as an attractor—particularly when care networks, vernacular knowledges, or community infrastructures manage to sustain themselves against the grain of commodification and systemic disruption. In such instances, they generate what we might call counter-attractors: relational and material hubs around which life reorganizes itself differently, according to logics of care, subsistence, reciprocity, and collective maintenance. A garden commons, a care cooperative, a feminist strike, a rent strike, a worker mobilization over conditions of labor, an NGO that saves migrants from drowning in the Mediterranean, an anti-war demonstration, a radical social center offering cheap food and plural convivial space, and a legal team offering free advice to the marginalized—these are not simply events or spaces but infrastructures of social reproduction. They are situated enactments of value that sediment alternative rhythms, reorient subjectivities, and reconfigure what life is allowed to mean. Their gravitational pull may be weaker, less infrastructurally supported, and constantly under siege, but it is nonetheless real. And when these counter-attractors are pluralized, linked, or mutually reinforced, they begin to shape counter-fields of possibility—zones within the wider field where the reproduction of life becomes visible, valued, and capable of reorganizing the terms of cooperation.

To see autopoietic forces as attractors is to understand that social power operates through gravitational structuring: the systemic orchestration of multiple mechanisms that bend the field of social cooperation around a dominant logic. Forms of governance, norms, incentives, and affects are not external to this structuring; they are its vectors. It is through their patterned interaction that certain choices come to feel rational, inevitable, or even desirable. Attractors mobilize social reproductive *powers-to* (potentia) toward either social reproduction or capital reproduction. In this light, struggles are attempts to realign *powers-to* around counter-attractors that propose a different geometry of life: different rhythms, values, or forms of cooperation.

Types of attractors: autopoietic, sympoietic, allopoietic

Not all attractors operate in the same way. Some are grounded in a tightly integrated capacity for self-reproduction (autopoietic). Others emerge from interdependent collaboration (sympoietic). Still others function as attractors only to the extent that the logic of their organization is imposed on them externally (allopoietic). Social cooperation is shaped by all three types, always in intermingled and nested ways. Figure 3.1 gives a graphical representation of these different systemic organizations, from which we may derive the notion of attractors.

The distinction between autopoietic, sympoietic, and allopoietic systems originates in the notion of organization in systems theory, not in the concept of attractors. Maturana and Varela used the first and the last of these terms to differentiate systems according to how they reproduce their own organizations, not how they shape their environments. But in the social field, where different systems interact, persist, and exert influence over patterns of cooperation, these modes of systems' organization function as attractors.

The autopoietic attractor, as previously described, is a force that sustains itself through its own recursive operations. It reproduces its logic internally and

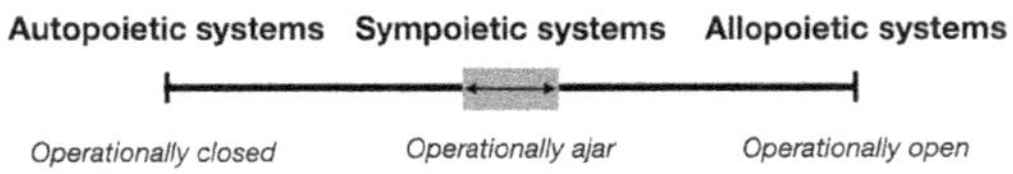

Figure 3.1 Types of systemic organization

reshapes its environment to reinforce that logic. Capital is the clearest example. Its autopoietic core—valorization, accumulation, and reinvestment—feeds back into itself, generating the conditions for its continued expansion. But this core does not float in abstraction: It becomes an attractor by modifying institutional norms, extracting and reallocating resources, and by continuously seeking to recalibrate social cooperation in its image—often succeeding but never without friction or residue. *It bends the field toward itself not only by decree and enclosure but by making its logic appear as the default condition of possibility.*

As Hayek (1973) distinguished between *taxis*—an order deliberately constructed—and *cosmos*—an order that emerges spontaneously from the interactions of many agents—autopoietic social systems embody a complex interplay of the two. Their operational closure generates self-organizing patterns and recursive behaviors that resemble *cosmos*, yet their reproduction also depends on designed instruments—laws, institutions, procedures—that function as *taxis*, guiding and stabilizing the system from within.

Capital, like all autopoietic systems, operates with a degree of central control but not as a central puppeteer in total control pulling strings from above. It generates identity through operational closure, reproducing its own logic while filtering and amplifying environmental signals in ways that reinforce its internal coherence. In complex social systems, this filtering and amplification (Chapter 8) takes the form of laws, policies, and enforcement. These act as external commands upon society, but they are not external to the autopoietic logic that produces them. Rather, they are internally generated projections of that logic—mechanisms through which the system seeks to secure its reproduction in given contexts. Like the muscles and reflexes of a body, they are responsive, coordinated, and directed toward systemic viability.

While autopoietic attractors are defined by operational closure—that is, by reproducing their own logic and interpreting inputs in ways that reinforce it—they do not function in isolation. In complex social systems, the reproduction of an autopoietic core often depends on, and actively integrates, other forms of systemic organization. Capital, for instance, sustains itself not only through self-referential circuits of valorization and accumulation but also through the appropriation and reconfiguration of social reproduction, ecological cycles, and public infrastructures. These become integrated into capital's reproductive logic through sympoietic processes under conditions of asymmetric power differential: interdependent, adaptive, and coproduced arrangements such as markets, lobbying networks, cultural imaginaries, or logistical ecologies. In this sense, capital's mode of reproduction is always mixed—part autopoietic (e.g., the firm or the financial circuit), part sympoietic (shared infrastructures and coproduced norms), and part allopoietic (hierarchical imposition or substitution through command).

Sympoietic attractors emerge from distributed, codependent processes of mutual reproduction. The term, drawn from systems theory and reanimated by Donna Haraway (2016), was originally elaborated by Beth Dempster (1998, 2000) and derives from the Greek roots *sym* (together) and *poiesis* (making). It refers to systems in which organizational changes emerge not from an internally closed or hierarchical logic but from continuous interactions between internal components and external environments. These systems are characterized by amorphous cooperation, fluid boundaries, and recursive adaptation. Rather than reproducing themselves through internally bounded operations, sympoietic systems maintain coherence through continuous structural coupling, where identity emerges from the interaction of diverse agents and environments—not from a pre-given logic or stable internal code but through mutual adaptation and relational responsiveness.

Thus, sympoietic systems, by contrast with autopoietic ones, are *operationally ajar*; their coherence is sustained not through operational closure but through ongoing structural coupling with other systems and elements. Their boundaries are not fixed but continually renegotiated through interaction.

The internal operations of a household, a neighborhood, or a care infrastructure are typically shaped through responsiveness to emotional ties, ecological rhythms, institutional conditions, and inherited knowledges—unless subordinated to the logic of systems such as patriarchy or capital, which may operate allopoietically by externally reshaping their function for extractive or normative ends, or autopoietically when such norms and hierarchies become recursively reproduced from within.

A commons is sympoietic when it emerges from the shared maintenance of land, water, code, or care—where no single agent controls the whole but where all participate in holding it together. Yet even within these systems, tools that facilitate autopoiesis may emerge: Families may reproduce internal norms, routines, or exclusions that stabilize identity through recursion; friendships may sediment codes and affective rhythms that generate continuity over time. In more durable or scaled forms of sympoietic organization—such as commons, care networks, or cooperative institutions—shared rules, cultural norms, or even legal frameworks can function as tools that sustain autopoietic coherence without overriding relational interdependence. These instruments do not impose identity from above; they support recursive self-patterning within a broader web of cocreation. Such systems often exhibit partial operational closure: not full autonomy but the ability to stabilize form through interaction.

This relational pattern is visible across daily life. Dancing, convivial conversation, and collective music-making—each is a sympoietic micro-system, sustained not by predetermined rules but by the improvised coordination of multiple agents. Social movements, too, arise from the interplay of actors, affects, discourses, struggles, and tactical improvisation. Their internal logics develop through co-adaptation and coproduction, not imposition. But even these systems may consolidate around certain narratives, symbols, or organizational forms—temporary autopoietic closures that give them coherence but must be continuously reopened to avoid becoming extractive or hierarchical.

Sympoietic attractors gain pull not through imposed coherence but by enabling relational autonomy and mutual resonance. Their field effect is quieter and more situated—but no less real. When a network of urban gardens makes a neighborhood more livable, when a care cooperative sets a new standard of dignity in labor, or when feminist struggles redefine time and value, we see the emergence of life-oriented attractors. These do not demand obedience; they invite participation. In doing so, they begin to reorganize what people consider meaningful, possible, or worthwhile—not through decree but through resonance.

The third type, allopoietic attractors, are reproduced not through the self-maintenance of internal system logic, nor through symbiotic cocreation but through the intervention of other systems from the outside to serve their ends. In Maturana and Varela's original terms, the organization of allopoietic systems is *operationally open*: Their organization is produced by external forces. Their organizational models depend solely on the relations established by those forces, and as a result, their boundaries are defined from the outside. A clear example is that of artifacts, whose form and structure depend on the subject who designs them.

In social terms, allopoietic attractors are logics of external imposition. They do not exert pull through self-reinforcement or mutual care but through command, extraction, and substitution. They do not reproduce their own coherence organically; instead, they intervene in the reproduction of other systems—hollowing out their internal logic while preserving their functional appearance. What may be left is a simulation of autonomy, oriented not toward the system's own flourishing but toward the reproduction of the dominant attractor's logic.

Capital, again, often operates allopoietically when it reorganizes domains of life not to sustain them but to subordinate them to its own logic of accumulation. Enclosures of the commons are allopoietic interventions that disrupt autopoietic and sympoietic processes in affected communities. Through the erosion of welfare infrastructures, the family is reconfigured as a flexible care unit adapted to the needs of precarious labor. When public childcare or health services are gutted, for instance, caregiving responsibilities are offloaded onto households—primarily onto women—allowing employers and the state to externalize the costs of social reproduction while maintaining labor flexibility. Education is not cultivated as a space for learning to live with the challenges of our time—learning to care, to think critically, and to navigate the demands of collective life—but is recalibrated into a credentialing pipeline for human capital, geared toward competition and employability. Ecosystems are not maintained in their relational integrity; they are treated as reservoirs of extractable raw materials.

In each of these cases, capital does not reproduce these systems; it appropriates their reproductive functions, hollowing out their internal logics while preserving their external appearance. The attractor functions here not as a gravitational pull toward life but as a centripetal force that drains autonomy, seeks to reassign purpose, and replaces endogenous value with imposed function.

But even allopoietic attractors are not pure. In practice, they depend on sympoietic relations to function—for example, the unpaid affective labor within families that sustains emotional well-being and care, or the civic trust and relational engagement that allow education systems to operate beyond formal compliance. Over time, allopoietic systems may also develop autopoietic tendencies, particularly when stabilized within state apparatuses or technocratic institutions that begin to reproduce their own internal logic. Welfare-to-work programs, for instance, often evolve into bureaucratic machines that multiply conditionalities, sanctions, and digital reporting—not to meet social needs but to sustain their own operational coherence. University administrations do the same when evaluative frameworks and funding metrics begin to shape academic life less around knowledge and more around auditability. In both cases, what began as an instrumental apparatus becomes a self-referential structure—a system that organizes life in order to preserve its own continuity—while at the same time reinforcing the broader reproductive logic of capital, to which it remains structurally coupled.

The architecture of social cooperation is therefore never composed of discrete or isolated attractor types. Instead, it is shaped by constellations—interlocking formations in which dominant attractors draw on, suppress, or reconfigure other modes of reproduction. What we inhabit is not a clean taxonomy but a contested force field, where autopoietic, sympoietic, and allopoietic logics interact, compete, overlap, or are nested within one another in the ongoing organization of social cooperation.

But the key thing to keep in mind is that these attractor types are not neutral; they are mobilized by opposing social forces that seek to orient the field in their favor: capital and social reproduction. Each of these forces operates through different reproductive modalities, deploying autopoietic, sympoietic, or allopoietic dynamics to stabilize their logic, reconfigure environments, and draw other systems into alignment. None of these attractor types is inherently virtuous or malign; each can be mobilized by either social force. Even allopoietic dynamics, for example, may be harnessed by social reproduction such as when laws impose wealth taxes to fund care infrastructures or mandate environmental and labor protections that constrain capital's logic. *These attractors are, in other words, politically plastic.* These attractor types are not mutually exclusive. In practice, they overlap in shared spaces, entangle through reciprocal influence, and at times mutate, with one taking on the traits or functions of another, often under the gravitational structuring of capital's dominant field logic. A commons may be co-opted into a corporate social responsibility campaign. A financial instrument may originate in community-based microcredit, only to be abstracted and fed back into speculative markets. A household may operate sympoietically one day and be violently reorganized through patriarchal or market pressures the next. Vernacular relations in a workplace may sour under allopoietic decisions from above, such as a boss imposing cuts or restructuring, fracturing solidarities, and installing divisions among colleagues.

Force fields: the medium of interaction

The value of the typology proposed in the previous section lies not in rigid classifications but in illuminating the shifting relations through which different systems may enact different reproductive logics. Subjects inhabit these systems, but if this is the case, then the typology of attractors must also help us grasp how different reproductive logics are not only enacted structurally but also perceived, embodied, and negotiated by those moving within them. We must therefore not only examine how attractors operate but also how they are experienced, observed, and navigated by subjects embedded within the field. This requires a shift in our point of observation—what cyberneticians call a second-order perspective (von Foerster 2003a,b). Rather than seeing systems as external objects acting upon unreflective or isolated observers, we must recognize that subjects themselves co-constitute the field through their actions, perceptions, and forms of structural couplings.

A force field is the medium through which subjects enact their world. The force field of social cooperation is the dynamic space where competing reproductive logics curve space, clash, and reorient life; where attractors contend; subjects respond; collective subjects seek to modify the pull of attractors; and the organization of the common as condition is continuously reshaped. From this vantage point, a force field is not simply a neutral medium; it is a space of interaction, distortion, and enactment in which different logics seek to attract, absorb, or repulse types of subjectivities. This is not *simply* the world as it is but the world as it is brought forth through engagement, through praxis. It is through this second-order observation that we begin to understand how the gravitational pull of capital can feel like necessity, how commons can emerge as counter-attractors, and how singular or collective subjects navigate this terrain—carrying with them intentions, histories, representations, and exposures to conflicting reproductive logics, value imaginaries, and ideologies.

As social space, the force field is not a neutral container; it is the dynamic terrain through which systemic reproduction occurs, where opposing logics bend, distort, and recompose social cooperation through attractors. The conceptual foundation for this approach lies in field theory, which offers a powerful framework for grasping how forces operate within a structured environment.

Field theory first emerged in physics, particularly through the work of Faraday and Maxwell, where it was used to describe how forces such as gravity and electromagnetism propagate through space. Rather than imagining physical bodies exerting direct effects on one another, these theories conceptualized force as unfolding through invisible fields—continuous, structured spaces that influence the behavior of every particle within them. In a gravitational field, for example, each object is affected by every other object's mass, and the strength of that influence varies with distance. What this implies is that forces do not merely operate through contact but through the configuration of space itself.

This insight was later transposed into the human sciences. In psychology, Kurt Lewin (1936) argued that behavior is a function of both the person and the environment, understood as a dynamic field. Individuals act within a totality of copresent forces—social, psychological, and situational—that together define the horizon of possibility and action. In sociology, Pierre Bourdieu (1993) extended the idea of the field by defining structured arenas such as the artistic, political, or academic fields, in which agents occupy positions and struggle over specific stakes by deploying different forms of capital—economic, cultural, and symbolic. In this sense, fields are not neutral backdrops but conflictual configurations shaped by historical sedimentations, institutional logics, and asymmetries of power.

What unites these perspectives is the recognition that relationality, structure, and dynamism are constitutive of fields. Nothing exists in isolation: behaviors, positions, and identities gain meaning only within the configuration of a field. Fields are not flat or homogeneous but differentiated by gradients and thresholds that orient action and possibility. Crucially, fields evolve—through the accumulated effects of struggle within them, and through external shocks that disturb their regularities.

Our concern here is not field theory in general but the more specific notion of the force field—a field structured by the presence and interaction of antagonistic, generative forces. In the case at hand, these are capital reproduction and social reproduction. To grasp them in field-theoretic terms is to recognize that their confrontation is not simply a matter of conflict between opposing entities but a metabolic entanglement unfolding through a shared medium. The field is not just where they clash; it is what is continually shaped by that clash.

This conceptual move allows us to reinterpret what we will later call the pyramid of capital not simply as a fixed hierarchy imposed from above but as the emergent shape of a force field—a dynamic geometry, an architecture of gradients and constraints—produced by the recursive, asymmetrical reproduction of capital on one side and the insurgent, fragmented but vital reproduction of life on the other.

The architecture of the force field

Once we understand capital and social reproduction as antagonistic yet interdependent forces, the next step is to grasp how they interact through the structured space they co-constitute. The force field is not a stable equilibrium but a charged, turbulent atmosphere, continually shaped and reshaped by the asymmetrical encounter between these two poles (Figure 3.2).

First, the field is structured by attractors. Each pole acts like a gravitational mass that warps the terrain around it, orienting time, value, behavior, and institutional form. Capital exerts a pull toward commodification, abstraction,

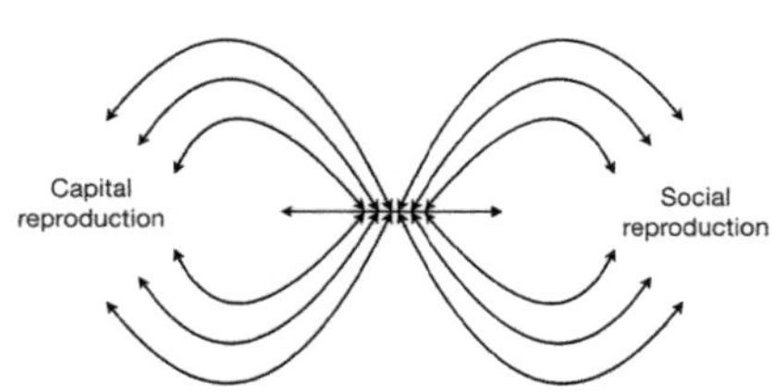

Figure 3.2 The force field of social cooperation, with social and capital reproduction as the two main attractors

and accumulation. Social reproduction exerts a counter-pull toward care, sustenance, and the renewal of life. A public health system, for example, may be pulled toward capital through privatization and performance metrics, and toward social reproduction through community control and universal access. The attractor is not an object—it is a structuring force, a systemic lure, a recursive logic that shapes its surroundings.

Second, these attractors generate gradients—zones of uneven force. Some regions of the field—like speculative finance or extractive infrastructure—are steeply aligned with capital. Others—like neighborhood mutual aid or ecological commons—tilt toward social reproduction. These gradients are not smooth inclines but fractured landscapes: sedimented by history, carved by policy, and thickened by institutional inertia. A workplace ruled by productivity metrics and a neighborhood held together by relational reciprocity are structured by different inclines—what seems "natural" in one may feel alien in the other.

Third, the field is dense with tensions and frictions. These arise where reproductive logics collide—not as exceptions but as systemic expressions of incompatibility. Affective burnout, ecological exhaustion, and institutional breakdown—these are symptoms of a field stretched thin. Tensions emerge as moral injury in care work, as exhaustion in unpaid labor, or as ecological collapse where extractive capital tears at life's conditions. Friction is not just a symptom of contradiction; it is its lived expression—and its potential ignition.

Fourth, the field is traversed by thresholds—points where accumulated tensions become unsustainable and phase shifts occur. These can erupt as crisis or build imperceptibly until conditions can no longer reproduce themselves. A financial collapse, a care strike, a mass resignation, a food riot, and a climate blockade all mark thresholds in the field's geometry. These are not terminal points; they are forks—where the balance between reproductions is recalibrated, for better or worse.

Fifth, the field is bent by curvature. Dominant attractors—especially capital—do not merely respond to contradiction; they act preemptively, seeking to curve the field around themselves. This curvature is enacted through policy, financial leverage, technological architectures, legal frames, or cultural logics that naturalize commodification. When disaster relief is routed through private contractors, or when credit scores determine access to housing and care, capital's curvature is made tangible. It remakes the horizon of social reproduction in its own image. But the field resists. It warps. It tears. And at times, it curves back—through sustained waves of struggle, through the slow sedimentation of commoning practices, through the enactment of alternative rhythms, needs, and solidarities that begin to bend the terrain toward social reproduction.

Together, these features—attractors, gradients, tensions, thresholds, and curvature—compose the internal architecture of the force field. They show that power operates not only from above but through the shaping of the very terrain in which action occurs. The field is organized—and contested—through the interaction of generative forces struggling to reproduce themselves. Social cooperation is shaped not only by command or coercion but by the modulation of the field's very feel: its rhythms, its gravitational pulls, and its zones of opacity or possibility.

Understanding the field in this way also clarifies how capital reproduces itself not only through accumulation but also through field orchestration: steepening gradients in its favor, absorbing frictions, displacing attractors, and recalibrating thresholds. This is what the throbs of command (Chapter 14) seek to manage: the rhythms, dangers, and instabilities of the field itself. But no throb can eliminate contradiction entirely. The field remains uneven, unstable, and full of possibility—a medium not only of reproduction but also of potential recomposition.

Class reframed: systemic identity versus subjective identity

Having redefined social forces as autopoietic systems, mapped their gravitational effects as attractors, and described the structured terrain they cocreate as a force field, we are now in a position to turn to the question of class—but to do so with altered eyes. In this framework, class does not refer primarily to a sociological group, a cultural identity, or even a shared position in the wage relation. It refers to something more fundamental: a systemic identity enacted by subjects who bear and reproduce the logic of an autopoietic force as it struggles to organize the field of social cooperation in its favor.

In much of political discourse, class has been conflated with subjective identity—as if it were a matter of how people see themselves, how they vote, how they dress, what they consume, or whether they belong to the "middle class." When I arrived in the UK in the early 1990s and worked for years in precarious jobs, I was bemused to discover that, because I drank wine, I was labeled "middle class," while a true working-class guy would drink beer. Alternatively, class is often treated as a sociological category, defined by income brackets, job types, or educational attainment. Even within Marxist traditions, the concept of class has been interpreted through divergent lenses: as a structural position in the relations of production (as in Althusser 1971), as a historically grounded identity forged through struggle (as in Thompson 1963), or as a cultural formation shaped by hegemony and ideology (as in Gramsci 1971).

While each of these perspectives offers valuable insights, they often remain entangled with the idea of class as something one occupies or becomes—a position or an identity. In this sense, each of these perspectives, in different ways, operates through a form of first-order observation; they define class as something that can be observed, categorized, or theorized from a position external to its enactment. Yet such views risk missing how class is not merely an object of analysis but a force field that subjects themselves navigate, embody, and are internally traversed by. Instead, what I propose—by moving to a second-order observational plane—is this: Class is a systemic identity enacted by subjects who reproduce the logic of an autopoietic force striving to organize the field of social cooperation. This systemic identity is not self-contained or static—it is realized through concrete practices, orientations, and relations, and it exists only in tension with a competing reproductive logic with which it is structurally entangled. It is within this antagonistic relation that class becomes legible—not as a sociological grouping but as a dynamic configuration of subjectivities and practices oriented, by choice or necessity, toward the reproduction of a particular systemic logic against another. In this sense, class is first of all an antagonistic relation, a relation of struggle that even traverses diverse subjects entangled in the circuits of social cooperation.

This reconceptualization does not deny the reality of class as it is conventionally perceived as a cultural identity, a sociological category, or a political self-description. Rather, it reframes these representations as situated enactments: partial and historically variable ways in which the deeper antagonism becomes visible, named, or misnamed within a given field. As developed in Chapter 4, representation is not a mirror of an underlying essence but the product of historical processes of structural coupling, interpretive framing, and collective enactments. In this light, class consciousness is not awareness of an objective position already given but an emergent mode of articulation of a reproductive force becoming reflexive within a contested field.

Of course, the very framing offered here is also a representation—one among others. But it is a representation forged not from a standpoint outside the field but from within it: a situated attempt to make legible the structural antagonism that organizes social cooperation. As discussed in Chapters 4 and 5, representations are not neutral reflections but enactments—ways of seeing and naming that arise through systemic couplings and affective investments. The concept of class developed here is thus not a mirror of a universal essence but a reflexive representation: one that seeks to give coherence and visibility to a reproductive force struggling to become conscious of itself within a contested field.

This understanding of class as the systemic identity of a reproductive logic—and as an antagonistic relation—is deeply indebted to the insights of the autonomist Marxist tradition. From Raniero Panzieri's (1976) emphasis on the technical composition of labor as a political imposition, to Mario Tronti's (2019) reversal that places working-class struggle as the motor of capitalist development, and Antonio Negri's (1984) conception of antagonism as constitutive of capital's transformations, class has been understood not as a fixed sociological entity but as a dynamic force of struggle. Harry Cleaver (2000), in Reading Capital Politically, makes this explicit when he defines class as a relation that exists only in and through its antagonism with capital. Feminist interventions—starting from the classic text of the Wages for Housework movement (Dalla Costa and James 1975)—extended this logic to the sphere of unwaged reproductive labor, revealing how class antagonism cuts across both the visible and invisible circuits of social cooperation, into the kitchen. My approach builds on and rearticulates this lineage by situating class not just within the relations of production but within the wider, pervasive force field shaped by competing reproductive logics and the attractors they generate.

But what is politically decisive, within the framework developed here, is that class is not primarily about what subjects are or what they identify with—it is about what reproduces them, and the fissures therein, whether conscious or not. Class, in this sense, is not a subjective label or a demographic trait, nor is it something that is worn—it is enacted. It emerges through the patterned reproduction of life and its conflicts. I am enacting both capital's reproduction *and* social reproduction at every moment of my entanglements within the circuits of social cooperation, although in different degrees across contexts and positionalities. Through my enactment of social praxis, I contribute to constituting the systemic identity of social forces—the reproductive logics that organize bodies, practices, and institutions across the wider field of social cooperation.

To speak of class as a systemic identity is thus to refer to a relation of struggle between conflicting reproductive logics. Class, in this view, is not the label of a subject group but the name for the social force through which social reproduction endures its autopoiesis in the face of capital's own self-reproduction. Class is always vis-à-vis. It is the antagonistic dynamic that unfolds as bodies, institutions, and life systems are pulled between incompatible demands: to reproduce life on its own terms and to serve the reproduction of capital. Class is therefore not just a condition; it is not just an instantiation of struggle—it is a fielded contradiction, inscribed in the very geometry of social cooperation.

To frame class in this way is not to retreat into abstraction but to make a qualified claim to objectivity—not in the sense of a neutral or universal truth but in the sense of a structured antagonism: one that traverses and ramifies through nearly every domain of social cooperation, articulating itself across institutions, infrastructures, affects, and everyday practices. It is objective because it is situated at the *frontlines* (De Angelis 2007) of reproduction—where different orders of value clash, where the measure of things is imposed and resisted, and where one form of autopoiesis seeks to subordinate another. Capital reproduction and social reproduction are not simply in tension; they are in struggle over the field itself—over what will be counted, sustained, and made possible. Class, as defined here, is the name of that struggle—not from the outside but from within. Its extensiveness is not reducible to a single location or a single subject but unfolds through the very organization of social cooperation under contested conditions of reproduction. Its reach is as global and pervasive as capital's own!

A social relation that can be traced, contested, and measured across the transversal field of social cooperation—within the lives of the waged and the unwaged, across the "Global North" and "Global South," between queer and cisgender lives, between citizens and *sans papiers*, and through formations of both right and left. Class is a social relation that, in its extension and reach, is nothing less than the living map of our entanglement and daily struggle over how life is organized, valued, and made possible. It is a cartography not of borders but of battles—fought in the streets and in the gut, in fire and in breath, in the quiet burn of care and the storm of collective refusal and claims of dignity. Across every terrain of social cooperation, these struggles leave their mark. Class traces the shifting front lines over how social cooperation is organized, extracted, sustained, and refused. And it is precisely this extension and reach that, on the one side, thread through and connect dispersed forms of labor and care to reproduce societal conditions of living, and, on the other, carry the potential of their recomposition into an organic force for remaking the world. It is perhaps for this reason that the tycoons and oligarchs plan their retreats on fortified islands or dream of exits to Mars: because they know, at their core, that if this Hydra (Linebaugh and Rediker 2000) of reproduction becomes self-aware—while climate catastrophe and social disintegration accelerate—if it sees not just with one eye but from many positions at once and organizes on that basis, it may not only resist their order but make the world anew.

This distinction becomes especially important today, when identity has become a key terrain of struggle and contestation. Race, gender, sexuality, religion, and cultural belonging all structure experience and power in profound ways. But class, in the sense proposed here, is not one subject's identity among others. Class is not like an identity constructed around being a woman, a factory worker, a member of the LGBTQ+ community, a football club supporter, or—as Giso Amendola provocatively put it in a recent seminar—one of "the faithful of the Madonna of Pompei." It is not a sociological grouping to be added to a pluralist inventory of particularities. It is the ontological antagonism that structures the field itself—the generative contradiction through which all other identities are, in various situated ways, articulated, mediated, lived, and enacted in specific contexts. It is the clash among the measures of value that traverse both subjects and the broader field of social cooperation.

To frame class in this way is to reject both economistic reduction and identity-based relativism. It is to recognize that what we might still call "the working class" is not a homogeneous social group but a distributed and conflictual position within the force field—a position defined by its entanglement with, and reproduction of, life under conditions not of its choosing. Its coherence does not lie in uniformity but in a shared implication in the metabolic tension between capital and social reproduction—a tension that traverses lives, institutions, and struggles in situated, uneven, but connected ways.

The political implication is direct: Class is not what you are but what reproduces you. It is not a subjective identification but a systemic process that shapes bodies, affects, infrastructures, and institutions. Class struggle, therefore, is not merely a clash between these workers and these bosses, or between these proletarians and these capitalists. It is a struggle over the terms, conditions, and meanings of reproduction itself—a struggle over what kind of force will organize the field, what measure of value will be employed, and what kind of worlds will be made possible through that organization.

In this sense, the distinction Marx (2010b) drew between class *in itself* and class *for itself* takes on renewed meaning. What I have described here as class *in itself* is not merely a sociological group or an unconscious mass—it is the distributed and antagonistic configuration of subjects whose practices and institutional entanglements collectively enact the systemic reproduction of capital's reproductive logic within a contested field. It is the social force through which that logic becomes operative in and across society, whether consciously or not. Yet this reproduction is not uncontested; it unfolds within a force field where other reproductive logics—rooted in care, solidarity, ecological repair, or collective autonomy—persist, resist, and sometimes coalesce into counterforces. But when the fragments of that force begin to cohere—when care, migration, climate struggle, Indigenous defense, and logistical refusal begin to resonate and move together—they mark the emergence of class *for itself*: the becoming-conscious of social reproduction as a collective capacity to remake the world on other terms.

To reclaim class in this way is not to return to an old orthodoxy but to open a new horizon. It is to see in the fight for LGBTQ+ parental rights not merely as a quest for equality but as a challenge to the reproductive norms imposed by capital in specific contexts. It is to recognize students' demands for participation in curriculum design and educational governance as a struggle over the reproduction of knowledge and subjectivity. It is to understand migrants' battles for access to health care, housing, and social services as efforts to assert their role in the social fabric against exclusionary policies. It is to see climate justice movements, Indigenous land defenders, and logistical workers' strikes as interconnected fronts resisting the commodification of life and asserting alternative modes of social reproduction. It is to hear, in the voices of women resisting gendered violence, denouncing femicide, or rising against war, rearmament, and genocide, not only a cry for justice but the defense of life itself against its organized destruction. Class, reframed in these terms, is not the residue of a bygone industrial age but the name of a living force striving to become conscious of itself and to forge organizational forms capable of recomposing its plural and fragmented expressions in a world that urgently needs such convergence.[1]

Part II

The making of the common

4

Daily life, social change, and enactment

Where the world touches us: the everyday between system and subject

If social reproduction movements are to sustain their autopoietic force beyond cycles of mobilization, their organizational endurance must be rooted in the textures of everyday life. The circuits, practices, and subject formations that emerge from struggles over reproduction determine whether alternative logics can take root or whether capital's structures continue to hegemonize experience. To understand where these dynamics unfold, we must begin with the everyday as the terrain where reproduction, subject formation, and hegemony converge, constraining and enabling transformation.

The everyday, however, is not merely a backdrop but an ongoing performance of social cooperation. It is through everyday lived practices that subjects enact and reproduce the worlds they inhabit, whether in conformity with or in defiance of dominant logics.

This chapter thus introduces the notion of *enactment* as a way to understand how social realities are brought forth through embodied practice, relational coupling, and the situated unfolding of life. If class marks the systemic identity of a reproductive force, enactment traces how that force becomes perceptible, affective, and reproductive of sameness or transformative in the rhythms, refusals, and reconfigurations of everyday cooperation.

In the everyday, in everyday life—that is, primarily in the sphere where the subjects have their habitus, their routines, their cycles, their repeated experiences—we find both the field of differentiation among subjects and the common ground across differences.

But the subject's routines and habitus do not exhaust the sense we can make of the everyday. My experience of the everyday emerges from the encounter between my specific subjectivity and the complex of societal operations to which it is necessarily articulated. For Henri Lefebvre (1991), the everyday does not simply refer to what happens every day in people's lives but is rather a complex social construction involving the material, symbolic, and cultural aspects of everyday life. If we look closely, the dynamics of power relations and dominant social structures are manifested in every moment of the everyday. The everyday is also the area where "everyday representations" such as images and cultural representations deeply influence our experience, shaping our perceptions of space, time, and social relations. These representations and narratives, which are the hybrid product of self-production and bottom-up processes of signification, together with top-down narrative forms produced by media, advertising, and institutions, help shape how we conceive of and experience the everyday. The everyday thus becomes a theater in which opposing dynamics of alienation and autonomy play out across subjects.

Everyday life thus becomes the site of a constant struggle: the struggle to experience autonomy, to participate meaningfully in shaping one's own life context, and to realize oneself beyond constraint. The innumerable material and symbolic hierarchies in which daily existence is entangled make alienation not the exception but the rule. For Henri Lefebvre, everyday life is where fragmented, alienated subjectivities unfold—trapped in repetitive routines and jobs that stifle human potential, fractured into multiple roles that often contradict each other yet together compose a lived identity.

This fragmentation is not accidental but organized. It takes shape through the separation of life into distinct, hierarchical domains, each governing a specific set of roles, expectations, and forms of value. Everyday life is thus divided into siloed spheres: work and leisure, public and private, production and consumption, man and woman, citizen and noncitizen. In recent decades, these silos have begun to blur under hybridizing pressures. Labor, through the spread of precarity and welfare retrenchment, increasingly infiltrates leisure, particularly as the burden of unpaid reproductive labor grows. The private sphere, reshaped by privatization and policy manipulation, seeps into the public sphere. Consumption becomes labor, marked by budgeting struggles, symbolic performance, and the stress of keeping up. Women, in breaking through glass ceilings, are often compelled to conform to masculinized norms of power without undoing the hierarchies themselves. The idea of the "human being" dissolves into abstraction amid the brutal distinctions between citizens and rightless subjects—migrants, the poor, the colonized, and the victims of war and genocide.

But the everyday is also the terrain where an inner struggle for meaning unfolds, preventing alienation from ever becoming total. It is here that memories resurface—of migration, war, and violence—recasting the present in the shadow of past trauma (Highmore 2002: 3). Yet the everyday can also rekindle an experience of the *sacred*: not as institutional religion but as a visceral sense of being part of something larger—an order, a reality, an excess of possibility that transcends the individual. This sacred is connection, interdependence, and belonging—to the universe, the divine, or a deeper social whole.

Today, however, our sense of the sacred is often flattened into forms of partial belonging: to a football club, a family, or a nation—forms readily co-opted by dominant logics. Football fans become fuel for big business; familial loyalty may harden into rivalry, amplified by distinctive consumption patterns; national pride is instrumentalized to feed competition, exploitation, and war. Yet the sacred can also be reclaimed through shared struggle: in the recognition of collective subjugation—of class, gender, and race—and in the emergence of common joy and shared pain, self-esteem, and self-determination. These are redemptive moments in which latent resources are activated, subjects reappropriate their potential, and new horizons open for the collective. As Bartolini and Consigliere (2019: 172) write, "the sacred, which largely exceeds the sphere of religion and does not necessarily coincide with it, is responsible for a radical proximity to the dimension of the possible."

After all, if we look closely, the everyday is a point of sensitive connection between part and whole: a weave of relational experiences punctuated by the rhythms of the subject, sequenced by the linear time of the practices, circuits, and systems of which they are a part. These, in turn, attune themselves to the circular rhythms that reproduce them—dancing together, interconnected within the order of things, which thereby reproduces itself as a macro-hierarchy over social cooperation.

But within this complex systemic machine, a different temporality can also break through: the time of phase change—of transformation—when, through a movement either external to the subject or emerging from within it, the circularity and linearity of the everyday deviate from their paths. This deviation, varying in intensity and quality, opens a space of simultaneity and immanence—a moment of "one huge instant. A totality that is lived and without the experience of time 'passing'" (Vaneigem 1983: 68).

And yet, there is no absolute escape from the cyclical time of reproduction, nor from the linear time of production to which our survival remains tethered. The temporal rupture offered by a phase shift is not an exit but a gap—a breach that makes possible a reconfiguration of the circuits and relations in which we are entangled, and of the times—linear and circular—that absorb us.

What, then, is to be done, starting from the everyday? "Since one must survive in order to live, virtual moments, possibilities, are necessarily rooted in that time. When we try to federate moments, to bring out the pleasure in them, to realize their promise of life, we are already learning how to construct 'situations'" (Vaneigem 1983). To construct a situation out of the everyday—out of its survival routines—is, first and foremost, to begin to unravel the very situation we find ourselves in. It is to explore avenues for action that take as their object of change the knots of seemingly unresolvable contradictions embedded in the interpretive, narrative, and practical cage of dominant values. This is where the naive questions—the ones through which the measures of things are defined, and can be redefined—come into play. Not to escape time but to recompose it. Not to flee the everyday but to inscribe in its folds a different rhythm. In this act, perhaps, lies the most radical sense of *carpe diem*: not to seize the day as it is but to grasp the possible in what is and make it the ground of an otherwise.

Part and whole

In this everyday, we find the indelible marks of the common as a condition. This condition can be viewed from two perspectives: that of the whole and that of the part. From the perspective of the whole, it reveals itself as the hegemonic structure of our social cooperation—namely, capitalism as it manifests in the present, across different contexts. Yet this "whole" is, in truth, only partial, for within it persists the non-capitalism of life. Still, this partiality—capital—mobilizes enormous social power and aspires to become total, reducing the entirety of life, including its space-time coordinates, to a function of its command and domination. Seen from the perspective of the part—that is, the subjects acting within this totalizing structure, pursuing and shaping their own forms of life—the common as condition takes on another dimension. While capitalist hegemony requires and seeks to mold a particular kind of subjectivity—fragmented and functional across its domains of command—as we have seen, the wider field of social cooperation exceeds capital's reach. Within this plural terrain, the subject is compelled to deploy differentiated forms of consciousness to make their actions intelligible—or at least viable—within each specific domain, navigating not only the demands of capital but also the divergent logics of care, reciprocity, resistance, and survival.

In this everyday life, the subject enacts intentionality and autonomy, albeit within a range of possibilities and capacities that vary across different contexts—yet autonomy and intentionality remain. There are always constraints on intentionality, which produce precisely a more or less wide range of possibilities and directions to be taken. These constraints are the surface that delimits the social cooperation systems in which we operate daily in multiple ways and in multiple roles. Their systemic organization makes its presence felt on our bodies as we operate in the everyday. Indeed, the everyday is never separate from the structures and cycles of social cooperation. "Out there," there is a complex objectivity of the everyday that at least delimits this intentionality within specific boundaries, forms, and languages that make them socially intelligible. For example, a child going to the local store to buy a lollipop interconnects this ordinary desire for sweets with a complex of social relations (Smith 2002: 273).

In principle, there are two opposing ways of viewing the subject within the everyday as a node in the network of social cooperation. One sees the subject as a self-governing micro-entity—a little sovereign in a micro-kingdom—endowed with autonomy and freedom of choice, speech, and consumption, though constrained by budgetary limits. This is the image of *homo economicus*: a self-interested, rational individual, cognitively and emotionally isolated, evaluating the world through prices and utility. Society, in this view, is nothing more than the aggregate of such individuals. The other perspective regards this notion of autonomy with a wry smile. Here, the subject is not sovereign but is shaped by and functional within larger systems—the economy, media, law, and governance—that determine their practices, preferences, and routines. The individual becomes a cog in the machine of reproduction.

At its core, this contrast reflects the classic tension between part and whole. Reductionism errs on the side of disconnection: It isolates a part from the whole, exaggerates its autonomy, and attributes to it a generative power disproportionate to the complexity of reality. Functionalism, on the other hand, flattens distinctiveness: It absorbs the part into the logic of the whole, reducing the subject to a passive executor of systemic demands.

Thus, reductionism represents a view of reality that is underconnected, failing to account for the complexity of interactions among parts. Functionalism, on the other hand, makes the opposite error of overconnectedness, in which individual parts lose their distinct identity. It emphasizes the totality so strongly that parts are seen solely as functions of the whole, reducing their autonomy.

Examples of reductionism abound: the idea that climate change can be solved through recycling; that poverty is a personal failing; that migration is caused by smugglers. Each isolates a node from the web of relations—erasing structures of production, extraction, and global asymmetry. But functionalist distortions are just as real: here, individuals are not merely reduced to a single attribute, but defined entirely by the functions they perform within a system. When people are seen only as human capital, as voters, or as demographic targets, their agency is subsumed under systemic logics that claim to speak for the whole.

In the first case, systemic change becomes unthinkable because the subject is too sovereign to need it. In the second, change appears impossible because the subject has no outside from which to act. Both miss the tension that defines our condition: We are neither fully autonomous nor wholly determined; we are entangled in a field of forces, navigating partial freedoms and partial captures.

Both reductionism and functionalism ultimately serve the status quo—a stance we cannot afford. Within this false dichotomy, transformation becomes inconceivable. Change cannot emerge from isolated, partial subjects locked in their respective spheres, with no constitutive relation to the whole. Nor can it arise from a totality that absorbs its parts into mere functions of itself—precisely the logic enacted by the pyramid of capital.

And yet, history is replete with ruptures—radical shifts in how social cooperation is organized. To engage with reality as something to be transformed, we must break out of this conceptual trap. The everyday is a fundamental dimension of the real, where meaning, reproduction, and resistance are continuously enacted. We must approach it with a perspective that honors both the distinction and mutual determination between part and whole—without collapsing critical thought and judgment into one or the other.

Social change between part and whole

The issue of change has two dimensions: from the perspective of the part, that is, the subject, and from the perspective of the totality of social cooperation.

From the perspective of the totality, social change entails the reorganization of social cooperation—that is, of the common as a condition. Jason Read (2022) puts it succinctly: "The transformation of the world must be grasped first and foremost as its reorganization: it is a matter of organizing the world in such a way that events, circumstances, and encounters favorable to human beings multiply in number and intensity to the point where human beings find in the world a human way of living."

But what does it mean to reorganize social cooperation—and how might it be done?

The difficulty lies in this: life itself, in all its diversity—both social and more-than-social—is inherently organizational. As Rodrigo Nunes (2021) argues, "life exudes organisation from all its pores." Social cooperation, then, is never a blank slate. It is always already organized, and in a multiplicity of ways. Yet, in its totality, these plural organizations are not neutral or evenly distributed. They are integrated, subordinated, and shaped by the hegemonic power of capital, which imposes its own logic of organization onto social cooperation. This logic is congruent with the reproductive aims of capital itself. It bends—or seeks to bend—the full complexity of the real, with all its contradictions, resistances, and contingencies, toward its own ends. In this light, capital appears not merely as a system of accumulation but as a social force that fosters an autopoietic organization of social cooperation—a self-reproducing machine that absorbs perturbations, especially conflict, in order to stabilize and recompose its own conditions of reproduction. The pyramid of capital, which we will explore in Chapter 9, is precisely this immense autopoietic machine: a dynamic system that perpetually reorganizes social cooperation in ways that seek to sustain its own survival. The historical task, then, is not simply to resist this machinery but to construct another—to build an autopoietic organization of social cooperation founded on different values, different meanings, and different ways of living together.

Let us now shift perspective: from the need to reorganize social cooperation as a whole, to the challenge of reorganization as it appears from the standpoint of the part—of one or more cooperating singularities. If the image of the common as a condition invites us to think about transforming the totality of social cooperation, the internalization of its order of things within each of us compels us to confront a more intimate problem: the relationship between the subject and their exteriority. The constitution of a "we" emerges through this terrain—not as an abstract unity but through concrete processes of communication and connection, material and immaterial, between plural subjects who seek to reclaim more and more areas of their lives from capitalist command. This resonates with Félix Guattari's view that genuine social change hinges on the reorganization of social relations—understood as a reconfiguration of the relationship between subjectivity and its exteriority. For Guattari (2000: 27), this exteriority is not limited to social structures but encompasses everything with which subjectivity interacts: "*whether social, animal, vegetable, or cosmic*." He argues that the ecological crisis—and the broader social crisis—reveals how this relationship has become compromised. Subjectivity, instead of being open and generative, is increasingly marked by "*a general movement of implosion and regressive infantilisation*" (Guattari 2000).

Social change, in this view, is the remodeling of the relationship between subjects and their exteriority—the material, social, and symbolic environments through which life is produced and reproduced at multiple scales. This remodeling involves becoming attuned to new configurations of meaning, including different ends, purposes, sensibilities, relational practices, and horizons.

On the side of the totality, the question of change appears as the reorganization of cooperation as a whole—as a shift in the general order of things that orients and shapes social life. On the side of the part—from the standpoint of the subject—change is defined as a new relationship with exteriority, with what lies beyond the self. This relationship operates across multiple levels: psychic, ecological, social, and beyond.

Change, then, plays out in the dynamic between part and whole—where the part is not merely functional within the existing totality but potentially constitutive of another and where the whole is not a closed system but one that incorporates—or seeks to incorporate—what exceeds it, turning new terrain into potential sites of capture.

It is important to distinguish these two perspectives. Though part and whole are inseparable, it is from the movement of the part that transformative horizons emerge—from situated practices and desires that recompose experience and point toward another possible totality. Yet without a critical grasp of the whole, the movement of the part remains myopic, unable to discern the contours of the very challenge it faces.

The relationship between part and whole, subject and totality, is dynamic: Each co-emerges and shapes the other (Thompson 2007: 423). This co-emergence allows us to think not only about the possibility of transformation but also about the persistence of dominant structures despite constant change. Every action by a part unfolds within a context that appears, from its position, as a totality. Yet within this apparent totality, there is always the possibility of opening a gap—a rupture. If such gaps multiply and reach a critical threshold, they may reconfigure the whole. But they may also be absorbed, stabilized, and neutralized within it.

Changing the meta-organization of social cooperation is thus the central task and challenge before us—yet such transformation can arise only from within the movement of the parts themselves, from those situated practices that prefigure and weave together another autopoietic meta-organization, one no longer grounded in the priority of capital reproduction but in the primacy of social reproduction in a broader sense.

Enactivism

Transformation, as we have seen, can only arise from within the movement of the parts themselves. Yet this does not mean that the part and the whole stand opposed or separate. To understand how transformation unfolds, we must grasp the co-emergence that binds them: the ways in which the activity of the part simultaneously draws upon and alters the structures of the whole. Let us now dwell on the general character of this relationship between part and whole by developing a framework that moves beyond the dichotomy that forces us to privilege one side of the equation—the subject or the world—as the sole site of change. Enactivism offers such a perspective, highlighting the dynamic and coproductive linkages between part and whole through its understanding of cognition as a process of signification, the continual creation of meaning.[1]

Briefly, enactivism offers a framework for understanding cognition as an emergent and dynamic process rooted in the interplay between autonomy, embodiment, and the co-emergence of parts and wholes. At its core lies the principle that living systems, including human and social systems, are *autonomous agents:* They generate and sustain themselves through processes of *autopoiesis*, a concept that we have already discussed in previous chapters. Applied to the living systems in general, autopoiesis describes how an organism maintains its identity by continuously producing and organizing its own components within a self-contained, yet environmentally embedded, network of processes (Varela et al. 1974).

This autonomy is not isolation; rather, it reflects an entanglement between the parts (the internal processes of the organism, human, or social system) and the whole (the organism, human, or social system). The parts gain their identity and function only within the context of the whole system they help sustain, while the whole exists only through the self-organizing interaction of its parts. Enactivism extends this view to cognition, proposing that cognitive processes arise as a natural continuation of this organizational dynamic, in which the organism enacts, or "brings forth," its world through its interactions with the environment (Varela et al. 1991).

This relational perspective fundamentally challenges traditional mechanistic or representational models of cognition, suggesting instead that the organism and its environment are inseparably co-defined. The enactive approach thus positions cognition not as an abstract computational process but as an adaptive process of sense-making—understood here as the organism's ongoing selection and regulation of environmental perturbations in relation to its own organization, goals, and embodied viability. By emphasizing the inseparability of organism and environment, enactivism reveals how life and mind co-emerge in the ongoing relational dynamics through which self and world are enacted. This co-emergent logic also extends to the subject: Our social, affective, and cognitive lives unfold through similar enactments of meaning within the relational fields that sustain us.

For the authors, cognition is a phenomenon that encompasses the entire living system, including both human and nonhuman organisms. Since this book addresses social change within social cooperation, I will use the term *subject*—whether singular or collective—as the elementary unit of analysis.

To illustrate the enactive dynamic of subject-world co-constitution, consider the act of walking in the mountains. One can follow a well-worn trail, reinforcing its existence through repeated passage—just as everyday practices often reproduce established social paths. Or one may forge a new trail across a meadow, initiating a shift in the landscape through deviation and repetition. In both cases, the subject engages in a process of sense-making, where cognition is not detached representation but embodied engagement. The path becomes a trace of relational entanglement: maintaining or transforming the terrain through which life moves. A fisher mends their net at dawn. They are not simply working; they are remaking the relation between ocean and sustenance, the self and the sea. Dock workers refuse to load weapons bound for a bombed country: They are not simply striking but recasting their relation to the victims of carnage and to the political and business interests sustained by it.

In this way, the subject does not simply operate within a pre-given world—they participate in enacting one.

In this perspective, cognition, or sense-making, is not confined to the brain; it is enacted through the subject's embodied, material, and relational interactions with the environment. Cognition emerges through a dynamic coupling of subject and context, where perception and action form an adaptive loop. Thinking is not simply internal processing that is later expressed in behavior—it is formed through that behavior. As McGann (n.d.) puts it, cognition is like a handshake: a reciprocal act that requires mutual engagement and subtle negotiation. Once we know how to "shake hands" with the world, we are able to sense its moods, tensions, and invitations. A street medic during a protest senses danger not through abstract calculation but through the pressure of breath, the tension in a crowd, the smell of smoke—cognition shaped by the pulse of struggle.

The contrast between enaction and representation illustrates two distinct cognitive paradigms. Classical cognitivism posits that the mind constructs internal symbolic models of an objective world—representations that function like codes in a computer, whose semantics are programmed from the outside. In this model, the brain manipulates images of a reality that it does not itself cocreate.

Enactivism offers a radically different orientation. Cognition is not an abstract computational process but a relational, embodied, and participatory activity: a process of *sense-making*, through which the organism continuously selects and regulates environmental perturbations in relation to its own organization and viability. The mind does not stand outside the world interpreting it; it inhabits the world, shaping it and being shaped by it. Cognition is a dance between body and world, between subject and field, through which meaning arises—and this dance is sometimes free and improvisational, sometimes choreographed by the inherited routines and bureaucratic scripts that constrain our movements before they are even made. Thus, a bureaucrat checks a form. A mother reads a child's face. Both interpret—but one reads signs from above, and the other enacts meaning through touch, tone, and trust.

Although enactivism emerged from cognitive science, its implications reach far beyond the biology of perception. It helps us understand how *subjects*, too, enact worlds of meaning within the social field. A worker retools a machine in the factory not just to meet a quota but to ease the pain in their wrist—tweaking the world to feel differently within it. A nurse lingers for a second longer before removing the needle—not for protocol but to ease fear—calibrating care through breath and eye contact. A team of civil servants rewrites an intake form—not only to reduce error but also to remove questions that shame—quietly redrawing the borders of belonging. A neighborhood mutual aid group remaps food distribution routes—not just for efficiency but to meet elders where they are—rediscovering proximity as care.

In each of these gestures, meaning and world are cocreated. To *constitute* the world is not to create it from nothing but to disclose it through action—to bring forth meaning through our embodied engagement with it. From a reflexive stance, the world ceases to appear as an object outside the self and instead reveals itself as dynamically co-emergent with it: I act in the world, and the world, in turn, transforms my action. Representations, then, are not fixed images of an external order but evolving traces of embodied enactment. Their significance lies not in mirroring reality but in orienting action—and in remaining open to transformation.

This shift is crucial for understanding social change. If what we take to be *the world* is itself enacted—shaped through our actions, institutions, and narratives—then transformation begins with altering our mode of engagement. We do not act in a static world; we enact it anew. As Marx (2010a: 103–4) wrote, "Men [*sic*] make their own history, but they do not make it just as they please . . . the tradition of all the dead generations weighs like a nightmare on the brain of the living."

Our ability to reshape the world is always mediated by inherited conditions. Yet, through reflexive enactment—by becoming aware of how our cognition cocreates reality—we can reanimate the past in the service of a different future. We conjure ghosts not to be haunted by them but to transform what they make possible.

Intentionality and consciousness

This approach integrates subjects and their exteriority within the enactive process of cognition, drawing our attention to two related notions: intentionality and consciousness, both of which are fundamental to the definition of the subject, as I will discuss in the next chapter. Let us briefly focus on these.

Intentionality—the mind's directedness toward an object—links subject and world. For Husserl, every conscious act is intentional, in the sense that thought and perception are always about something—not only when that something is a concrete purpose of acting but also when it is imaginary or abstract. For example, when you think about a tree, your thoughts are intentionally directed toward the tree. In the enactive view, this directedness is not disembodied but enacted through living interaction: a lived orientation expressed through the body and action, even if this action consists only of the internal bodily processes that make that thought possible. Merleau-Ponty had already extended this insight, showing how perception and movement disclose the world through embodied interaction. In this sense, intentionality is not only mental but *sensorimotor*, a process of *bringing forth*.

This active directedness parallels Spinoza's (2018: 102) *conatus*—the striving by which each being persists in existence. Both conatus and enactivist intentionality describe vitality as a dynamic relation: Being unfolds through action that sustains its own conditions of life. If Husserl's intentionality is reflective, Spinoza's is pre-reflective and material—a striving enacted even before thought takes form. A refugee crossing a border and a gardener tending soil—each embodies this striving to persist, to live.

Cognition, understood as the ongoing, first-order interaction between the subject and the environment, is the process from which both intentionality and consciousness emerge. While intentionality expresses the outward-directed orientation of the subject—a movement through which the world is enacted and interpreted—consciousness is the reflective aspect that arises at the point of encounter, when experience itself becomes explicit and the intertwining of subject and world comes into view. Consciousness is thus the site of representations—not static images of an external world but lived appearances that arise through this relational interplay.

Emotions mediate between the two: They orient conscious attention and infuse meaning with value. In neuroscience, for example, emotions are considered essential in structuring consciousness, influencing perception, attention, and memory. Thus, Antonio Damasio (1994, 1999) argues that emotions help give meaning and value to conscious experience by directing attention to what we consider important. Thus, through emotions, we perceive events and situations not only cognitively but also evaluatively, based on their impact on us. In parallel, consciousness enables us to recognize, interpret, and regulate emotions. In this sense, consciousness and emotions influence each other: Emotions orient conscious experience toward subjective values, while consciousness allows emotions to be reflected upon and acted upon.

Within this framework, *judgment* appears as the evaluative moment of enactment—the process by which subjects attribute value to their world. Judgment plays a fundamental role in the process of enactment because it is concerned with the subject's definition, classification, and control of their environment through categories of "good" or "bad," "useful" or "useless," "pleasant or painful," and "profitable or costly." Judgment is not a detached mental act but a situated articulation between embodied beings and the conditions they inhabit. A tenant weighing whether to confront a landlord, a neighborhood assembly resisting a new road—each enacts judgment through a felt calibration of dignity, risk, and care. A corporate entity deciding how to cut costs by relocating likewise enacts judgment—one guided by the systemic logic of accumulation, where value is measured in margins rather than in lives affected. As we shall see in Chapter 7, value praxis begins here: in the ways subjects enact evaluations that reproduce or transform their worlds.

5

The subject

Individual and subject

In the last chapter, we interrogated the question of social change by grounding it in the everyday and arrived at a vision of a general cocreative relationship between part and whole. There, through the lens of enactment, we saw how cognition, intentionality, and judgment arise within embodied interaction—how subjects and worlds are co-constituted through the very processes that bring meaning to life. The move to this chapter follows directly from that insight: If sense-making is enacted, then the subject itself must be understood not as a pre-given entity that acts upon the world but as an embodied becoming that *emerges through* its engagements with the world.

Within this framework, I now turn to the exploration of the subjects who operate, cocreate, and coproduce the different spheres of their world. The subject, as a part within a larger totality, is embedded in bodily, conscious, and affective action through enactive processes—dynamic engagements with their exteriority. It is around this relational redefinition that Félix Guattari glimpses the possibility of social change, seeing transformation as emerging from shifts in how the subject navigates and reconfigures its connections to the world. Social cooperation is constituted by the continuous relational intertwining of these subjects, their mutual exchanges and disruptions at different scales, which produce the entanglements between the two broad circuits of reproduction identified in Chapters 2 and 3: capital reproduction and social reproduction.

But what is, or rather, who is the subject? I offer here a working definition that follows from the enactive account developed earlier: *The subject is a sensory and sensuous body that operates within the world's various contexts, both perturbing and being perturbed, equipped with a set of capacities (powers-to) and vectors of intentionality that together compose its subjectivity.*

The subject is, first and foremost, a sensory and sensuous body that enacts the world through its sensorimotor activities, both internal and external. Second, as we shall see in Chapter 7 on praxis, it is a body articulated with other bodies, with which it enacts the world in determinate forms, scalable through organizational processes of various kinds—networks, coalescences, circuits, and social systems—that amplify capacities, powers, and intentionalities.

When we speak of subjects, then, we are not referring only to the strictly human subject (or to *bios*) but also to those social assemblages—collective subjects—that, through specific forms of social cooperation and organization (Chapters 2 and 3), enact capacities and intentionalities, thereby giving substance to social forces. The notion of the subject used here and in the following chapter therefore applies not only to individuals but also to groupings that, at different scales, act as *macro-intentional singularities*—subjects that operate in the world through their capacities and powers-to and that, when viewed from the standpoint of the particular circuits of reproduction in which they are entangled, can be understood as subjects of *social reproduction* or *capital reproduction*.

The action of the subject is always embodied in a twofold sense. First, because cognition—the generation of meaning through which organization is possible—"depends upon the kinds of experience that come from having a body with various sensorimotor capacities." Second, because "these individual sensorimotor capacities are themselves embedded in a more encompassing biological, psychological, and cultural context" (Varela et al. 1991: 173), hence a social and ecosystemic body. In this chapter and the next, however, the focus will remain on the human subject, while, through the discussion of praxis in Chapter 7, we will turn to the constitution of collective subjects of social cooperation.

The subject, at every moment of their interaction with the world, enacts a certain subjectivity. By subjectivity, I mean, with Alquati (1994: 22), "the system of beliefs, visions and conceptions, representations, knowledge and culture for certain aspects and valences; and of desires, of certain aspects of the imaginary and as well as of passions and will, options, etc." Such a system is dynamic, "characterised by historicity and sociality and therefore evolving, in a processual way." Moreover, let us keep in mind that subjectivity, like the subject, is scalable and does not refer only to an individual singularity, to the person, but also to singularity that is "collective . . . at various layers of breadth and levels-of-reality" (Alquati 1994).

The question of subjectivity is a fundamental issue for social transformation. There is no transformation in the relationships that constitute social cooperation among bodies without transformation of subjectivities, and conversely, there is no transformation of subjectivities without transformation of social relations among bodies. The problem of whether the chicken or the egg—subjectivity or the relational system of subjectivities—came into being first is resolved in a systemic, processual conception of reciprocal feedback between the state of subjectivity and the state of social relations in given contexts. This is, I think, one way to think about enactment, as discussed in the last chapter.

Subjectivity, understood in this sense as a system (a set of internal elements that relate to each other in given forms) of which subjects are bearers, is already a first reason why we speak of subjects and not individuals. *Individual* comes from the Latin *individuus*, meaning "not divisible," and refers to any single being with characteristics (individuality) that make it unique and differentiate it from all other beings of the same logical class, such as a species.

However, at both the social and biological levels, individual boundaries are ambiguous and, to some extent, blurred. What we call the individual is always shaped by interactions with other species and other human beings. This interconnectedness makes it difficult to pinpoint what is truly indivisible in the individual, while simultaneously grounding individual uniqueness in a common basis—a shared condition. For example, one is always born into a world structured by particular belief systems—frameworks that provide a basis for making sense of reality and navigating it. However, each person's unique life trajectory, shaped by social interactions and the layering of experiences, leads to a singular assemblage of subjectivity. Yet, paradoxically, it is through differentiation and communication that the conditions for a common feeling, a new collective subjectivity, and cultural transformation emerge.

From a biological point of view, such sharing stems from the fact that, as parts of Gaia, we interact with other parts, from which we draw (and internalize) all sorts of nourishment and means of life. Hence the question: Is the food we are digesting right now part of an individual body or not? At the biological level, nucleic acid analysis has shown how animals and plants interact significantly with symbiotic microorganisms that disrupt the sharp boundaries that have hitherto characterized the definition of a biological individual in different subdisciplines. In this sense, for example, anatomical or physiological criteria are not sufficient to consider animals as individuals, precisely because a large variety of symbionts serve and complement many physiological functions, such as metabolism. Our bodies are home to numerous organisms that, while struggling to survive in them, also perform important functions. Our relationship with the human microbiota, that is, the collection of microorganisms inside the human body that can reach, in total, the astounding weight of two kilograms, is a good example of mutualism, that is, cooperation between different types of organisms that brings an advantage to each of them. The microbiota has a protective function against the proliferation of other pathogenic bacteria, regulates our immune system, enables the production of some of the vitamins essential to our bodies by promoting the absorption of nutrients introduced through food, and stimulates intestinal nerve cells by facilitating the natural contraction and relaxation mechanisms of the colon during the digestion phase. In addition, the very development of animals is incomplete without symbionts, which constitute a second mode of genetic inheritance and provide a range of genetic variation within which natural selection can operate. Finally, the development and regulation of the immune system occur through an interaction that leads to microorganisms being integrated into animal cells (Gilbert et al. 2012).

If, at the social and biological levels, individual boundaries are ambiguous and, to some extent, blurred, when I use the term individual in this book, I do so to identify only an element of a logical class. To the extent, however, that this individual, so understood, is seen as embedded in its real interactional context and is no longer seen merely as an element of a logical class, it is no longer an individual but an individual subject, or a singularity—that is, a social subject whose difference cannot be reduced to something common, a difference that remains different (Hardt and Negri 2004). Yet the differentiation of singularities is always premised on shared conditions, as common infrastructures, histories, and modes of social reproduction and cooperation form the ground upon which differences emerge. In this sense, commons and diversity are not opposing forces but two sides of the same coin, with the common providing the basis for singular expression and singularities reciprocally shaping and reconfiguring the common. To the extent that singularities are articulated among themselves, they constitute moments of the collective power of a multitude.

What, then, remains of the individual? It remains that an individual, without further specification, is an element of a logical class, and a logical class is itself an aggregate of individuals who relate to each other in specific ways that are distinct from the ways in which they relate to members of other logical classes. In this sense, an individual is a node in a network of social relations and circuits of social production but a node of social production only conforms to and is functional within the circuits in which it is embedded. In this sense, we might follow Guattari (2000: 36) in saying that the individual is "something like a 'terminal' for processes that involve human groups, socio-economic ensembles, data-processing machines, etc." The individual is a terminal, and the subject, even when acting functionally as a terminal, is more than just a terminal. A computer terminal is a piece of equipment consisting of a keyboard and a screen, connected to a central computer system—that is, a place where information comes in and goes out—but selection, encoding, and signification take place elsewhere, away from the terminal, in the case of this example, in the computer. The individual as terminal within social systems thus offers an image of relative passivity: that of a peripheral functional organ of a system (or plurality of systems), however necessary, but subordinate to algorithmic logic, meanings, and values defined elsewhere.

Unlike the individual, the subject is generally understood as the agent who performs the action, as opposed to the object of action and transformation. The subject is a dimension of the process of the historical alteration of the world, which also concerns the agent-human as its particular (and also anomalous) moment (Alquati 1994: 5).

As in enactivism, the subject is defined here in relation to the world—as an agent that transforms it through its activity and is, in turn, transformed by it. Defining the subject solely as an individual, in the sense of being undivided, downplays the feedback dynamics between the subject and the world. This perspective overlooks the social dimension—the ways in which external contexts shape the subject and, conversely, how individual subjects influence their surroundings.

There are three key reasons why the individual subject should always be understood as a specific and unique singularity, shaped by a distinct accumulation of experiences. First, subjects are internally divisible—they navigate multiple trajectories of performance and experience depending on the external social systems with which they are structurally coupled at different times and in contexts, as well as on their psychic loops in relation to these systems. Second, unlike individuals who are merely functionally integrated into systems and passively conform to their parameters, subjects do not simply perform the required feedback. Instead, their coupling with external structures generates internal creative processes, enabling them to produce both positive and negative feedback within these systems, mobilizing agency, power, signs, and affects. Third, subjects are scalable from the realm of the psyche to the social, both in their individual experience of social multiplicity and in the collective forms of experience they share through cultural and communicative processes. "Expanding subjectivities beyond the realm of the psyche, we need to theorize and analyze them as collectively experienced and not only a means of understanding and making sense of the world, but also as a major force shaping the world that we live in" (Singh 2018: 762–3).

Operational modes of the subject

But now let us ask: How does the subject stand in relation to the world in such a way as to be both the transformer and the transformed? Alquati here provides a very useful classification of what we may call operational modes through which the subjects operate in the contemporary capitalist world.

The first of these determinations indicates the human actor who activates systemic roles, who performs specific systemic functions, and who follows, without ambivalence or antagonism, the scripts provided by the system in which they are embedded. It is perhaps similar to Guattari's individual as terminal, although only externally, because the subject's internal operations always distinguish it from a terminal:

> 1. Actor-human, rather accepting: it is the agent-human in that it activates systemic roles, charged with specific systemic functions.

Second, there is the agent, the subject who incorporates the ambivalence constituted by their participation in a multitude of systems, and by the experiences, memories, and value traces—cosmological and sense-making—that this participation has left in their internal mechanisms of adaptation, within the individual or collective psyche. In this sense, being an agent is the recognition that our individual and collective bodies are traversed by the multiple perturbations of multiple systems and the logics of reproduction within which they are embedded, and with which they interact in multiple adaptive circuits:

> 2. Intermediate agent or person: characterized by a peculiar ambivalence specific to capitalist civilization, it is the human agent that today remains beneath the actor, subsists within it, and sustains it, while already possessing and reproducing a certain degree of autonomy. In doing so, it imposes on the system—through its processes and exchanges—both informatics and a part of latency. It is the most relevant bearer of human ambivalence.

The passage, I think, describes a paradoxical human condition under capitalism, where people are both shaped by and shaping the system. The "intermediate agent/person" is neither fully an autonomous actor nor merely a passive functionary but exists in a liminal state—one that sustains the system while also imposing its own imprint on it. "Informatics" represents the structured exchange of information in which they are embedded, while "latency" represents an underlying or hidden potential that may become disruptive or transformative.

Finally, for Alquati, there is the subject-against.

> 3. Subject-human in the proper sense (or subject-against): I propose and intend it . . . as the agent-human insofar as he tends to develop and qualify his autonomy also as an alternative, which forces him today into

> antagonism. And thus he pursues ends not only different from those of the system, but ends which then, because of capitalist intolerance and totalitarianism, and all the more as he ascends to the highest levels of his reality (not at the bottom then), become ends somewhat at odds with the tolerated constraints and more so with the ends of the specific capitalist system (in the aforementioned totalitarianism). Therefore, the now rare human-subject is, in fact, always antagonistic toward the established social system; otherwise, for me, it is not a human-subject in the strict sense.
>
> —Alquati (1994: 5–6)

Counter-subjectivity for Alquati is thus a subjectivity connoted in an antagonistic manner, that is,

> the system of beliefs, visions and conceptions, representations, knowledge and culture for certain aspects and valences; and of desires, of certain aspects of the imaginary and as well as of passions and will, options, etc. . . . that "antagonistically and effectively connote the agent-human . . ." a subjectivity that one must "always . . . consider as contextualised . . . and thus outside of various ambiguous subjectivisms, and prophecies."
>
> —Alquati (1994: 22)

For the subject-against, being against is not a feature of a fixed ideological matrix but the result of intentionalities that are at odds, in given contexts, with the registers tolerated at the different levels of the order of things in which they operate: the pyramid of capital. To highlight this aspect, I will refer to this subject as an alter-subject, which includes, but is not exhausted by, its being against.

I propose that actor, agent, and alter-subject should not be understood as fixed representations of specific subjects but rather as operational and existential modes of subjectivity that manifest in given contexts. While they may correspond to certain characteristics of singularities, it is more useful to consider them as dynamic positions within a continuum (Figure 5.1), shifting according to situational demands and relational configurations. This continuum applies both across different singularities and within the varying

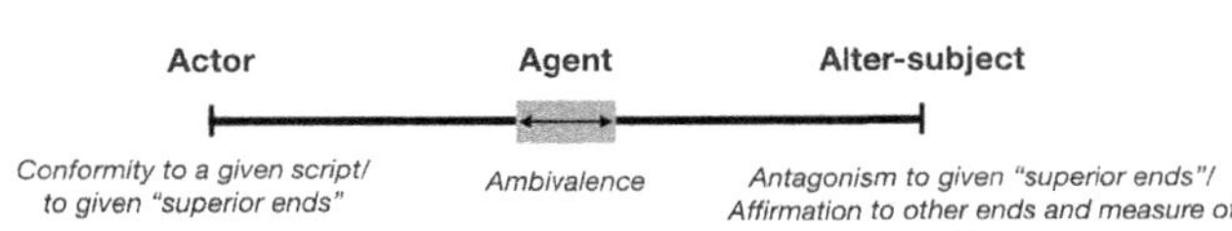

Figure 5.1 Range of variations of subjectivity vis-à-vis dominant systems

experiences of the same singularity across different contexts. It goes without saying that different subjectivities, shaped by their histories, dispositions, and material conditions, are more or less prone to aligning themselves with different modes in different situations.

An example can be found in the mechanisms of capital valorization, where subjects largely operate as actors following a script directed by external forces—whether through managerial hierarchies or market signals. However, this scripted role is not absolute; ambivalence emerges through the body's needs and desires, which push against the constraints imposed by capital. This tension—between following the script and experiencing one's own limits and aspirations—creates a space of ambivalence, where the potential for alter-subjectivity arises as subjects begin to recognize and question the structures shaping their actions.

Yet this same space of ambivalence is also where creativity can be recuperated by capital for its own purposes. Adam Smith's (1970) example of the child worker in the pin factory, who innovates a shortcut in performing a task so that he can go play, illustrates this dynamic well. In his text, Smith accounts for the child's ingenuity, initially driven by the desire for leisure but not for the fact that, as may be expected, such ingenuity is soon absorbed into capital's logic of efficiency and productivity—when what was, for the child, an inventive way to free up time becomes, for capital, a new method for increasing output and reducing unit costs. As we will see in Chapter 12, capital thrives on this paradox, capturing the very creative forces that could otherwise disrupt its logic and turning them into engines of further accumulation. Thus, while ambivalence holds the potential for transformation, it is also the terrain where capital constantly reabsorbs and repurposes forms of agency and invention for its own reproduction.

This tripartition of subjectivity, unfolding across a spectrum, can be mapped onto different scales and more collective dimensions—including, ultimately, the Marxian conception of class. As we saw in Chapter 3, Marx (2010b) distinguishes between a *class in itself* and a *class for itself*. In our terms, the former refers to the *acting* class—the class of all those subjects (or moments within subjects' experience) whose participation in social cooperation is shaped and measured by the logic of capital. In contrast, a *class for itself* emerges when a collective consciousness arises, posing alternative purposes and different measures of value against those imposed by capital. Between these two poles lies the broadest space of ambivalence.

However, the macro-systemic forces of the *pyramid of capital* continually push to define class merely as an *acting* class, either by channeling individuals into adaptive processes of *desubjectification* or by absorbing ambivalence in order to extract useful praxis and imaginaries for capital's reproduction.

The key political challenge, then, is how to develop adaptive political paths that foster *resubjectification*—at least by engaging with those elements of ambivalence that may open up new horizons of *alter-subjectivity*.

To *resubjectify* the acting class "means radically transforming it—from within and against, at least in certain of its internal moments" (Alquati 1994: 13). Crucially, for new subjectivities to emerge, a *human subjectivity* must already exist—just as counter-subjectivity can arise only from an existing subjectivity capable of resisting and redefining its place within social cooperation.

Subjectivity and consciousness

The problem of resubjectification, or the creation of new subjects, is linked to the question of consciousness.

Building on Alquati's understanding of subjectivity as a dynamic and relational process, we can conceive of consciousness as a state of awareness and responsiveness that draws on the resources mobilized by subjectivity but directs them toward navigating a given environment. In this sense, consciousness is not a static property of the subject but an ongoing process shaped by interactions within social cooperation and the structures of capital (Alquati 1975, 1993). In the previous chapter, consciousness appeared as the reflective moment within the enactive process of cognition—the point at which experience becomes explicit in the encounter between subject and world. Here, the focus widens: The same reflexive dynamic now operates at the level of social cooperation, where consciousness takes the form of organized orientations through which subjects, individually and collectively, navigate their worlds.

In the daily life interactions of subjects with different social systems at different scales—a multitude of systems—a plurality of forms of consciousness interact in such a way that they often form a hierarchy of consciousnesses: ways and selections by which subjects draw on the resources mobilized by subjectivity to orient themselves toward navigating a given environment, which we attribute, in short, to different forms of rationality. In the end, within the complex social systems of capitalist social cooperation, the hierarchy of consciousnesses, rationalities, and thus modes of evaluation and judgment is an arrangement of priorities and constraints; it is an order of things.

Consciousness is thus the "map" that individual subjects construct from the resources of subjectivity in order to orient themselves within the territories of the external operations of the world (in particular contexts) and thus act in determinate forms. The map and the territory are obviously distinct, since, as is well known, a map is not the territory it represents, although when it has a territory-like structure, it is quite useful (Bateson 1987). Yet, in the enactive sense, this "map" is not a detached representation of an external reality but a living pattern of orientation that arises through the subject's ongoing engagement with its environment. Moreover, Bateson argued that it is impossible to know what a territory is, since any understanding of a territory is based on a circuit of sensory channels that represent the territory and report this reading imperfectly. Consciousness is thus a selection of belief systems, visions and conceptions, representations, knowledge, culture, and values, as well as of desires, of certain aspects of imagery, and also of passions and wills, options, and so on. In this sense, different forms of consciousness always offer an image of the world, and, depending on the shape of this image, subjects distinguish particular kinds of boundaries, contours, rather than others, and blind spots and undertake different ways and directions of navigating the world in the processes of their enactment.

The particular function of consciousness is to orient the coupling (or uncoupling) between subjects and the systems within which they operate, an orientation that always subtends certain purposes of the subject, whether expressly intentional on the part of the subject or emergent from the form of the subject-system interaction itself. At the same time, it underlies the emergent purposes of the practices, circuits, and systems within which subjects operate in different spheres.

In what form do we couple, for example, students and educational systems, workers and production systems, caregivers and care systems, citizens and political systems, and consumers/workers and economic systems? It is obvious that a particular relational form of subject-system coupling corresponds to a particular kind of consciousness congruent with the system and, conversely, that a particular kind of consciousness corresponds to a particular way of coupling singularities to form larger systems of which they are a part. But this correspondence, and this congruity, does not imply that this consciousness and this coupling are the only ones possible. I can observe my own activity as I operate within a profit-seeking circuit and understand how the operations of this circuit are designed to minimize costs and maximize profits according to the logic of efficiency—that is, according to the logic of a particular kind of consciousness that connects my singularity to profit-seeking systems. But from my point of view—that is, as an ambivalent being who very concretely experiences the effects of this organization on my body—I am not only conscious of the relationships in which I am immersed, but I am also, to some extent, conscious of the contradiction and incongruity between these measures and the needs and desires of my body. Consciousness is not a fixed, given thing but is constantly evolving under the rhythms of the perturbations received by the subject within the various spheres of social cooperation, the dynamics within the subject triggered by these perturbations, and then externalized by it through communication, resistance, or exodus.

In maps of the world, among the types of consciousness, there are also ways of perceiving the world and thus orienting the subject's action that take care to include the effects of social cooperation not only on the body of a given singularity but also on other bodies, as well as on the body of the Earth and on ecology, which that way of organizing social production entails. These other consciousnesses—these critical consciousnesses—then yearn for a different way of coupling singularities and systems; a different way of *drawing on the resources mobilized by subjectivity and of orienting oneself toward navigating a given environment;* a way obtusely open to the question of the transformation of this environment and to posing the question of adaptation as a transformation not only of the subjects, given the environment in which they operate, but also of the environment itself, given the problems of social reproduction faced by these subjects. The lives, battles, and community construction that have produced these critical consciousnesses in history would demand that we find some ways to articulate them in such a way as to contribute to the orientation of a broad, plural movement for radical social change.

We can take a cue here from Mark Fisher (2016, 2020) to identify some types of critical consciousness that are directly related to the question of social transformation beyond the "realism of capitalism," for which there is no alternative: forms of critical consciousness that broke the dialectic of capital in the 1960s and 1970s but that, with the emergence of neoliberalism, have been marginalized, divided, or subsumed by the mainstream from neoliberal realism. Mark Fisher identifies three types of critical consciousness—class consciousness, feminist consciousness, and psychedelic consciousness—but to these, I believe, we should add *at least* ecological and Indigenous consciousness.

Class consciousness concerns the awareness of exploitation in the relationship between capital and labor, in all its hierarchical forms, wage and non-wage, within the multiple mechanisms of capitalism. This consciousness, in different forms, has mobilized struggles for decades and, in many places, continues to do so, pushing for improvements in working and living conditions. Feminist consciousness is about bringing the body to the center of political practice—its relationships, affects, everyday life, sexual diversity, care, and reproduction.

To these two should be added ecological consciousness, which is about the interconnectedness of all forms of life, the being-nature of the human, and thus the tragic consequences of living in and enacting a world of ecologically destructive capitalist growth and endless accumulation. Ecological consciousness makes us realize that all political practice is always also a form of ecological practice.

Indigenous consciousness must also be added. By this, I indicate not only the ecological consciousness of which the Indigenous one is often the bearer but also a consciousness that unfolds "with a commitment to shared space and coexistence. One is indigenous to the extent that one participates in the material and social reality that one inhabits" (Lucha Indígena 2022: 3). Let us, however, give a broad and articulated sense to "inhabiting." One inhabits a place, but through the circuits of social cooperation, one also inhabits a world and everything in between, as we envisaged in Chapter 1.

Finally, we return to Mark Fisher, who points us to a further kind of consciousness necessary for social transformation, one that concerns a quality of feeling that allows us to recognize the plasticity of the real—its potential for transformation and mutation—which is precisely the opposite of capitalist realism. The awakening of a psychedelic consciousness, which may not necessarily be related to substance use, is accompanied by the perception of shifting and blurred boundaries and thus implies a critique of fixed subjects built around rigid identity markers such as race, class, gender, or species (Battistutta 2022). Psychedelic consciousness disrupts the boundaries between subjects and between the subject and the environment in which they operate. These boundaries no longer present themselves as walls, as a sharp division between inside and outside through a rigid filtering mechanism, but as a threshold (Stavrides 2016): a boundary whose function is not only to divide the inside and the outside but also to connect them in new ways. Psychedelic consciousness directs us to problematize the illusory and arbitrary nature of all our distinctions. At the same time, however, we must always recognize the need to draw distinctions in order to orient ourselves and act out of hierarchies in this world. Threshold boundaries thus allow us to keep an open mind and get on with the business of life, allowing specific social forms to be contaminated by other forms while remaining open to a wide field of possibilities whose containment, for all intents and purposes, depends on what we consider acceptable or unacceptable, what we value more or less, and the value system we manage to construct and operationalize in social cooperation, both within and in contrast to the upper levels of the pyramid (Chapter 16).

The different forms of critical consciousness outlined above offer ways to challenge capitalist realism by revealing the contingency of existing structures and the potential for transformation. However, these forms of consciousness do not emerge in a vacuum; they develop through concrete social practices, struggles, and modes of collective organization. It is here that Romano Alquati's work becomes particularly relevant. His analysis of consciousness as a relational and situated process highlights the ways in which awareness is shaped by material conditions, social cooperation, and the dynamics of production and reproduction. If Fisher points us to the need for a consciousness that can break with the fatalism of capitalist realism, Alquati provides a framework for understanding how such consciousness is produced, how it evolves through inquiry, conflict, and organization, and how it can be embedded in processes of subjectification and class composition. By linking consciousness to the materiality of everyday life and the structural tensions between adaptation and resistance, Alquati allows us to see consciousness not simply as an ideological awakening but as an embodied and processual phenomenon, one that is constantly shaped by, shaping, and possibly challenging the hierarchies and constraints of capitalist social cooperation.

Romano Alquati (1975, 1993) conceives consciousness not as an abstract or purely individual entity but as a relational and situated process, rooted in the materiality of social practices and the dynamics of production relations. For Alquati, consciousness is neither an immediate given of subjective experience nor a mechanical reflection of economic structures; rather, it functions as a form of mediation between the subject and the social context in which it is embedded, emerging through processes of subjectification and collective struggle (Borio et al. 2002).

More precisely, Alquati conceptualizes consciousness as a processual and collective phenomenon, developed through interactions with the material and symbolic structures of capital and social cooperation. It is formed and transformed through labor experiences, conflicts, practices of inquiry and *conricerca*, and collective organizational forms (Alquati 1975). *Conricerca*,[1] in particular, is not merely a methodological tool for Alquati but a device through which workers can construct autonomous consciousness, deconstructing the narratives imposed by capital and producing new forms of knowledge and political organization. Consciousness is therefore not a fixed datum but a continuously evolving process, marked by tensions between adaptation and resistance, between the internalization of dominant logics and the possibility of rupture and reappropriation (Wright 2002).

Alquati (1975) links this conception of consciousness to the concept of class composition, emphasizing that consciousness is not configured solely at the individual level but primarily within the collective dynamics through which subjects become aware of their role in the processes of production and social reproduction. Thus, consciousness is not merely an ideological recognition but an enacted and embodied practice, developing within the materiality of everyday life and the processes of subjectification, both inside and against capital (Roggero 2019).

This dynamic understanding of consciousness, rooted in material conditions and collective struggle, points directly to the question of how social reproduction can be organized beyond capital's imperatives. If consciousness is both shaped by and actively shapes the structures of social cooperation, then its transformative potential lies in its capacity to orient and sustain an autopoietic organization of social reproduction on its own terms, rather than as a subordinated function of capital's self-reproduction.

6

Subjectification and the subject-holon

Subjectification

If the previous chapter explored what the subject is, this one asks how it becomes. Subjectification is the name of this becoming—the continual formation and transformation of subjects within the forces and relations that shape social cooperation—while the *subject-holon* names the relational condition of this becoming: a subject that is at once a whole in itself and a part of wider totalities, co-constituted through the very systems in which it participates.

In everyday life, subjectification is the ongoing process through which the subjects take shape in relation to exteriority, adapting to and negotiating the forces—psychic, social, economic, and ecological—that condition their becoming. This dynamic adaptation—what we have previously referred to as enaction—describes how subjectivity emerges through ongoing interactions with its surroundings, shaping and being shaped by the systems in which it operates.

In daily life, each of us operates, to a greater or lesser extent, in a multiplicity of systems, relating to them in different ways depending on context. Think of the number of social systems with which we are engaged daily while wearing the hat of consumers, workers, passengers, citizens or noncitizens, mothers or fathers, sons or daughters, friends, students or teachers, doctors or patients, or social networkers. Each of these domains, practices, circuits, and systems demands of us subjectivities adapted to its rituals, dynamics, and narratives; requires us to structure our behavior around specific norms (subject as actor); nudges us to avail ourselves of our ambivalence to navigate contradictions (subject as agent); or serves as the situated context for deploying our "no," so that we can call upon resources layered within our subjectivity and imagine other horizons, relationships, and forms of praxis (alter-subjects). Whether the systems in which the subject operates are intersubjective or machinic—that is, whether they function through a more open-ended, sympoietic logic or within the tighter constraints of an autopoietic framework—significantly influences the possibilities for action and transformation.

The concept of subjectification refers to the processes through which individuals become subjects, shaped by social, political, and economic forces while also exercising agency within these constraints. Within social cooperation, individual subjects, understood as singularities, are exposed to multiple processes of subjectification to the extent that they are "structurally coupled" to a variety of systemic circuits, each with different demands for adaptation and congruence. By "structural coupling" (Maturana and Varela 1987), I mean the sustained interactions over time that occur between different subjects and between subjects and systems and that both presuppose and produce some form of congruence between subjects and their externality, without which there can be no cooperation. Vectors of subjectification are established through structural coupling between subjects, constituting various circuits and social systems of social cooperation. Structural coupling is a generic term that always implies some form of relationality.

Subjectification is thus generally the name for the production process of the subject, participating with capacity and intentionality in the relational dance with the world. Subjectification involves endless processes of becoming subjects through particular relations with the environment or the "exteriority" of the subject—processes in which subjects influence (or perturb) their exteriority and, at the same time, the exteriority influences (or perturbs) the subjects. This process of mutual constitution between subject and exteriority takes on different organizational, relational, and dynamic forms depending on the spheres of operation and the range of options that characterize the ongoing process of the constitution of social cooperation.

Subjectification, power, and resistance

The notion of *subjectification* marks a significant shift from the classical concept of the subject in contemporary thought, particularly in the works of Foucault and Deleuze and Guattari. Traditional accounts of the subject—whether in Cartesian rationalism, Kantian autonomy, or even existentialist thought—often assume a relatively stable, self-contained individual endowed with agency and self-reflection. However, thinkers such as Foucault (1977, 1978, 1982) and Deleuze and Guattari (1988) challenge this view by emphasizing the processual, relational, and contingent nature of subject formation.

For Foucault, subjectivity is not an innate or fixed quality but the effect of power relations and discursive formations. He introduced the concept of *subjectivation* (*assujettissement*) as a central element of power relations, demonstrating how institutions, discourses, technologies of power/knowledge, and disciplinary mechanisms produce subjects who internalize norms and modes of self-regulation (Foucault 1977, 1982). In this view, the subject is not pre-given but produced through historical, social, and institutional apparatuses.

Whereas Foucault's notion of *subjectivation* focuses on the ways power makes subjects through subjection, Deleuze and Guattari (1988) expand the analysis toward *subjectification*, emphasizing the creative, processual, distributed, and machinic dimensions through which subjectivity is continually produced and transformed. Rather than seeing subjectivity as a singular identity, they conceive of it as multiple, dynamic, and always in the making, shaped by assemblages of desire, power, and material conditions. They introduce the notion of machinic enslavement, in which subjectivity is not merely determined by ideology or discourse but also by material infrastructures, economic systems, and technological dispositifs.

Both perspectives emphasize that subjectification is not merely about being a subject but about *becoming* one—a process that is never complete, always contingent, and shaped by forces beyond individual consciousness. This shift has crucial political implications: Rather than focusing on a pre-given subject resisting domination, contemporary thought explores how new modes of subjectivity can be produced, contested, and reconfigured within different social and economic structures.

Following Foucault and Deleuze and Guattari, several theorists have further developed the concept of subjectification, each introducing distinct perspectives on power, agency, and resistance. Judith Butler (1990, 1997) extends Foucault's notion of subjectivation through her theory of performativity, arguing that gendered and political subjects are produced through repetitive discursive acts. For Butler, subjectification is paradoxical: While individuals are constituted by norms, they also have the capacity to subvert and resignify them through performance and reiteration. Etienne Balibar (1994, 2001), on the other hand, foregrounds the tension between subjectivation and emancipation, emphasizing the historical processes through which subjects emerge in relation to citizenship, political struggle, and the dialectic between individual rights and collective belonging. His work critiques the deterministic tendencies in Foucault and Deleuze and Guattari by insisting on the potential for political subjectivity to disrupt established power structures. Jacques Rancière (1995, 2004) offers another perspective, shifting the focus from subjectification as a process of subjection to one of dissensus—the emergence of political subjects through moments of rupture and contestation that challenge the established distribution of the sensible. Unlike Deleuze and Guattari, who emphasize impersonal machinic processes, Rancière highlights the role of subjective agency in political aesthetics and the redistribution of visibility and voice.

Finally, Maurizio Lazzarato (2011, 2014) extends the discussion of subjectification to neoliberal capitalism, exploring how debt and financial mechanisms shape contemporary forms of subjectivity and expanding Deleuze and Guattari's analysis by distinguishing between social subjection and machinic enslavement. Here, he argues that contemporary capitalism not only disciplines individuals through social roles and identity assignments but also integrates them into technical, financial, and media assemblages, reducing them to functions within automated systems. He criticizes a one-sided focus on signifying semiotics (e.g., Butler, Rancière), arguing that much political theory neglects asignifying mechanisms such as financial flows, algorithms, and infrastructures—a critique he extends to contemporary theory at large. Yet, from an enactive standpoint, even these so-called asignifying, machinic processes still enact meaning: Every operation that orients behavior or cooperation regulates relations according to particular values or thresholds of viability. Capital's machinic assemblages are no exception: They, too, enact worlds of significance, translating flows, codes, and affects into regimes of value that sustain accumulation.

Put differently, machinic enslavement is a configuration of *system-level consciousness*: Capitalism enacts its own "map of viability" through algorithms, logistics, and institutional routines. It does not escape sense-making; it automates and formalizes it around exchange value. Hence, subjection and machinic enslavement are co-constitutive: The ideological–institutional frames that legitimize capture and the functional mechanisms that materialize it jointly organize social cooperation for capital's reproduction. To challenge this process, we must move beyond the opposition between signifying and asignifying mechanisms and recognize how both function within a structured regime of valorization that must itself be contested.

This dynamic of valorization—through which capitalism continuously reorganizes social differences into functional hierarchies—is what Mezzadra and Neilson (2013) describe as translation: Capitalism reconfigures differences rather than simply excluding them. Borders, for instance, stratify labor markets—turning migrant status into intensified exploitation while disciplining citizens. In this way, horizontal differentiations (citizen/noncitizen, worker/unemployed, consumer/nonconsumer) are continually translated into vertical hierarchies that expand labor pools and fragment solidarity.

This reveals how subjection and machinic enslavement reinforce one another: The ideological and legal apparatuses that organize subjected forms of participation—borders, laws, and cultural narratives—are inseparable from the machinic infrastructures that operationalize them. Together, they embed social life within a regime of valorization in which exchange value dictates the terms of inclusion, exclusion, and subordination. This translation of horizontal differentiations into vertical hierarchies expands labor pools while fragmenting solidarity: Exclusion itself becomes a mode of inclusion, as noncitizens or informal workers are incorporated on precarious terms that discipline the rest and secure capital's reproduction, thereby tightening the reproduction of capital's order.

At the same time, this process blurs the boundary between control through representation (subjection) and control through function (machinic enslavement). The worker, for instance, is both defined by ideological and institutional narratives and captured within machinic circuits of labor extraction and value production. This dual integration ensures that capital's autopoietic reproduction remains flexible—constantly recalibrating the symbolic and functional dimensions of subjectivity to sustain accumulation.

Gender makes the same dynamic legible. The feminization of care locates women in systematically devalued labor; its commodification (domestic work, nursing, childcare, etc.) renders this labor indispensable to capital's self-reproduction. Thus, gendered subjection and machinic enslavement coproduce devaluation and capture.

Thus, rather than treating subjection and machinic enslavement as distinct or opposing forms of control, we should recognize them as mutually constitutive mechanisms that ensure capital's self-reproduction. Their entanglement highlights the central challenge of resisting capitalist subjectification—not only through ideological critique or attempts to escape machinic capture but also by contesting the hierarchies of value that sustain this system. Breaking free, therefore, requires more than detachment from dominant representations: It demands the active reorganization of social cooperation around other measures of value by refusing exchange value as the ultimate criterion of participation in collective life.

Such reorganization is itself an enactive process—the collective redefinition of what counts as meaningful, viable, and valuable within the ongoing coupling between life and its systems of reproduction. Lines of flight, in Deleuze and Guattari's sense, remain crucial moments of deterritorialization, when subjects break from established formations of power and meaning. Yet these must be joined by *lines of landing*—processes of reterritorialization that root new forms of cooperation in alternative orders of value praxis. Without such grounding, flight risks dissolve into transient rupture rather than transformation. Reterritorialization, in this sense, means creating sustainable and autonomous infrastructures of life-making: collective capacities, institutions, and practices through which alternative subjectivities can persist and proliferate beyond capital's grasp.

The subject-holon and intermittent consciousness

If transformation requires not only rupture but durable reorganization, then the problem is not simply one of escape, but of endurance. Much contemporary analysis influenced by Deleuze and Guattari rightly emphasizes subjectification as ongoing becoming, deterritorialization, and multiplicity. While this perspective remains indispensable for grasping how subjectivity exceeds fixed identities, it leaves open a further theoretical question: what conception of the subject can account for the fact that we act, reproduce institutions, and reorganize cooperation over time—without reducing subjectivity to a fixed essence? The issue, then, is not to define a subject that serves the desire for change, but to clarify the kind of subject that already operates within social cooperation—one capable of both reproducing existing orders of value praxis and, under certain conditions, reconfiguring them. Entirely dispensing with the subject risks obscuring the locus of enactment itself: the structured yet open process through which social cooperation is maintained, contested, and transformed. If social transformation demands not only deterritorialization but the reorganization of value praxis, we must rethink subjectivity beyond the binary of subjection and machinic enslavement—as an open, dynamic, and relational process: autopoietic, yet structurally coupled to broader social and ecological systems.

It is at this juncture that the concept of the subject-holon becomes necessary. Borrowed from Bland and Bell's (2007) discussion of agroecological agency and reworked within my systemic framework, it allows us to conceptualize subjectivity beyond the opposition between subjection and machinic enslavement. If transformation entails not only moments of escape from dominant structures but also the reorganization of social cooperation around different orders of value praxis, this is because subjects are neither fixed identities nor mere functional nodes. The subject-holon names this condition: an open, dynamic, and relational process—partially autopoietic, yet structurally coupled to broader social and ecological systems—through which social cooperation is both reproduced and, at times, reconfigured. Because its autopoiesis is always partial and relational—dependent on systemic conditions it does not fully control—the subject-holon inhabits a field of structural coupling in which the stabilization of existing value orders and their reconfiguration remain copresent possibilities, emerging from shifts in the balance of forces that shape value praxis.

As discussed in Chapter 4, the problem of change has a dual dimension: It unfolds from the perspective of the subject as a part and from the perspective of social cooperation as a whole. Change, then, emerges in the dynamic between the subject as a part and the totality to which it belongs (in its "local" enactments at different moments, as well as in social cooperation as a whole), but this is not a functionalist relationship. The subject is not merely an effect of social structures but also a potential constituent force that can shape alternative totalities. The question of the subject in social change thus corresponds to the perspective of the part that, through its articulations and struggles, pushes toward new horizons from which a different whole can emerge (or may at least have a chance to). To conceive of such a subject as both integrated and transformative requires a framework that does not reduce it to a passive victim of the system, nor elevate it to a voluntaristic force of change but one that is open to interrogate its operations and possibilities within the materiality of a condition and the enacted horizon of its possibilities—even when that horizon is limited to modest improvements in basic living and cultural conditions.

By starting with the everyday, as we did in Chapter 4, we can understand the subject as a node of articulation between intentionality and autonomy, on the one hand, and systemic constraints and relational entanglements, on the other. The subject does not simply react to external forces but actively interprets, negotiates, and often resists them. The subject is both perturbed by and an agent of perturbation. What mediates the subject's activity vis-à-vis their context of interaction is thus a cognitive stance on the part of the subject—some form of consciousness, a local representation within a broader circuit of enaction. This epistemic expedient allows us to overcome the paradox between reductionism and functionalism—that is, the flattening of reality into the primacy of a part or, conversely, the emphasis on an organic totality in which the parts exist merely as functions of the whole, without also existing for themselves. Rather than reducing social life to individual will (as in liberal theories of agency) or to an organic totality (as in functionalist sociologies), the subject-holon reveals how subjectivity emerges through dynamic interactions that can both sustain and disrupt dominant structures.

The concept of the holon, introduced by Koestler (1967), captures this double character of the subject: At times, it is a whole, with autonomy, intentionality, and creative capacity, while at other times, it is a part, subject to constraints and imperatives dictated by broader structures. A holon is both a system and a subsystem—composed of multiple elements that interact dynamically within itself while also being embedded in larger systems.

This applies directly to subjectivity. The subject is not a singular, indivisible entity but an assemblage of capacities, experiences, and social relations that interact with multiple spheres of social cooperation. Different spheres of interaction mobilize different aspects of subjectivity, requiring selective engagement with different norms, values, and practices. Just as subjection and machinic enslavement are co-constitutive, the subject's position within capitalist reproduction and its potential for alternative praxis are equally interwoven.

Because the subject operates across multiple relational spheres, their consciousness is necessarily *intermittent* (Bland and Bell 2007). The subject shifts between different modes of engagement, depending on the context. When doing the weekly grocery shopping, the subject maps their needs against economic constraints, enacting the logic of market choice under conditions of scarcity. When caring for a child in distress, the subject activates practices of care that are incommensurable with market logic. In moments of collective joy—sharing music, food, and conversation—the subject experiences moments of communism, even if ideologically opposed to it. The process of enaction pluralizes, making the subject a participant across different worlds.

Yet, as we will see in Part III, capital's autopoietic logic does not leave these spheres untouched. The pyramid of capital, as a macro-systemic machine within which all subjects operate, hierarchizes these realms, attempting to make all forms of subjectivity functional for its own reproduction. This is where the question of alternative value praxis becomes decisive.

The subject-holon not only helps us understand how subjectivity is shaped within capitalist reproduction but also reveals the spaces of possibility for social transformation. It invites us to move beyond merely resisting subjection or machinic enslavement to examine the organizational and material conditions necessary for the emergence of new forms of subjectivity that can create and engage with an autopoietic organization of social reproduction vis-à-vis capital reproduction. Subjectivity is a process of becoming that is also a field of organization: one in which, to varying degrees and through different modalities, sites of contestation and construction emerge, where different modes of subjectivity, actor, agent, and alter-subject come into play.

As I have discussed, these modes are not fixed identities but positions within the broader organization of social reproduction. Sure, capital's autopoietic reproduction works by absorbing ambivalence, structuring adaptation, and translating exclusion into graded forms of integration (Mezzadra and Neilson 2013). But thinking of the subject as a subject-holon allows us to see how subjectivity oscillates between being instrumental to capital reproduction and a yielding to rupture, between functional integration and transformative possibility. This oscillation is not merely a theoretical tension but the material basis for reterritorialization on the terrain of social reproduction. It is precisely because subjectivity is never fully captured—because it is intermittent and moves between complicity and resistance, between adaptation and invention—that social transformation remains possible. Social transformation is not only about breaking from machinic capture but also about constructing infrastructures of social reproduction that sustain life beyond capital's measure.

By understanding subjectivity through this lens, we bridge the gap between critique and construction—between oppositional politics and the task of practical reorganization of social cooperation on a different value basis. The subject-holon is not only a conceptual tool for analyzing subjectivity within capitalism but also a practical framework for envisioning pathways beyond it.

The intentionality and capacity of the subject-holon: the mediation of congruence

The subject discussed here is not a mere holon—a nested set of parts and wholes—but an intentional holon. Social subjects at all scales of aggregation are *intentional* holons, where intentionality is understood as the intentionality to persist (in the psychological, social, economic, or even ecological sense as a species), that is, to reproduce at various levels of being within a given context. In this sense, the subject-holon "is bounded by its intentionality to persist, and the imperative to do so in multiple, immeasurable, and ever-changing contexts motivates, indeed makes possible and inevitable, change" (Bland and Bell 2007: 280).

It is here that intentionality thus delimits a subject-holon within the magma of social cooperation. The subject is an intentional holon operating in a context that is a contextual bundle of systems. Clearly, in addition to intentionality, the subject-holon must bring into play capacities or *powers-to* procure change, which may prove more feasible in certain areas of its contextual bundle but not in others. But the capacity, the *power-to* of an entity, does not allow us to distinguish that entity as a subject-holon, an intentional holon.

Bruno Latour (1999, 2005) has rightly argued that objects have capacities and have consequences. However, to these capacities he corresponds an action on the world. But a pen, a lathe, a computer, or a tractor, unlike a human being or a mule, does not have intentionality, which is instead ascribed to it externally. That is, in terms of our discussion in Chapter 3, through an allopoietic organization that makes them part of a particular social autopoiesis. It is through this external intentionality that it is also possible to modulate the very capabilities of these objects, to make them part of an artistic installation or objects of use as they are designed. The point, then, is that it is intentionality that defines a subject-holon, not its capabilities.

Following Bland and Bell (2007: 288), intentionality can be understood as "the active imagination and pursuit of a set of goals" through which subject-holons "try to maintain themselves as a set of mutually involved parts, and this usually requires that they also try to maintain themselves as parts involved in a whole." This implies an ongoing imaginative oscillation between inner and outer contexts, through which subjects continually reproduce both themselves and their environments. Artifacts do not try to maintain themselves; they lack autopoiesis. Human beings, social groups, and living systems do try.

Understanding intentionality in terms of goal or purpose aligns with the enactivist approach discussed in the previous chapter. As we have seen, enactivism seeks to overcome the dichotomy between intentionality as an object of reflection (à la Husserl) and intentionality as goal-directed activity through an embodied, situated, and dynamic interpretation of consciousness and cognition. Enactivism starts from the idea that cognition is not a merely representational or internal process but is instead an active process of interaction with the world. The reflexive dimension is not rejected but is articulated within a broader framework that includes corporeality and interaction with the environment. Intentionality is embodied in a double sense: within the body of the subject operating in an environment and within the social environment in which the subject operates. This means that cognitive processes cannot be separated from the bodily and sensorimotor capacities of the subject, nor is intentionality only a matter of consciousness directed toward an object; rather, it is woven into the body's practice in the world: within its social and thus relational practices, within its circuits and systems of social cooperation, and within the range of social meanings that are given to praxis in specific spheres. In this sense, intentionality is both a possible object of reflection—analyzed in the phenomenological sense as consciousness directed toward something—and a mode of reflection embedded in social practice. It is inherently teleological, oriented toward purposes and goals that emerge within a world of meanings shaped by the practices, structures, circuits, and systems in which the subjects are embedded and through which they operate.

Every subject holds a set of goals, and each goal entails at least one context of interaction. For individuals, these goals center on the pursuit of well-being—material, psychic, and relational—within the web of social relations that shape life. Families, broadly conceived, also operate as intentional networks, not only in terms of economic sustainability but also as structures that mediate and reproduce affective ties while structuring care and responsibilities. Communities and movements articulate intentionalities of collective purpose. Multinational corporations express intentionality as the pursuit of an expanding market share, increasing stock value, and upholding the promise of profitability to shareholders. States, in turn, navigate their intentionality through the maintenance of internal power in response to domestic instability while managing external balances in relation to other states. The intentionality of social movements manifests through the practices they adopt in pursuit of recognition, the achievement of specific goals, and the formulation and execution of tactics and strategies of struggle.

Subject-holons, whether individual or collective, are bearers of active intentionalities. They enter into relationships, exchange materials and meanings, and experience these exchanges through their embodied and social being. Because they operate within a plurality of contexts, each governed by distinct relational practices and intentionalities, they must continually weave a form of congruence among these multiple orientations. This search for coherence—internally among their own parts and externally with the environments they inhabit—is ongoing and unstable, perpetually reshaped by changing conditions and evolving intentionalities. However, the nature of this sought-after congruence is not fixed; it depends on the subjectivity of the subject-holons, their aspirations, and the scope of their intentionalities. More than that, this congruence is never stable, as it is continually challenged by the evolving nature of their constituent parts, the transformation of their intentionalities through experience, and the shifting conditions of the contexts in which they operate.

The nature of this congruence varies with a subject's aspirations and position. A multinational corporation, for example, seeks the congruence of a competitive machine, subordinating the well-being of its parts to market adaptation. Its working bodies, by contrast, seek congruence in the pursuit of dignity and a good life. In both cases, intentionalities strive to sustain themselves through practices and relations unfolding across different circuits of cooperation. The search for congruence among intentionalities is thus inseparable from movement across the domains of value praxis—a movement that, as we shall see in the next chapters, grounds the very formation of social cooperation in practice. Through everyday praxis and its articulation in structures, circuits, and systems (Chapter 7), the multitude of subject-holons continuously generates both themselves and the diverse contexts in which they operate.

A visual representation of the subject-holon

The insights discussed in the previous chapter and in this chapter can be put to work in the formation of a conception—at once precise and flexible, as well as scalable—of the subject, one who finds herself operating to varying degrees in relation to different spheres of life within which they play a role as a coproducer.

The relationship between the subject and their exteriority is the fundamental unit that constitutes social life in a variety of forms. From the point of view of their constitution, therefore, by subjects we have understood systems of interacting heterogeneous elements (subjectivities) that mobilize capacities (or powers-to), develop intentionality, and are engaged in continuous adaptive relations with their environment (with their "exteriority" in Guattari's terms or in terms of the milieu or context in which they are embedded). In this sense, subjects are thus always systems of different parts conceived in a relational context. We denote these subjects/systems by "S/E": S for subject (which subtends an internal system of interconnected parts, a subjectivity), "/" to denote a certain boundary or contour with a certain porosity produced by the specific internal relations—and forms of consciousness of these relations—in relation to "E," the exterior, the context in which the subject is called to interact, a context that is also plural and divided into different spheres of operation. By S/E, therefore, I intend to name an entity that, in its general and not specific characteristics, has a transversal character across all social cooperation and all areas of the mixed constitution of social cooperation we call capitalism.

In Figure 6.1, I illustrate the subject-holon in a way that captures all its essential elements. This is the same representation that Maturana and Varela (1987) propose in their analysis of the cell as a system, in their effort to answer the question of what constitutes life, and which I translate here, with due caution, to the human subject within social relations:

In the definition and figure, we have thus already identified the two basic relational realms of this subject: one internal to it and the other in relation to the outside. It is necessary to keep these two realms analytically separate in order to give room for any sense of the subject's operativity and randomness.

In the figure, the inner realm of the subject is symbolized by the empty space within the circle, an empty space that is filled with relations between elements and the processes constituting the subject's subjectivity, related processes, dynamic forces at play, and experiences. In turn, from these internal relations, processes, and experiences emerges the circle, understood as the boundary of the system, a porous and selective "membrane" that allows the operational distinction between what is inside and what is outside, a distinction without which it is not possible to speak of any degree of the subject's autonomy.

The arrows between the subject-holon and its context indicate the flow of perturbations and feedback between the environment and the subject-holon and vice versa; that is, they indicate a situated force field. The arrow pointing inward from the wave toward the subject may carry forces of subjection, capture, or support—such as legal constraints, financial pressures,

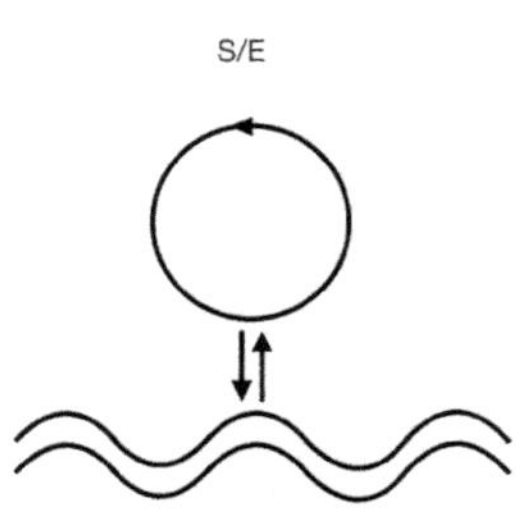

Figure 6.1 The subject/system

or solidarity. The arrow pointing outward from the subject to the wave represents the subject's action: resistance, complicity, or innovation. All of these, of course, occur across different situated gradients.

The wave at the base of the figure represents the set of contexts or environments in which the subject-holons find themselves operating, a context made up of other subject-holons (whether human or machinic), which also mobilize their powers and point to specific ends, the latter aligned with, opposed to, or congruent with the meta-ends of the subject-holon in question. What congruences? What disjunctions? What conflicts? These are questions the subject cannot avoid asking if they want to activate themselves as political subjects of change.

The subject's environment is not unique but composite, consisting of numerous spheres of interaction. In their everyday life, the subjects move within these various spheres and adopts forms of relations and orders of value praxis that are, to some extent, congruent with the sphere within which they operate. At the same time, in each interaction at a particular level, the subject adopts, to varying degrees, forms of consciousness corresponding to their action not only at that level but also resonating across other levels. These crossings among domains of value praxis—where distinct norms, affective registers, and measures of value overlap—constitute the very terrain on which congruence and conflict are enacted. The troubles, stresses, and worries, as well as the joys and the sublime, that I have experienced in one sphere I bring into myself in another sphere, providing a background contrast and thus modifying my sensibility and judgment, thereby shaping my way of acting, my intentionalities, and my capacities in operating in that sphere. Through these transfers between domains—say, from care to work, or from production to affection—the subject continuously reweaves their internal field of value. The same applies to the cognitive models adopted; the selections and distinctions that lead to ideological bias; the layers of toxic narratives that pollute my body; and all the real that has been absorbed within me, assimilated, and readapted within the operation of my subjectivity in continuous communication with the singular and structured subjectivities of the world.

A more complete representation of the subject-holon

The contexts of social cooperation in which the subjects operate are not neutral or homogeneous. They are traversed and structured by different "regimes" of value—modes of organizing, evaluating, and making sense of practices and relations. These regimes operate as distinct domains of value praxis, each shaping how subjects relate to the world and to others through particular logics: relational value, use value, exchange value, and command. A fuller discussion follows in the next two chapters.

Here it is enough to note that, from the standpoint of everyday life, these four domains are rarely separate; they coexist and interpenetrate within every act of cooperation, though their relative weight shifts with context. They are not separate silos or independent spheres of society. They are all dimensions of reality in every moment of social cooperation, although, in different contexts, they have more or less prevalence and impose themselves with varying intensity both on our consciousness and on the relational forms required by a system of conformity in a given field and context.

These domains of value praxis do not coincide with the "spheres" of culture, politics, or the economy. Subjects do not enter the economy when they leave home and go to work. They do not enter politics only every four or five years when they go to vote. They do not enter culture only when they enter a museum or a theater. *When subjects move between what we generally identify as distinct social zones, they move through differently ordered configurations of value praxis.* These configurations can achieve a relative autonomy when particular orders of value become institutionalized—forming what we then perceive as "the economy," "politics," or "culture"—yet their boundaries remain porous and dynamically interlinked within the broader field of social cooperation. These spheres we call the economy, culture, politics, and so on are all transversal to, and interpenetrating with, the four major areas of the value praxis of social cooperation. For example, what we call the "economy" is not a neutral field of production and exchange but a territorially organized pattern of cooperation shaped by the dominance of exchange and command value, subordinating use and relational values to capital's logic of accumulation. "Politics" is not confined to institutions or statecraft but pervades all levels of the pyramid where norms, decisions, and thresholds are contested—where value orders are imposed or resisted. "Culture" is not merely the expressive or symbolic realm but the terrain where subjectivities are formed and judgments enacted, mediating congruence or dissonance with prevailing value regimes. Rather than treating these as discrete spheres, this framework shows them as transversal modalities of social cooperation—each a field of struggle over the values that organize life.

This interplay of overlapping value domains is not abstract—it is lived, navigated, and negotiated daily by subjects embedded in multiple contexts. For instance, consider a single mother who works as a nurse. At work, she must subordinate her caring practices to strict productivity metrics while managing patients (exchange and command values). At home, she provides care to her child, drawing on practices of love, patience, and presence (relational values). Meanwhile, the TV is switched on, and the cartoon program her child is watching is full of advertising for junk food (capturing desires *for* exchange value). Her own sense of purpose as a caregiver involves balancing these different demands, developing a sense of judgment, and searching for moments of joy and rest within them. Her experience reveals how the subject-holon continually oscillates among domains of value praxis, translating and mediating their logics through everyday action.

What congruences are required by these exteriorities? How does the subject respond to these demands of congruence? This presence of different orders of value domains in the subject's exteriority is what gives rise to the intermittence of the subject-holon—a ceaseless negotiation between the search for congruence and resistance across the contexts of social cooperation in which they operate. The subject's exteriority presents itself not simply as a differentiated plurality of contexts of interaction but as a dynamic terrain traversed by transversal currents of order of value praxis. Contexts such as school, factory, public space, family, social center, global market, or world order are shaped by the simultaneous and uneven presence of relational, use, exchange, and command value logics. On the other hand, these value currents do not merely surround the subjects—they traverse them, animating their internal dynamics of subjectification and constituting the very basis of the form of their structural coupling with broader circuits of cooperation. Subjectification thus expresses the subject's internal work of orientation—its effort to enact congruence, dissent, or resistance among competing value orders. Figure 6.2 illustrates this entanglement, showing how the subject-holon navigates and is shaped by these copresent value domains across the multiple fields of social cooperation.

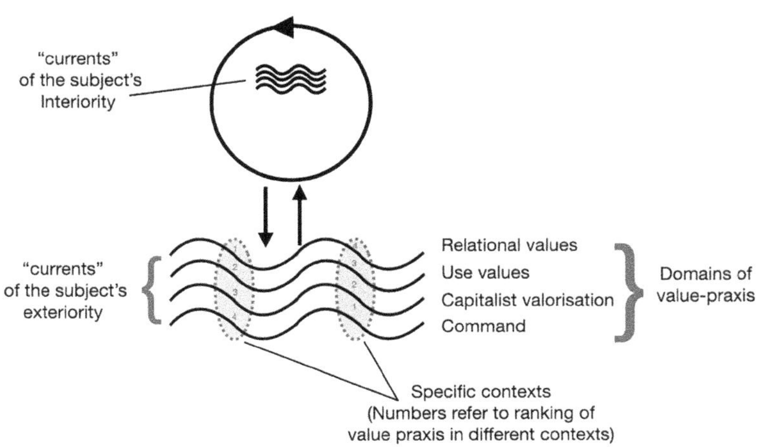

Figure 6.2 The subject-holon and the dimensions of value praxis

These four domains of value praxis are copresent and take shape at every moment of social cooperation, across different situations and contexts: inside and outside the family, the community, or the workplace; as a salaried or non-salaried worker; as a public official, private citizen, or the *sans papiers*; as a woman, man, LGPTQ+, young, old person, of any nationality or ethnic group; whether fascist, conservative, or communist; whether European, American, Brazilian, Israeli, Palestinian, Arab, Chinese, Russian, or Ukrainian. At every moment and in every specific context, these domains take a specific ordering, a more or less broad relative relevance, and an operative hierarchy of values that consciousness must somehow grasp in order to gain orientation within a given sphere of value praxis, whether to operate with some congruence toward it or to resist it and seek to a different ordering.

7

Value praxis or the coupling of the subjects with their exteriority

How do we cooperate?

The preceding chapter defined the subject as an assemblage of intentionalities and capacities whose relations emerge through the enactment of praxis across multiple, overlapping domains of social cooperation. The subject-holon is not a fixed identity but a dynamic, enactive node—shaped by its exteriority while also perturbing it through the rhythms of relational, use, exchange, and command values.

This understanding deepens the discussion from Chapter 4 on enactment, where sense-making was shown to arise through embodied interaction with the world. Here, we turn to value praxis as the organizing principle of these interactions: the way in which subjects, in their everyday practices, enter into systemic couplings that reproduce or challenge the social order. If subjects are the enacting agents, value praxis is the dynamic field within which they act and by which they are shaped—yet also a field they continuously constitute through patterned rhythms of cooperation, conflict, and meaning-making.

How do subjects cooperate within the complexity of social cooperation? The particular forms in which subjects are coupled with their exteriority are not reducible to intersubjective relations. The great bulk of our structural couplings—the processes through which we cooperate and reproduce our lives—do not occur through direct subject-to-subject interaction alone but through couplings with complex machinic organizations: algorithmic systems, standardized social structures, functional circuits of material and semantic flows, and regulatory systems that orient our actions toward goals and forms often beyond our conscious control. This is the realm where social autopoiesis comes into play today. However complex or disembodied these machinic organizations may seem, their foundational elements are rooted in the everyday—in the bodies of subjects and of Gaia—and in the multiple threads of relational weaving that compose the terrain of social cooperation. This terrain, with all its structured asymmetries and generative contradictions, demands mapping.

In this chapter, I begin that mapping. This is not a further diagnosis of dominant tendencies—these have already been extensively studied, and they are etched into our collective neuroses and sense of impotence. Rather, those very tendencies call upon us, as ambivalent and intermittent subjects, to mobilize countertendencies and generate alternative forms of social cooperation, especially within the diverse terrain of social reproduction.

In Chapter 4, we approached cognition as a process of sense-making rooted in the embodied interaction between subject and environment. This perspective goes beyond traditional views of cognition as information processing, highlighting instead the active, relational, and enactive ways that living systems bring forth their world. Sense-making is not confined to internal mental states; it emerges through a dynamic interplay between perception and external constraints—what Varela termed "enactment." Meaning is co-constituted between subjects and their contexts. Because cognition is inseparable from sensorimotor action, it is always already praxis—an adaptive and situated engagement with the world. Praxis, in turn, involves selection: the prioritization of some meanings, practices, and outcomes over others. Drawing from Bateson, this selection process forms the basis of learning and systemic organization, but it also defines value: Each act of engagement affirms certain configurations of meaning and negates others. Thus, value praxis refers to the way value is enacted, sustained, and contested within social cooperation. Value praxis is the way in which subjects generate meaning embodied in action that shapes the structures, circuits, and systems of material and social reality. Let us unpack this.

Praxis

Understanding cognition as sense-making—when rooted in enactive and embodied interaction with the world—aligns closely with the concept of praxis, understood as the enactment of meaning through situated, purposive activity. Praxis is not merely the application of thought but the space in which subjects generate meaning through their actions, through ongoing engagement with the social and material world. Across philosophical traditions, praxis bridges thought and practice in distinct ways. For Aristotle (1985), in the *Nicomachean Ethics*, ethical action is guided by *phronesis* (practical wisdom) and aimed at *eudaimonia* (flourishing). In Marx's (1975) early writings, praxis is transformative activity: the unification of theory and practice directed at changing material conditions—hence his declaration, "The philosophers have only interpreted the world in various ways; the point is to change it." Lukács (1972) extends this into the terrain of class struggle, where praxis becomes the proletariat's self-conscious engagement in historical transformation, a form of action that reveals and contests the reification of social relations.

The Frankfurt School approaches praxis critically: Adorno questions its instrumentalization, Marcuse sees it as a vehicle for liberation, Habermas emphasizes communicative action, and Honneth focuses on struggles for recognition. Hannah Arendt (1998), by contrast, frames praxis as political action in the public sphere, where individuals engage in speech and interaction to shape collective life. Paulo Freire (1988: 36) underscores praxis as essential to liberation from oppression, arguing that only through critical reflection and transformative action can the subject break free from subjugation: "Oppression is domesticating . . . to no longer be prey to its force, one must emerge from it and turn upon it. This can be done only by means of praxis: reflection and action upon the world in order to transform it."

Across these perspectives, praxis involves recursive action and reflection—an iterative engagement through which novelty and transformation can emerge. But transformation for whom, and toward what end? In the revolutionary traditions of Marx, Lukács, the Frankfurt School, and Freire, the answer is generally clear: emancipation from oppression, alienation, and exploitation. In contrast, the enactivist perspective that we have surveyed conceives praxis as embodied and situated action, emerging from the dynamic interplay of mind, body, and world—but it does not explicitly identify relations of domination. There are no exploiters or exploited in this view, only co-emerging agents and an adaptive environment. In contrast, my approach refuses such neutrality. Every act of sense-making unfolds within value-laden relations of power—relations that organize who can act, who must adapt, and on what terms. In my account, both of these horizons are held together. Praxis is the generative principle of social reality: Different forms of praxis generate different forms of social reality, whether emancipatory or rooted in the same oppressive sameness.

Praxis is always value praxis

Praxis—any type of praxis—understood broadly as the dynamic unity of mind and doing (theory and practice), and hence of enacted cognition, is also the embodied enactment of values in situated social action. Since value is not an abstract concept but a lived and enacted orientation, praxis is the process through which values materialize and embed themselves in social reality. By *value*, I refer here, in a general sense, to the meaning attributed to action—a meaning that ultimately guides action itself. Anthropologists remind us that value is the way in which people represent to themselves the importance of their actions (Graeber 2001). By constructing this representation of importance, subjects develop a guiding framework for what is worth doing.

However, value does not originate in isolated individuals detached from society. As Graeber (2001: 68) notes, any action "becomes meaningful (in Hegelian terms, assumes 'a concrete and specific form') only if integrated into a broader system of action."

The articulation between individuals and wholes, between parts and totalities, implies that in pursuing value, we also reproduce *wholes*—networks of coproduction—that themselves embody value. Therefore, *different kinds of value pursued, different value domains activated* (relational, use, exchange, or command), *and different orders among these domains reproduce different types of wholes*—different self-organizing systems and dimensions of social cooperation.

By value praxis, I therefore refer to social practices—as well as their corresponding networks of relations, structures, circuits, and systems—insofar as they are shaped by specific orders of value domains in different fields of social cooperation. Such praxis is always materially embodied: in the lived body of the subject, in the organized flesh of the social body, and in the ecological body of Gaia that grounds all forms of life and cooperation.

Crucially, value praxis is not only the enactment of values by individuals but also the reproduction of the broader wholes—systems, institutions, and modes of social cooperation—that those values sustain or transform. It names the reciprocal movement between the subjective and the systemic, between individual meaning-making and societal reproduction, in which practices are embedded in larger value frameworks that shape, support, or constrain future action. This articulation of parts and wholes takes place as individuals engage in discursive and embodied selections, determining what is "good" and "bad" within a situated configuration of value domains and registers and acting accordingly. These selections are not isolated choices but operate within structured environments—material, institutional, and symbolic—that frame what is visible and valuable.

Crucially, value praxis is not static but dynamic: The values enacted through everyday practices feed back into the social body, shaping the evolution of norms, institutions, and circuits of cooperation. In this recursive loop, the meanings of "good" and "bad" are either reinforced or contested, depending on how agency and systemic structures interact.

To speak of value praxis, then, is to speak of how social forms, organizational structures, patterns of coproduction, relations of power, and modes of social reproduction emerge—and are continually reconstituted—through practices shaped by, and shaping value. Through this interplay, value praxis defines the selections that crystallize into the circuits and systems of social cooperation, shaping not only personal trajectories but the broader contours of collective life.

What we call *capitalism* is the sedimented result of these recursive forces of value praxis: the historical layering of norms, structures, and systems formed through the couplings, ruptures, and struggles among divergent forms of value praxis, which has resulted in a hierarchical order of values that puts the domain of command and exchange value above use and relational value.

In what follows, we begin to explore how this struggle-ridden praxis creates, sustains, or transforms the circuits, structures, and systems that give shape to social cooperation and that ultimately constitute the pyramid of capital. In the sections that follow, I begin with a basic conception of praxis as a practical-relational nexus at the intersubjective level, and build toward more complex forms such as structures, circuits, and systems.

Praxis or the practical-relational nexus

The subjects pursue their multiple objects—what we have called *intentionality*—and they can do so only by entering into specific social relations with other subjects. Whether these relations are interpersonal or mediated by the representatives of social institutions is secondary at this point. What matters is that *intentionality* and *relatedness* are the two fundamental axes through which the subject mobilizes their *powers-to*.

Intentionality orients action; relatedness enables it by amplifying individual capacities into social powers—while simultaneously shaping, constraining, and adjusting intentionality itself. These two dimensions—*intentionality* and *relatedness*—are phylogenetic features of human sociality. They exist in every epoch, every culture, and every context. Yet because they are *phylogenetic*—rooted in the biological, historical, and cultural evolution of the species—they always take on different forms depending on context.

In this sense, an Indigenous community in the Lacandonian jungle and a transnational corporation commanding a global supply chain both enact intentionality and relatedness—but in radically different and often opposed ways. The former may foster modes of reciprocity, embeddedness, and ecological care; the latter tends toward instrumental control, abstraction, and commodification. Yet these oppositions emerge from a shared ground: the human capacity to orient action and build relations. It is in the modulation, appropriation, or contestation of these capacities that divergent worlds are formed.

Together, *intentionality* and *relatedness* define what Thompson (2023: 62), a critical theorist,[1] calls a *practical-relational nexus*: "our capacity to form relations and to act out our intentions via our practical relations with others and the world as a whole." To describe these as *phylogenetic* capacities is to indicate that they are species-specific features of human beings—biologically grounded but shaped and expressed through diverse forms of socialization. Through ontogenetic development, these capacities are mobilized differently by distinct institutions and social processes.[2] This means that entities such as markets, states, schools, families, cooperatives, multinational corporations, Indigenous communities, or social movements are not simply expressions of collective intentionality (as argued by Searle) but *organizational shapes* of these underlying relational and intentional capacities (Thompson 2023: 62).

A fundamental characteristic of human social cooperation—both in the diachronic sense of historical development and in the synchronic dimension of cultural differentiation (Graeber and Wengrow 2021)—is precisely the *capacity to shape and reshape these ontological foundations of our social being* in a multiplicity of forms (Thompson 2023: 65).

Social ontologies—that is, the ontologies of social entities and institutions that emerge from specific forms of cooperation—result from different modulations of the practical-relational nexus. In turn, the configuration of this nexus in any given context depends on *social power*: the capacity to determine, organize, and sustain the practices, relations, structures, systems, and ends that constitute a social reality.

Social power is not merely about mental representations or what Searle (1995) calls *status functions*—the attribution of roles or institutional facts through collective agreement. Rather, it refers to the concrete ability to shape the *practical*, *relational*, and *teleological* dimensions of the social world. By teleological, I refer to the orientation toward purposes—those socially instituted ends and systemic priorities that govern what counts as meaningful, valuable, or desirable in a given context. As discussed in Chapters 2 and 3, these purposes are not neutral but are always structured by value regimes, and thus shape what is reproduced or transformed through social cooperation. Each dominant purpose functions as an attractor within a broader force field, drawing subjects and practices toward particular systemic configurations while repelling or marginalizing others. These force fields are shaped by the structured configuration of value praxis—relational, use, exchange, and command—whose logics are dynamically interwoven yet hierarchically ordered, as well as by the distribution of social power that stabilizes or destabilizes that ordering.

This concrete power to shape social reality includes the power to organize and modify the relational architectures of society, to shape the categories and values that underpin social life, to distribute resources within a community, and to influence the ontogenetic development of individuals within it.

In other words, social power is the capacity to enact what we earlier (Chapter 2) called *the measure of things* in social cooperation—that is, to bring forth and stabilize the logics through which value is assigned, relations are ordered, and purposes are pursued.

How this power is distributed is crucial. When shared relatively equally among members of a community, it tends to foster cooperative and collaborative structures. When unequally distributed—allowing a subset of actors to shape social reality for their own benefit while extracting material, emotional, or financial surplus from others—it constitutes a form of *domination*. Domination should not be confused with *authority*, which refers to recognized and consented forms of power that do not necessarily involve exploitation or surplus extraction. Understanding social power is therefore essential to any account of how social realities are formed, maintained, or transformed.

While Marx's category of labor captures the metabolic and productive activity essential to human life, praxis—as I define it—is broader. Praxis refers to any embodied, relational, and purposive action that enacts values within a social context. Labor is thus a subset of praxis: It is praxis directed toward producing use values, whether for survival or profit. As Marx (1976: 133) famously wrote, "*Labour, then, as the creator of use-values, as useful labour, is a condition of human existence which is independent of all forms of society; it is an eternal necessity which mediates the metabolism between man and nature, and therefore human life itself.*" But praxis also includes forms of action that generate value beyond the scope of labor as classically conceived—caring for a grieving friend may generate consolation and mutual recognition; forming a community choir brings a new collective into being; a refusal to comply with extractive demands produces a stance of resistance and antagonism. These acts may not yield distinct use values—whether commodifiable or not—but they nonetheless contribute to the reproduction and transformation of social life in meaningful ways.

Praxis as value praxis: teleology, normativity, and relatedness

The practical-relational nexus—or simply, praxis—is the generative force of the social world. It is the process of enactment through which subjects "bring forth a world." Depending on how intentionality and relatedness are modulated and configured, we may call it work, social labor, or commoning. But in its general, transhistorical, and transcultural form, praxis has inescapable features: purpose, which orients action; normative coordination, which organizes practices and expectations; and relatedness, which embeds each subject in a web of social and ecological interdependencies.

The first key feature of praxis is that social reality—whether in the immediacy of daily life or in the systemic totality we call capitalism—is not merely a reflection of thoughts, attitudes, or norms. It is embedded in social practices, and thus in purposes. Praxis, as embodied enactment in the world, is always purposive: It enacts ends. Institutions such as marriages, friendships, universities, markets, multinationals, states, and community centers are not merely collections of norms or sets of relational models. They manifest distinct configurations of practices, relations, and purposes that sustain them as structured social forms. These forms endure because specific, norm-governed practices generate and reproduce them, creating relational structures that persist over time and across participants.

A reader might ask: What is the purpose of friendship? Does such a question instrumentalize what should be spontaneous or affective? Not necessarily. Purpose need not mean external utility or a measurable outcome—it can also refer to the implicit ends that guide and sustain a relation from within. In the case of friendship, the purpose may be mutual recognition, shared joy, or simply the continuation of the bond itself. These are not imposed goals but emergent orientations that become meaningful through the relation's own unfolding. Even the most intimate or non-instrumental relations are structured by tacit ends that guide practices and shape expectations over time.

Social practices are thus inherently teleological—structured by ends that shape the means by which they are pursued. "A practice," as Thompson (2023: 66) writes, "is inherently teleological in that it is structured by some end: an end retrogressively can be seen to determine or in some sense organise the means used to realise it." A practice is not just an action; it is an activity oriented toward a purpose to be realized in the world. This distinguishes it from automatic acts like sneezing or yawning, which primarily serve biological functions and occur outside the subject's intentionality. Yet even such acts, once situated within a social context, can acquire meaning—signaling fatigue, boredom, or disapproval—and thereby enter the field of praxis as socially interpreted behaviors. Try to organize a collective yawn at a manager's meeting.

Ends may be discrete and finite—such as cooking a meal or assembling a weapon—or extended and recursive, as in Rödl's (2007) notion of infinite ends. These include not only producing *this* meal but also cultivating a pattern of healthy meals; not only producing *this* bomb but also maintaining a global market in arms. Similarly, the purpose of sustaining a friendship involves ongoing engagement in relational practices, not a singular act. In each case, ends shape the practices enacted and are embedded in broader circuits of social reproduction. As discussed in Chapters 2 and 3, such circuits often exhibit autopoietic dynamics; systems reproduce themselves by recursively enacting the conditions of their own continuity. In this sense, teleology is not incidental but intrinsic to social reality—purpose is embedded in the very mechanisms through which institutions, norms, and relations sustain themselves over time.

Second, any purposive practice—any praxis—is also normatively coordinated. Because praxis is inherently social, it requires the establishment of norms that organize expectations, behaviors, and mutual recognition. Norms, here, are not limited to formal rules but include any shared expectations that guide interaction in a collectivity. These expectations range from tacit habits to codified rules and can apply in contexts as diverse as a circle of friends, a workplace, a revolutionary cell, or a bureaucracy.

Such norms must be *congruent with the purpose* of a given praxis. A practice oriented toward care will require different modes of coordination than one oriented toward control or accumulation. As such, purpose constrains and orients normativity. The coordination of action within any institution thus reflects not just practical logistics but value-laden selections—about what should be done, how, and for what end—the measure of things.

Moreover, practices and norms are mutually constitutive. Norms shape actions into practices, giving them recognizable form; practices, in turn, instantiate, reproduce, or contest the norms that guide them. This dynamic is recursive and embodied, as discussed in Chapter 4. It underpins both institutional formation and social learning: Individuals internalize norms by performing practices within relationships, acquiring roles and orientations that are socially intelligible.

Over time, repeated and patterned interactions among practices and norms produce institutions: structured, value-laden forms of coordination aimed at reproducing specific ends. Institutions are thus expressions of enduring configurations of purposes and norms, sedimented through cooperation, and maintained through shared expectations.

Third, praxis always unfolds within relational fields. As Thompson (2020: 66) puts it, praxis "becomes a generator for social reality when it is paired with our capacity for relatedness: for interacting with another through some kind of attachment or cooperative behavior." Purposeful, norm-governed practices cannot be enacted in a vacuum. They arise and unfold within relationships—between subjects, between subjects and institutions, and between subjects and nature.

The kinds of relations that structure praxis are not neutral. They are shaped by power. Social power determines who can influence norms, shape practices, and define which ends are considered legitimate. As explored earlier, subjects, in entering coordination with their exteriority, must synchronize with a register of relational norms—whether toward others, toward nature, toward institutions, or toward the world at large. These relational norms are not merely conduits of interaction; they carry and encode value orientations. They guide the meaning that subjects give to their actions, enabling and constraining which practices are selected and how they are performed.

These three constitutive dimensions—teleology, normativity, and relatedness—demonstrate why all praxis is value praxis. Purposeful action always presupposes value: an end *worth* realizing. Norms are always value-laden: They define what counts as appropriate, acceptable, or desirable. Social relations are saturated with value: They define the quality, asymmetry, and moral texture of cooperation.

Thus, the purposes praxis enacts reflect what is valued in a given context—personal, cultural, political, or systemic. The norms that coordinate it express hierarchies of value—what is sanctioned, promoted, or suppressed. The relational fabric in which it unfolds embodies shared or contested valuations—of worth, dignity, authority, equality, or domination.

Praxis is therefore never neutral. It is the process through which values are enacted, stabilized, resisted, and transformed in social life. All praxis is value praxis.

Praxis and the architecture of social cooperation

The *practical-relational nexus*—that is, praxis understood as the entangled unity of purpose, normativity, and relatedness—serves as a generative algorithm for the emergence of more complex social realities. Practices are goal-oriented activities through which individual or collective subjects pursue specific ends. Relations refer to the connections and interdependencies among subjects that enable, guide, and constrain those practices, including the development of social powers and the embedding of norms. These two moments—practices and relations—are mutually constitutive: Practices shape relations, and relations, in turn, condition what practices are possible and how they unfold. Neither has primacy; their interplay is recursive and coproductive.

This dynamic gives rise to richer and more structured forms of association, generating systemic relatedness and an orientation toward collective purposes. From this interplay of practice, norm, and relation emerge the more complex articulations of social life. To grasp these articulations, we need a vocabulary that includes *structures*, *networks*, *circuits*, and *systems*—terms that help us trace the anatomy and physiology of social cooperation and how our lives and our acts of sense-making are entangled within them.

Before introducing these, it is crucial to clarify that they are not discrete types of social entities but analytical lenses—ways of observing and interpreting real formations each highlighting different yet coexisting organizing logics. A school, for example, may be understood as a structure (insofar as it stabilizes roles and practices), as an institution (insofar as it formalizes and enforces norms), as part of circuits (e.g., of knowledge transmission, credentialization, and reproduction), or as a subsystem within broader configurations (e.g., the education system, the state, or the machinery of social or capital reproduction). These modalities of organization are copresent in most domains of social life.

What matters is not to fix these categories in place but to attend to the dominant modality at play in a given context: Structures emphasize patterned role-norm coordination; circuits foreground the flow and relational coupling among value, information, or practices; and systems describe recursive, self-regulating configurations of cooperation and control.

These distinctions will become especially important when we analyze the pyramid of capital, a layered and hierarchical macro-system in which social cooperation is captured, coordinated, and stratified. Toward the base of the pyramid, we find structures rooted in everyday life—households, schools, farms, and clinics—whose practices and relations are shaped by immediate needs and local norms. These structures are linked through circuits of production, reproduction, and value extraction—flows of labor, money, care, and information—that often cross institutional boundaries and domains.

At higher levels, these circuits are organized and governed by systems—such as financial markets, state apparatuses, or planetary command regimes—which function as meta-systems: They not only coordinate circuits but also impose their systemic priorities on everything beneath them. In this configuration, the diverse structures and circuits of social life are effectively treated as subsystems—monitored, steered, and recalibrated to serve the overarching imperatives of capital accumulation, institutional stability, and social control.

This is one of the defining features of the pyramid of capital: its top-down pressure to organize social cooperation as a nested hierarchy of subsystems, where value praxis is constantly reconfigured under the dominant logics of the upper levels.

This praxis-centered understanding of social cooperation is not only descriptive but also diagnostic and strategic: It reveals the embedded value logics through which practices are coordinated but also opens the question of how such coordination is governed—through what rhythms, asymmetries, and regulative forces. As will be developed in Chapter 14 through an analysis of the throbs of command, these regulative logics constitute the infrastructural pulse of governance: They selectively stabilize certain forms of value praxis while suppressing or assimilating others, thereby shaping the architecture of policy and systemic reproduction itself.

Structures and institutions: regularized patterns of social praxis

A social structure can be understood as "a *regularized* pattern of practices that are enacted by specific normative relations" (Thompson 2020: 67, my emphasis). Structures are either instituted or developed through continuous recursion, or more likely, a bit of both. This means that some structures are consciously designed—whether by institutions, collectives, or authorities—while others sediment gradually through repeated practice, often without central coordination. Instituting a structure—whether setting up a company, a cooperative, a reading group, or a radical activist collective—means defining the models of social relations through which an organization makes its selections and distinctions. However, structures are not only instituted; they also emerge and evolve recursively. Over time, the relations through which practices are articulated solidify and reify into social structures, as each cycle of practice reinforces, modifies, or challenges the established patterns. Social structures, then, are not merely repeated; they are recursively shaped by the interplay of action and norm, selection and distinction.

Regularized patterns of practices are always enacted through social relations that have some degree of rigidity. These relations are not neutral conduits but shape how decisions are made and how coordination occurs. Their configuration expresses a particular distribution of social power—what gets done, by whom, and for whom. As practices and norms exist within and through a relational context, social relations influence how decisions are made, who does what, when one talks, how to organize tasks in social cooperation, and how moral judgment arises. For individual subjects, particular types of social relations provide the framework for a motivated coordination in which each subject aligns with the expectations of a shared behavior, or deviates from them, or even dissents and resists them. In this sense, the type of social relations involved in a given structure is the way social power is actualized and, in this respect, gives the *form* to social cooperation.[3]

We can observe the effects of social structures—the regularized, habitual, and consistent patterns of practices—in different contexts. They are sedimented in the spatial organization of a city or a territory, as well as in the temporal definition of tasks and routines. An urban context that has destined its public space predominantly to commerce and private cars is the result of such routinized patterns of practices within a normative framework that sees private transport and business as more important than, say, public transport and the convivial use of public space. A supermarket allocates commodities along a spatial configuration that seeks to solicit and encourage their purchase. In workplaces, temporal examples include daily routines such as the nine-to-five schedule or performance reviews. In the gig economy, structures refer to standardized routines and interactions that emerge despite the ostensibly flexible and individualized nature of gig work. These patterns often develop through algorithms, user ratings, contractual terms, and platform-mediated rules, creating a framework for both workers and clients. They align with platform policies, economic incentives, and worker behaviors, shaping how tasks are performed, evaluated, and repeated over time. In a school, the structure includes rules, roles, and expectations: Teachers teach, students learn, and administrators oversee operations. These roles are not random but are guided by norms, such as the expectation that teachers provide knowledge and students follow a curriculum, do their homework, and obey the rules of attendance. Structures stabilize these practices over time, ensuring that purposeful activities—such as teaching and learning—occur in a predictable way *within* the given normative framework and defined purposes. Similarly, in a workplace, the structure defines hierarchies, responsibilities, and workflows, shaping how tasks are carried out and coordinated among workers. Likewise, legal systems follow regular procedures for trials, while policing adheres to established protocols. Religious and spiritual practices involve consistent rituals, such as weekly worship, prayer routines, or chanting. Governments operate through regular elections and legislative processes. Different protest movements involve regular campaigning and lobbying, marches or riots, and meetings with specific formal and informal procedures for decision-making gatherings. Social customs, such as holiday celebrations and manners, are also examples. Health-care practices include routine checkups and vaccination schedules. These are as much a part of structure as the hierarchical chain of command in a hospital or a health district. Families follow regular mealtimes and household chores, distributed according to the social relations. Economic practices such as shopping habits and banking routines are regularized, as are digital behaviors such as social media use and privacy protocols. Because of their normative basis, structures embody what we earlier called a "measure of things": *They sediment social priorities and value distinctions into recurring practices.* These patterns create order and predictability in the social lives of subjects across different dimensions of cooperation—even amid the chaos and unpredictability they also generate.

Social reality is inherently dynamic because it is grounded in the practical-relational nexus: the evolving interplay of practices, relations, structures, and norms. This nexus is never static but continuously transforms as subjects interact with their exteriority—others, institutions, and the environment. A defining feature of this dynamism is reciprocal causality, whereby individuals influence others and are, in turn, shaped by them. Through this mutual shaping, social structures generate a fluid and adaptable social landscape.

When subjects occupy roles within a structure, they are expected to enact patterns of behavior aligned with established norms and practices. These roles both reflect and reproduce the structure's internal logic. At the same time, by performing these roles, subjects participate in reinforcing, modifying, or contesting the very structures that shape them. Structures thus exert causal power while remaining permeable to change.

In this way, social structures constitute a distinct ontological sphere: a relational reality in which subjects are transformed through the roles they inhabit and the practices they perform. As Thompson (2023: 68) observes, "Friends treat one another differently than strangers," just as employees relate differently to bosses than to colleagues—"and they do this as a result of the mutual ways in which they organize and enact their relational practices with one another." Social structures thus instantiate relational patterns of practice that can crystallize into broader systems of cooperation and control.

But the space between social structures and systems is occupied by other concepts that are important for describing the complexities of social cooperation. The first of these concepts is that of institutions, which I touch on briefly here, while I discuss circuits, networks, and systems in the next two sections. While structures arise from patterned and relational practice, institutions formalize and stabilize these patterns into durable frameworks with social legitimacy, enforcement mechanisms, and systemic functions. Institutions are identifiable once social structures are in place and acquire an "ontological independence" from any individual subject that enacts them. Institutions are thus structured systems of norms, rules, and practices that guide and organize social behavior within a society. They imply some form of social, legal, cultural, or organizational mechanism ensuring the consistency and predictability of these practices in the face of both the emergence of new practices and deviant behavior. Thus, when rules, norms, or expectations are not met, there may be consequences (e.g., sanctions). For example, in a school, regularized patterns of practice include scheduled classes, attendance procedures, and standardized teaching methods. These are formally enforced through mechanisms that filter out (or repress) deviant behavior. In a family, kids can be warned: "You are not getting to play unless you eat your vegetables!" Enforcing a structure within an institution means enabling a system. Institutions, of course, may differ in terms of formality and consistency, enforcement, and flexibility.

The regularization of practices implies a higher degree of formality and systematic consistency compared to the general expression of "patterns of practices." Regularized practices are often institutionalized—that is, regulated by norms or rules with some formal oversight—whereas "patterns of practices" may simply emerge through habit or custom without formal oversight, or even give rise to new patterns of practice in response to changing conditions, innovations, or the emergence of new purposes. One of the most frustrating aspects for those involved in innovation within institutions, for example, is having to bend innovation to existing rules and norms of social structures, which, due to their regularized and institutionalized patterns, resist change.

Networks and circuits

Structures stabilize practices over time, ensuring that purposeful activities occur in a predictable way within a specific normative framework. These practices always occur through networks—that is, through webs of connections that form between individuals or groups engaging in practices for some shared purposes—supporting the execution and reproduction of social cooperation.

Network scientists see the network from a bird's-eye view; they perceive its nodes, that is, interconnected entities, and the connections (edges) between them. They also see networks as embodied in social and biological structures. Information of all kinds, whether symbolic or material, flows through the network. It is therefore important to distinguish between open and closed networks. An open network refers to a set of connections in which flows disperse without necessarily returning. A closed network, by contrast, is a closed loop within a network in which the flow returns to its point of origin—creating feedback, function, and the potential for adaptation. Networks are thus the medium of information and, hence, of meaning and sense-making (value again). Information can be unidirectional and dispersed, as in open networks (like an advertisement that hit me when opening a web page and that I no longer even remember), or it can return to a point of origin and form a circuit (like an advertisement to which I reacted by immediately purchasing the product).

Examples of open networks are many. For example, a communication network in which messages are sent from a central hub to various nodes without the need for responses to these signals to return to the hub. Or the many neural networks that transmit signals from the sensory organs to the brain without a return signal. Computer networks such as the internet, in which the paths from a server to a client and vice versa, do not necessarily form a continuous loop. In social media networks, users are connected according to friendships or follows, but these connections rarely form a closed loop in which interaction between users is continuous. If a selection of subjects in this network starts to communicate and exchange impressions or gifts—that is, interact in a continuous, cyclic movement—we have established a closed network. Its closure does not refer to the number of elements it contains but to the return of information to its point of origin, enabling feedback and adaptation.

The substantial difference between open and closed networks—or circuits—is that *circuits perform functions and pursue purposes.* While an open network represents a field of potential relations, a circuit actualizes a selection within that field, turning possibility into operation. This act of selection—where a relational path closes into an operative feedback loop—is what Bateson called "the difference that makes a difference." It marks the moment when potential becomes actuality, and when function, adaptation, and purpose emerge. Integrated with other circuits, each operation contributes to higher-order functions—meta-functions—within broader systems of cooperation. *Circuits, then, are the elementary operational units of social praxis: selections within networks that enact purposes, embody value, and enable coordination through feedback.*

To give some intuitive examples, I open the fridge and find that it is empty (this is the state of the fridge that sends me feedback). I go to the supermarket and buy food, which I have selected after processing the quality/price feedback according to my budget. I return home and put the food in the fridge. The fridge is full, and I can cook (a new loop). It sounds trivial, but through this loop, a selection of several elements in a network structure is made. I select the type of shop, the type of food, and the type of transport used. Acting on how these selections are made is obviously crucial for social change, but so are the contexts (such as budget) that constrain those choices. And once food fills the fridge, it opens up a new selection or circuit: that of cooking. My social role within that circuit is also determined: the "consumer" and the householder. Another simple example: There is a pothole in the road. A citizen reports it (feedback) to the municipality. The municipality sends a team of workers. The pothole is filled. The citizen is happy to have triggered a successful process. Of course, this loop may never close, as the potholes in Rome prove, despite many complaints. The citizen calls a municipal official; then they call another municipal official, who then calls yet another one, and their energy is dispersed into thin air. When the feedback falls into thin air, somewhere a filtering has taken place, and the elements that wanted to connect in a loop revert to being simply abstract elements of a network. The purpose is never pursued, and the function remains unexecuted.

Thus, a circuit describes the flows of practices, outcomes, or resources—such as information, goods, or energy—that move through the connections in view of a purpose. It also describes the sequence of steps in operations that must occur for a purpose to be achieved. In the appendix to this chapter, I discuss two important meta-circuits constituting social cooperation: capital circuits and the circuit of the procommons.

At this point, feedback becomes a critical factor in maintaining, adjusting, or transforming the circuits within a network. Feedback refers to the information or results that flow back into the network, influencing future practices and connections. For example, in a classroom, a student's exam performance provides feedback to the teacher about the effectiveness of their teaching methods and to the student about their own understanding. This feedback can lead to adjustments, such as the teacher modifying their approach or the student studying differently. In a supply chain, feedback comes in the form of inventory levels or delivery delays, prompting businesses to adjust production schedules, transportation logistics, or supplier relationships. In a market, feedback occurs in the form of prices and, hence, costs or anticipated profit. A massive social movement provides feedback to those in power that something needs to change. Feedback becomes a critical factor in maintaining, adjusting, or transforming the circuits within a network. It refers to the information or results that flow back into the network, influencing future practices and connections. Feedback can be positive (amplifying a process or deviation, which may lead to escalation or systemic instability) or negative (counteracting deviations and contributing to equilibrium or system resilience). Feedback is the nuts and bolts of systems.

Systems

As discussed in the appendix to this chapter, the capital circuit and the circuit of the procommons represent the sequences through which value is generated, exchanged, and transformed. Yet these sequences do not always complete themselves automatically—they may stall, rupture, or be actively disrupted (Cleaver 2024). Systems emerge precisely to stabilize and regulate these sequences, ensuring that the necessary transitions are completed and that circuits function with continuity over time.

A system, then, is a self-organizing network of interrelated circuits and structures that maintains the continuity of these processes within a given environment. While circuits enact specific operations and structures stabilize patterned relations, systems integrate and regulate these elements toward broader systemic ends—selecting, maintaining, or discarding circuits depending on shifting priorities and environmental feedback. By integrating multiple circuits and coordinating their interdependent roles, systems introduce regulatory mechanisms that sustain and reinforce circuits beyond their immediate operational scope. Through feedback and adaptation, they persist, evolve, or transform in response to internal variations or external perturbations[4] (Bateson 1987; Luhmann 1995).

The scale at which systems operate varies widely, from localized formations to global macro-systems. At each level—whether individual, organizational, or societal—structures, circuits, and systems interact in nested configurations. This holonic perspective (Koestler 1967) highlights how smaller systems both adapt to and shape the macro-systems in which they are embedded, generating bottom-up perturbations that may, in turn, destabilize or reconfigure the larger systemic formations.

Unlike circuits, which define the sequential flows of operations necessary for a given purpose, and unlike structures, which stabilize patterns of practice, systems represent a higher level of organization that actively regulates and sustains the interplay between circuits and structures—not simply to pursue the purposes defined within each circuit but to selectively prioritize and coordinate these purposes according to the system's overarching logic. In the case of capitalism, this logic is governed by the imperative of capital accumulation and control. While each capital circuit (M–C–M′) already embodies the capitalist purpose of valorization, the capitalist system as a whole must continuously select, filter, or reorder among competing circuits—favoring those that best align with its need to maintain dominance, coherence, and autopoietic reproduction amid systemic turbulence.

Systems achieve this coherence through regulatory feedback loops, allowing them to persist and adapt even under changing conditions (Ashby 1956; Bateson 1987). These feedback mechanisms ensure that systems do not function as rigid, top-down entities in a purely mechanistic sense but as self-organizing processes in which coordination emerges through iterative adjustments rather than external imposition. In the force field hegemonized by capital, however, this coordination is asymmetrical: systems privilege circuits aligned with accumulation, converting all other domains—such as ecological, relational, or use value—into subsystems instrumental to capital's logic.

However, this self-organization is not necessarily horizontal or egalitarian. In hierarchical social systems, feedback loops operate within structured asymmetries of power, where lower-order circuits—such as those sustaining use value and relational values—become functional for higher-order circuits of accumulation and capitalist valorization (M–C–M′). As explored in the discussion of the pyramid of capital, these hierarchies shape the conditions under which circuits of social reproduction are subordinated to, or attempt to escape from, the overarching logic of accumulation.

One key aspect of social system self-organization is distributed coordination through feedback loops, enabling systems to regulate themselves by integrating responses from individuals, groups, institutions, and external conditions (Meadows 2008). Because circuits define the purpose of a system, feedback mechanisms must work to sustain, modify, or transform those circuits in response to environmental shifts and internal pressures.

At the core of this regulation lies functional teleology—the system's ability to define, adapt, and maintain its organizing purpose through the integration of circuits and structures, aligning operational flows with system-wide ends (von Bertalanffy 1968). Social systems, in particular, display a dialectic between stability and transformation, as they absorb perturbations, incorporate emergent practices, and reconfigure their internal logic in response to crises, restructuring processes, or shifts in power and meaning (Jessop 2016). For example, labor markets do not operate through centralized control; instead, they adjust dynamically through interactions between workers, employers, unions, and state policies, forming an evolving equilibrium that shifts in response to wage levels, labor demand, and regulatory interventions (Hollingsworth and Boyer 1997). The same applies to financial markets and to capitalism as a whole. This dynamic stabilization enables systems to persist while remaining open to reorganization, shaping the conditions for both systemic reproduction and potential transformation.

This feedback-driven adaptation also highlights the emergence of systemic patterns from individual and collective actions. Social systems are not fully planned; rather, they emerge from the aggregation of individual behaviors, norms, and institutional interactions, forming self-reinforcing cycles. For instance, urban transportation networks do not develop solely from government planning but also from commuter behaviors, economic incentives, social conflict, and evolving infrastructure investments, leading to the self-organization of transit flows and settlement patterns.

Such systems are neither fully planned nor purely spontaneous. They coalesce through the patterned aggregation of behaviors, institutional logics, and feedback dynamics, giving rise to emergent properties. An essential characteristic of systems is emergence, whereby new properties, behaviors, or functions arise that cannot be reduced to the sum of their individual components (Capra and Luisi 2014). The interaction of circuits, structures, and feedback loops generates systemic properties that shape the possibilities and constraints within which individual agents and subsystems operate. These emergent properties define the ontological distinctiveness of social systems, as they produce forms of organization, meaning, and coordination that go beyond the intentional actions of individual actors. While feedback mechanisms sustain systemic coherence, emergent properties often lead to unpredictable transformations, opening possibilities for new modes of cooperation, conflict, or systemic restructuring.

Beyond capital's systems: toward the autonomy of social reproduction

As discussed in Chapters 2 and 3, social reproduction must be capable of reproducing its own norms, practices, and circuits, drastically reducing its dependence on and subordination to external systemic priorities of capital accumulation. While capitalism stabilizes and expands itself through M–C–M′ circuits, reinforcing its systemic logic through hierarchies of value praxis, many circuits of social reproduction—especially those rooted in care, ecological regeneration, and mutual support—remain structurally precarious, and public institutions and systems of welfare are increasingly eroded. Embedded within and often dependent on capitalist systems of regulation, they lack the systemic autonomy needed to operate on their own terms.

To sustain and expand life-affirming forms of social cooperation beyond capital's extractive logic, these circuits must develop their own structures, circuits, and systems of stabilization—networks of feedback, coordination, and self-regulation that can ensure persistence, adaptation, and the capacity to scale. Without such self-organizing mechanisms, they remain vulnerable to capture, erosion, or forced reintegration into the logic of accumulation.

The challenge, then, is not only to multiply alternative practices but also to construct the organizational conditions necessary for their long-term viability. This chapter has outlined how praxis, structures, circuits, and systems interrelate in shaping social cooperation, showing that value praxis is always embedded in broader organizational logics. The key question moving forward is whether these alternative circuits of reproduction can generate their own systemic stability—an organizational capacity not merely to resist but to reorder the value hierarchies imposed by capitalist command. This requires not just new practices but the deliberate formation of counter-systems—organizational ecologies capable of sustaining non-extractive, life-centered forms of cooperation.

Appendix to chapter 7: Circuits of capital and the procommons

This appendix expands on key concepts introduced in Chapter 7, particularly the distinction between different types of circuits that organize contemporary social cooperation. Rather than interrupting the flow of the main argument, I have placed this material here to offer a more detailed exposition of the systemic logics at stake—especially the contrast between capitalist circuits (such as M–C–M′) and those oriented toward social reproduction. Here, I introduce the notion of the *procommons circuit*—a conceptual tool for grasping the hybrid, contested, and often fragile assemblages through which life is sustained outside, alongside, and against the dominant circuit of accumulation.

It is important to discuss two types of circuits inherent in contemporary social cooperation. Circuits are sequences of necessary state transitions through which social practices must pass to achieve their purposes. In Chapter 2, we identified two broad autopoietic processes that structure social cooperation: capital reproduction and social reproduction. These processes unfold through distinct circuits—M–C–M′, the circuit of capital, and, *within* social reproduction, a market-mediated moment expressed by C–M–C.

In these formulas, M represents money, the general equivalent used to facilitate exchange, while C stands for commodities—goods or services that hold use value for those who acquire them. M–C–M′ describes a movement in which money (M) is invested in commodities (C)—such as raw materials, labor power (LP), or machinery—only to be resold for a larger sum of money (M′), including profit. The end of the circuit becomes the condition for its reproduction. This accumulation cycle is self-expanding and defines the logic of capital reproduction.

By contrast, C–M–C represents a different logic, in which a commodity (C)—such as LP or a product—is sold for money (M), which is then used to acquire another commodity (C) for consumption or use. However, this circuit does not encapsulate the totality of the social reproduction circuit, as much of it occurs beyond market exchange. Social reproduction also involves non-commodity-based processes, such as state redistribution, mutual aid, and household labor, which sustain life but do not operate through the logic of exchange value. These belong to the procommons circuit, which I will discuss in greater detail later.

Thus, while C–M–C represents a necessary interface with markets, it is only one moment of social reproduction. The procommons circuit encompasses a broader range of cooperative practices and provisioning mechanisms, many of which function without direct monetary mediation. Understanding this distinction is crucial for grasping how different circuits interweave to shape the dynamics of social life.

As pointed out by Marx (1976), and by Aristotle before him, both circuits involve money, but for different purposes. In C–M–C, money mediates the exchange of commodities to satisfy needs. Its logic is selling (C–M) in order to buy (M–C). By contrast, in M–C–M′, money is both the starting and the ultimate goal; expanded through profit extraction, it is buying (M–C) in order to sell (C–M).

The capital circuit (M–C–M′) is the core of capital reproduction. It begins with money (M) invested in commodities (C), which are then sold for an increased sum (M′). When repeated, this circuit forms an endless accumulation spiral, continuously absorbing resources and labor while externalizing social and environmental costs. Expanding this to industrial production, we get:

$$M\text{–}C\ \{MP; LP\} \ldots P \ldots C'\text{–}M'$$

where MP (means of production) and LP (labor power) are essential inputs, and P (production) is the stage in which labor, under capital's command, generates surplus value. As shown elsewhere (De Angelis 2007), this logic extends to global capital's major productive processes.

The commodity circulation circuit (C–M–C), by contrast, is the circuit through which most people acquire the means of subsistence. Here, money is not the goal but merely a medium for accessing necessary goods in a market-dependent economy. Whether freelancers selling services, small farmers selling produce, or workers selling LP, all must sell (C–M) to buy (M–C). However, once acquired, these use values flow into domains of social reproduction, where reproductive labor, rather than capital accumulation, is the organizing principle. This labor has a degree of autonomy from the logic of capital, as its structuring principles emerge from the relational values that shape these circuits. While these domains are often structured by patriarchal norms that naturalize unpaid or undervalued labor—particularly that of women and marginalized groups—social reproduction is never fully subsumed. It generates an excess beyond capitalist imperatives, shaped by resistance, reciprocity, care, and collective forms of organization that reconfigure its meaning and value, sometimes affirming and sometimes subverting dominant social relations. While C–M–C operates through markets, social reproduction also occurs through noncommodity transfers, such as state redistribution (Polanyi 1968), gift economies (Mauss 1990; Godbout 2000), and mutual aid networks. These alternative exchanges highlight that market transactions are not the only way to circulate use values.

Building on feminist critiques discussed in Chapter 3 (also see De Angelis 2017), which emphasize the unpaid reproductive labor overlooked in Marx's analysis, we can see that C–M–C is only a moment within a broader circuit—one that includes the unpaid labor of social reproduction (R) necessary to transform commodities into actual means of life. This leads us to define the procommons circuit, which integrates commodity exchange with noncommodity forms of resource sharing.

Unlike capitalist circuits, which prioritize accumulation, procommons circuits pursue the reproduction of life to different degrees, including human capacities, care, culture, and ecological sustainability. As discussed earlier, praxis is inherently teleological, structured by a purpose that orients action. In the procommons, this teleology is not dictated by the imperative of profit but emerges from relational and use values, which are foundational to social reproduction. However, this does not mean that procommons circuits are always functional or effective in sustaining life. Most of today's procommons formations operate under conditions of scarcity, fragmentation, or dependency on capitalist circuits, whether through market mediation, state regulation, or historical hierarchies such as patriarchy and racialized exclusion. These conditions limit their capacity to sustain life, introduce contradictions, and create internal tensions between cooperation and survival imperatives and between solidarity and selective exclusion. Yet, even within these constraints, the relational values that guide these circuits can generate an excess—gestures of care, forms of resistance, and alternative modes of cooperation—that defy strict capitalist rationality.

The procommons circuit can be summarized as follows:

$$pC\text{–}R\text{–}pC',$$

where pC (procommons) is a social system that consists of

- A (an association of people and their relationships) and
- CW (commonwealth or shared resources), which may come from markets, solidarity exchanges, or state redistribution.

The circuit involves a reproduction process (R) that renews these elements over time, ensuring the sustainability of the procommons.

At the beginning of the cycle, the procommons exists as a collective of people (A) and shared resources (CW). Some of these resources are derived from markets, particularly through the proceeds of labor or commodity sales. By the end of the cycle, the procommons reemerges as pC′, a renewed set of people, relations, and resources. However, unlike capitalist circuits, this

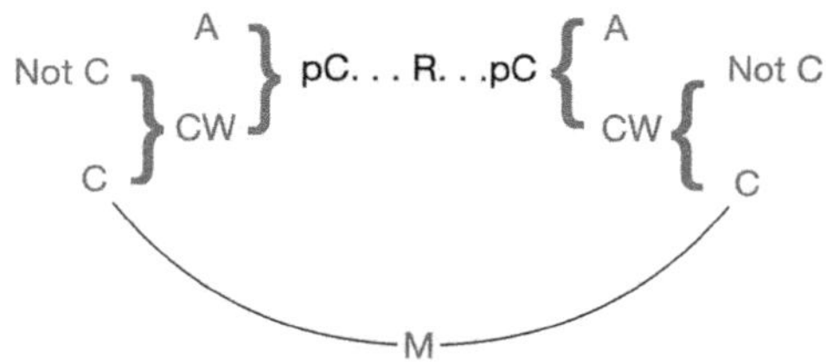

Figure 7.1 The circuit of the procommons

renewal is not driven by profit but by the ongoing reproduction of life and social relations. A full representation of the procommons circuit is shown in Figure 7.1.

A key point here is that C–M–C is only a subsystem of the procommons circuit, as it refers solely to moments in which money is involved. At least in principle, procommons reproduction does not depend entirely on markets. Instead, it integrates both commodity-based and noncommodity forms of provisioning, such as solidarity economies, communal resource management, and redistributive mechanisms.

Noncommodity resources (NC) include material and immaterial resources directly produced, maintained, or shared within a procommons or exchanged as gifts with other procommons. This category encompasses self-produced goods and services (e.g., food prepared within a household, a collective garden, cooperative housing, peer-to-peer care, knowledge-sharing within activist networks) as well as reciprocal relations among multiple procommons (e.g., intercommunity food exchanges, neighbor or friend exchanges, shared infrastructure between worker cooperatives, solidarity-based digital commons, mutual aid networks). The degree of openness, reciprocity, and coordination in these transversal exchanges influences the resilience and autonomy of procommons formations. The more robust and regularized these practices are, the greater the autonomy of the procommons from dependency on capitalist markets.

Noncommodity resources also include monetary transfers—receiving external financial support via redistributive mechanisms (e.g., state-provided welfare, grants). While such transfers can buffer against market dependency, they are often subject to external constraints, political conditions, or institutional volatility.

Commodity resources (C) include those acquired through market interactions, the means for which are obtained by earning wages or selling surplus production (C–M–C). While often necessary, reliance on markets exposes the procommons to capitalist logics, such as competition, price fluctuations, and commodification pressures. However, non-capitalist markets can be embedded in procommons in ways that seek to balance out producers' and consumers' well-being, as well as ecological conditions.

To sustain itself, a procommons must rely on a combination of these modes of resource acquisition, to different degrees in different contexts. The capacity to sustain and expand autonomous provisioning is central to the resilience of the procommons against the encroachments of capital accumulation.

8

Domains of value praxis

The immanent fabric of value praxis

We have seen that the generative, ontological principle of social reality—the force that shapes and orients social cooperation—is praxis. Praxis has three constitutive features: purpose, which guides action toward an end; norms, which enable coordination; and relatedness, which organizes social power through interaction with others—human, machinic, and ecological. Every act of praxis thus involves a selection of ends, means, and relations. As Gregory Bateson (1987) emphasized, selection draws distinctions, and these define what is included or excluded, what is considered good or bad, and what is desirable or deviant. Hence, selection is a value operation.

In this light, praxis is always value praxis: an embodied, situated process through which value is enacted, reproduced, or contested. The meaning we attribute to our actions is never purely subjective; it arises within structured environments shaped by norms, expectations, and social organization. Yet the internal and systemic dimensions of value do not always align: tensions, dissonances, and arrhythmic pulses between affects, judgments, and institutional structures often generate the very pressure for change. These frictions become salient through feedback—when enacted experience rubs against dominant norms or expectations—illuminating the force fields in which subjects are embedded. But the existence of such pressures does not guarantee transformation: For change to occur, dissonance must be enacted collectively, reach a threshold of resonance, and generate a counterforce with sufficient coherence and critical mass.

To speak of value praxis, then, is to address how social formations—including structures, circuits, and systems—emerge from and reproduce the judgments, priorities, and distinctions enacted in everyday life. This recursive process cannot be reduced to a moral position. Value praxis can stabilize domination or generate alternatives; it can affirm commodification or care. What matters is not simply whether a practice appears ethically "good" or " bad" in isolation but how it participates in a broader value domain—and how, through that domain, it sustains or challenges the systemic configurations in which it is embedded.

This chapter develops the concept of value praxis by distinguishing four key domains of cooperation: relational, use, exchange, and command. Each corresponds to a different organizing logic of social life: *Relational value* is grounded in the quality of bonds and mutual recognition; *use value* centers on the practical fulfillment of needs and purposes; *exchange value* refers to the equivalences established through markets and commodification; and *command* arises from asymmetries of power and the capacity to enforce coordination through authority or coercion. These are not discrete spheres but copresent organizing logics—fields within which specific configurations of norms, practices, and relations coalesce. In every social situation, multiple domains may be at play simultaneously, yet from the standpoint of first-order experience, one typically dominates perception and behavior. A second-order perspective, by contrast, brings into focus their entanglement and tension—making visible the layered dynamics of value that shape the architecture of social life.

These domains are not fixed modes of organization but value fields whose relative dominance shapes how social cooperation is configured. The prevailing domain in a given context helps determine the orientation of purpose, the form of normativity, and the structure of relations. In capitalist societies, the command and exchange domains tend to dominate, subordinating relational and use value to the systemic imperatives of accumulation and control. Yet all four domains are continuously enacted, recombined, and contested across different fields of social life. As Thompson (2023: 71) argues, social life is composed of overlapping "social schemes," each defined by distinct forms of practice, relation, and purpose. These schemes do not map directly onto institutions such as schools, families, or corporations, but they give rise to them through specific configurations of value domains. Institutions, in this sense, are condensations of multiple value domains and the political negotiations that stabilize them.

Let us take an example: care workers in a public hospital. Their daily praxis engages relational value (care, empathy, attentiveness), use value (meeting patient needs), command value (following institutional protocols), and exchange value (receiving a salary). The dominance of one domain over others—say, when funding cuts prioritize efficiency over care—reconfigures the meaning and orientation of the entire activity. Because subjects are holonic—that is, composed of multiple intentionalities and capacities that shift across different contexts—they often navigate competing value domains in a single day, or even a single act. A teacher may oscillate between care, discipline, and bureaucratic compliance; a migrant worker between solidarity, necessity, and coercion. These transitions require distinct forms of consciousness and selective adaptation to prevailing norms. What appears as a seamless role performance is often a fragile balancing act – a continuous search for congruence – between diverging systemic pressures. In this navigation, ambivalence becomes a form of survival: a way to sustain oneself across conflicting demands and to preserve internal coherence while inhabiting fractured social realities.

This is why it is crucial to view value domains not as separate spheres but as interacting logics of organization. Each practice enacts multiple domains, but systemic configurations (such as the capitalist pyramid explored in the next chapter) tend to prioritize some over others, turning value plurality into value hierarchy. Institutions do not simply reflect one value domain; rather, they emerge from specific articulations of multiple domains, stabilized into roles, routines, and rules. Their form reflects a historically and politically contingent ordering of value relations, which they, in turn, help reproduce. Whether in families, firms, or public services, it is this ordering that gives institutions their systemic identity.

These distinctions also inform the analysis of policy and governance discussed in Chapter 14. Governance is not neutral; it always enacts and enforces particular value configurations. The "throbs of command" identified there—purpose, agency, crisiscraft, displacement, instrumentality, and threshold recalibration—are all forms of regulating value praxis across domains. Understanding the distribution and dominance of value domains is thus key to understanding how policy selects, stabilizes, or disrupts specific circuits of social cooperation.

This approach offers a way to read both the macro-structures of capital and the micro-practices of everyday life through a common lens of value praxis. It helps clarify how domination is reproduced not only through direct coercion or ideology but through the patterned selection and reinforcement of specific value domains in given contexts.

By naming these domains and tracing their articulations, we prepare the ground for the analysis in Chapter 9. There, we will broadly examine how the capitalist pyramid functions as a macro-system for organizing social cooperation through the hierarchical ordering of value domains. But first, we need this conceptual grounding—to make visible the relational, use-based, exchange-based, and command-based logics that structure social life, and to clarify that every moment of praxis, no matter how intimate or routine, participates in systemic reproduction.

Value registers

Each domain is shaped by specific value registers—culturally and historically embedded patterns that define what is meaningful, legitimate, or desirable within the domain. Value registers are not fixed; they evolve, conflict, and mutate through everyday struggles, political interventions, and historical shifts. They serve as internal selectors within each domain, shaping how norms, practices, and relations are enacted—and contested. The significance and operation of these registers are never absolute; they depend on the broader configurations of value domains in which they are actualized. The same register may take on different meanings, effects, or tensions depending on how it interacts with other registers and the systemic context in which it is embedded.

In the relational domain, value registers include both affirming principles such as care, love, respect, honor, or trust, and their negations or opposites—such as neglect, betrayal, contempt, or dishonor. These registers structure how individuals engage with one another based on mutual recognition, emotional attunement, or social solidarity—but also how these are denied or weaponized. A care register may guide intimate caregiving, while a respect register may define interactions in formal mentorships or intergenerational settings. A register of honor may foster solidarity and mutual recognition in some cultural settings, while in others it can be mobilized to enforce patriarchal authority or exclusionary hierarchies.

In the use-value domain, registers shape how utility is understood and pursued. Self-sufficiency, effectiveness, craftsmanship, sustainability, or improvisation may all serve as value registers. These may orient practices toward durability, adequacy, or direct fulfillment of needs—such as the careful maintenance of communal tools or the adaptive reuse of materials in contexts of scarcity. While effectiveness remains central to use value, its related notion of efficiency is far more ambivalent; for instance, when it is aligned with relational registers—such as care or solidarity—it may support practices that liberate time for life or increase the accessibility of goods without commodification. By contrast, when the register of efficiency is aligned with exchange value, it often subordinates use and relational values to productivity, performativity, or accumulation.

In the exchange-value domain, registers mediate how equivalence, profit, or participation in markets are normatively framed. These include speculative accumulation, cost-effectiveness, fair trade, ethical consumerism, or value for money. A social enterprise may invoke a register of social responsibility to differentiate itself from purely profit-driven models, while speculative investors may enact a register that prioritizes volatility and arbitrage. Conflicts among these registers shape not only economic behavior but also social imaginaries about what the market is and should be.

In the command domain, value registers define the legitimacy, form, and scope of authority. These include discipline, meritocracy, administrative neutrality, legal-rational authority, charismatic leadership, as well as coercion or obedience. Different governance regimes privilege different registers: Liberal democracies often highlight the separation of powers and the rule of law; military regimes prioritize command and discipline; managerial hierarchies rely on efficiency and procedural compliance. Yet even within one system, registers can clash—such as when appeals to democratic legitimacy confront bureaucratic opacity or executive discretion.

Crucially, value registers are sites of dynamic tensions. They not only define the boundaries of acceptable practice but also serve as terrains of struggle over meaning, legitimacy, and power. A school may be structured by competing registers of discipline and care; a climate movement may navigate between urgency and inclusivity; a family may oscillate between obligation and affection. These frictions are not merely obstacles; they are generative points through which social cooperation is renegotiated.

Many of the most pressing struggles in social life—over wages, working conditions, ecological breakdown, access to public services, or the treatment of migrants—do not arise within a single domain of value. Rather, they emerge at the intersections where value registers from different domains collide, pulling practices, norms, and priorities in conflicting directions. While each domain contains internal tensions—such as between reciprocity and hierarchy in relational life or between sufficiency and optimization in use—*interdomain* frictions are often where systemic contradictions become most visible and politically charged.

Consider the wage struggle. This is not merely a negotiation within the exchange domain over price or productivity. It is a conflict between the register of cost minimization (exchange) and other value registers: relational ones such as dignity, recognition, and solidarity; use-value registers tied to livelihood and reproduction; and command registers invoking entitlement, legal protection, or institutional legitimacy. A wage, then, is not just an amount—it expresses competing visions of value and worth in social cooperation.

Ecological struggles further highlight these interdomain tensions. When forests are razed, rivers poisoned, or territories sacrificed to extractive industries, what is at stake is not only material survival (use value) but also relational registers that bind humans to one another and to the more-than-human world. These include care, respect, and responsibility toward ecosystems, future generations, and the cycles of life—what we might call the relational grammar of Gaia. These registers clash with the exchange logic of commodification and speculative accumulation, which abstracts nature into units of value and sacrifice zones.

Similarly, conflicts over public services—health care, education, and transport—often pit relational and use-value registers (care, inclusion, and well-being) against command and exchange-value registers that enforce efficiency, control, or privatization. The restructuring of hospitals or schools in the name of performance metrics displaces forms of relational meaning—trust, empathy, and mutual accountability—central to their social purpose.

Migration and bordering practices expose further entanglements. The relational value of hospitality, the use value of refuge and livelihood, and command registers of rights and asylum compete with sovereign logics of closure and market-based calculations of utility. Migrants are framed simultaneously as threats, workers, kin, or neighbors—depending on which value domains dominate a given discourse or institutional arrangement.

Across all these cases, what is contested is not just a policy, a wage, or a resource but the organizing *hierarchy* of value domains. These struggles are about whose values count, how cooperation is structured, and what kinds of lives are made possible or impossible. They reveal that domination is not simply enforced by rules or ideology but enacted through the hierarchical prioritization of certain domains of value praxis over others—an ordering articulated through specific value registers—and that resistance often arises through the reassertion of subordinated value grammars, especially those rooted in relational life, communal care, and ecological interdependence.

By attending to value registers, we deepen our grasp of how value domains are operationalized in everyday life—and how they can be reconfigured. Registers provide the language and criteria by which practices are evaluated, challenged, and affirmed. While the richness and contestation of value registers are crucial to understanding how value is enacted in practice, I cannot pursue their complexity further here; my aim is to clarify the broader architecture of value domains as a necessary step toward analyzing how they are hierarchically organized within the pyramid of capital. In what follows, I examine each of the four value domains in turn—relational, use, exchange, and command—not as isolated spheres but as overlapping fields of praxis, each with its own organizing logics, tensions, and value registers.

Relational values domain

The domain of relational values is the domain of existential and social experience. Relational values shape interactions not only between individuals but also with Gaia, the self, and the sacred. Their purpose is the relationship itself—valuing connection, recognition, and mutual presence as ends rather than means. These values emerge through interaction and cooperation, taking form in the ways communities and individuals give meaning to relationships.

Relational values include trust, care, solidarity, loyalty, fairness, respect, and others but also encompass their negations—indifference, alienation, and violence. They define how people assess roles and intentions, extending beyond transactional concerns and anchoring social life in emotional, ethical, and symbolic dimensions (Chan et al. 2016; Klain et al. 2017). Relational values also encompass what some scholars describe as *eudaimonic* values—those linked to living a good life and cultivating personal and collective flourishing. They are not limited to individual preferences but emerge from reflection on justice, reciprocity, care, and virtue. These values are derived from ongoing interactions and responsibilities not only with other humans but also with nonhuman beings, landscapes, and ecosystems.

However, they are not inherently virtuous. Loyalty can breed complicity; solidarity can foster exclusion; respect can entrench hierarchy. Trust can empower or deceive. Indifference, often seen as absence, is a form of relational value that structures alienation, withdrawal, and invisibility. It institutionalizes social distance, as seen in bureaucratic or market-based systems, and may also serve as a strategy of self-protection in dehumanizing contexts.

Relational values also shape the self. Self-respect, self-trust, and even solidarity with oneself are conditions of autonomy. They regulate the subject's capacity to assert agency and remain coherent under systemic pressure. Just as trust and care are necessary in interpersonal relations, they are vital to the subject's relationship to their own integrity and survival.

Violence and coercion likewise mark relational configurations. Patriarchal, colonial, or racialized systems often sustain themselves through violence—not merely as a failure of relation but as a mode of ordering it (Bourdieu 1998; Fanon 2004; Federici 2004). The threat or anticipation of violence shapes behavior even in its absence. Relational values, then, are not neutral; they are fields of contestation through which domination or emancipation can be enacted.

These dynamics unfold across both direct and mediated relationships. In close bonds—family, friendship, and caregiving—values like trust and reciprocity structure action. In broader social fields—institutions, imagined communities (Anderson 2006)—they orient belonging and recognition (Yuval-Davis 2011). Mauss's (1990) analysis of the gift as obligation, and Esposito's (2009) notion of *munus*—the shared duty or gift that binds individuals to others—underscore how relational values form the ethical glue of cooperation, structuring duties rather than possessions.

Specific value registers like care, loyalty, fairness, and recognition operate across settings—from households to institutions. Care, for example, guides parenting and healing; loyalty guides long-term commitments; solidarity guides collective action; fairness guides institutional trust. These registers vary in intensity and meaning depending on the social and historical context. Respect may signal formal hierarchy or mutual regard; care may be shallow or deeply reciprocal. Registers shift, conflict, and evolve. A bond of reciprocity may deepen into solidarity—or erode into detachment.

Relational values are always enacted within broader systemic configurations. Under capitalism, they are frequently corrupted by exchange and command. Love, for example, becomes commodified in care economies, where emotional labor is extracted under precarious conditions. Nationalism converts love into allegiance, subordinating solidarity to state command and mobilizing it against perceived outsiders.

Spiritual and artistic praxis also expresses relational value. Spirituality guides individuals in cultivating a relationship with something greater than themselves, whether it be a deity, the cosmos, shared conditions, or Gaia, while fostering empathy, community, and ethical life. Artistic expression builds shared meaning and recognition, generating second-order observation and perturbation. As relational aesthetics and participatory art demonstrate, art can become a field of cocreation, community, and critical reflection—positioning subjects within webs of relationships, revealing the social through the aesthetic. This has been explored by authors like Max Haiven (2014), who foregrounds art's role in contesting capitalist imaginaries and opening commons-based alternatives, and Massimiliano Mollona (2021), who emphasizes how art intersects with struggles over collective life and value, particularly in precarious and politicized settings.

Relational values, then, are not static virtues but shifting, contested dynamics of recognition, connection, and exclusion. They structure the affective and ethical infrastructure of social cooperation—and their suppression, erosion, or distortion signals deeper systemic contradiction and struggle.

Use value

The domain of use value refers to value praxis grounded in usefulness—the ability of things, services, or processes to satisfy needs, serve purposes, and support life. It is here that concrete labor, embodied knowledge, and material transformation converge to produce and reproduce the conditions of social cooperation. This is not simply about utility in an abstract sense but about the situated, relational, and context-specific enactment of usefulness—what is effective in sustaining life, social relations, and collective purpose.

Historically, the concept of use value has been central to political economy. Classical economists such as Adam Smith and David Ricardo described goods as having both use value and exchange value, treating these as coexisting attributes. Karl Marx radicalized this framework by focusing not on goods in general but on *commodities*—goods produced for exchange within capitalist relations. In this context, exchange value takes precedence: Production is not organized to meet needs but to generate profit. Abstract labor—the homogenized, socially measurable labor time that underpins exchange—overrules concrete labor, the actual, diverse activity that produces use values. Thus, under capitalism, human activity is reduced to units of equivalence, distorting the social purpose of usefulness.[1]

Yet use value does not disappear; it remains the ground of all commodity production. Every exchange presupposes use, and every act of reproduction requires material transformation. Use-value praxis involves not only the production and consumption of goods but also the application of knowledge, technique, and embodied skill. It is embedded in the effective performance of tasks: the craft of a potter, the healing practice of a midwife, the maintenance of a bike, the operation of a computer numerical control machine in a factory, the work of a nurse in a hospital ward, or the labor of an AI trainer refining algorithmic performance. From the preparation of a meal to the calibration of scientific equipment or the repair of a public water system, use-value praxis unfolds wherever material and immaterial needs are addressed through situated, competent doing. Effectiveness—rather than efficiency—is the guiding register here: not doing more with less but doing well what needs to be done in alignment with situated needs and purposes.

These practices rely on specific value registers that guide the social meaning of utility. Registers such as *durability*, *repairability*, *craftsmanship*, *sufficiency*, *resilience*, and *communal provisioning* all shape how use value is enacted. For example, in a rural cooperative, the register of repairability might structure how tools are designed and shared. In an urban public kitchen, sufficiency and adaptability may guide how food is prepared and distributed. In an urban makerspace or fab lab, craftsmanship and modularity may guide how prototypes are designed for iterative improvement. In each case, usefulness is not only functional but socially mediated—determined by who benefits, in what context, and under which relational conditions.

Use-value praxis is inseparable from knowledge. This includes both technical expertise and vernacular, embodied forms of knowing—how to sew, cook, irrigate, design, mend, build, or code. It also encompasses collaborative and experimental knowledge practices, such as how to conduct research, share findings, or collectively solve problems. In scientific communities, the commitment to replicability and peer validation supports shared learning, even as the commodification of research through paywalled journals and intellectual property regimes undermines such openness. Open-source software development similarly operates through value registers of transparency, collective authorship, and continuous adaptation—registers that can clash with the proprietary logic of tech corporations that enclose knowledge for profit. Registers such as craftsmanship, repairability, sufficiency, and resilience shape how utility is enacted in material contexts, while registers like open access, replicability, peer review, and collective learning structure the production and circulation of knowledge.

Thus, knowledge in the use-value domain is effective insofar as it meets shared needs and sustains life, but its social meaning and accessibility are shaped by its articulation with other value domains. When knowledge serves relational values, it circulates as a commons—shared, taught, and adapted across generations or networks. This is visible in the transmission of Indigenous ecological knowledge, community-based public health initiatives, or collaborative scientific platforms such as Wikipedia or OpenStreetMap. When captured by exchange value, knowledge is enclosed—commodified through patents, trade secrets, or intellectual property regimes that turn collective learning into private assets. When subordinated to command, knowledge becomes a means of surveillance, enforcement, and hierarchical control—shaping how resources, people, and environments are governed. In predictive policing, for example, or in algorithmic management in warehouses, knowledge does not simply solve problems; it enforces priorities defined elsewhere.

The value of knowledge, then, is never intrinsic; it depends on what it is useful for, for whom, and under what value regime. Whether knowledge functions as a commons, a commodity, or a tool of control is not given by its content but by the social configuration in which it operates.

Use value also implies a dynamic and pervasive relation between production and consumption—not as discrete stages but as immanent, co-constitutive moments of every act of praxis (Marx 1973: 90–4). To use something is not merely to consume it but to consume it productively: Drinking water hydrates the body so it can work; repairing a tool enables future tasks; eating a meal fuels care or study. But more fundamentally, every act of *production* is also an act of *consumption*: the potter shaping clay expends bodily energy, just as the machine operator draws on electricity, and the teacher burns metabolic calories while preparing a lesson. Conversely, every act of *consumption* is also productive—it configures bodies, regenerates attention, or creates affective states. Writing a book, for instance, consumes energy, materials, and time while producing meaning, argument, and political orientation.

This dual character of praxis reveals the metabolic nature of use value: It binds together expenditure and regeneration, material transformation and subjective formation. It also destabilizes simplistic separations between production and reproduction. Indeed, *every productive act is reproductive*, in the sense that it sustains, extends, or transforms the conditions for further doing. But as we have seen in Chapters 2 and 3, reproduction can serve different systemic ends.

In this light, the metabolic circuits of use value are always contested. They may be harnessed to reproduce capital—through extractive labor, commodified care, technocratic control, or the stimulation of endless demand detached from real needs—or they may serve to reproduce social and ecological life on more autonomous, solidaristic, or sustainable terms. The question is never whether use value is being produced but how it is produced, for whom, and to what end. This is because use value is not neutral—it is a site of struggle between competing logics of reproduction.

Precisely because use value remains indispensable—because no circuit of capital can function without a material or symbolic utility anchoring it—it becomes a terrain of strategic capture. Under capitalist conditions, many goods and services are not organized to meet actual needs but to maintain the momentum of accumulation. Planned obsolescence, disposable design, wasteful packaging, and hyper-specialization systematically degrade usefulness to generate turnover. Things are made to break, to expire, and to be replaced—not because they no longer serve their purpose but because their continued durability would disrupt profit flows. More deeply, capitalism produces entire landscapes of waste—not only in the form of material excess but also in the treatment of people, skills, communities, and environments as expendable. Deindustrialized workers, displaced populations, polluted ecosystems, and redundant infrastructures are not collateral; they are outcomes of a system that measures worth by exchange, not by contribution to life. Waste is not a by-product in capitalism; it is a governing logic (Armiero 2021).

This critique resonates deeply with Georges Bataille's (1988) insight that human societies cannot be reduced to instrumental reason. In *The Accursed Share*, Bataille argues that excess—expressed through ritual, gift, sacrifice, or art—is not wasteful in a pejorative sense but a constitutive force of social life. These practices are not anomalies but essential expressions of what it means to live collectively: They affirm shared meaning, symbolic continuity, and forms of value that escape reduction to utility or profit. In contrast to a restricted economy fixated on scarcity, Bataille outlines a *general economy* grounded in surplus energy and the necessity of its expenditure. From this perspective, excess is not a problem to be eliminated but a condition to be navigated—through generosity, ritual, or symbolic expenditure, which reaffirms social bonds and collective significance.

Yet capitalism inverts this dynamic. It does not eliminate excess but reorganizes it into systems of extraction, commodification, and destruction. What traditional societies treated as a sacred offering, capitalism renders into disposable surplus. In place of ritual sacrifice, we find systemic discard. People, capacities, and ecologies are wasted not to affirm collective meaning but to sustain accumulation. Capitalism demands expansion, and in doing so, produces planned obsolescence, overproduction, and ecological exhaustion—not as dysfunctions but as structural imperatives. Its mode of sacrifice is impersonal: What is offered up is not symbolic wealth or surplus energy but life itself—human and nonhuman alike.

Thus, under the capitalist regime, the sacred is displaced: no longer oriented toward the community, Gaia, or a transcendent sense of meaning, it is redirected toward capital itself. Capital becomes the deity to which everything is sacrificed—time, energy, ecosystems, and future generations. In this inversion, the meaning-making power of excess is hollowed out. Giving presupposes endless extraction; expenditure turns into waste; sacrifice becomes annihilation.

Bataille's insights invite us to rethink the domain of use value not simply in terms of need satisfaction or effectiveness but as a contested terrain in which the meaning of surplus, necessity, and life itself is constantly fought over. They call attention to a deeper political question: who or what is deemed necessary, and who or what is rendered expendable? The organization of use values is never neutral. It encodes hierarchies of worth—defining which lives, knowledges, environments, and capacities are maintained, and which are sacrificed to sustain the system's relentless motion.

Thus, the domain of use value is both foundational and embattled. It anchors the very possibility of meeting needs, yet it is constantly subordinated, redirected, and distorted by other domains. Its registers—when guided by effectiveness, reciprocity, and care—can sustain communities and ecosystems. When overridden by exchange or command, they are instrumentalized, hollowed out, or turned against their own purposes.

Understanding use-value praxis today means recognizing this ambivalence. The same labor that feeds a community may be deployed in military logistics. The same infrastructure that sustains urban life may collapse under austerity. The same technologies that heal may exclude, surveil, or control. Usefulness, then, is never neutral—it is a site of struggle over what is necessary, who decides, and for whom.

Exchange value

We now enter the third domain of value praxis: exchange value. This domain links social cooperation to calculative equivalence and monetized abstraction. In its simplest form, exchange value refers to the price a good or service commands in the market. But when embedded in value praxis, it becomes more than a mechanism of trade: It configures social relations through commodification, valuation, and profit-driven interaction.

Exchange value always emerges in conjunction with use value, which provides the material basis of any commodity. Yet their logics of valorization diverge. When a good or service is produced not primarily for use but for sale, it becomes a commodity: a use value oriented toward others, mediated by money, and framed by market expectations. This marks a shift in social cooperation—one that becomes capitalist when the systemic purpose of production is profit, and all other forms of value must adapt to its logic. To be sure, not every act of selling signals capitalist production. A street vendor, a waged worker, or a community producer may sell goods or services to meet needs or sustain life. The sale of labor power often aims at securing the means of reproduction, not at generating profit. What distinguishes capitalism is not the existence of exchange but the structural dominance of profit as the organizing principle of social cooperation.

Following Braudel's (1982) distinction between markets and capitalism, we must remember that market exchange is not inherently capitalist. Historically, markets have functioned within relational and ethical frameworks that moderated accumulation: guilds, commons, customary regulations, and moral economies constrained price manipulation and protected livelihoods. Even today, alternative practices such as solidarity economies, local food networks, and cooperative production show that exchange can be embedded in relational norms of fairness, reciprocity, and ecological care (De Angelis 2017; De Angelis and Diesner 2020).

Capitalist valorization emerges when the logic of exchange value becomes hegemonic—subordinating use value and coercing all social cooperation into a single metric of worth. Under these conditions, exchange value no longer simply mediates transactions; it becomes an autonomous logic that restructures purpose, labor, consumption, and production itself. Profitability—not need, relation, or effectiveness—becomes the primary criterion of value.

This shift produces systemic distortions. From the standpoint of use, goods exist to fulfill human needs with minimal social and ecological cost. But from the standpoint of hegemonic exchange, their worth lies in their capacity to generate surplus value. Production for use becomes subordinated to production for profit. This logic normalizes labor exploitation, ecological degradation, and overproduction, while masking this violence under the veil of economic rationality.

The triumph of hegemonic exchange value is often framed as natural or necessary. Classical and neoliberal economists, from Smith to Friedman, claim that the pursuit of profit in competitive markets drives innovation and progress. In this view, use value is a happy by-product of a profitable enterprise. But history tells another story. Humanity's greatest innovations—language, agriculture, penicillin, the wheel, fire, and eyeglasses—did not emerge from the profit motive. They arose from collective experimentation, need, and care.

Even today, transformative innovations often emerge from nonprofit contexts: open-source projects like Linux and Wikipedia; scientific breakthroughs like the Human Genome Project, and mutual aid networks and maker communities that responded to the COVID-19 pandemic. What links these examples is not price incentives but shared purpose and social cooperation.

Yet these infrastructures are not immune to capture. The story of GNU/Linux illustrates how collaborative innovation can be absorbed into corporate ecosystems. Initiated by Richard Stallman in the 1980s and expanded through Linus Torvalds's Linux kernel in 1991, the GNU/Linux system was designed to be free, decentralized, and transparent. But over time, companies like IBM, Google, and Red Hat integrated it into platform capitalism. What began as a commons became the infrastructure of surveillance, data extraction, and corporate control (Zuboff 2019).

This dynamic underscores the ambivalence of exchange value. On the one hand, markets enable circulation, comparison, and provisioning. On the other, when abstracted from use and relations, they erode the commons, extract from social cooperation, and turn freedom into a vector of capture. The shift from shared development to proprietary platforms is not incidental—it is how hegemonic exchange value operates when unbound by other domains.

That is why the struggle over exchange value is not simply about prices or trade. It concerns the very architecture of social cooperation. When exchange dominates, other values—care, utility, and autonomy—must justify themselves in its terms or risk marginalization. Often, this justification means becoming functional to the logic of profit, appealing to the god of "efficiency" to demonstrate worth. Education becomes an investment, art a commodity, attention a revenue stream, and even activism a brand.

Yet the field of exchange value is not monolithic. Value registers within this domain can be diverse and contested: cost-effectiveness, value for money, fair trade, ethical consumerism, and speculative arbitrage. These shape not only economic behavior but also the imaginary of what the market is—and what it should be. Struggles over wages, working conditions, public procurement, and consumer ethics all reflect contestations over these registers, often pitting exchange value against relational, use, or command-oriented logics. Moreover, hegemonic exchange value imposes a particular temporality: one of urgency, fast turnover, and short-term maximization. This time logic often clashes with the slower rhythms of care (relational value), the durability of ecosystems (relational and use value), or the reflexive calibration of governance (command). It produces a dissonant acceleration that reshapes social cooperation around speed and extraction. As will be discussed in the last three chapters, these frictions generate arrhythmic patterns—temporal disjunctions that destabilize social life, fragment experience, and intensify systemic stress.

Through credit and debt mechanisms, hegemonic exchange value also colonizes the future. Anticipated use—such as housing, education, or health care—is transformed into present financial obligation. A student takes on decades of debt for the promise of employability; a family signs a mortgage—a word derived from the Latin *mortuum vadium*, "death pledge"—to secure a home, binding their future labor to the profit margins of banks. Entire nations are locked into austerity regimes to repay sovereign debts accrued under extractive terms. In each case, future needs, work, and even planetary conditions are subordinated to present profitability. Social cooperation, rather than reproducing the conditions of life, becomes a necrological instrument, sustaining accumulation through the calculated sacrifice of time, autonomy, and ecological possibility. This dynamic extends the reach of exchange value into domains once shaped by relational commitments, social guarantees, or intergenerational ethics.

Perhaps most troubling is the commodification of elements never meant for trade—what Polanyi (1944) called fictitious commodities. Under hegemonic exchange value, land becomes real estate, time becomes a unit of billable hours, emotions become sellable content, and attention becomes the currency of platform capitalism. These transformations erode relational value by instrumentalizing what was once freely shared, lived, or gifted. This is especially evident today in the commodification of emotional labor. Acts of care, friendliness, and attention—central to relational value—are increasingly formatted into service metrics, ratings, and monetized interaction. The result is a disfigured form of relation, in which even empathy is scripted for profit. Meanwhile, the extraction of data and behavioral surplus signals how hegemonic exchange value now operates through the very act of living. Our movements, preferences, and connections are mined as value streams, often without consent or awareness. What once remained in the realm of relational or subjective experience becomes monetizable residue.

Finally, we must acknowledge the limits of exchange value as a coordinating logic—precisely the role championed by liberal thinkers from Smith to Hayek. While Adam Smith still grounded market behavior in moral sentiments and relational interdependence, contemporary capitalism severs that grounding, advancing a logic that misreads life as a cost, care as inefficiency, and justice as an externality. Hayek (1945), in turn, defends the market as a decentralized information processor, capable of coordinating dispersed plans through the price mechanism alone. But this vision is predicated on a profound erasure: the possibility of direct communication, collective deliberation, and shared rule-making—the very practices that underpin tacit knowledge, relational trust, and the reproductive labor necessary for any social order. Tacit knowledge, relational trust, and reproductive labor are not merely technical functions; they are embedded, enacted, and cultivated through embodied practices of shared life. Hayek's idea of spontaneous market order thus presupposes a radical disorder of life. Like Garrett Hardin's (1968) parable of the "tragedy of the commons," it assumes that people cannot—or should not—communicate their purposes and must instead be disciplined by signals abstracted from their own cooperation (Ostrom 1990; De Angelis 2017). Both thinkers thus eliminate the social capacity for mutual adjustment, negotiation, and care—misrecognizing these not as resources for autonomy and collective reason but as threats to efficiency and thereby providing ideological legitimacy to their enclosure. In doing so, the market becomes a tool for coordinating cooperation only on the basis of its logic of fragmentation, masking its own dominance as neutrality. What is selected and transmitted through prices is not a neutral reflection of social needs but the filtering of life through the priorities of exchange value alone—what can be monetized, extracted, or rendered calculable. This is not merely a misrepresentation of economic life; it is a performative logic that, once enacted through policy and institutions, entrenches market rule, amplifies dispossession, and disfigures the fabric of social cooperation. Understanding the domain of exchange value, then, is essential not in order to reject markets outright but to expose the conditions under which they must be bounded. Such bounding does not arise from the market itself but from the logics of relational value and use value—the values of care, need, and effectiveness—that ground the ongoing work of social reproduction. Only by reclaiming the plural possibilities of value can we reorient exchange toward cooperation rather than extraction, and reassert the primacy of life over profit.

Command

To the three dimensions of value praxis—relational, use, and exchange—we must add a fourth: command. This domain does not generate value directly but operates as a structuring force within social cooperation, shaping which values take precedence, how they interact, and under what conditions they become operative. Command emerges from the contested interplay of *powers-to* (potentia) oriented toward different purposes, establishing the parameters of coordination, regulation, and meaning. Where these powers clash within a structured force field, their asymmetrical stabilization gives rise to forms of power-over (potestas), through which social priorities are set and the domains of value praxis are hierarchically ordered.

Unlike the other dimensions, command configures, limits, and reorganizes the production, circulation, and recognition of value. It determines not only how value is distributed but also what counts as socially valuable at all. It operates at both a material and symbolic level. Materially, it structures access to resources—who controls what, for whom, and on what terms—effectively establishing the dominant "measure of things" through which bodies, labor, nonhuman nature, and time are organized and made meaningful within social cooperation. This measure is not abstract: It is enacted in embodied and ecological practices, shaping how people's and nature's capacities, roles, and contributions are valued or disregarded. Symbolically, command defines the terms under which value is recognized, shaping the social imaginaries that orient cooperation and legitimize particular arrangements of meaning and power (Castoriadis 1987). As such, command assigns, rather than produces, value: It determines whose labor, time, and contributions are recognized, and under which value regime.

A helpful metaphor comes from programming. In Python, the command $x = 5$ does not create the number 5 but assigns it to a variable, integrating it into a system of references. Similarly, command in value praxis does not produce care, utility, or profit directly; it designates their meaning, priority, and interaction. Registers of command—law, governance, bureaucracy, and military authority—organize how relational, use, and exchange values are enacted. For example, legal norms shape economic behavior; bureaucratic criteria govern access to services; public policy defines who is entitled to what and under what conditions.

Even in nonhierarchical settings, command is necessary. It allocates roles, establishes procedures, and maintains coherence. What matters is not only how command is structured but also how it is performed—whether it emerges through deliberation, mutual accountability, and shared responsibility or whether it reproduces asymmetry and domination or enables autonomy and cooperation.

In shaping value relations, command configures the coherence of social cooperation. It sets priorities and allocates resources. In a workplace, command might prioritize productivity over well-being; in a municipal budget, it might favor real estate development over green space; in social movements, it might privilege visibility and mobilization over internal care and sustainability. At scale, it determines whether planetary limits are overridden for financial growth or whether social care is elevated above accumulation—or vice versa.

Crucially, command over use values—such as food, land, housing, infrastructure, energy, or money—organizes dependency and privilege. Those who command provisioning systems gain leverage over others' needs and capacities, consolidating power and reinforcing existing hierarchies. The ability to allocate, restrict, or withhold useful goods and services becomes not merely a matter of economic exchange but a structuring force in the distribution of social capital, political influence, and institutional access. These decisions shape the broader order of things, determining whose needs are prioritized, who is integrated into systems of value production and distribution, and under what conditions social cooperation unfolds. Depending on how it is configured, command thus functions not only as a means of coordination but also as a terrain of domination and exclusion, embedding relations of power in the very structure of value enactment. Because it structures how values are assigned and recognized, command is never neutral—it is a site of struggle that organizes both the reproduction of inequality and the possibilities for resistance.

Command exists on a spectrum. At one extreme, it manifests as coercive, hierarchical domination—seen in totalitarian states, colonial rule, and capitalist exploitation (Weber 1978; Agamben 2005; Mbembe 2019). At the other extreme, it takes the form of participatory coordination, as found in commons-based governance, cooperatives, and direct-democratic assemblies (Ostrom 1990; Graeber 2013).

What distinguishes these two poles is the degree of power asymmetry. When command is structurally orientated toward reproducing asymmetry, limiting agency, and subordinating value production to elite priorities, then it becomes domination—that is, a configuration of command that reorders relational, use, and exchange values to serve its hierarchical ends.

Domination is a specific modality of command in which power not only operates asymmetrically but is structured to reproduce asymmetries as a central principle of cooperation. Unlike nondominative forms of command, which organize social coordination without necessarily entrenching inequality, domination functions through institutionalized mechanisms that restrict agency, control access to value, and sustain hierarchies. Domination is not necessary for social cooperation but is a historically contingent form of power that emerges within specific material and institutional formations. Capitalist exploitation, for example, represents a form of command that tends toward domination, as workers are structurally subordinated to capitalists through wage dependence, dispossession, and workplace control (Marx 1976). Similarly, colonial rule imposed domination by subjugating entire populations through political, economic, and cultural control (Fanon 2004).

In both cases, command is instrumentalized to maintain subordination. In a later chapter, we will examine how the current global pyramid of power functions as a system of domination, aligning with these coercive and asymmetric structures. Rather than merely structuring cooperation, it actively enforces systemic inequalities through economic, political, and institutional mechanisms that restrict agency, prioritize accumulation, and reinforce dependency on a global scale.

In this middle range of the spectrum, hybrid forms of command arise—configurations that combine participatory or procedural elements with entrenched asymmetries. Bureaucratic systems, for example, may rely on impersonal rules and legal-rational legitimacy (Weber 1978), yet still reproduce structural inequalities by obscuring who sets the rules and whose interests are served. Bureaucratic command, as analyzed by Weber, is not inherently "in-between" these poles: It is a rationalized form of control that can serve both participatory and authoritarian systems. Its impersonality, rule-bound procedures, and administrative ordering make it structurally flexible—able to support democratic access and accountability or to operate as efficient machinery of domination. Managerialism and technocracy often claim neutrality but centralize decision-making and prioritize quantifiable outcomes over relational or ecological values. Even governance mechanisms within democracies or cooperatives can enact domination if they institutionalize exclusion, suppress dissent, or enforce norms that subordinate alternative value logics. These hybrid forms demonstrate that domination can be embedded not only in overtly authoritarian regimes but also in administrative, algorithmic, or consultative processes that appear inclusive while reproducing control.

While command can take multiple forms, its configuration determines whether it reproduces domination or enables cooperation. Bureaucratic command, for instance, need not be authoritarian, yet under neoliberalism, it often becomes technocratic—delegated to experts, audit cultures, and algorithmic procedures that obscure political choices behind a facade of neutrality (Dardot and Laval 2014; Brown 2015). Feminist theorists have long shown that such forms of command systematically devalue reproductive labor and care, externalizing them to households or communities without recognition or support, thus entrenching gendered hierarchies at the heart of social reproduction (Federici 2004; Fraser 2016).

Ecologically, command extends to nonhuman life. The capitalist drive for "cheap nature" subordinates ecosystems to extractive imperatives, treating rivers, forests, and species as resources to be allocated or sacrificed for profit (Moore 2015; Tsing 2015). In the digital domain, command is increasingly embedded in infrastructure itself. Algorithmic governance, platform capitalism, and predictive systems automate prioritization and control, shaping behavior while obscuring responsibility—thus reinforcing asymmetries behind the veil of optimization (Terranova 2004; Bratton 2016; Zuboff 2019). These forms of command may appear decentralized or benign, yet they organize cooperation along lines that fragment solidarity, restrict agency, and deepen inequalities. The question, then, is not whether command exists but how it is enacted: whether it amplifies autonomy and mutual responsibility or consolidates domination under the guise of efficiency, growth, or technical necessity.

Cybernetic theory helps illuminate command not as direct control but as a mechanism of filtering and amplification that ensures systemic coherence (Wiener 1948; Ashby 1956). Control, in this sense, is not primarily about issuing directives but about managing flows of information, feedback, and resources to maintain alignment with a system's dominant logic. As a filter, command selects which values, behaviors, and priorities become operational, while excluding or marginalizing those that do not serve the system's objectives. As an amplifier, it reinforces certain practices or norms—such as productivity, efficiency, and competition—ensuring their reproduction and systemic prominence (Figure 8.1).

In a corporate system, for example, command may amplify profit maximization while filtering out worker well-being, leisure, or unquantifiable forms of care. In contrast, a commons-based initiative may amplify sustainability, reciprocity, or local stewardship while filtering out market-driven incentives. These filtering and amplification processes are not

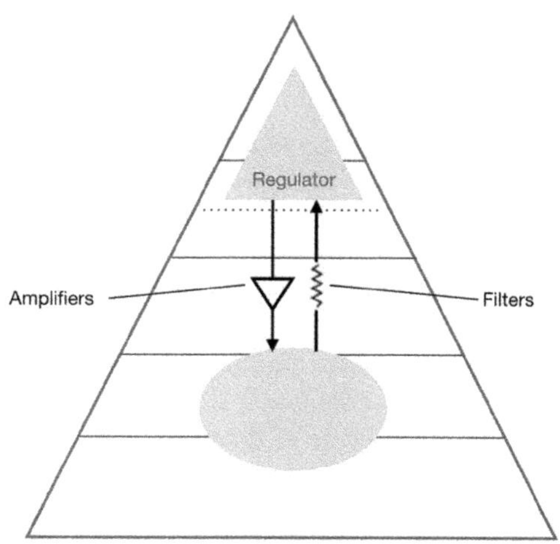

Figure 8.1 A synthetic view of regulation

neutral: They shape the coherence and adaptability of social cooperation according to specific priorities. Whether command reinforces domination or enables autonomy depends on which values it filters out and which it amplifies—and how these selections are made, by whom, and for what purpose. Again, this is what we called the measure of things in Chapter 2.

Reading power through the prism of value praxis

Widely different theoretical traditions have contributed to our understanding of how command operates within social organization. Notably, systems theory (Luhmann), sovereignty (Agamben), governmentality and discipline (Foucault), and the social imaginary (Castoriadis) each offer important perspectives on the structure and dynamics of power. Yet none fully account for command as a domain of value praxis—as a structuring force field that arises from the contested interplay of *powers-to* (potentia) and that configures how relational, use, and exchange values are prioritized, coordinated, or subordinated within social cooperation.

Niklas Luhmann's (1977, 1995) systems theory conceptualizes power not as a possession or coercive force but as a communication medium that reduces complexity by stabilizing expectations within functionally differentiated systems such as law, politics, or the economy. Command, in this view, is a coded operation internal to each system, allowing decisions to cohere with systemic logic. My framework incorporates this insight, recognizing that command can indeed serve to stabilize cooperation through structured mediation. However, it goes beyond Luhmann by emphasizing that command is also a *dynamic and material site of conflict*, where competing *powers-to* confront one another, and where the filtering, structuring, and operationalization of values are actively contested. In this sense, command is not only a stabilizer of systemic reproduction but also a field of struggle over how value is enacted and reconfigured.

Giorgio Agamben's (1998, 2005) theory of sovereignty focuses on exclusion—the creation of zones of exception in which legal norms are suspended and life is stripped of political recognition. This illuminates how command can render subjects invisible or disposable. However, while Agamben powerfully theorizes exclusion, he tends to underplay how command also structures the *conditions of inclusion*: the terms under which people are integrated into value regimes, recognized, and governed. In reality, inclusion and exclusion are mutually constitutive, as toxic narratives, conditional rights, and differentiated recognition often operate together to shape the terms of belonging. My approach incorporates this dual logic, showing how command configures inclusion not as a given but as a contested and stratified process embedded in the broader force field of value praxis.

Michel Foucault's (1977, 2002, 2008) concepts of discipline and governmentality reveal how power operates through decentralized regulation, bodily normalization, and subject formation. These analyses are indispensable for understanding how command takes institutional and micro-social form. However, they do not fully explain how command reconfigures the hierarchy of value domains. Under neoliberalism, for example, command does not simply produce entrepreneurial subjects but intensifies the dominance of exchange value within social cooperation, subordinating other values—such as care, autonomy, or sustainability. While exchange value was already hegemonic under capitalism, neoliberalism amplifies its reach and naturalizes its priority. My framework extends Foucault by locating command within the dynamic architecture of value praxis, where it not only shapes subjectivities and norms but recalibrates the relational balance of social cooperation itself.

But command as value praxis goes further. It names the contested field through which the structure of cooperation is configured—how relational, use, and exchange values are ordered, prioritized, filtered, or suppressed. It is both symbolic and material, both regulatory and imaginative, and both enabling and coercive. To understand command in this way is to move beyond the administration of power and into the core terrain where the meaning, distribution, and reproduction of value are fought over and restructured.

Cornelius Castoriadis (1987) illuminates command as a symbolic process. Societies, he argues, self-institute through the social imaginary, generating the meanings and norms that ground institutional life. This allows us to understand command not as externally imposed but as socially cocreated and contingent. However, Castoriadis largely foregrounds the symbolic dimension of self-institution, without detailing how these imaginaries are materialized in systems of value allocation and coordination. My framework builds on his insight that societies create their own orders but insists that these orders are not purely symbolic—they are enacted in infrastructures, provisioning systems, institutional architectures, and contested value configurations. Command is not just an imaginary—it is a struggle over how imaginaries become operational.

Taken together, these traditions illuminate essential dimensions of command: its stabilizing role within systemic logics (Luhmann), its sovereign production of exclusions (Agamben), its regulatory and disciplinary functions (Foucault), and its symbolic and institutional creativity (Castoriadis). While Agamben, Foucault, and Castoriadis each presuppose conflict—whether as resistance to power, the ontological violence of exclusion, or the generative tension of self-institution—Luhmann's systems theory largely sidelines conflict, framing command as the coded reproduction of systemic coherence. What remains underdeveloped across these perspectives, however, is a theorization of command as a material and symbolic structuring of value praxis in social cooperation. My framework addresses this by treating command as the contested terrain through which relational, use, and exchange values are filtered, prioritized, and made operational. It is through command that inclusion and exclusion are not only formalized but enacted via access to resources, recognition, and the institutional frameworks and norms that organize cooperation. Hegemonic command does not merely govern—it enforces a dominant logic of value, subordinating alternative orders to its reproduction. To understand command in this light is to recognize it as the shifting ground where imaginaries, institutions, and material relations are both stabilized and struggled over.

In the next chapter, we will see how this contested field of command crystallizes into the mega-structural architecture of the capitalist system: the pyramid of capital—a machinic formation of systemic domination.

Part III

The pyramid of capital and beyond

9

The pyramid of capital

From primitive accumulation . . .

Capitalism is rooted in a long, bloodied history of wealth expropriation, exploitation, war, colonialism, oppression, and genocide. This is not a contingent or unfortunate background but a foundational process in the historical constitution of capitalist society. As Karl Marx reinterpreted against the myths of classical political economy, the origins of capitalism lie in what he called "primitive accumulation"—a term already used by thinkers such as Adam Smith to refer to the buildup of capital through individual saving and thrift. Marx, however, revealed it to be a history of brutal dispossession, exemplified by the English commons' enclosures of the seventeenth to the nineteenth centuries: a violent separation of coproducers from their means of subsistence and social reproduction.

This separation did more than deprive communities of use values such as shared access to land, tools, and resources. It tore through the dense web of relational bonds that had sustained collective life and cooperation. Enforced through draconian laws that criminalized bottom-up attempts to resist destitution—whether through migration, gleaning, or collective land reclamation—this process transformed the social body into a fragmented laboring population, increasingly exposed to the discipline and measurement imposed by capital.

The commons that were enclosed were not idealized spaces of harmony but the outcome of centuries of struggle and resistance within feudal systems of domination. Their destruction marked not only a material dispossession but also a strategic dismantling of alternative modes of life and sources of collective power. Among the strategies used to undermine these communal structures was the persecution of so-called witches—often community healers, midwives, and older women who embodied relational knowledge and social cohesion. The witch hunt thus functioned not only as gendered violence but also as a targeted assault on the relational and reproductive networks that sustained communal life (Federici 2004).

The process of primitive accumulation did not merely destroy these relations; it recomposed them into new forms of dependence. What had been an articulated and complex social body was fragmented and commodified, reshaped into a laboring force increasingly subjected to the discipline of capital. This transformation laid the social and material groundwork for the English Industrial Revolution, which depended on a population dispossessed of its means of reproduction and rendered available for factory labor under conditions of wage dependency and spatial displacement (Thompson 1963; Wood 2017). This new social body could now be governed by the abstract and extractive logic of capital's "measure of things"—a regime of valuation that subordinates life to profit, relations to competition, and need to exchange.

Yet this regime was never passively accepted. From its inception, capital's measure of value—its imposition of quantified time, productivity, and exchange abstraction—met with resistance. As Thompson (1967) shows, the transition to industrial time discipline was fiercely contested, not least through the widespread riots and collective acts of sabotage aimed at the new temporal order marked by the factory clock. These rebellions around the clock were not only protests against labor conditions but refusals of an imposed regime of life measurement that fractured earlier temporalities of communal and seasonal rhythms.

From the enclosure of English commons to the genocide of Indigenous peoples in the Americas and to the transatlantic slave trade that devastated African societies, capitalism emerged as a global system through a violent triangulation of dispossession. These historical vectors were not isolated events but interlinked processes that restructured social cooperation across continents. Alongside them, the gendered separation of production and reproduction and the suppression of alternative knowledges and reproductive forms of power served to discipline bodies, erase collective memory, and impose new regimes of value and labor (Harvey 2003; De Angelis 2007). Each moment of dispossession extended and deepened capital's reach—reordering diverse social formations into a planetary hierarchy governed by its logic.

Rather than a distant origin, primitive accumulation remains an ongoing engine of systemic reproduction, continuously reconfiguring the conditions of life to sustain the hierarchy between capital and social reproduction. It should not be viewed merely as a phase of early capitalism but as a recurring strategic pattern that underpins and propels capitalist expansion—especially in response to crisis, major waves of resistance, or the exhaustion of existing frontiers. Each time, it violently reorganizes social cooperation under conditions favorable to a new round of accumulation (Perelman 2000; De Angelis 2007). Primitive accumulation, in this sense, does not consist of isolated historical events but of phase shifts within the circuits of social cooperation—points of transformation in specific space-times through which both human and nonhuman natures are further integrated into the processes of capitalist valorization. These transformations refunctionalize entire domains of life to sustain and extend capitalist normality.

At its core, primitive accumulation is about reasserting control through dispossession: reordering social cooperation and disciplining bodies, temporalities, and territories into the machinic regime of capitalist value. While the extensive colonization of planetary territories continues—particularly in zones newly opened to resource extraction, infrastructure expansion, or speculative urbanization—other frontiers today are increasingly intensive: social, technological, ecological, and affective. They include the frontiers of care, data, genetic material, time, attention, and subjectivity itself.

. . . to systemic normality

If we look closely, every pore of our daily lives bears the traces of primitive accumulation—traces that shape even how we perceive the world. There would be no sense in living the way we do—trapped in hectic routines, chasing visibility, competing to survive, undermining each other's livelihoods, destroying Gaia, and fomenting war—if not for the systemic architecture that compels us to subordinate life to the priorities of capital. These absurdities are not personal failures but the lived expression of a deeper condition: a material, affective, and libidinal dependence on a system that continues to reorganize social cooperation through dispossession.

At the core of this condition lies a logic of separation—first unleashed by primitive accumulation and then sedimented into the fabric of capitalist normality. This is the separation between needs and the means of existence, and between activity and autonomy. It is also the separation by which the measure of things—what counts as value—is imposed externally rather than enacted collectively among subjects of social cooperation, who are turned into competitors, and between the social body and the body of the Earth. What began as the violent rupture of primitive accumulation has since been routinized and internalized, crystallizing into the everyday imperative to work, economize, and compete.

Ultimately, separation is rooted in the systemic hierarchy of value praxes between the reproduction of capital and that of life. This hierarchy is not abstract. It structures the silent background of hunger, ecological collapse, burnout, displacement, and social fragmentation. It is a regime of valuation that renders some lives exploitable or disposable and others inherently valuable.

Not all suffering can be traced directly to this system—complexity involves contingency. And yet, even resistance can be folded back into the system. Subjects are not passive; they adapt, interpret, internalize, and resist. But when these responses remain individual or their struggles are fragmented, they often end up reproducing the very constraints they contest. What must be examined, then, is not only surface-level adaptation but also the recursive reproduction of the structural logic itself: the ongoing reorganization of life through renewed separations—between knowledge and action, care and value, subsistence and property. Like the original enclosures, today's infrastructures fragment subjectivities and redirect collective energies toward capital's priorities.

This recursive logic is embedded in institutions, norms, and imaginaries. It reproduces what might be called the contemporary order of things: a systemic interface where everyday life unfolds under historically accumulated power relations. Here, social cooperation is not free but channeled through separations that stratify meanings, functions, and lives into hierarchies of value and command. These separations generate a fundamental divide between those structurally aligned with capital reproduction and those oriented toward sustaining life. But this divide is often fuzzy. It runs not just between groups but within them and through institutions, households, and even individual subjectivities. Ambivalence is not only a feature of subjectivity but also pervades, in different degrees, the social field.

In this framework, class is not simply a sociological category like income or occupation. It is a contradiction embedded in daily practices, decisions, and constraints. It is a tension internal to the very organization of social cooperation. Class is better understood as an emergent social ecosystem—structured by the frontline between two opposing logics of reproduction. This frontline is not a single battlefield but a fractal terrain, threaded through workplaces, homes, infrastructures, and bodies. It surfaces in open conflict—strikes, revolts—but also in the micro-decisions of daily life: how we spend time, care, consume, or rest. As argued in Chapter 3, social classes are best seen as antagonistic autopoietic forces—living systems pulling in opposing directions over what is valuable and how life should be organized. What appears as neutral normality is actually sustained by this unresolved conflict. Class struggle is not an exception—it is the very condition of the system.

It is within this plane of systemic normality—where individual lives intersect with institutional structures—that countless micro-conflicts unfold: negotiations over value, recognition, time, and survival. These are not mere disruptions; they contain the potential for recomposition and expansion, for connecting across differences and scales in ways that may challenge the very foundations of the system. If the threat of enclosures—broadly defined—is the sword of Damocles hanging over every collective struggle, then the capacity for revolt, refusal, and the constitution of other orders of life is the immanent presence of a dragon that may yet awaken—a reminder to those in power that their world and privilege rest on fragile and contested ground.

To understand how this contested normality is reproduced despite crisis and resistance, we must now turn to the systemic architecture that organizes social cooperation itself. I locate this in the autopoietic organization of the contemporary capitalist macro-system, structured across distinct levels of value praxis and oriented toward specific systemic ends. This is the pyramid in which all subjectivities engaged in social cooperation—whether exploited, complicit, resisting, or hopeful—are caught and constrained. Even the most virtuous horizontal networks and the most desiring subjectivities for another world are not outside it but within its recursive logics.

In this task, I draw inspiration from Romano Alquati's so-called *Modellone*, which offers a useful entry point into the complex structure of contemporary capitalism, allowing us to grasp its relational and systemic command structures. Engaging with Alquati's *Modellone* is no easy feat.[1] First, because it is a research hypothesis in continual becoming—not a stable endpoint or a fixed conclusion. In this sense, the *Modellone* is not intended to "explain" capitalist command, which can only be explained historically. Rather, it allows us to organize a shared path of reflection and antagonistic research—what Romano Alquati called *co-research* (*conricerca*). This is a collective reflection and inquiry that problematizes the structural organization of contemporary capitalism.

But this problematization of structure is not an end in itself; it is not simply meant to reveal an external, objective reality. Its aim is to frame the autopoietic dynamics that preserve and reproduce capital's dominance, in relation to the development of counter- and alter-subjectivities that—across different domains and scales—seek to impose limits on it and to constitute a *common* as the basis for a mode of production or a mode of social cooperation that is fundamentally different—different, that is, from the command of capital's reproduction over that of society.

It is this recursive organization of separation—across time, scale, and domain—that constitutes the architecture of systemic normality. The pyramid of capital is nothing other than the materialization of this logic: a hierarchy of separations that interlock and seek to stabilize capital's command over social cooperation. It is precisely in this spirit that I draw inspiration from Alquati's *Modellone*, without claiming to offer a complete or faithful description of it, or a full exegesis of his thought—which, given the volume and fragmentary nature of his work, would require a far greater undertaking. There are two main reasons for my interest in Alquati's *Modellone*. First, because it was developed with the intention of problematizing contemporary capitalism in order to identify potential paths for its overcoming. Second, because it is perhaps the only attempt I know of—by a Marxist from the Italian *operaismo* tradition—to engage with theoretical tools from systems theory and complexity science (including the works of Maturana and Varela), avoiding reductionism and functionalism, in order to grasp the mechanisms of capital's command over the world at a time (the 1980s) when those mechanisms were being reconfigured in a neoliberal direction.

Today, in the midst of capitalism's systemic crises, the impasse of neoliberalism, and the rise of a new authoritarian configuration of command that deepens, rather than overturns, the neoliberal project, it is worth revisiting this analysis—following Alquati's intuition as a point of departure.

The pyramid and capitalism as a macro-system

Let us begin with Alquati's general concept of capitalism—an intuition I will take as a point of departure before integrating it into my own analysis of value praxis and its various dimensions. Capitalism, and even more so contemporary capitalism, is a stratified and hierarchical complex social macro-system. Its complexity arises first and foremost from the enormous number of elements—material and immaterial, human, nonhuman, and artificial—that compose it, and from the countless relationships these elements weave among themselves. There are also countless vantage points from which to describe such a complex pyramid. But it is precisely this systemic complexity that contributes to obscuring the structure of command over the segmented bodies of the multitudes that function as nodes within this meta-systemic web in the everyday life of things—through which the rationalities and goals of capital are enacted and onto which capital externalizes its costs.

This opacity—this pervasiveness of capitalist command—combined with the material necessity of survival for the various subjects within it, contributes to its normalization, making the sense of being trapped within binding systemic circuits all the more tangible. Alquati (1989: 47) writes:

> A system is said to be complex when, by placing ourselves within one of its parts or subsystems, we are unable to see or observe the interdependence between all the other parts—or even the mere existence of those other parts. This latter condition is thus an even stronger one. In a hierarchical system such as ours, it also depends on the level of reality one looks at, and from which one is looking, and with which theoretical tools.

It is precisely this *systemic opacity*—the performative effect of a complex hierarchy in which each level masks the dynamics of other levels—that the model of the capital pyramid seeks to confront.

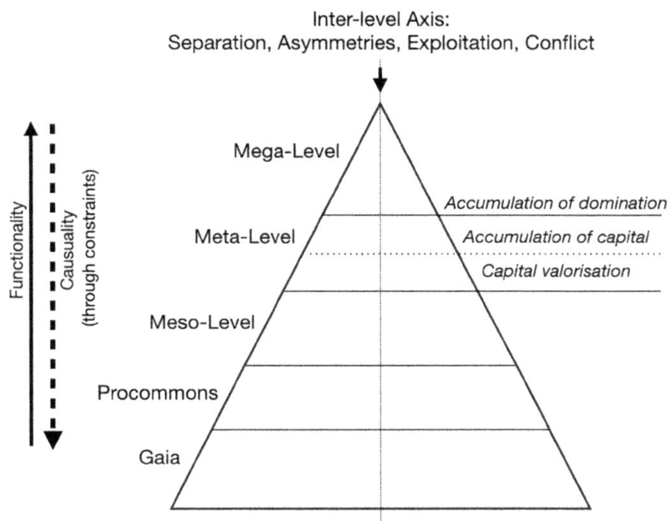

Figure 9.1 The capitalist macro-system

Source: My elaboration building on Pentenero (2018).

The stratification here can be represented as a pyramid of hierarchical levels. But this pyramid does not resemble the textbook representations of ancient social hierarchies—such as those of Ancient Egypt, with pharaohs at the top, slaves at the bottom, and scribes and priests in between. Nor is it like those found in socialist iconography, showing a succession of layers (bourgeoisie, military, clergy, petty bourgeoisie, etc.) supported by the proletariat at the base. Not that such representations of class stratification based on wealth, privilege, and flows of command and control are irrelevant today—in a general sense, they are, in fact, still very much valid. However, it is crucial to keep in mind that such stratifications are embedded in and reproduced at every level of the pyramid described here.

The Modellone developed by Alquati—on which I draw and which I represent in Figure 9.1—is not a simple succession of social classes. Rather, class formations are transversal within a succession of systemic levels (which, in my terms, correspond to different domains of social and value praxis). Their articulation continuously reconfigures the large antagonistic "macro-parts" traditionally named the bourgeoisie and the proletariat. I interpret these as the bearers (actual or potential) of the macro-forces we identified earlier: those oriented toward the reproduction of capital and those oriented toward social reproduction.

Each level is a domain of value praxis—that is, a configuration of practices, norms, and relations within a teleological horizon or a domain of ends. What distinguishes these levels is the dominance of different value registers within which the signification processes of praxis are reproduced. Each level has two axes. Taken horizontally, these systemic levels correspond to spheres tangibly lived by the subjects of social reality. Taken vertically, they compose the complexity of social cooperation under capitalist hegemony.

The order among these systemic levels is hierarchical, meaning that higher levels generally "cause" lower ones in the sense that they set the constraints under which the latter operate, while lower levels functionally serve the goals of higher ones. This resonates with insights from systems theory and enactivism, in which constraint does not eliminate autonomy but channels and shapes it. As in autopoietic systems, the freedom of components is conditioned by the boundary conditions of the whole. First, it enables command to be exercised through the illusion of freedom—such as the consumer's "freedom" of choice within a budget constraint shaped by structural conditions, or the "freedom" to decompress from the burnout of overworked urban life by rushing into overcrowded, overpriced tourist resorts. There, one trades office deadlines for airport queues and stress relief for curated consumption—before returning, sun-scorched and financially lighter, to the same exhausting routines that made the escape feel necessary in the first place. Second, it allows the lower levels a certain degree of autonomy—within limits imposed by higher levels—thus enabling the system as a whole to capture the social productivity generated at each level in a specific form, while masquerading as an organization of individual freedom.

We must therefore understand how constraints operate not as obliterations of autonomy but as ways to direct it. Consider, for example, the constraints that capital imposes on nonhuman nature. Every act of environmental destruction—deforestation or extraction—does not eliminate Gaia's autopoiesis but disrupts the elements and relationships within specific ecosystems. Gaia continues its self-organizing process but under disrupted conditions that increasingly undermine the symbiosis necessary for human and multispecies flourishing. Capital does not halt autopoiesis—it captures and redirects it, externalizing costs while deepening dependency. In the same way, the privatization of public services, the dismantling of welfare, or episodes of primitive accumulation do not eliminate the reproductive autopoiesis of human subjects. They simply reorient it in ways more compatible with capital.

Although the capital pyramid is presented here as a synchronic organization of command over social cooperation, this macro-system is not static. It is constantly evolving, driven by turbulences that unfold within each level, between levels, and across scales. I cannot study this dynamic in detail here, apart from occasional references, but it is important to note that such turbulences express shifting force fields generated by the often conflicting interaction of social forces that pursue different "measures of things" across all levels and scales of social cooperation.

Class struggle, in all its forms and intersections with other struggles, is not only the originating constitutive interaction of the macro-system but also the dynamic to which it must continually adapt in order to reproduce itself as a capitalist macro-system in each historical phase. *From the standpoint of capitalist valorization, any social struggle*—whether over wages, labor, welfare, women's rights, environmental justice, migration, or the rights and recognition of gender and sexual minorities—*that increases the cost of social reproduction appears as a class struggle*. In order to reduce this cost, capital selects which segments of the social body will bear the burden of capitalist valorization.

Put simply: more demands for social rights? Then lower wages. Higher wages for the lowest strata? Then fewer rights. If a historical phase sees a recomposition of traditional class struggles (around wages, labor conditions, and welfare) with struggles for rights (by students, women, minorities, and gender-nonconforming subjects), the macro-system reacts with a regulatory shift. The move from Keynesianism to neoliberalism in the late 1970s, for instance, came not just as a response to economic crisis but as a way to channel and reabsorb the explosion of freedoms and aspirations that had emerged in the preceding decades. The expansion of social and individual rights was met with the advancement of market logic, aiming to integrate those freedoms into circuits of capitalist valorization. Today, in a different key, the climate emergency threatens to catalyze a new recomposition of the social body around demands for survival and solidarity—while, at the same time, we witness an authoritarian backlash. From Trump's America to illiberal shifts in Europe, this socially conservative turn increasingly attacks the very rights once co-opted by neoliberalism, exposing the fragility of freedoms when they cease to serve capital.

One of Alquati's (1989: 6) hypotheses is that the macro-system "tends to simplify itself, to compress and integrate further: in the sense of reducing—until they disappear over time—differences in scope and level, thereby collapsing many phenomena and variables that still appear distinct today." This aligns largely with the pervasive expansion of capitalist rationality and materiality into all aspects of life, human activity, and subjectivation. The collapse of distinct levels, which Alquati foresaw in the 1980s, has certainly intensified over the past forty years. However, in my view, it has not eliminated "differences of scope and level"; rather, it has functionally blurred them—compressing distinctions without abolishing the hierarchy of command and value. Alquati's pyramid can thus be understood as a structure akin to those collapsible, telescopic travel cups—compressing without eliminating the substance they are made of.

While internal and external forces (nonhuman nature) push the macro-system toward continuous evolution, it also pursues a horizon: its own self-preservation as a capitalist macro-system. Following Alquati, we call this "macro-systemic accumulation"—the forward movement, growth, and qualitative transformation of the macro-system as a whole. Macro-systemic accumulation is thus "expanded reproduction of the neo-macro-social-system" (Alquati 1989: 7), the increase of a system of social relations, always marked by specific asymmetries, and therefore increasingly shaped by separation and exploitation.

Accumulation, then, is not just the accumulation of capital value in the conventional sense but the accumulation of specific and asymmetric social relations—relations of domination and struggle (see also Cleaver 2000). The macro-system is traversed by contradictions that manifest differently at each level. These contradictions are not only logical but real: "some of the fundamental constitutive moments of the capitalist macro-system tend to be incompatible with others—not only in specific periods" (Alquati 1989: 24).

These contradictions are often the result of separation turning back on itself—between production and reproduction, economy and ecology, and growth and well-being. The logic of separation, once systematized, generates tensions that cascade across domains. Among these contradictions are environmental destruction versus economic growth; economic growth versus polarized wealth; increased labor productivity versus worsening living and working conditions; intensified labor demands; migration flows and their criminalized management; the tension between the reproduction of capital and social reproduction; and the promotion of an ideology of freedom alongside conditions of social cooperation based on scarcity, work compulsion, and adherence to the capitalist measure of things.

Capitalism, however, is not dissuaded by contradiction. Rather, it turns contradictions into motors of adaptation. On the one hand, through its ideological self-understanding (its policies, rationalities, and blind spots), it displaces systemic responsibility and individualizes the causes of contradiction, blaming individuals for low wages, poor working conditions, environmental collapse, and poverty. On the other hand, it turns this ideological representation into the foundation for constructing models to address the contradictions—without abandoning its central goal: the preservation of itself, its fundamental structure, and its privileges through accumulation and therefore specific social relations based on alienation and exploitation. One contemporary example is the "green deal"—an attempt to address the climate crisis not by confronting the core contradiction between endless growth and ecological destruction through transformative, care-based, and sustainable imaginaries but by doubling down on technological innovation. These technologies, while improving energy efficiency, fail to reduce overall energy consumption, emissions, or extractivism when deployed within a growth-driven paradigm. The meta-goal of accumulation remains unchanged, as does the reproduction of capital, while sub-goals are reoriented toward so-called green technologies—whose production, in accordance with expanded accumulation, entails further ecological destruction. Even these limited measures face mounting resistance—from fossil fuel lobbies, nationalist governments, and austerity-driven elites intent on preserving short-term profitability.

The role of contradiction within capitalism is thus central. It runs through the entire pyramid, but it is at the highest level—the level of domination—where, once contradiction reaches a critical threshold capable of generating the perception, desire, and practice of systemic alternatives, it becomes a potential motor of further development—whether through quantitative accumulation (growth) or qualitative transformation (the expansion of capitalist relations).

As Alquati (1989: 24) puts it:

> This means nothing less than that in this system, the presence of contradictions is not only frequent; in a certain sense, the system is founded on contradiction: real contradiction ends up functioning as the very motor of the (Neo)Macro-system.

Here emerges the macro-function of the collective capitalist, which we will encounter at the highest level of the macro-systemic pyramid (Chapter 14). In acute moments of contradiction such as ours—especially following the 2007 crisis, ecological catastrophe, and war regime—the collective capitalist seeks to formulate strategies to defuse contradictions, reorganize them spatially, and project them forward.

Importantly, this collective capitalist should not be merely understood as a unified boardroom of decision-makers but rather as a dispersed system of command. It is a structurally emergent formation whose main function is to manage the recursive organization of separation—maintaining hierarchy while adapting to resistance, turbulence, and crisis. Even war operates as a mechanism through which capital reorganizes its reproduction and sustains its dominance. Yet it never abandons the system's macro-finality: the maintenance of domination through accumulation.

What we need to trace now is how this architecture of constraint and separation translates into distinct regimes of value praxis—layered within the pyramid but always in motion. What follows is a conceptual and analytical journey through the macro-systemic pyramid of capital—a layered model that reveals how different levels of social reality are structured, connected, and governed. We begin by situating this pyramid as a meta-context that shapes and perturbs local contexts and subjectivities. We then explore how value is produced across its levels through distinct yet interrelated domains—relational, use, exchange, and command. Finally, we ascend the pyramid level by level—and we will do this more fully in the next five chapters—tracing how each domain configures value praxis, mediates power, and reproduces the social order.

Context and meta-context

The pyramid of capital is composed of levels, but in its totality it functions, in a certain sense, as the *meta-context* to which all subjects—operating within different specific contexts (geographical, social, cultural, etc.)—are in some way connected. In other words, it is not a backdrop but an active, recursive system; it constrains, perturbs, and reorganizes local contexts through the stratified logic of value, command, and separation. While we live in particular locations, institutions, and relations, we do so within a system that defines the possible forms, meanings, and constraints those contexts can take. It is a context that exceeds the particular contexts in which we act, while at the same time influencing and perturbing those specific contexts and, thus, the actions of the subjects within them, as well as their material constraints, subjectivities, imaginaries, and rationalities.

For example, I can host a Zoom call with dozens of people from disparate locations around the world, each embedded in distinct societies and cultures, yet we are all able to grasp, even if differently and unevenly, the meaning of "capitalism" as a structural force that traverses our different contexts—shaping markets, values, infrastructures, and institutions—while also allowing for locally specific articulations. This scalar interplay between the global and the local, the abstract and the situated, also characterizes how the levels of the pyramid operate. For instance, the level of Gaia—the totality of the operations of nonhuman nature—is the meta-context of this or that particular ecological sphere in which I live and relate on a daily basis. The level of the procommons is the meta-context for any given domain of direct social relations. The meso-level—where many institutions, infrastructures, and services are organized—is the meta-context for the production and coordination of particular use values within society. The meta-level of capitalist valorization serves as the meta-context within which individual capitals operate—shaped by regulatory norms, financial flows, and technological paradigms that set the conditions of competition or collusion. The level of command is the meta-context within which different centers of command—whether geopolitical, geoeconomic, or geocultural—interact, collude, or clash in shaping the strategic direction of the macro-system, mobilizing tools ranging from military power and financial instruments to narrative control and planetary-scale governance.

Value production across the levels of the pyramid

The pyramid is a map constructed to represent social cooperation—our doing and acting in common—under capitalist hegemony. It is, therefore, a map of how value is produced in a general, complex sense. Each level constitutes a distinct systemic domain of praxis (i.e., a relation between part and whole) and value production. At each level, the part–whole relation is structured differently, according to the range of registers within that value domain. In the procommons, the whole is a web of direct relations; at the meso-level, a field of utility; at the meta-level, a circuit of exchange; and at the command level, a system of hierarchical control. These different configurations not only produce different types of value—they organize the very intelligibility of what counts as value. There are two exceptions to this. The bottom level of Gaia does not produce value in any sense—not even relational or use value—because its internal processes are not shaped by human praxis. Rather, Gaia provides the material, energetic, and ecological preconditions for all human activity and value production. It is the ground, not a level of social praxis. In relation to these different levels, the procommons, the meso-level, and the meta-level each translate this condition into specific processes of social valorization: the procommons through relational value, the meso-level through use value, and the meta-level through exchange value and capitalist valorization. This means that, at each specific level, the "measure of things" within social cooperation is oriented by a particular dimension of value praxis, which defines its dominant registers. At the top of the pyramid, the level of command also does not produce value per se but instead operates as a meta-level of ordering—it disposes and ranks values across all other levels, imposing the reproduction of a hierarchy that determines which forms of value are recognized, prioritized, and legitimized within social cooperation. Like Gaia, command constitutes a limit condition—but one of control rather than support. It orchestrates the structural asymmetry among value registers, reproducing separation between forms of cooperation while subordinating them to the telos of accumulation.

The whole with which we relate at every moment of our doing is stratified into such levels—systemic domains—each with its own prevailing logic of value production and meaning attribution. While these domains interact with and influence one another—both in our cognition and in the systems we enact—each level combines a configuration of subjectivity and totality across a spectrum of value registers.

To illustrate, imagine that I prepare dinner for my guests. The dishes I cook are use values—for me and for those I host. Their production involves sequences of action shaped by specific selections: the recipes I follow, the ingredients I choose, the money I spend, and the embodied labor I expend. These operations are embedded in concrete bodily activity, interwoven with emotional and affective states, memory, and practical judgments about value. This process takes place largely within what I call the meso-level of praxis—the domain where use values are produced and circulated according to socially embedded forms of utility. Yet the dinner does not serve merely to satisfy physiologically induced hunger. Not only are its preparation and final consumption embedded within specific cultures, but its ultimate function may also be to create a space for conviviality, shared time, and relational resonance. This dimension shifts the center of gravity to another level: the procommons, where value is configured primarily through the registers of relationality. Crucially, these levels are not separate—they are entangled. The anticipation of conviviality affects how I measure ingredients or time; the desire to nourish a relationship shapes the use-value choices I make, just as the pressure of time scarcity or rising food prices may limit the ingredients I can buy. This intertwining reveals how relational, use, and exchange values do not merely coexist—they constrain and reconfigure one another. What appears as an act of personal care is cut across by broader systemic structures.

At the same time, my capacity to prepare this dinner is also mediated by a different, often more dominant level: the meta-level of capitalist valorization. Here, my time, energy, and access to ingredients are filtered through the constraints imposed by wage labor, commodity prices, and the demands of exchange value. This level does not simply coexist with the others—it conditions them. It shapes what I can afford, how much time I can dedicate, and how I relate to the use values I produce and share. Moreover, the level of command may have influenced my preparation indirectly through regulations, geopolitical supply chain disruptions, or austerity policies that reduced public infrastructure, limited food availability, or intensified my time poverty—forcing me to adapt my dinner to what is realistically feasible within a constrained social environment. In short, the entire multidimensional and complex machinery of the world—from planetary ecologies and social bonds to market forces and geopolitical command structures—has converged, together with my labor, to produce *this* dinner, on *this* table, in *this* moment.

In this sense, each level presents itself as a horizon of systemic totality for the subject: a structured field in which practices are embedded, constrained, and made meaningful. This means that the meaning of a gesture or decision shifts depending on the dominant value framework in play. A shared meal can appear as relational care, nutritional provision, or consumption—a single action refracted through multiple systemic lenses. Every act of value production is tied to specific ends, but these ends are shaped by the meta-purposes of each domain or level. That is, each level embeds registers of value that frames how meaning is given to action. At the level of the procommons, value is framed in terms of relationality; at the meso-level, in terms of usefulness; at the meta-level, in terms of exchange and profit; and at the level of command, in terms of the autopoietic self-preservation of the capitalist system itself. In short, the value we collectively produce through social cooperation is a composite of these domains, and each domain defines a field of "frequencies" through which our actions resonate socially. To act within social cooperation is to navigate, shape, and be shaped by these overlapping and often conflicting regimes of value.

Domination, then, is not merely an external imposition but a systemic hierarchy among these domains and their corresponding praxes—a hierarchy that determines which forms of value dominate and which are subordinated. This hierarchy is reproduced not only through institutional structures but also within our own imaginative and affective bodies. We enact it daily—sometimes resisting, often complying, and frequently oscillating between registers belonging to different domains, the contradictions of which we embody. We experience its effects in our labor, emotions, and relationships—with Gaia, with others, with institutions, and with digital platforms. This is not simply an abstract framework—it is the texture of our lives under capital. It is the condition under which we organize our daily circuits, decisions, and dreams. It is a common condition, a mega-corrupted common—capitalism as a hegemonic form of social cooperation with a mixed constitution, in which relational, useful, and reproductive values are subordinated to the commanding telos of accumulation.

These level-specific registers give rise to a range of relations, norms, processes, and, above all, teleologies that impose restrictions or prohibitions on certain behaviors, objects, people, or topics while favoring others. Each level, therefore, is the theater of a spectrum of social selection. These selections function as boundary conditions: what is visible, sayable, or doable in one domain is taboo in another. This hierarchy of constraints regulates the distribution of legitimacy across practices, bodies, and desires. Acting as socially produced taboos, these restrictions are considered sacred, inviolable, or socially unacceptable at a given level—even if they become central or normative at another. The limits socially imposed in one domain are often reconfigured—or even nullified—and replaced by other limits in another. Since social being is constituted at the intersection of these various levels, this often results in deep incongruities.

For instance, it may be socially unacceptable at the level of the procommons or the meso-level of use value, in a particular context, to throw garbage on the street or to dispose of paper, plastic, and glass in bins other than those designated for recycling. Yet ecological destruction is the norm at the level of capitalist valorization. This is evident in the fact that since the United Nations Framework Convention on Climate Change in 1992—that is, the official recognition by world governments of the problem and their formal commitment to address it—global carbon dioxide emissions have increased by more than 60 percent. This rise in emissions has been accompanied by a significant intensification of extreme weather events. For instance, in 2024 alone, over 150 unprecedented climate disasters were recorded, including severe heatwaves, floods, and storms, resulting in massive destruction and displacement (Carrington 2025). Compounding this issue, the Trump administration has initiated extensive rollbacks of environmental regulations, including plans to dismantle thirty-one key pollution rules projected to save nearly 200,000 lives, thereby undermining efforts to mitigate climate change and protect public health (Milman and Noor 2025). Meanwhile, in Europe, even the pretense of greenwashing is being sidelined, as governments intensify militarization and shift political priorities away from climate policy and ecological transition.

Similarly, while violent behavior may be socially unacceptable within the procommons, and while at the level of use value the state and its laws are often regarded as the ultimate arbiters of conflict, at the mega-level of command the violence of war and genocide is actively mobilized as a strategic instrument of realpolitik—deployed in defiance of UN resolutions and international law—to consolidate or expand particular forms of power. This level is often coupled with the energy mobilized by corrupted forms of the procommons—collective identitarian formations organized for exclusion rather than solidarity—such as those rooted in the Israeli settler movement and the extreme right. These formations do not simply defend their own; they justify domination by dehumanizing the other. As recently reported, for example, Likud MK Nissim Vaturi stated that "every Palestinian man is a terrorist and should be killed. They are not human. They are not even animals. They are subhuman" (The New Arab Staff 2025). Such language, which is not an isolated case, fuels and legitimizes policies of dispossession and extermination as expressions of communal survival set against the communal survival of the stigmatized "other."

These geopolitical examples reveal how the pyramid's upper levels—command and meta—can override or suppress the values of the lower ones. The violence exercised in contexts like Gaza is not only physical but systemic: It reflects a hierarchy of value that renders some lives disposable, some destructions permissible, and some solidarities criminal. This asymmetry between a common sense rooted in relational care and that driven by geopolitical domination is brutally evident in the case of Palestine—where the fate of the Palestinian people and the world's response to it lay bare the split between registers of value. Since October 2023, Israel has dropped more than 70,000 tons of bombs on the Gaza Strip, surpassing the combined tonnage dropped on Hiroshima, Nagasaki, and Dresden during the Second World War (EuroMed 2024; Youvan 2024). This relentless bombardment has devastated Gaza's infrastructure, destroying schools, hospitals, and refugee camps. A recent study published in *The Lancet* (Jamaluddine et al. 2025) estimated that between October 7, 2023 and June 30, 2024, approximately 64,260 people died from traumatic injuries alone—a figure suggesting that the Palestinian Ministry of Health underreported mortality by around 41 percent. Of those deaths, women, children (under 18), and older adults (aged 65 and over) accounted for 16,699 or 59.1 percent. Notably, this estimate does not include noninjury excess mortality such as deaths resulting from a lack of access to medical care, clean water, or essential supplies. Concurrently, a total siege has been imposed, cutting off essential supplies such as food, water, fuel, and medicine, and leading to catastrophic humanitarian conditions in which clean water is unavailable to most residents. Also, in the first three months of 2025, Israeli military raids and escalating settler violence in the occupied West Bank have displaced around 40,000 Palestinians and devastated infrastructure, reflecting an intensification of Israel's settlement expansion strategy. At the same time, governments worldwide, led by the United States under President Trump, have sought to criminalize protests—dimensions of the procommons manifested in movements aiming to pressure governments into action. In the United States, the administration has implemented measures targeting pro-Palestinian activists. Universities have faced pressure to suppress pro-Palestinian demonstrations, with institutions such as Columbia University conceding to federal demands to restrict such activities in exchange for funding. Internationally, several European governments have imposed restrictions or outright bans on pro-Palestinian demonstrations, citing concerns over public order. Yet despite repression, protests have multiplied across continents, from student encampments to port blockades and generalized strikes, showing that the demos—life overflowing—cannot be easily contained (De Angelis 2025b). These actions represent a concerted effort to stifle dissent and curtail expressions of the procommons that challenge prevailing geopolitical agendas. The entanglement and asymmetry among value registers are not simply theoretical—it is the daily battlefield of meaning, survival, and resistance. To navigate this terrain is to engage in a struggle over the very measure of things.

Levels

While the next five chapters address each level in detail, what follows is a brief synthetic overview of the macro-systemic pyramid of capital (represented here in Figure 9.1). I will climb from the lower levels upward, sketching their interconnections and reconstructing the whole. In this exercise, I will follow Alquati only in terms of the general schema and key insights and in some of his reflections—those that I find most clear and incisive within his work, especially considering the fragmentary nature of the available material on his *Modellone*. Along the way, I will interweave my own investigation with additional insights and arguments.

To make sense of this ascent through the pyramid's levels, it is important to remember that each level of the capital pyramid is immanent in our everyday reality. These levels do not float above social reality—they are embedded in it. The pyramid is not a distant schema but the layered architecture through which we live, move, and make meaning. *Gaia* is the complex system that reproduces the air I breathe, the fragment of nature that I metabolize through my social and biological functions, and that constitutes the body I am made of. The *procommons* are the dimensions of my many forms of relationality—with the world and with myself—in their various temporalities and spatialities. The *meso-level* consists of the material and immaterial use values I draw utility from in each moment of daily life, as well as the concrete labor required to produce them, whether it is my work or that of the immense multitude of cooperators I am connected with (even if I ignore the form of such a connection). The *meta-level* is the social machine propelled toward accumulation and extraction, a machine that seeks to govern my life rhythms and access to social wealth, that enforces its measure of things in the bodies of cooperating subjects, in the circuits and systems of the social body, and in the body of the earth. *Command* is the form of ordering among these different levels. What varies across the contexts in which we operate is the ordering between these levels. And so, what appears as my singular navigation through space, rhythm, and constraint is, in fact, a journey through entangled levels—each one present in the background of every action, shaping what can be done, imagined, or refused. Each level of the pyramid embeds a specific configuration of value domains—relational, use, exchange, and command—articulated through particular institutional, normative, and practical arrangements. These configurations are not static. They are shaped both by the global ordering logic imposed by the pyramid as a whole and by the resistances and struggles that emerge from within each level. Thus, the hierarchical order of value that appears to flow from the top downward is, in fact, continually contested from below—reconfigured through everyday practices, refusals, and counter-organization. In this sense, the pyramid is not simply a structure but a dynamic field of tension, where the imposition of value orders is constantly negotiated, destabilized, and, at times, transformed. The pyramid of capital should not be understood as a rigid ontological hierarchy *out there*, nor merely as an abstract analytical framework. Rather, each of its levels exists *immanently* within the totality of social cooperation, in every moment of it. These "domains" are not separated but stratified, interacting layers that co-constitute every moment of social life. This means that in the praxis within any coalescence, institution, system, or circuit—whether a community, a school, a hospital, a household, a digital platform, or a factory—each level is present, albeit with different degrees of salience or dominance. What varies is the *weight* or *grade* of each level in the composition of practices, norms, and value praxes that define the system in question. The pyramid, therefore, underlines the specific dominance over social cooperation as a whole—the capitalist form of dominance that defines our current condition.

Likewise, at the level of individual enactment, subjects navigate these strata continuously: They breathe Gaia, engage in relational vernacularity (procommons), produce and consume use values, enter markets of exchange and face the measure of capital, and are positioned within systems of command. We do this, of course, in different degrees (we even breathe differently!) in different social and institutional contexts, largely depending on the salience, configuration, and ranking of the different levels in those contexts—the specific worlds we are enacting and bringing forth. But these levels do not alternate sequentially; rather, they overlap and co-inform each action, each relationship, and each social configuration. What alternates sequentially is our embeddedness—through our daily life—in coalescences, institutions, circuits, or systems, whose practices are characterized by different rankings among these levels and involve different weightings or gradations of each level. The pyramid is therefore not only a model of systemic structure—it is a map of the multidimensional space within which social cooperation and subjectivity unfold. To say that the levels of the pyramid are immanent is not to say they are always equally perceptible. Their presence is not uniform but contingent—surfacing with varying clarity depending on how we move, relate, and enact our being in the world. Each level operates like a layer of resonance in the collective field of social cooperation. We pass through the registers of these domains daily, but only sometimes do we attune ourselves to their specific frequencies. To be *attuned* is to reach the bandwidth at which a particular logic begins to resonate within us—to feel the pull of relational care, the rhythm of the useful, the hum of commodification, or the pulse of command. This is not the posture of a detached observer but of a subject already implicated—whose attention, care, or resistance modulates the rhythms of value that structure daily life. Like tuning an instrument, attunement is not automatic; it requires orientation, listening, and adjustment. It is a way of sensing the mode in which value is being produced and mediated in a given encounter. Sometimes we are immersed in the warmth of proximity; other times, we are struck by the cold abstraction of metrics. These shifts in resonance express the deeper systemic grammar of separation—between life and capital, reproduction and accumulation—that the pyramid enacts not abstractly but through embodied constraints. But in each case, the level becomes experientially real not because it is imposed from above but because we meet it—whether in friction or in flow—with the sensibilities it calls forth. In this sense, the levels of the pyramid are not simply analytic strata—they are experiential territories that become visible through practices of attunement and dissonance. To live critically and collectively is to develop a capacity for this tuning: to discern where we are, what forces shape our actions, and how we might change the song.

In the chapters that follow, each level will be unpacked not simply as a domain of function but as a site of struggle over meaning, value, and the future of social cooperation itself.

10

The level of Gaia

Foundation and horizon

Gaia's level

The lowest level—the base of the systemic pyramid of capital—is not itself a level of social cooperation but its ultimate precondition. It is the domain of ecosystemic processes: the reproduction of life at all scales, including plant and animal life; the transformations of water; the turbulence and rhythms of the atmosphere; and the countless biochemical interactions that sustain the biosphere. Every action carried out at higher levels of social cooperation is conditioned by and interacts with this level and, in doing so, perturbs it. The concept of *social metabolism* names this interface—the ongoing material and energetic exchange between human societies and this deeper substrate of nonhuman life (see Figure 2.1).

This level refers to the nonhuman nature with which social cooperation enters into entangled and transformative relations. Strictly speaking, it is not yet Gaia, for Gaia includes humans. And yet I refer to this level as Gaia to highlight the relative autonomy of these living processes: their capacity to operate beyond and despite human disturbance, their irreducibility to human ends, and their foundational role in making life, including social life, possible.

This ambiguity is intentional. While, at the base of the pyramid, Gaia may appear as the "lowest" level—the passive substrate of exploitation and disturbance—seen from another perspective, Gaia is the *entire edifice*: the full ecological totality within which all levels of social cooperation unfold. Gaia is not merely the ground of our systems—it is the living, dynamic condition that includes and exceeds them. It is the outside of our bodies that is also inside, the common matrix of existence—resisting full capture by any social formation, including capital. This conceptual shift—from viewing Gaia as the lowest layer to recognizing it as the all-encompassing system—will reemerge in the final chapter, when the pyramid is reoriented from the top down, and Gaia appears not merely as a base but as the meta-systemic field within which all levels of social cooperation are embedded and conditioned. Then Gaia will no longer be a forgotten foundation but the breath that holds the entire edifice of social cooperation in suspension—whether in its pyramidal or any other geometric form—the great living field within which every level of cooperation stirs, collides, and dreams.

This lowest level is not a domain of value production in the strict sense. It does not operate through social cooperation, nor is it governed by human ends. Rather, it is the condition of possibility for any such cooperation: the substrate of biogeochemical cycles, trophic chains, symbiotic interdependencies, and geophysical flows that render the planet habitable. These processes do not answer to human measure, yet human systems increasingly exert pressure on them—extracting, dumping, and disrupting—often with cascading and irreversible effects.

And yet, these processes are not inert or passive. They are self-organizing, adaptive, and relational. They make up what can be described as the autopoiesis of the Earth system—the generative movements of life that exceed and precede the human. This autonomy of Gaia is not a metaphysical claim but a reminder of limits—limits that are ecological, thermodynamic, and ultimately civilizational.

This dual positioning—Gaia as both the enabling base and the encompassing whole—creates a productive ambiguity that is central to this framework. To place Gaia at the base of the pyramid is to treat it as a domain external to value praxis: an "out there" that enables but does not itself participate in social cooperation. This is the first-order stance I adopt here—not because it is the only perspective but because it aligns with the structure of value as enacted in human domains. It allows us to map how social cooperation is stratified, organized, and governed through dominant hierarchies of meaning and purpose.

This stance, however, should not be mistaken for a claim of epistemic finality. *Rather than attempting to universalize this analytic framework of human value praxis*, I offer it in a spirit of porousness—open to being affected and reshaped by other cosmologies and practices. In many Indigenous and relational worldviews, Gaia—or the beings within it—is not merely the substrate of life but a participant in it: an agent, a relative, and a co-subject. Meaning arises not only from human valuation but from reciprocal, interspecies enactments shaped by ritual, kinship, and care. These worldviews challenge the very boundaries upon which dominant value systems rest: between subject and object, self and world, life and meaning.[1]

In contrast, many modern frameworks—such as environmental economics and ecosystem services—attempt to assign Gaia a form of "value" by translating its processes (pollination, carbon capture, biodiversity) into monetizable metrics. But in this framework, such efforts do not constitute value production. They represent not an emergence of meaning from Gaia but the *projection of exchange logic* onto a domain that remains outside human social cooperation. These frameworks ultimately reinforce the reduction of Gaia to capital-compatible function, without transforming the sensibility of praxis itself.

What I propose instead is a reflexive shift in sensibility toward Gaia as a living whole—a form of awareness that does not collapse Gaia into the human but repositions human action within Gaia. Such reflexivity cannot itself produce value, but it can reorient value praxis by transforming how it feels, what it prioritizes, and how it relates to limits. As Latour (2017) and Stengers (2015) have each suggested in their distinct ways, Gaia is not a passive ground but a transformative presence—one that resists instrumentalization and demands a shift in sensibility, politics, and belonging. As we will see in the final chapter, this attunement is essential if social cooperation is to remain with ecological threshold and compose different horizons of reproduction and care. This attunement is not abstract mysticism but a condition for rethinking the very material exchanges that sustain our collective existence.

From this view, social metabolism becomes the interface: the space of exchange, transformation, and often conflict between human social cooperation and the wider Earth system. It is the name we give to the systemic relationship between society and nonhuman nature—a relationship that is mediated by energy, material flows, and information, and organized according to the prevailing logic of the social system. Since the Earth system includes humans as a part of it, this is not merely an external conflict but one that traverses and constitutes the subject itself—as ambivalent and internally divided—just as discussed in Chapter 6. Under capitalism, this mediation is shaped by the imperative of endless accumulation, producing a metabolic rift between what is extracted and what can be regenerated and between what is produced and what can be absorbed without systemic breakdown.

The spectrum of value praxis in the metabolic interface

Social metabolism thus encompasses the full spectrum of value praxis in relation to nonhuman nature—ranging from the most virtuous to the most vicious—from those who recognize nonhuman life not only as the material basis of human existence but also as part of a spiritual sense of belonging to a greater whole, to those who treat it solely as a resource to be extracted or dumped upon. The hegemony of capital over social cooperation pulls the overall metabolic relation toward the vicious end of the spectrum—so much so that ecological devastation and climate change now pose existential threats to human life on Earth. Capital's insensitivity to relationality at this level is also at the root of the atrocious suffering inflicted upon nonhuman animals—especially those confined within the mass extermination camps of industrial farming.

Metabolic exchanges between this level and those above it produce cumulative impacts that increasingly disrupt the autopoietic processes of nonhuman nature. As a result, the ecological equilibria of the Holocene—which for over 11,000 years sustained the fragile conditions for human and social development—now teeter on the verge of collapse.[2] This planetary imbalance is not simply environmental—it is a crisis of the entire system of social cooperation, revealing how deeply the current mode of value praxis disrupts the living foundations upon which it depends.

Capitalism as an ecological regime

In Chapter 2, we defined *societal* reproduction—as distinct from *social* reproduction—as the ensemble of processes, social relations, and material and energy flows that unfold through social cooperation with the ecosystem in all its dimensions. This general formulation carries two main implications.

First, this approach links social cooperation to the general reproduction of society, a process sustained through a plurality of productive forms, organizational ends, and systems of measure. The emergent configuration of societal reproduction can be named capitalism, insofar as society is reproduced through a mixed constitution of productive forms under the hegemony of a particular social force: capital and its reproductive meta-purpose.

Second, society reproduces itself historically by generating the conditions of its own existence through internal forms of interaction—forms that necessarily correspond to how it relates to nonhuman nature. This correspondence constitutes what we call *social metabolism*: the mediated, patterned exchange between human *societal reproduction* and the broader Earth system. In this sense, society as a whole reproduces itself through its metabolic exchange with the nonhuman. This exchange, and the processes through which it unfolds, are what we refer to as social metabolism.

Let us now examine this metabolic interface more closely—between the reproduction of society as a whole (the common as condition, shaped by capitalism) and the reproduction of nonhuman nature (Gaia or the ecosystem).[3] I will briefly discuss two key dimensions: a general one, concerning the historical relationship between capitalism and nonhuman nature; and an analytical one, which will help us distinguish how the ranking of value praxes embedded in the pyramid of capital ultimately gives shape to social metabolism.

From a historical standpoint, the relationship between society and nonhuman nature has often been theorized in terms of dialectical co-determination. Already in the mid-twentieth century, Alfred Schmidt (1971)—in his seminal reading of Marx—emphasized that human history unfolds *within* nature, not *against* it. Nature is not an external object but a constitutive condition of human praxis. Later, with the rise of ecological science, James Lovelock (2000) proposed the Gaia hypothesis: The Earth is not merely a passive environment but a *self-regulating system*, composed of both living organisms and their inorganic surroundings, whose dynamic interactions maintain conditions for life. This insight resonates with a shift in both ecological science and political thought: the need to understand nature not as a passive background but as a dynamic actor.

From this perspective, Gaia is not only a name for the biophysical substrate of life but a conceptual rupture that challenges the modern, dualistic image of nature as inert and controllable. Gaia breathes, evolves, and adapts—she is not just a backdrop to human action but a metabolic participant. Thus, if Schmidt invites us to think of society as always already natural, Lovelock asks us to think of nature as always already social in its planetary dynamics.

Jason W. Moore (2015) weaves these insights into his critique of capitalism. In his world-ecology framework, capitalism is not simply a system acting *within* nature—it is a way of *organizing* nature itself. Capital depends on what Moore calls "cheap nature": It relentlessly seeks to appropriate not only underpaid labor but also undervalued ecological work—sunlight, soil, food, and energy—treating them as externalities to be absorbed without cost. This renders capitalism both materially and epistemologically extractivist: It draws life from Gaia while denying that this life has its own logic, temporality, and limits. This drive for "cheap nature" is not a neutral or automatic process—it is historically contingent and deeply entangled with class struggle. This is illustrated, for example, by Andreas Malm's (2016) discussion of the transition from water power to coal in early industrial capitalism, which was not primarily driven by considerations of technological efficiency or resource abundance. Rather, it was a strategic response to class struggle. Water power, though renewable, was geographically fixed and often embedded in social relations that limited capitalist control. Coal, by contrast, enabled greater spatial and temporal flexibility: It could power steam engines located in urban centers, closer to pools of cheap, disciplined labor, and outside the constraints of rural, socially rooted water mills. In this sense, the fossil economy emerged not out of technical necessity but out of the capitalist imperative to command labor and mobility.

The transition to fossil fuels, in other words, was not only about resource extraction but also about labor discipline and control—showing how innovations in energy regimes often emerge as counterstrategies to insurgent forms of social reproduction. This reveals the continuity between energy regimes and labor regimes—both shaped by the imperative to command time, mobility, and reproduction. This drive for "cheap nature" is not simply an economic imperative but a political strategy shaped by class conflict. Energy transitions, in this view, are often orchestrated not only to extract more from nature but also to reassert domination over the social body. Similar dynamics can be seen today in the green-energy sector, where the deployment of renewables is increasingly tied to the reorganization of land, labor, and territory: large-scale solar and wind projects dispossess Indigenous and rural communities (Pearce 2025; Torres 2025), while embedding new forms of labor discipline and logistical control through digitalized infrastructures of monitoring, data extraction, and automation. Far from simply decarbonizing production, the green transition often reproduces the same relations of command that earlier fossil transitions established—recasting ecological transformation as another terrain of class struggle (Dunlap 2020a,b; IEA 2021).

Capitalism, then, is not merely destructive of nature—it actively *remakes* nature through its own reproductive logic. In this sense, each historical phase of capital accumulation generates a distinct ecological regime—a mode of metabolizing and abstracting nature, shaped by its embedded social struggles. Its metabolic interface with Gaia is not one of mutual adaptation but one of dominance and abstraction. Capitalism, then, cannot be understood through a Cartesian framework that separates nature and society—as if it were a purely economic or social formation acting upon an external nature. Rather, as Jason Moore argues, capitalism is a historical-social formation that coevolves with nature through specific modes of appropriation, domination, and abstraction. In this sense, capitalism does not simply have an ecological regime—it *is* an ecological regime. To speak of capitalism, or of any dominant mode of production, past or future, is to speak of a succession of ecological regimes: historically specific configurations that structure the processes of accumulation and what Moore calls the *production of nature*.

Yet the reproduction of nature under capitalism does not occur without rupture. Its logic of control and abstraction generates not only ecological transformation but also deep structural disconnections—between cycles of life and circuits of value and between ecosystems and economic imperatives.

The metabolic rift

This means we should not think of capitalism's history as one of mere impact on a separate "natural" system. Instead, we must investigate the generative relationship between capital's logic of infinite accumulation and nature's dynamics of continuous reproduction. This relationship unfolds through recurrent environmental crises that are inseparable from economic crises. Both are moments of disruption in the broader process of social metabolism—a dynamic that John Bellamy Foster (2000), following Marx, famously theorized as the *metabolic rift* between human society and the ecological systems that sustain it.

The rift names a structurally produced disconnection between human society and the nonhuman nature on which it depends—an estrangement not incidental but inscribed within capital's modus operandi. Marx observed that capitalist production tends to centralize populations and labor in urban-industrial cores, while treating the biophysical world—particularly soil, nutrients, and ecosystems—as expendable resources. The result is a rupture in the cyclical flows that once returned matter to the land. Marx foresaw this rupture in terms of soil depletion and the fragmentation of ecological cycles—symptoms of a broader capitalist indifference to regenerative time. As Marx (1976: 637–8) puts it:

> Capitalist production . . . disturbs the metabolic interaction between man and the earth, i.e. it prevents the return to the soil of its constituent elements consumed by man in the form of food and clothing; hence it hinders the operation of the eternal natural condition for lasting fertility of the soil. Thus it destroys at the same time the physical health of the urban worker, and the intellectual life of the rural worker. But by destroying the circumstances surrounding that metabolism . . . it compels its systematic restoration as a regulative law of social production . . . Capitalist production, therefore, develops only the techniques and degree of combination of the social process of production by simultaneously undermining the original sources of all wealth—the soil and the worker.

This rift is not a mere accident—it is a systemic feature of capitalist development, one that undermines the material and energetic foundations of societal reproduction itself. The break between nature's cyclical rhythms and capital's linear drive to valorize renders sustainable metabolic exchange structurally impossible. It is this irreparable fracture, nested deep within the reproductive processes of capital, that anticipates the contemporary ecological catastrophe. At stake is nothing less than the reproduction of life itself—what Marx captured in the twin images of the soil and the worker. Social reproduction is ecological reproduction—and vice versa. To disrupt one is to threaten the other.

Social metabolism

Let us now turn to a more precise understanding of what is meant by *social metabolism*. In biology, metabolism refers to the set of chemical reactions that occur within each cell of a living organism and that provide the energy necessary for vital processes and the synthesis of new organic matter. The term is used to describe all the biochemical transformations required to sustain the life of cells and organisms. At a smaller scale, metabolism encompasses the chemical and energetic changes that enable an organism to maintain itself, grow, move, and regenerate. In medical science, the concept is scaled up: Metabolism is understood as the process through which the human body converts external nourishment into internal energy. Importantly, the biological (i.e., cellular) basis of the process remains unchanged across these different scales.

The term *metabolism* here always refers to internal processes—chemical or energetic transformations—that occur within a system, in this case, a living one. Crucially, every metabolism presupposes both an internal organization and a continuous exchange with an external environment.

It is evident that each of us constitutes a point of exchange with the ecosystem—a node in the ongoing metabolic interaction between human life and nonhuman nature. Every action we perform, from sustaining our bodily functions to sending a message on WhatsApp or clicking a "like" on social media, and from our daily biological rhythms to our participation in the productive networks that span the planet, involves a metabolic relation with the nonhuman world.

However, it is essential to distinguish this metabolic interaction at the individual level from the broader systemic one. At the level of the organism, each of us draws from nature the oxygen, water, CO_2, and minerals necessary for life. This is referred to as endosomatic metabolism—the internal, biological metabolism of humans. When measured per capita, this flow is relatively constant over time, though it increases proportionally with the global population (Giampietro et al. 2012: 187).

What concerns us more directly here, however, is exosomatic metabolism—that is, the collective metabolism of social cooperation.[4] This refers to the five key metabolic functions through which society engages nonhuman nature: extraction, circulation, transformation, consumption, and excretion of matter and energy. It is this exosomatic metabolism that has grown exponentially throughout human history and has reached pathological proportions under capitalism, especially since the post–Second World War acceleration. This metabolic excess has plunged us into a condition of ecological catastrophe, of which climate change is merely the most visible symptom. Moreover, exosomatic metabolism is increasingly marked by deep and growing inequities, both across different geographical regions of social cooperation and between economic classes (OXFAM 2023). Addressing the ecological crisis without confronting this profound carbon inequality risks exacerbating global injustices. According to OXFAM, the richest 1 percent of the global population were responsible for 16 percent of global consumption emissions in 2019—*equal to the emissions of the poorest two-thirds of humanity combined*. This disparity underscores that climate mitigation efforts must prioritize equity; otherwise, they would impose greater burdens on those least responsible for emissions, deepening existing socioeconomic divides. Also, as Joan Martinez-Alier (2002) has shown, many ecological conflicts are conflicts over metabolism and valuation—over who bears the costs of environmental degradation and who has the power to define what counts as "development." Stefania Barca (2022) extends this analysis by placing labor at the center of ecological struggle, showing how working-class and subaltern communities often serve as both the exploited labor force and the frontline defenders of ecosystems. Her notion of "workers of the earth" reframes waged and unwaged labor not only as a victim of extractivism but also as a potential agent of metabolic repair. In the end, the ecological crisis must be understood as a crisis of social reproduction, in which the forces that sustain life—both human and more-than-human—are systematically devalued and exploited under capitalist metabolism.

When we speak of social metabolism, then, we must keep in mind this double reference: first, to a set of processes, and second, to the fact that these processes occur within a system of social cooperation, which itself exists only through its exchange with the ecosystem. Social metabolism thus designates all the organized processes through which energy, matter, and information flow between the whole of social cooperation and the ecosystem that sustains it (De Molina and Toledo 2014).

Following De Molina and Toledo, social metabolism operates through *five major metabolic functions*—appropriation, transformation, distribution, consumption, and excretion—by which society exchanges energy and matter with nature. These functions constitute the material "hardware" of social cooperation: the metabolic circuits that link the social and ecological realms.

This includes the exchange of energy and matter at the points of convergence between society and nature (the biosphere), that is, at the points of appropriation (agriculture, extraction) and disposal (pollution); the processes within society (circulation, transformation, consumption). Yet social metabolism is not reducible to material throughput alone. The organization of these five functions is shaped by symbolic, cultural, and political processes that select, rank, and prioritize among possible metabolic pathways. This immaterial dimension—though intangible—structures how appropriation occurs, what transformations are pursued, how distribution is arranged, and what forms of consumption and disposal are normalized. It is here that value regimes and their measures of things enter the metabolic whole.

The "operating system" of social metabolism

If the organized exchange of energy and matter constitutes the "hardware" of social metabolism, the informational dimension acts as its "software," the domain through which societies design, regulate, and give meaning to metabolic functions. De Molina and Toledo (2014) identify eight "software" elements, which are grouped into two broad categories: cosmovisions (ideologies, knowledge, and technologies) and juridical relations (implicit or explicit norms, political rules, cultural rules, economic rules, and property relations).

These elements—ideologies, norms, knowledge systems, and rules—are not abstract superstructures; they have concrete effects on extraction, waste, and production. They orient social production, shaping its practices, possibilities, and horizons. As De Molina and Toledo (2014: 64) write, "in every society there is a particular articulation of the five metabolic functions that is commanded by a corresponding set of social relations, which configure each one of the functions."

In other words, the "software" determines how the hardware of metabolism operates. But within this software lies an even deeper layer—the "operating system" (OS) of social metabolism—which governs how cosmovisions and rules are selected, combined, and ranked.

It is the nature of this "command" that defines the socio-ecological interface: the intersectional zone where the autopoietic dynamics of society—whether in the register of the autopoiesis pursued by capital or of social reproduction—interact with those of nonhuman nature (De Molina and Toledo 2014: 256–92).

What remains implicit in the metaphor—but essential—is this OS: the meta-logic in command that determines which cosmovisions take precedence, how rules are interpreted, and which purposes institutions and circuits pursue.

The OS is not merely another cultural layer but the systemic configuration of dominant value domains—today, primarily shaped by the logic of capital accumulation. It governs the interface between society and Gaia, ensuring that metabolism is steered by imperatives of growth, profit, and control rather than by the needs of social or ecological reproduction.

As discussed throughout this book, the systems comprising social cooperation are structured ensembles of value praxes—norms, purposes, and practices through which meaning is socially attributed to action. This has direct implications for how "information" is read, selected, and coded within these systems, because every metabolic process is filtered through particular regimes of signification and judgment that reflect dominant value hierarchies.

In Chapter 7, we defined value praxis as the ensemble of practices, norms, and teleologies through which meaning is given to action within specific domains of social cooperation—whether relational, useful, commodified, or governed. The metaphor of the OS now allows us to restate this: A social OS is not merely a cultural layer; it is the structural logic that hierarchically orchestrates and ranks different value praxes within a given societal configuration. It is a historically situated configuration of value hierarchies—an architecture of systemic coordination and control that shapes the flow of social metabolism by aligning cooperation with a dominant meta-purpose, whether capital accumulation or social reproduction (including ecological regeneration).

For information to be decoded and acted upon within this framework, it must be inserted into a context that gives it meaning—a context configured by the OS. In other words, the significance of a piece of information depends on the entangled hierarchy of meta-purposes that organizes social cooperation: the relative weight given to capital reproduction versus social reproduction. Within this hierarchy, information flows through productive circuits only insofar as it aligns with the dominant logic. It is interpreted through epistemologies, rationalities, and measures of value that reflect existing power relations and ultimately contribute to the selection of practices across domains of social life.

Every instance of social cooperation must navigate a contested terrain of perceptions, logics, and value systems—none of which are neutral, and many of which are in tension or outright conflict. It is through the dominance of one reproductive logic over another that information acquires operational meaning. Following Gregory Bateson (1987), we can say that information is the "difference that makes a difference"—but what counts as difference, and what kind of difference is allowed to matter, depends entirely on the interpretive architecture of the OS in place.

Within a productive circuit, for example, the relevant "difference that makes a difference" is tied to a productive goal (e.g., the creation of a use value), which itself is subsumed under a dominant reproductive logic—either the reproduction of capital or the reproduction of life. When capital dominates, information is parsed in ways that prioritize profitability, efficiency, or market expansion. But this same information, placed in the context of a commons-oriented OS, might orient practices toward regeneration, care, or collective flourishing.

Often, capital reproduces itself by exploiting divisions within social reproduction—by pitting needs, values, and subjects against one another. Consider the competitive pressures that force workers into a race to the bottom on wages and conditions, or the false trade-offs between health and employment, where addressing toxicity or harm is said to threaten jobs. Or consider the silent toll of ecological degradation endured by communities economically dependent on the very industries causing harm. In all these cases, the capitalist OS parses incoming information—social signals, environmental feedback, labor struggles—according to its own reproductive logic, neutralizing countervailing codes of care, solidarity, or sustainability.

Within the same hardware and software configuration—that is, within shared infrastructures, institutions, and normative frameworks—conflicting operating systems can coexist but not peacefully. Just as in computing, where dual-boot systems or virtual machines may run rival OSs in tension, in the social world, different meta-logics—such as capital reproduction versus social reproduction—can inhabit the same institutional shell. As I have argued in Chapters 2 and 3, the struggle between social and capital reproduction pervades the entire field of social cooperation.

This conflict plays out with particular violence in relation to ecosystems and Gaia. A forest, for example, may be defined in scientific and legal terms as a carbon sink and biodiversity reserve—a commons. But it may simultaneously be targeted by a capitalist OS that values it as a resource for timber, mining, or monoculture. The two OSs—one oriented toward the reproduction of life, the other to accumulation—clash for control over how the ecosystem is valued, accessed, and transformed. In the Amazon, community agroforestry practices rooted in Indigenous cosmovisions are bulldozed—often literally—by extractivist regimes that treat the forest as raw material. Similar clashes erupt in the oceans, where subsistence fishing is displaced by industrial trawling in the name of GDP growth. Similarly, in climate policy, high-tech "green growth" models intensify global inequality, while grassroots and Indigenous alternatives propose radically different relations to land, energy, and time. In each of these examples, what is ultimately contested is not simply a resource or policy but the operative logic that defines the terms of engagement between society and nature.

These are not just policy disagreements. They are OS-level conflicts—struggles over the meaning of value, the allocation of energy, and the very horizon of collective reproduction. These conflicts pervade every domain of value praxis in social cooperation insofar as they are hierarchically ordered by the mega-systemic machine of the pyramid of capital.

Entropy, praxis, and the organization of social metabolism

De Molina and Toledo develop a thermodynamic theory of social metabolism that, while informed by cybernetic ideas such as feedback, consciously shifts from equilibrium-based control models toward a materialist, political reading of entropy, struggle, and systemic transformation. Drawing on Prigogine's (1996) concept of dissipative structures, they understand societies—like all living systems—as complex, evolving formations that maintain internal order by importing low-entropy energy and materials—sunlight, fossil fuels, and food—and exporting disorder (entropy) into their environment. This process enables societies to conserve or increase complexity, not by avoiding disorder but by displacing it.

In thermodynamics, energy is the capacity to perform work, and work is any transformation—physical, chemical, or social—that alters a system's state. In this context, entropy refers to energy that is no longer available for transformation, while negentropy is the ordered energy that sustains complexity. What we referred to in Chapter 7 as value praxis—socially meaningful activity—is thus also a specific form of energy transformation. It is not simply mechanical effort but the channeling of energy into value-oriented action: into care, production for profit, or resistance. Praxis arises not only from cultural norms or institutional structures but from the energetic substrate—bodily and ecological—that underpins them.

To grasp the entropic implications of social metabolism more precisely, we must focus on the material basis of praxis—energy itself, in its bodily and systemic forms. We must distinguish between two forms of energy. Bodily energy derives from endosomatic metabolism: the conversion of nutrients into affective, cognitive, and muscular capacities. It grounds lived praxis. External energy, meanwhile, comes from exosomatic metabolism: the appropriation of energy from nature (e.g., fossil fuels, food, sunlight) to power infrastructures, machines, and institutions. Social metabolism depends on both forms, but the way this energy is transformed—toward entropy or negentropy—depends on the value praxes that structure social cooperation.

This is where De Molina and Toledo's framework gains political depth. Their extension of Prigogine's thermodynamic equation makes this clear:

$$\text{SSt} = \text{SSin} + \text{Ssout},$$

where SSt = total social entropy; SSin = internal social disorder; and SSout = disorder displaced externally.

Specific forms of autopoietic logic can preserve their internal order (lower SSin) by exporting entropy (raising SSout) onto other groups or ecosystems. Inequality, then, is not only an ethical or political issue—it is a thermodynamic strategy. The maintenance of social complexity—of institutional form, economic productivity, or urban life—often requires the displacement of disorder through ecological degradation, labor exploitation, or geopolitical violence. Entropy becomes a measure of this asymmetry.

Information plays a crucial role here. As De Molina and Toledo argue, information functions as negentropy: It organizes social action, reduces uncertainty, and sustains complex cooperation. Yet the production and interpretation of information are not neutral. They are embedded in ranked systems of value—the ensembles of practices, norms, and purposes through which meaning is socially attributed to actions (as discussed in Chapter 7).

Whether information counteracts or amplifies entropy depends on the dominant value praxis that guides social cooperation. When the telos of capital accumulation prevails, knowledge and norms are organized around profitability, competition, and control, producing *informational entropy*—the degradation of meaning systems that no longer serve the reproduction of life. Conversely, value praxes grounded in care, reciprocity, and ecological regeneration generate *informational negentropy*: relational and cognitive orders that foster coordination, solidarity, and commoning rather than commodification.

From this perspective, the OS of a society is not simply its cultural framework but the structural configuration of value praxis that ranks and organizes informational flows, bodily energy, and external resources. The OS determines which work is valued and which is made invisible; which uses of energy reduce systemic entropy, and which accelerate social and ecological disorder. A care-oriented OS channels energy into practices of relational and ecological regeneration, while a capitalist OS displaces entropy outward—intensifying inequality, ecological degradation, and social fragmentation

This thermodynamic framing casts the struggle between competing reproductive logics as not only social or ethical but material—rooted in how energy, labor, and information are organized across systems. The distinction can be understood as a divergence between two competing autopoietic logics—each organizing the flow of energy, matter, and information in distinct ways toward different reproductive purposes. While both processes draw on the same material substrate and informational capacities, capital reproduction operates as an autopoietic system geared toward endless accumulation, externalizing entropy and deepening socio-ecological inequality. Social reproduction, by contrast, as developed through the *problematic* of its autopoietic organization (Chapters 2 and 3), seeks to maintain and regenerate the conditions of life, embodying a negentropic orientation that values interdependence, care, and ecological balance. These divergent logics configure not only metabolic flows but the very meaning of information, as each system selects and enacts value praxes according to its own reproductive horizon.

This thermodynamic framing reveals that the struggle between reproductive logics is not merely social or ethical but material—rooted in how energy, labor, and information are organized and valued. The distinction can be understood as a divergence between two autopoietic logics—each organizing the flow of energy, matter, and information toward different reproductive ends. While both draw on the same material substrate, capital reproduction operates as an autopoietic system geared toward endless accumulation, preserving its internal order by exporting entropy and deepening socio-ecological inequality. Social reproduction, by contrast, seeks to maintain and regenerate the conditions of life, embodying a negentropic orientation that values interdependence, care, and ecological balance. These divergent logics configure not only metabolic flows but also the very meaning of information, as each system selects and enacts value praxes according to its own reproductive horizon.

Yet even this negentropic orientation of social reproduction entails an entropic displacement because when it is confined within the private or exclusionary forms structured by capital, social reproduction also expels disorder outward, offloading costs onto ecosystems or vulnerable others. To preserve life, however, social reproduction must instead direct this entropic displacement toward the circuits of capital itself, transforming its defensive and fragmented logics into collective, transversal practices capable of forcing capital's autopoiesis to internalize the disorder it generates by making it pay the social and environmental costs it generated. In doing so, it compels accumulation to absorb its own externalities rather than displacing them onto the living. In this sense, an alternative configuration of social cooperation rests on reversing the direction of entropy flow, transforming capital from an extractor of vitality into the principal sink of systemic disorder. These divergent logics configure not only metabolic flows but also the very meaning of information, as each system selects and enacts value praxes according to its own reproductive horizon.

To imagine capital as the principal sink of systemic disorder is to picture a world in which the turbulence of accumulation can no longer be expelled onto the living. The circuits of capital themselves begin to overheat, absorbing the waste, instability, and exhaustion that they once displaced.

Stock exchanges and data centers—those crystalline architectures of order—begin to register the material consequences of extraction and inequality not on their own but through the frictions, resistances, and refusals that force disorder to appear within the metrics of accumulation.

Climate strikes, insurgent migrations, divestment campaigns, sabotage, debt defaults, and the physical shocks of ecological collapse all act as signals of entropy that the system can no longer externalize. What once counted as "externalities" now returns as volatility, uninsurability, and ungovernable crisis. Supply chains buckle under the weight of the ecological feedback they helped unleash; speculative finance finds its returns eroded by the very disruptions it amplifies. Energy grids, markets, and institutions that once channeled entropy outward now face it inward, forced into processes of contraction, transformation, or dissolution.

In this inversion, capital no longer expands by translating disorder into accumulation. Instead, it becomes a zone in which disorder circulates until the system can no longer externalize the instability it generates and is forced to confront it internally.

The heat sink, in this sense, is not a managerial fix but a developmental threshold: the point at which capital's metabolism loses its capacity to expel entropy and must reorganize under the pressure of the disorder it once displaced. The task that emerges at this threshold is not technical adjustment but a reorientation of social cooperation itself—of how flows of matter, energy, and meaning are organized in relation to the sustenance of life.

Yet this inversion does not occur in a vacuum. Social reproduction remains deeply entangled with capital's infrastructures and circuits of provision, so when capital becomes the principal sink of disorder, the shock reverberates across the entire social metabolism. The issue, therefore, is not collapse but recomposition: how to reorganize social cooperation so that the crisis of capital does not become the crisis of life.

From Gaia to the pyramid

The image of capital as the principal sink of systemic disorder brings us back to Gaia—not as a passive substrate but as the living matrix through which all levels of social cooperation unfold. Entropy and negentropy, in this sense, are not only physical processes but *social gradients*, distributed across relations of production, exchange, and command. When capital's autopoiesis begins to internalize the disorder it once expelled, the reverberations travel across the entire architecture of social cooperation. Gaia, the procommons, the meso-level, the meta-level, and the level of command each express distinct configurations of energy, meaning, and value, translating these thermodynamic tensions into social forms.

To trace these dynamics, we must now move from the systemic metabolism of capital to its stratified organization—the *pyramid of capital.*

This structure channels entropy and order unevenly: Negentropic control and accumulation are concentrated upward, while disorder and depletion are displaced downward onto bodies, communities, and ecosystems. Within this hierarchy, every level is both a site of reproduction and a conduit of entropic transfer, mediating the flows of energy, labor, and meaning that sustain the whole.

From this perspective, the pyramid is not simply a hierarchy of power or function but a thermodynamic hierarchy of value praxis: an architecture that encodes how societies metabolize matter, energy, and information according to dominant reproductive logics. To transform the metabolism of society, then, is to transform this architecture itself—to realign its flows of energy and sense-making toward the reproduction of life rather than the accumulation of capital.

As we have seen, these competing autopoietic logics not only shape the systemic processing of information but also manifest differently across the stratified architecture of social cooperation. Within the pyramid of capital, each level—from the foundational exchanges with Gaia to the structuring apex of command—embodies distinct configurations of value praxis, which in turn carry specific entropic or negentropic implications.

To pose the question of a transversal organization centered on social reproduction is to intervene in the relational and use-value terrain of the procommons and meso-level, where social praxes can generate low-entropy systems prioritizing both collective well-being and virtuous metabolic exchanges with Gaia. Many commons already do this through reproductive labor or subsistence exchange that nurtures more-than-human interdependencies, guided by relational values of care, reciprocity, and shared sustenance. Yet extending and scaling up these praxes requires embedding their principles within larger circuits of use-value production on which we greatly depend—the major areas of use-value production discussed in Chapter 12. The meso-level, structured primarily around the production and circulation of use values, bears strong potential for negentropic contribution—especially when oriented toward socially necessary, ecologically embedded goods and services. However, since this level functions as a subcomponent of capital valorization, its selective processes and productive organization remain subordinated to accumulation imperatives. Its metabolic profile is thus skewed toward entropic dissipation: massive extractivism, resource-intensive manufacturing, linear supply chains, waste cycles, and policies oriented toward perpetual growth at all costs.

The hegemony of the meta-level ensures that use and relational values are systematically abstracted and subsumed by the equivalence logic of dominant markets. Accumulation becomes the dominant reproductive aim; financial resources are reinvested in line with this aim, and metabolic flows are calibrated far less by social needs than by profitability. The logic of capital at this level maximizes its own negentropic social order through the maximization of throughput—accelerating extraction, consumption, and disposal—while systematically externalizing ecological and social costs, thereby generating entropy at the procommons and Gaia levels.

Although the command level at the top—the strategic and institutional infrastructure that seeks to stabilize and orient the whole pyramid (Chapter 14)—does not produce material value per se, its entropic relevance is considerable: It codifies and enforces the systemic logic of accumulation, fuels destructive wars, and protects the property rights and rights of action of large appropriators and polluting organizations (big capital) by ranking value praxes and institutionalizing them through law, policy, finance, and global governance. The command level thus allocates rights to generate entropy—*entropic privileges* (e.g., through permits, subsidies, or military force). In doing so, it secures the reproduction of capital at the expense of planetary and social thresholds. Yet this level also holds the potential to reorient systemic purpose—should its governing logic shift—from a driver of entropic acceleration to a coordinator of regenerative transitions. However, this potential depends on reconfigurations emerging from below—through movements and transformations in the procommons and meso-levels that build transversal organizations and grow their social force to challenge the prevailing command logic while asserting alternative horizons on the terrain of social reproduction. Such transformations, if sustained and amplified, would reverberate across the entire pyramid—reshaping the dominant hierarchies of value, reorganizing production, and reorienting and reconfiguring command itself. Across the layers of the pyramid, then, the metabolic consequences of value praxis are not incidental—they are structurally patterned. What begins as an epistemic ordering of value becomes a material gradient of entropy and regeneration, inscribed in bodies, institutions, ecologies, and time.

The pyramid of capital is not just a hierarchy of function or control but a thermodynamic hierarchy of reproductive logics—where the balance between entropy and negentropy, accumulation and regeneration, depends on which value praxes are enabled or suppressed across levels. To reconfigure the pyramid is thus not only a political task—it is a metabolic necessity for life itself, pointing to the need to rethink metabolism as a social and ecological practice rather than a throughput dictated by capital's need for expansion.

11

The level of the procommons

The immanence of the procommons

Any level of the pyramid permeates the totality of social cooperation immanently. At the level of the procommons, this immanence takes on a particularly embodied and affective form. Unlike command or meta-level abstractions, which often operate through institutions and codes, the procommons is felt directly in the texture of everyday life—in shared meals, caring gestures, emotional interdependence, spontaneous cooperation, or the affective resonance of a gaze or a voice. But it is also present in tension, misunderstanding, and the micro-conflicts that mark any dense web of relationships: a quarrel between neighbors, a rupture of trust, and the pain of exclusion. These moments—whether of warmth or friction—may appear ephemeral or informal, yet they are the ground from which all higher-order systems grow. They constitute the relational medium through which all other levels pass and acquire form.

Even when they are not visible as formal institutions, procommons dynamics are always present—sometimes as fleeting interactions, sometimes as stabilized vernacular infrastructures of care, trust, and mutuality. These interactions are not outside capitalism, but they are not reducible to it either. Their presence is transversal: They undergird family life, seep into workplaces, interrupt circuits of commodification, and animate solidarity in both analog and digital spaces. What makes them a level rather than a generalized background is the fact that they entail a specific configuration of value praxis, one grounded in forms of relationality, reciprocity, and the embodied reproduction of life, often in tension with the dominant logic of accumulation.

Yet, to grasp the full significance of these relational dynamics, we must move beyond their immediacy and consider how they are embedded in a wider systemic architecture of social cooperation. We will therefore identify this domain of value praxis, where relational values are experimented with and forged as the procommons—"pro" in a double sense. As *proto*-commons, coming before regularized patterns of commoning that give shapes to commons (De Angelis 2017) but also in the sense that they are *pro*-commons, beneficial, and foundational for the creation of commons. Procommons encompasses all those dimensions of social life in which relational values become important to us, in which we recognize relationships—with one another, with different life-forms, and with ecosystems—as constitutive of the quality of our life in common and, therefore, of the quality of our social powers. As we saw in Chapter 9, this dimension of care, relational embeddedness, and attunement to more-than-human life is inseparable from the metabolic exchanges with Gaia that underlie all levels of social cooperation.

Since the levels of the pyramid are systemic levels of multitudinous coalescences of subjects in relation to one another, operating within different registers of the praxis of value depending on the level, at the lowest level of social cooperation we do not find a social class, as it is generally defined in terms of income bracket, wealth, or access to the means of production; nor do we find a professional status or educational level, gender identity, or anything else. And yet the relational spaces at this level are where the effects of that differentially distributed inclusion (Morini 2022: 10) are concentrated—an inclusion that policies of workfare, a precarious labor market, and, more generally, class or other forms of power stratification have amplified in recent decades, together with all the other polarizing systemic dynamics of capitalism. We therefore find a multitudinous landscape of difference, articulated through circuits and systems of immediate life reproduction—what we call the procommons. This is the environment in which singular subjects, each with a bio/psychic body, live in varying states of intermittence and ambivalence as subject-holons. They perturb and are perturbed by their relational surroundings, engaging the world directly through embodied experience, without the mediation of formalized institutional roles.

Thus, the subject in the procommons breathes the polluted air of the Po Valley, relates to other singularities through forms of interaction that are not reducible to institutional scripts, and contributes to the formation of direct relationships—sometimes fleeting, sometimes enduring, with autopoietic potential. These relational dynamics are not necessarily outside institutional contexts; rather, they traverse them. Even within schools, hospitals, or workplaces, the procommons persists in the affective undercurrents of cooperation, care, resistance, or tension—those micro-movements through which subjects experience each other not only as roles but as living presences. In this sense, the procommons is the immanent relational stratum through which institutions are inhabited, subverted, or quietly reconfigured from within.

This lowest level of social cooperation is preoccupied with life itself—with the ongoing search for its meaning, and with the means and ways of its reproduction under the variegated conditions inherited from history, distributed by chance, and continually reshaped by the movement of the capitalist whole. Here, in the social basements of the macro-systemic pyramid, we reproduce our lives under different circumstances, of course, but first and foremost by doing things and sustaining our social relationships—living this experience through a turbulence of sensations, emotions, rationalizations, and the search for meaning. The subjects here are, first, individual people in the multiplicity of their relationships with the world, and second, the micro-aggregates of social cooperation to which their interrelated doing gives rise. These procommons formations—systemic assemblages of the most disparate kinds—include various types of family units, networks of friends, neighborhood communities, cultural associations, churches and parishes, local branches of trade unions and political parties, and all the forms of grassroots aggregation that participate, in one way or another, in the material or spiritual reproduction of life in different territories or digital spaces. But these micro-aggregates also permeate contexts of work, centers of power, and consumption. Even in the contemporary world, so distant from the premodern era, this level remains the point of entry for material (Braudel 1973), relational, and spiritual life. It is the privileged site of vernacular life: the sphere of social, productive, and reproductive activity—what is left, what is inherited, and what we still manage to create despite everything—that operates largely outside the market, its rationality, and its systems of measurement. It draws on direct social relations—those mediated only by the senses, perceptions, and consciousness of the subjects who enter into relationship and by their mutual constitution of a shared universe of value. This emphasis on the immediacy of embodied encounter does not exclude forms of mediation—digital or otherwise. A conversation in cyberspace can still be a direct encounter insofar as it expresses the singular voices of subjects. What matters is not whether communication is mediated by screens or signals but whether the relation unfolds between persons—rather than between a person and a role, an apparatus, or a system speaking through them.

The procommons is marked by encounters in which subjects appear to one another not primarily as functions or representatives of institutions but as singularities engaged in shared presence and mutual recognition. In this sense, the procommons is the domain where relational values—anticipated in Chapter 8 as the ways meaning is generated through intersubjective relations—are most directly lived, negotiated, and contested. These values do not express only care, trust, or reciprocity but also conflict, resentment, or exclusion: all registers of value that arise from the intensity and immediacy of being-with-others. This is the ground where relational values breathe—where meaning is spun not only through gestures of care, warmth, and mutual trust but also through the frictions of envy, the ache of exclusion, the flare of anger, and the silence of betrayal. These are not deviations from relation but its darker rhythms—just as essential, just as constitutive. In the procommons, relational values are not lofty ideals; they are embodied pulses of everyday life, stitching together the fragile fabric of being-with, in tenderness or in tension. Whereas Luhmann would relegate such affective intensities to the psychological system—external to the realm of social communication—what is at stake here is something else; following enactivist perspectives, these embodied affective modes are not peripheral to social systems but constitutive of them. In the procommons, relation is not abstract code but the very interweaving of sentient bodies, where emotion, perception, and modes of intersubjective resonance become the medium of social life.

This embodied relational field is thus not idyllic—it is the very site where social cooperation pulses with contradiction. At this level, social cooperation ranges from the fulfillment of the reproductive needs of life in a broad sense (therefore not only cooking and caring but also creating culture, messing around, playing, meeting, and socializing) to the production and dissolution of micro-hierarchies, always surrounded by processes of micro-conflict and escape, the migration of human singularities in search of living spaces for their development, and the congruence between their desires, their passions, and the relational ecologies in which they are inserted. It is at this level that the search for genuine relationships takes place, where mutual respect and care are the glue that holds them together. It is at this level that the desire to dismantle all oppressive systems, even in their macro-hierarchies, is born and develops. It is here that the desire to create a more just and cohesive society begins. It is at this relational level that the need for love is born and nurtured—one that may evolve into specific configurations of care, commitment, trust, and respect, which nourish dignity, open spaces of resistance to domination, and unfold as an end in itself: a collective praxis that is transformative at both personal and collective levels, as bell hooks (2001) reminds us. But it is also at this level that all kinds of violence, abuse, and feminicide take place, and where racial and xenophobic hatred is cultivated.

These tensions and aspirations take form through everyday rhythms—through the concrete, embodied practices by which social cooperation unfolds, dissolves, and reorganizes itself in the relational field of the procommons. These rhythms—pulsing between spontaneity and control—mirror the hierarchies of rhythm analyzed in Chapter 8, where temporalities become a key mode through which capitalism stratifies cooperation. Rhythms of purposeful doing and lived stillness mark the more or less fragmented forms of social cooperation across the multiple places of living and socializing. Even practices often dismissed as idle—such as binge-watching a TV series—can carry ambiguous forms of lived stillness: at times offering shared rituals of rest, emotional attunement, or narrative immersion; at others, slipping into affective drift, where attention is captured rather than held, and the rhythms of life dissolve into the background hum of algorithmic pacing. As Yves Citton

(2017) reminds us, in the ecology of attention shaped by digital capitalism, even rest becomes a site of struggle, where presence risks being replaced by passive capture. Between industrious intention and the slow pull of drifting, the procommons pulses with ambivalence—sometimes reclaiming presence, sometimes losing itself in the fog.

In this context, social labor often presents itself spontaneously as "commoning," in which the measure of things is managed in many ways by the actors of this social labor themselves, through their impromptu communicative exchanges or coordinated forms, microsystemic feedback, and direct and assembly-based relationships. This may not yet give rise to the commons as an institutionally stabilized resource regime (Ostrom 1990) or as social systems (De Angelis 2017) but commoning as an emergent form of social labor—immediate, affective, and often unmeasured—may or may not give rise to more formalized commons. And this communal activity takes place within various temporalities; it dissolves and recreates social organization, like a network of friendships that reproduces itself over time, giving rise to continuous relationships of "structural coupling" between subjects. When such activity is interrupted, the "molar" subjects it constitutes (a network and circuit of relationships) evaporate, leaving only a trace in the memory and experience of the "molecular" subjects who participated in it—the people.

The vernacular

The procommons resonates with what Ivan Illich (1981) called the vernacular: a dimension of social life rooted in shared practices, embodied relations, and self-sufficiency. In Illich's view, the vernacular refers to forms of life that emerge outside the market and centralized institutions, where value is created not through formal exchange but through reciprocity, embeddedness, and direct relation. Although initially conceived with reference to preindustrial societies, where households or communities sustained themselves through collective practice, the concept helps illuminate how cooperation continues to unfold today—often informally, under the radar, or in defiance of institutional logics.

Yet the vernacular, as Illich draws it from the premodern world, must be approached critically—it was deeply structured by relations of domination. The Roman *vernaculum*—that which belonged to the household—also included enslaved people born into servitude. The traditional home, far from a universal space of care, was often built upon patriarchy, hierarchy, and exclusion. What we recover, then, is not a mythologized past but the latent possibility of a present and future vernacular: forms of life-making and cooperation that resist commodification and challenge the abstractions of the market and the state.

In this spirit, the "moral economy" described by Thompson (1971) shares deep affinities with the vernacular. Both concepts refer to relational value systems that emerge within communities to govern fairness, obligation, and mutual care. These relational forms of normativity arise within specific socio-historical contexts, often as a counterpoint to the encroachment of capitalist discipline and market abstraction. They are not ideal types but lived negotiations of justice, sufficiency, and interdependence.

This brings us to the idea of *home*, a term that haunts the vernacular with both promise and burden. Etymologically linked to dwelling and rootedness, home evokes intimacy, memory, and belonging. Yet in a world increasingly shaped by global supply chains, migration, digital interconnection, and social fragmentation, home no longer coincides with the fixed household, let alone with male ownership or the nuclear family. Most of our reproductive needs today are met not in the household but within broader circuits of social cooperation—schools, clinics, neighborhoods, apps, and deliveries. Even care and emotional support often circulate through digital platforms, crossing spatial and generational boundaries.

One key to understanding this shift in the concept of home lies in Zygmunt Bauman's (2000) notion of liquid modernity, in which stable social forms give way to fluidity, impermanence, and detachment. In this light, home becomes less a physical place and more a shifting relational territory, expanding and contracting across online and offline presences, with practices of care and belonging that are often partial, distributed, or precarious. The idea of home as a space rooted in self-production and direct relationships is drastically reduced, since most material and immaterial needs are met within vast networks of social cooperation, often globalized and made even more pervasive by digital platforms.

In this sense, home is increasingly linked to relational spheres and networks of mutual support—what Hardt and Negri (2004) might describe as a "multitude" in motion, or what Turkle (2011) calls "intimate publics" of digital life. Cyberspace thus becomes both an extension of our daily living and a site of ambiguity, where community, care, and commodification constantly blur. Platforms offer spaces for solidarity—support groups, digital cooperatives—but also environments shaped by surveillance, commodified attention, and algorithmic control. As Zuboff (2019) details in *The Age of Surveillance Capitalism*, even our most intimate interactions become datafied, enclosed within extractive infrastructures that monetize care, attention, and sociability itself.

Against this backdrop, reclaiming the vernacular and rethinking home become political tasks. It is not about returning to the past but about cultivating spaces—physical and virtual—where cooperation, mutuality, and relational value can flourish despite systemic pressures. From this perspective, "home" becomes plural: a shifting constellation of practices and relations rooted in care, resistance, and the desire for autonomy from commodified norms. It is not confined to domestic walls but stretches across kitchens, networks, neighborhoods, collectives, and digital communities.

To reclaim home on a new ground means to reinsert it within wider cooperative networks that overflow the domestic sphere, disrupting the isolating, patriarchal, and xenophobic logics that have long haunted the idea of home. It means creating spaces—both material and symbolic—that support life, difference, and connection. In an increasingly fragmented and nomadic world, home can still become a terrain of hope, conflict, and reappropriation: a site where the vernacular is reinvented through care, memory, struggle, and imagination.

Sustenance

If the vernacular notion of home invites us to reimagine spaces of care, reciprocity, and autonomy beyond the market and the state, then the concept of sustenance offers a way to name the values and practices that make those spaces livable. I believe it is important to recover the sense of sustenance linked to that of home, since the vernacular, as discussed earlier, can be understood as a particular social modality of sustenance. By sustenance, I mean the pursuit of a good life—of individual and collective well-being—within the rhythms of everyday life and the biophysical limits of Gaia's body. The search for well-being has various dimensions: physical (bodily health), mental and emotional (managing stress and emotions, psychological resilience), social (the quality and support of relationships), material (access to use values), spiritual (meaning and deep values), cultural (access to education and the arts), environmental (sustainability and care for the planet), and social in the broadest sense (the reduction of inequalities and the promotion of social justice). All contribute to forming a complete picture of well-being for the individual and the community. By sustenance, therefore, I mean a wide range of activities, many of which are not directly associated with the production and consumption of use values—that is, the creation and use of concrete goods or services to satisfy human needs—but which can still be significant for individual and collective well-being, the construction of identity, social cohesion, and other aspects of social life. Linked to an inclusive and broad idea of sustenance, there can only be that of sufficiency—a simple and intuitive idea that reflects the sense that if a subject, community, or society does more and more in an activity, or consumes more and more resources, it may reach a state of sufficiency but also one of excess (Princen 2005: 6). Princen interprets sufficiency not only as a material value but as a logic that guides individual and collective decisions in the search for well-being—a logic that obviously clashes with the idea of unlimited growth in a limited world, as pursued by capitalism and its prophets.

This understanding of sufficiency as a logic rooted in limits—limits that are not mere constraints but conditions for sustaining and enabling life—opens onto the affective and relational dimensions of the procommons, where sustenance is measured not only in resources and needs met but also in the quality of presence, attention, and care. When we live life attuned to the immanence of the procommons, use value recedes into the background, while the vernacular—and the experiences of the subjects—moves into the foreground. Here Ivan Illich (1981: 57) reminds us that, the vernacular was, for the Romans, "the sustenance derived from patterns of reciprocity inherent in every aspect of life, as distinct from the sustenance that comes from exchange or vertical distribution." We must understand this idea of sustenance as concerning both body and mind, both material and spiritual needs. The level of the procommons is therefore the level at which, in very different and often interstitial forms, we sustain our lives *also* through—or in search of—horizontal human relationships that do not involve either the market or the state. In this dimension, we are within a crucial affective dimension of sustenance—what we might call *the warmth of proximity*—since its enactment implies the sensory touch of the nearby, the embodied experience of moving through the undercurrent of social and human kinship, and the hum of mutual presence: the subtle yet vital resonance that arises from shared presence, mutual care, and the unmeasured generosity of everyday life.

Likewise, we might speak of the *breath of grounding* to name the affective dimension of our relation with Gaia. Just as the warmth of proximity emerges in the nearness of others, this form of sustenance arises in the quiet reciprocity between bodies and Earth—through the scent of wet soil after rain, the texture of stone underfoot, and the cadence of seasonal light. It is not instrumental, though it makes life possible; it is not distant, though often ignored. To be attuned to Gaia's presence is to feel held within a wider metabolism, one that envelops us in relations, rhythms, and limits not of our making, yet inseparable from our becoming. This, too, is a mode of mutual presence—subtler than speech, older than measure—through which life signals its conditions and offers its embrace.

From an experiential point of view, the warmth of proximity today is not absent but increasingly compressed—its space and time constrained by the encroaching logics of the upper levels of the pyramid. In many Western urban areas, the field of direct relationships is fragmented not by disappearance but by the incursion of capital's measures: the clock, the screen, the price tag. Where once local and neighborhood communities played a more central role in material and spiritual sustenance, today their temporalities are constantly interrupted by the accelerated rhythms and quantified imperatives of productivist organization. Yet the procommons have not vanished. Rather, they continually reorganize themselves within the turbulence of the present—reshaping into new types of family units, emerging in networks of friendship both within and beyond digital platforms, forming within associations, through emerging social movements and commons, and asserting themselves wherever forms of sociality and shared care take root.

But for sustenance to become materially and socially real, it must draw upon use values—and thus upon forms of social cooperation aimed at their production. Yet, as we have seen, the notion of sustenance exceeds that of use value alone: It encompasses relational, affective, and symbolic dimensions that are not always directly tied to the production of goods or services. Sustenance practices, then, unfold across two closely interwoven levels of the pyramid: the procommons and the meso-level. Both of these are rooted in the Gaia level, and both are essential for sustaining life. In the procommons, these practices emerge within relational forms of vernacularity—that is, within the countless value relations constituted through direct interaction. At this level, the production of use value—instrumental to sustenance—is shaped by the embodied and situated relationships among subjects. It is a shared dance of doing and judging, of giving and receiving, through which the modalities, configurations, and measures of things are established—often in ways that are informal, negotiated, and not without tension or power.

At the adjacent meso-level, this relational dance recedes into the background and becomes the contextual substrate for more structured processes of producing and circulating use values. Here, use value becomes the meta-purpose: not being-together as such but *doing-for*—producing for the satisfaction of needs, however socially defined. And since all determinations of what counts as "useful" are themselves socially contested, it is the wider field of forces—cultural, technical, psychological—that define the social measure of what is useful. In this terrain, sustenance takes the form of practices, institutions, and infrastructures geared toward the production of use values. Yet because the meso-level operates under the gravitational pull of the meta-level—where capitalist valorization prevails—the procommons' search for sustenance becomes, to varying degrees, functional to the production of use values in capitalist form. This functionality is not merely ideological; it is materially conditioned by the growing dependence of everyday life on market provision—housing, food, transport, education, and even care itself increasingly require monetary access. At the same time, the immediate labor of reproduction is shaped by the structural withdrawal of public support: Austerity, welfare cuts, and the precarization of social services force subjects to internalize risk, fill in gaps, and absorb crisis. In this dual movement—growing dependence and shrinking support—the procommons is compelled to orient its activity toward circuits of commodification. What begins as a search for sustenance is continually reabsorbed into the logic of market mediation—subject to the metrics of productivity, streamlined by efficiency, and disrupted by the imperatives of advertising and capitalist abstraction that aim to capture desire.

Every social endeavor, including the broad field of social reproduction within the procommons, requires tools and means—and these must often be procured beyond the boundaries of the subject or collective that needs them. The dance of life at the level of the procommons, and the social cooperation that sustains it, thus unfolds under the weight of higher systemic constraints. These constraints—rooted in the meso-, meta-, and command levels—impose limits, shape conditions, and often disrupt subjectivity itself. In this context of social cooperation under capitalist hegemony, two historical dynamics unfold. First, a proliferation of monetary circuits emerges around the simple circulation of commodities (C–M–C), in which a multitude of subjects sell a commodity—be it a good, a service, or their labor power to a company or other systemic actor—in order to obtain monetary means (M) that can be transformed into means of life and reproduction (M–C), often reinserted into procommons circuits (as we have seen in the appendix of Chapter 7). These transactions are varied and ambivalent. Buyers, too, are often embedded in similar reproductive logics. Second, these same circuits increasingly become subordinated to the logic of valorisation (M–C–M′), as capital penetrates and reorganizes the temporalities and relations of the procommons. What begins as simple circulation oriented toward reproduction is gradually restructured by efficiency metrics, surveillance, and accumulation imperatives, compressing relational density and fragmenting vernacular time.

Take, for instance, my local baker. He sells me bread that I use to nourish those I care for, and he does so in order to acquire the money he needs to reproduce his own life within his procommons. Then, in the middle of that exchange, time begins to stretch. Our long digressions about philosophy, theology, and the Gregorian chants, compared to the ambient hum of Brian Eno or the chants of Tibetan monks, slow the wrapping of bread, the clicking of receipts, and the handover of coins. As if, right there—in the narrow space between transaction and interaction—a transversal procommons emerges to reclaim its time, to suspend the tempo of the market in favor of another rhythm. Try instead to have a conversation lasting more than a few seconds with a cashier at a large urban supermarket, their actions regulated by the rhythm of capital's own metabolic circuit (M–C–M′), their gestures timed by surveillance and efficiency metrics, and their presence stretched thin across a grid of productivity. Here, the procommons recedes under pressure—its relational density compressed, its temporalities fractured by the measure of capital.

The procommons is not only a site of compression; it is also where transversal potential can begin to crystallize—where the interruptions of capital's temporality become openings for alternative rhythms of life and cooperation, a theme we will return to in Chapter 16.

In any case, the market—the buying and selling of goods—can only be primarily the buying and selling of useful things, although the meaning of usefulness is varied and often relative. So we arrive at the next level, the meso-level, at which use values—and the concrete labor they depend on—come into the foreground. But before we shift focus entirely to production, we must recall that any such activity—however structured—is still rooted in these vernacular, affective, and embodied grounds. The procommons forms the threshold through which life moves from relation to production, from being-with to doing-for.

12

The meso-level

The contested terrain of use-value

This chapter explores the meso-level of the pyramid as the domain where social cooperation is organized primarily around the production and circulation of use values. Unlike the procommons, where relational value is foregrounded, the meso-level centers on purposeful doing—on the concrete labor that generates goods, services, and institutional functions deemed socially useful. Yet this usefulness is never neutral: It is shaped by the competing pulls of social reproduction and capital accumulation and thus by the deeper value conflicts that traverse the pyramid. Drawing on Romano Alquati's reformulation of economic life into four major spheres—artefacture, destructive/realizing consumption, reproductive consumption, and institutional politics—this chapter maps the meso-level as a contested terrain. A fifth sphere, agriculture, is added here due to its unique ecological entanglements. Together, these areas illuminate the ambiguity of usefulness, as the meso-level becomes the hinge where the logics of care and command collide.

While, at the level of the procommons, material and immaterial sustenance is immersed in the relational values employed by the pluralities that constitute it, at the meso-level, this relational field goes into the background, and various pluralities relate in specific ways *in order to* create use values for others—social use values. At this level, subjects aggregate, forming assemblages of various types and on various scales (generally through structures, circuits, and systems discussed in Chapter 7), with the main purpose of producing things or services useful to others, carrying out social functions that have to do with the satisfaction of a variety of needs beyond those met in the context of the procommons. But at this level, work still has a value and a meaning linked to the reproduction of life, to its materiality and purpose, and to its context, and this awareness is reflected in the fact that, at the meso-level, we remain within the sphere of the useful defined by the concrete labor of social cooperation and the useful purpose of its products. This valency of the useful does not present itself to experience in pure form, since it is hybridized with other domains of value practices, not only subject to the influences of the relational fields of the procommons but particularly to those of the higher meta-level and capitalist command, which exercise a strong influence in orienting work techniques and organizational methods. However, if I'm hired as a factory worker, the first thing they tell me is not that my job is to make money for the boss or the shareholders but to make the machine work, and I, in turn, must know how to operate it for its useful purposes. If I'm a delivery rider, they don't explain that the purpose of my bringing pizzas around the city is to make money for the shareholders of the platforms that organize my work but that I must be able to navigate the city to bring a pizza to those who are hungry and have purchasing power. In both cases, however, we know—and will see at the meta-level—that the logic of capitalist valorization and accumulation, which we specify at the meta-level above, is copresent with that of use value; indeed, it dominates it and contributes substantially to shaping it. But it is important to distinguish the specificity of the meso-level, in that it indicates a specific dimension of the praxis of value. If, in the procommons, what matters most is the value we give to the relationship, in the meso-level what matters most is the value we give to use, both as producers of goods and services and as consumers or users.

Effectiveness

In Chapter 5, we defined consciousness as the state of awareness and reactivity that draws on the resources mobilized by subjectivity but orients them toward navigation in a given environment. If you want to navigate the environment created by the meso-level, you must therefore follow a fundamental cardinal point, its guiding star: the use value, and therefore the activity, the work in its useful character, that is, with perceptible and at least broadly narrated purposes. This level of social organization, the meso-level, therefore "is the level of active-useful and different processes that run through the entire existing social order" (Pentenero 2018: 23). At this level, individual and social work is seen in its concreteness: it must bring results; means and ends are serialized in productive sequences suited to the purpose; and the measurement of things must, in principle, reckon with this purpose among other possible ones.

In this sense, this level can also be defined as the level of *effectiveness*. By effectiveness, we commonly mean the ability to achieve a useful, pre-established objective—an idea that we will contrast, at the meta-level, with the idea of efficiency, that is, the ability to achieve a pre-established objective with the least amount of resources, time, and energy. On the contrary, it is the underlying level of the procommons, dominated by the concern for relational values and by the sense of retributive justice it generates, that provides us with the sense and the criteria to establish whether a salary is an adequate remuneration for the useful work carried out; or whether the work carried out in the factory or on the streets is alienating or not, degrading or not, satisfying or not, rewarding or not; or whether a certain type of good or service is or is not congruent with the needs to be satisfied or with one's own dignity. Here, too, specific configurations of the measurement of things are obviously at stake. The meta-level, therefore, is torn between two attractors: one from below, which judges the useful in terms of relational values and ideas of sustenance, and one from above, which judges the useful in terms of its profitability.

It is evident that what is socially useful at any given moment depends on a balance of social power that determines not only *what* is produced—why society's collective resources should be devoted to certain ends—but also *how* production occurs: through which expenditures of material and energy and under what techniques and labor relations. From the perspective of the relational values of the procommons, the social utility of producing cluster bombs or nuclear armaments is deeply questionable, and yet it persists. Likewise, from the standpoint of sustaining the procommons, the growing energy consumption and emissions caused by an ever-expanding industrial output of "useful things" appear irrational—and yet they continue.

This persistence arises because the meso-level is structurally entangled in feedback relations with both the upper and lower levels of the pyramid. It mediates between the reproduction of bodies (health, education), the circulation of goods, and the territorial management of production and administration (the state). Yet this mediation is not neutral: It is organized through infrastructures, institutions, and policy frameworks that systematically privilege accumulation over care, and profitability over sufficiency. The meso-level therefore serves as the hinge through which capital's logic extends across society, continually reproducing its priorities while drawing legitimacy and resources from the very social and ecological fields that it simultaneously exhausts.

What counts as *useful* is thus not a neutral or technical matter but the outcome of a struggle over value definition—over which needs, purposes, and relations deserve to mobilize society's collective energies. The meso-level is the battlefield where this struggle takes material form: in investment decisions, technological design, labor organization, and the distribution of public goods. Each production cycle condenses this contest between opposing value logics—one oriented toward accumulation and competitive growth, the other toward reproduction and shared well-being. Within the current organization of social cooperation, however, this balance is structurally tilted toward capital: the infrastructures and incentive systems that shape production ensure that the "useful thing" most often serves profitability rather than life. Every artifact, policy, or commodity thus embodies, within its very form, the hierarchy of values that ordered its making.

From a thermodynamic perspective, this systemic tilt manifests as an *entropic bias* in the social metabolism: Collective energy is channeled into circuits that sustain capital's self-reproduction rather than life's regeneration. Each "useful thing" can be read as a condensation of energy and meaning—a local crystallization of the broader metabolic order. Its material form embodies the flows of energy and labor that sustain it, while its social function reveals the hierarchy of values through which these flows are organized. In this sense, production at the meso-level is not only an economic or technical process but a metabolic translation of the prevailing operating system. It channels energy and information through the filters of value praxis, reproducing either the entropic logic of accumulation or the negentropic logic of social and ecological regeneration. To contest what is considered *useful*, therefore, is to contest the very metabolism of society—to decide whether collective energy will be dissipated in the pursuit of profit or recirculated in the sustenance of life.

This struggle over what counts as *useful*—and for whom—finds an echo in the long history of utilitarian thought. Perhaps the fact that the meso-level is squeezed between two different meanings of utility helps explain why utilitarianism—the political and economic philosophy that emerged in the late eighteenth century and developed in the nineteenth through the works of Jeremy Bentham (1988) and John Stuart Mill (2002)—has always lent itself to two major interpretations: one rooted in the disciplinary logic of labor and social control within classical political economy, and another oriented toward democratic emancipation, as in the radical rationalism of William Godwin (2013). Yet mainstream economic thought systematically flattens these distinctions, conflating use value with exchange value and collapsing the rich, contested terrain of usefulness into the abstract metrics of market demand. In doing so, it not only obscures the tension between social necessity and capitalist valorization but also performs an apologetic function: It naturalizes the market as the sole arbiter of what is useful, thereby justifying the commodification of every human and nonhuman activity that enters its circuits. This erasure of the qualitative horizon of use value—its embeddedness in concrete lives, purposes, and relational judgments—is a central ideological operation through which capitalism presents itself not as a contingent social formation but as the rational and efficient fulfillment of needs.

Mapping the spheres of use-value production

Traditional administrative classifications of economic sectors—such as primary (agriculture and mining), secondary (industry), and tertiary (services)—were developed mainly for statistical and governance purposes. These categories treat economic activity as discrete and functionally neutral, failing to capture the social and political tensions that shape how use value is produced, for what ends, and for whom. They obscure the fact that the same kind of activity—such as education, food production, or infrastructure building—can follow radically different logics: It can sustain relational life and shared purpose (the procommons), or it can be subordinated to the demands of capital accumulation (the meta-level).

Against this flattening of qualitative distinctions, it becomes essential to adopt a different lens—one that does not focus on sectors as administrative categories but on spheres of social cooperation. This approach makes visible the competing forces that shape the production of use value and reveals the dual pull at the meso-level: on one side, toward usefulness rooted in social reproduction, care, and collective life; on the other, toward usefulness reduced to profitability, discipline, and extraction. It is not the nature of the activity that determines its function but the direction in which it is pulled—toward the procommons or the meta-level. The distinction, therefore, is not between one vocabulary and another but between two different ways of conceiving economic life. Administrative classifications group activities according to their technical content or output; Alquati's spheres, by contrast, are defined relationally—by the position activities occupy within the social division of labor of capital and by the orientation of their usefulness within a contested field of value reproduction. They are not sectors but force-field zones, internally heterogeneous and traversed by tensions between social and capital reproduction.

Alquati's approach offers a more dynamic and politically attuned mapping of the meso-level. He invites us to read economic life not as a neutral technical structure but as a field of struggle over the meaning and purpose of value. From the perspective of the social division of labor within the pyramid of capital, the meso-level is "horizontally divided into spheres: productive, reproductive, realization, political, and their possible overlaps" (Pentenero 2018: 23). Each sphere of concrete social cooperation is a site where specific forms of social utility are elaborated, contested, and captured—both serving the reproduction of the overall system and opening spaces in which this functionality can be challenged.

This framework highlights the fundamental ambiguity of usefulness at the meso-level: Every activity may serve either the reproduction of life or the reproduction of capital, depending on the forces that shape it. Alquati's lens thus helps us see economic activity not as fixed or neutral but as a terrain of struggle between different value orientations.

In this terrain, Alquati reformulates the old workerist triad of factory, society, and state into four major areas. The first he calls "artefacture," a term that refers not only to manufacturing but also to the broader human–technical coproduction of artifacts, encompassing the complex technical division of labor from primary sectors such as mining to certain services like transport and advertising, while excluding financial services, which belong to the meta-level. "Destructive/realizing consumption" designates domains where production is subordinated to destruction (e.g., war). "Reproductive final consumption" refers to labor and systems that reproduce humans. "Institutional politics" encompasses the regulatory and organizational structures that coordinate these spheres, mediate reproduction, and interface with command—whether through public policy, welfare systems, administrative control, or geopolitical alignment (Chapter 14). These terms, though specific, enable us to identify divergent trajectories in the production of use value and to trace how each sphere is pulled between social reproduction and capitalist accumulation (Alquati 2021: 24). To these, due to its specificity and ecological entanglement, the area of agriculture must be added.

The following review of these five spheres is necessarily selective and schematic. It does not aim to exhaust their complexity but to highlight key nodal tensions where social reproduction and capital accumulation intersect and diverge. While each sphere operates through distinct organizational forms and material processes, all are traversed by the problematic of social reproduction. Whether through wages, working conditions, environmental health, care infrastructures, or political rights, each area reflects the struggle over how life is maintained, valued, and organized under systemic constraints. We now examine how this contested orientation toward use value plays out across different meso-level spheres of cooperation.

Before delving into the five spheres, it is essential to briefly consider the transversal impact of digital platforms and artificial intelligence across the entire meso-level. While neither platforms nor AI constitute separate spheres, they increasingly act as infrastructural substrates that organize, mediate, and reconfigure how social cooperation is conducted across artefacture, agriculture, reproduction, destruction, and governance. Platforms standardize interfaces, algorithmically sort access, and extract data from every act of participation, thereby blurring the lines between coordination and control. AI, meanwhile, introduces new layers of automation and prediction that can either enhance or replace human capacities, often reinforcing asymmetries in knowledge, power, and value extraction. Crucially, the expansion of AI also entails a massive ecological footprint: Training large-scale models requires vast computational resources and energy, often sourced from carbon-intensive infrastructures (Bender et al. 2021; Crawford 2021). These energy demands are frequently outsourced to data centers located in regions with cheap electricity and weak environmental regulations, thereby deepening global inequalities. Together, platform infrastructures and AI systems instantiate a form of meso-level rationalization that is highly responsive to meta-level imperatives, optimizing production, streamlining services, and reconfiguring political administration according to profitability and surveillance. Yet they are also potential sites of contestation, reappropriation, and alternative design, where new forms of social cooperation and value attribution may be forged.

Artifact production

Artifact production, writes Alquati (2021: 25), "is about the specific working of artefacts and the provision and sub-consumption of living-human-capacity to produce the utility/use value of perceptible goods." This refers to the complex processes through which use values destined for final consumption are generated—perceptible goods that are shaped through the work of humans and machines, integrating energy, means of production, and raw materials into new forms of social utility. In this process, fragments of nature—transformed through mining, extraction, and technical conversion—are consumed alongside human and nonhuman capacities. What results is an "intermediate consumption" of labor and nature that underpins the production of goods seemingly destined to satisfy needs at all levels of the social pyramid, from the relational sphere of the procommons to the instrumental demands of meta-level planning.

Yet, from the point of view of social reproduction, this intermediate consumption is also a consumption of bodies—of workers, ecosystems, and future regenerative capacities. Crucially, because the products of this labor are not only use values but also exchange values, these bodies are subjected to acceleration and intensification and exposed to the pressures and rhythms of meta-level imperatives. The result is a form of extraction not only from nature but from subjectivity itself. Studies underscore how this dynamic unfolds in the workplace. For example, in the UK, over 828,000 workers reported work-related stress, depression, or anxiety in 2019–20 alone (HSE 2023). The perception of job insecurity correlates with reduced safety motivation and higher accident rates (Probst and Brubaker 2001). Such findings illustrate how the acceleration of artifact production under precarious conditions undermines both the physical and psychological well-being of workers—an intensification of labor inseparable from capital's imperative to valorize. This underscores how artifact production is not only a site of technical or economic coordination but one deeply implicated in the field of social reproduction, from working conditions and bodily exhaustion to the social utility or noxiousness of what is produced and its broader impacts on health, dignity, and care.

Artefacture also encompasses energy infrastructures, digital networks, and public utilities—artifacts that are central to the organization of social life. But the selection and configuration of these infrastructures are not guided primarily by social utility or procommons values; rather, they are shaped by the imperatives of accumulation. A strong current of critical thought—from classical Marxism to critical theory and the political history of technology—has long emphasized how technological and infrastructural developments under capitalism are shaped not by collective need but by the imperatives of accumulation. For instance, David F. Noble (1984) meticulously traced how industrial technologies, especially in manufacturing, were developed to discipline labor and centralize managerial control. As Marx (1976) observed in *Capital*, technological change under capitalism aims at increasing productivity and surplus value, not satisfying needs. Marcuse (1964) criticized the use of technology to manufacture artificial needs and intensify dependency on consumerism. David Harvey (1982, 1989) shows how infrastructural decisions—from urban highways to financial networks—are designed to support capital circulation, often at the expense of social cohesion and environmental integrity. There are numerous examples of this, from the Three Gorges Dam in China, which displaced over 1.3 million people in the name of development, to the American high-speed rail system, which has frequently been blocked in favor of car infrastructure due to lobbying by the automotive sector.

Today, these critiques remain deeply relevant. These dynamics are not relics of the past; they are being rapidly rearticulated through the integration of AI into artifact production. AI has become a central driver of change within this sphere. From predictive maintenance and supply chain optimization to the automation of design and fabrication processes, AI systems promise increased productivity but often deliver heightened precarity, labor fragmentation, and algorithmic control. Platforms such as Amazon Web Services and Alibaba's logistics AI operate as infrastructure for entire value chains, reshaping production logics while capturing rents and data. The introduction of generative AI in sectors such as design, engineering, and media artefacture also raises the question of authorship and creative labor, as machines increasingly coproduce outputs once reserved for skilled workers. These developments deepen the entanglement between artifact production and the meta-level logics of extraction, even as alternative techno-political imaginaries seek to reorient these tools toward convivial, commons-based uses.

Under the pressure of the meta-level's logic, industrial production adheres to a linear and accelerated temporality—one that privileges efficiency and profitability over ecological or social rhythms. As discussed in Chapter 10 on social metabolism, this model remains extractive, severing feedback loops between production and regeneration. Efforts to move toward a circular economy—such as those promoted by Braungart and McDonough (2002) and the Ellen MacArthur Foundation (2013)—aim to slow resource depletion through recycling and reuse. However, despite some progress in sectors such as construction and electronics, these practices remain marginal. Currently, approximately 6.5 percent of global economic activity follows circular models (Haas et al. 2015). The low degree of circularity has two main reasons. First, 44 percent of processed materials are used to provide energy and are thus not available for recirculation through reuse or recycling. Second, socioeconomic stocks are still growing at a high rate, with net additions of 17 Gt per year. Even optimistic projections suggest it will remain below 25 percent by 2050 (Tisserant et al. 2017). The deeper problem lies in the subordination of these innovations to the overarching logic of growth and capital accumulation at the meta-level and the level of command. So long as circular practices remain tethered to profitability, they cannot fundamentally restructure the metabolic rift between capital and nature.

From the standpoint of the procommons and the relational values of social reproduction, these efforts are not meaningless; they express attempts to redirect artifact production toward truly useful and sustainable ends. But when subordinated to capital accumulation, they are unable to secure a coherent and regenerative metabolic logic. Industry continues to consume labor and resources at a rate that outpaces their renewal. In this sense, artifact production today remains one of the key battlegrounds between the demands of capital and the needs of life. Experiences of worker-recuperated enterprises and forms of self-managed production show how production can be reorganized through commoning logics, breaking the subordination of usefulness to profitability (Azzellini and Vieta 2025).

Agriculture

A specific and nontrivial difference between agriculture and artifact production concerns their relationship with time and natural cycles. Agriculture is intrinsically linked to biological and climatic rhythms. Its practices depend on natural factors such as the seasons, soil fertility, rainfall, and the life cycles of plants and animals. This *traditionally* involves a circular temporality, in which activities are cyclically repeated in accordance with natural rhythms. Traditional agriculture is therefore linked to *natural cycles* and biological rhythms defined by Gaia: sowing, harvesting, and the resting of the soil mark a *circular temporality* in which, ideally, the Earth is able to regenerate itself. Practices such as crop rotation and organic fertilization help maintain soil fertility and support a more harmonious relationship between human communities and the environment. However, the introduction and expansion of industrial practices accelerated since the middle of the last century—such as extensive monocultures and the use of synthetic fertilizers and pesticides—have disrupted regenerative logic, articulating within agriculture what, as discussed in Chapter 10, is a systemic *metabolic rift* between natural and social systems. In this way, intensive agriculture, on the one hand, retains a residue of *natural circularity* and, on the other hand, approaches a model of continuous production that entails high costs for ecosystems and perpetuates producers' dependence on the capitalist structures of the global market.

Such dependence is exacerbated by the more recent introduction of *biotechnology*, with the aim of genetically modifying crops and animals to obtain higher yields or reduce growth times. Vandana Shiva (1991, 1997) has long emphasized how these innovations, often presented as technical solutions to hunger and scarcity of resources, end up concentrating the control over seeds and production in the hands of large multinationals, further altering the ecological and social balances. Patented seeds exemplify the tightening grip of corporate control over agriculture: Through legal restrictions encoded in intellectual property rights, farmers are prevented from saving or replanting seeds, forcing them into cycles of continual purchase and dependence. This enclosure of the genetic commons erodes the autonomy of farmers and transforms seeds into vectors of capital accumulation (Kloppenburg 2004). This trend is even more starkly illustrated by the development of so-called Terminator seeds—genetically engineered to be sterile after one planting, making reuse biologically impossible. While these technologies have faced international opposition and have not been widely commercialized, they reveal the direction of a system increasingly alienated from ecological cycles and traditional practices such as resowing, seed exchange, and varietal selection. The result is a model of farming that approaches the extractive logic of artefacture, furthering the severance of social reproduction from Gaia. This underscores a key feature of the meso-level; its productive logic is not intrinsic to any one activity but emerges from the pull of systemic forces—toward the procommons or the meta-level.

The environmental implications of biotechnology are significant. Critics argue that the introduction of Genetically Modified Organisms (GMOs) can disrupt local ecosystems and lead to unintended consequences, such as the emergence of superweeds resistant to herbicides. Reliance on chemical inputs associated with certain biotechnological practices can further degrade soil health and biodiversity, contradicting the principles of sustainable agriculture. In addition, there is a growing discourse on the need for inclusive governance frameworks that prioritize the voices of marginalized communities—particularly smallholder and family farmers, who together represent the vast majority of farmers worldwide and are disproportionately affected by biotechnological advancements. According to the Food and Agriculture Organization of the United Nations (FAO), family farms constitute over 90 percent of all farms globally and are responsible for producing approximately 80 percent of the world's food. Within this category, smallholders—those managing less than two hectares—produce about one-third of the global food supply while operating on just 24 percent of agricultural land (FAO 2014; Lowder et al. 2021).

Digital platforms and AI are also reshaping agriculture through so-called smart farming systems. These include AI-powered crop monitoring, predictive analytics for yields, automated irrigation, and precision agriculture technologies, often promoted under the banner of sustainability. Yet while they offer tools for optimization, they also consolidate corporate control over farming practices. Data extracted from fields are increasingly commodified, with platforms acting as intermediaries between farmers and inputs, markets, or knowledge systems. This risks intensifying dependency and enclosure. However, there are emerging counter-experiments—such as open-source farmbots or commons-oriented food sovereignty platforms—that challenge this trajectory by embedding AI within agroecological frameworks, aiming to augment rather than displace situated, relational, and vernacular knowledge systems.

Responding to these challenges requires rethinking dominant models of agricultural development. This includes recognizing the importance of agroecological approaches that ground agriculture in ecological principles, combining traditional knowledge with participatory, transdisciplinary science to codevelop farming practices that work in harmony with natural systems. As various scholars have shown (Shiva 1991, 1997; Altieri 1995; Gliessman 2015), agroecological practices foster systems that are ecologically sound, socially just, and resilient. Agroecological practices not only regenerate ecosystems but also cultivate networks of solidarity between producers and consumers—virtuous circuits in which use values and relational values converge through shared commitments to nourishment, locality, and care. Such an approach not only respects the rights of farmers but also promotes biodiversity and embeds the production of use values in agriculture within the relational field of the procommons.

Ultimately, while agriculture remains tied to biological cycles, its industrial intensification under capitalism erodes this connection, aligning it with extractive logics that mirror the worst ecological impacts of industry. In stark contrast, agroecological approaches reclaim agriculture as a space of regeneration, solidarity, and resistance, pointing toward a radically different metabolism of life.

Destructive/realizing consumption

Destructive/realizing consumption is that area of social cooperation where "work is almost exclusively destructive" (Alquati 2021: 27). Unlike artefacture, where products useful for sustenance are produced *even if* nature is destroyed, here use values are produced, but not use values that *from the broad point of view* of the procommons can be considered necessary for *sustenance*. The aim of this area is the creation and use of "destructive capacity and also a little capacity in general and across the board" such as "technoscience (increasingly across the board)" (Alquati 2021: 27). In this context, then, "there is . . . an end-consumption, a specific work of end-destructive consumption, aimed mainly at a hyper-industrial destruction that creates surplus (as is often the case in war, for example). Here, Production (with a capital P) is almost 'only' upwards" (Alquati 2021: 27), toward the meta-level, destroying its underlying foundations—that is, the procommons and Gaia's level—and toward the mega-level of command as domination: the maintenance and restructuring of the geopolitical and geoeconomics configuration of global capitalism.

The area of destructive/realizing consumption "produces almost only capital and capitalist domination and indirect techno-scientific development (and religion), which for our social system is the most important thing, the realisation of its greatest purpose. Capital is accumulated by destroying different utilities and thus realising the enlargement of markets" (Alquati 2021: 27). This destruction has two main effects. First, it "contributes to the production and accumulation of capital" (Alquati 2021: 28). Second, it

> has some secondary effect of innovativeness of methods and substances, and not only of artificial and cold means and machines, but also of living human resources, of technological and organisational innovation, of reproduction of human capacity. Consider the fact that most of the new organisational models and new technologies, materials and energies, and the reproduction of new human resources are first experimented with by the army: it is military technoscience, as Paul Virilio argues.
>
> —Alquati (2021: 27)

In the sphere of destructive/realizing consumption, AI plays a crucial role in enabling both the efficiency and scalability of militarized infrastructures. From autonomous weapon systems and drone surveillance to predictive policing and data-driven border controls, AI is deployed to accelerate the destructive capacities of contemporary command systems. Defense platforms and private contractors leverage machine learning to manage battlefield logistics, simulate war scenarios, and conduct cyber operations, turning destruction into a programmable function. A stark example is the Israeli military's use of AI in Gaza, where systems such as *Habsora* ("The Gospel") were employed to generate thousands of bombing targets at unprecedented speed—optimizing for throughput rather than human discernment and resulting in catastrophic civilian casualties—an instance of destructive/realizing consumption governed by algorithmic efficiency rather than ethical deliberation (Abraham 2023). Meanwhile, the same algorithms are repurposed in civilian domains—monitoring social unrest or managing emergency responses—further blurring the boundary between security and war. These systems often become self-reinforcing: As social reproduction is dismantled, AI-enhanced destruction is presented as the only form of order.

Destructive/realizing consumption ascends toward the meta- and mega-levels, reflecting both its profitability and its role in maintaining the global order. Consider the profit opportunities emerging from the war in Ukraine. The country's reconstruction is now estimated at $524 billion, with immediate needs for 2025 requiring $15 billion (World Bank 2025). In response, major powers have pledged substantial support: The G7 committed $50 billion, financed partly through interest on frozen Russian assets; the European Union pledged up to €35 billion for economic and energy infrastructure; the UK signed a century-long partnership focused on energy, green steel, and critical minerals; and Italy, in collaboration with UNESCO, is rebuilding Odesa's cultural sites (Amante and Lawder 2024; Tamma 2024; Murray 2025).

These investments highlight lucrative openings for firms in infrastructure, energy, and urban development. The United States has shown particular interest through a proposed bilateral agreement to co-invest in Ukraine's critical minerals, establishing a Reconstruction Investment Fund backed by 50 percent of future revenues from monetized public resources (Miller et al. 2025). Such arrangements reveal how geopolitical strategy is tightly woven with economic interests, making destructive/realizing consumption a core dynamic of global capitalism.

This sphere has expanded dramatically over the past two decades. Global military spending rose for the ninth consecutive year in 2023, reaching $2.4 trillion—up 6.8 percent, the sharpest increase since 2009—representing 2.3 percent of global GDP (SIPRI 2024). Countries such as the United States, China, and Russia lead this trend, with European states now pledging to raise defense spending to 3 percent, and even 5 percent, of GDP. Rearmament in Europe heavily benefits the US military industry: between 2020 and 2024, over 64 percent of European NATO arms imports came from the United States, making Europe its largest weapons market. This dependency includes systems such as the F-35 fighter jet and extends to satellite infrastructure, prompting European efforts such as the Galileo project to regain strategic autonomy (Ciesnik 2025). Yet this reorientation, which goes hand in hand with expanded security logics and increased criminalization of dissent, will further divert resources from social reproduction.

Reproductive final consumption

The sphere of reproductive final consumption is the sphere in which living-human-capacity is reproduced in organizational forms on much larger scales than those already found in the procommons. How? By consuming, in a hyper-industrial way, resources and means of final consumption and artificial machines fabricated elsewhere; nature's bounty; and "warm reproductive utilities provided by peculiar partners, such as services to the working person" (Alquati 2021: 28). Therefore, reproductive final consumption can be divided into two further subareas: "reproductive final consumption of sensitive goods" (e.g., medicines) and "reproductive final consumption of intangible services to the company and the worker" (Alquati 2021: 27), such as the care work of doctors and nurses or the training work of teachers and students. Through this reproductive final consumption, "through use and/or enjoyment," tangible and intangible utilities are incorporated "into the living social-human-body," that is, into the labor force, into the living human capacity. However, within the pyramid, the latter is primarily seen as a commodity, both singular and collective. Therefore, "warm living-human-capacity" is produced in such a way as to make it as functional as possible for acting within the measure of the things of the meta-level, subjects of course to the resistances and autonomous relational patterns coming from the procommons.

I want to briefly focus on the two major subareas of this reproductive consumption, that is, two forms of reproduction of living human capacities. One subarea involves the maintenance, or simple reproduction, of human working capacity—such as entertainment and health care—where labor is restored without enhancement (Alquati 2021: 30). The other subarea, on the other hand, is "the great final sub-area of formative reproduction or enlarged reproduction and therefore reproduction with (hyper-industrial) increase of the living human active/working capacity itself . . . In both these two reproductive sub-areas . . . the reproduction of capacity, of its value, is realised" (Alquati 2021: 30). Whether it is value for procommons and Gaia or for the meta-level and the level of command is the fundamental distinction to always keep in mind. What is generally called the area of education and health are two instances of the subareas Alquati is talking about here.

In recent decades, dominant education policies and trends across the United States, the UK, and Europe—through school choice, privatization, performance metrics, and technocratic governance—have increasingly restructured education toward the meta-level, aligning it with the production of human capital for the labor market. This reflects what Ivan Illich (1971) denounced: a system in which institutionalized schooling alienates learners from lived experience, narrows knowledge to measurable outputs, and imposes conformity to dominant values under the guise of education. Yet the pedagogical imagination of the procommons has not disappeared. Paulo Freire's (1988) legacy of education as liberation continues to animate grassroots student movements and radical educational practices that reclaim learning as a dialogical, participatory, and transformative praxis. These approaches foreground relational values, including mutual recognition, critical reflection, and the cultivation of capacities not subordinated to profit or competition.

Education, then, as a formative space of the meso-level, is also a site of struggle between two opposing poles: on the one hand, the logic of capital, which orients learning toward employability, standardized outcomes, and market efficiency; on the other, the logic of the procommons, which sees education as a relational and emancipatory process grounded in shared meaning, critical awareness, and collective life. Yet this struggle does not remain external to the procommons; it is also internalized and contested within it, as seen in the rise of right-wing educational movements that appropriate the language of community and autonomy to advance exclusionary, hierarchical visions. The struggle over education is thus a struggle over the meaning of usefulness itself: whether it serves the reproduction of capital or the flourishing of shared life.

The proliferation of digital platforms and AI tools in education—learning management systems, adaptive testing, automated grading, and even AI tutors—reflects a deeper shift in the meso-level configuration of reproductive consumption. These systems often obscure the pedagogical relationship behind metrics and efficiency, treating education as a sequence of data points to be optimized. Yet they also open ambivalent spaces: While some platforms reinforce the meta-level logic of human capital production, others are codesigned to support horizontal, relational, and community-driven learning. The key distinction lies in whether these tools augment mutual learning and care or whether they mediate and depersonalize them in the service of extraction.

The field of health, like that of education, is situated at the meso-level and traversed by a structural tension between two opposing attractors: on the one hand, an orientation toward the procommons, where health is understood as a relational good and a collective process of care; on the other, the pull of the meta-level, which tends to subordinate health to the imperatives of capitalist valorization. In recent decades, dominant health policies in many contexts—from Europe to the United States—have progressively shifted toward this second pole through processes of privatization, outsourcing, and the reduction of public services.

This process produces two converging effects. On the one hand, health becomes a commodity, accessible according to logics of profit and purchasing power, with an expansion of the private and insurance sectors that replace or supplement public services. On the other hand, the retreat of public provision and the precarization of health services shift an increasing share of care work into the informal and domestic sphere, intensifying the reproductive burden placed on families and on emotional and community networks. But the problem is not only quantitative: It is not just about how much care work is "offloaded" onto the procommons but about the material, relational, and emotional conditions under which this work takes place—often in isolation, with little support and insufficient resources. As Emma Dowling (2021) argues, this shift marks not merely a redistribution of care work but a transformation in the conditions under which it is performed—precarious, unsupported, and emotionally taxing.

To this must be added another critical dimension: the quality of care. Even within formally public health systems, the adoption of criteria based on efficiency, productivity, and financial performance has led to an increasingly business-oriented mode of management, often fueled by quantitative evaluation tools, incentive systems, and managerial metrics. This orientation can undermine the quality of care, particularly in primary medicine, where time per patient is reduced and pressures mount to "do more with less" (Martínez-Faneca et al. 2020; Martínez-Faneca and Fabrellas 2023). The consequences include the neglect of prevention, relational impoverishment, and the deterioration of trust between health-care workers and patients.

In health care, platforms and AI are transforming diagnostic routines, administrative processes, and patient monitoring. While such innovations can reduce friction and enable more precise interventions, they also introduce new forms of abstraction, datafication, and depersonalization. Patients become data profiles to be tracked, analyzed, and managed—often in ways that bypass direct human contact or relational judgment. The promise of AI-enhanced medicine is thus bifurcated. It can either extend the reach of care in underserved areas and support medical professionals in their relational tasks, or it can deepen the commodification of health, turning care into a transaction mediated by opaque algorithms. As in education, their social function depends not on the technology itself but on the political, institutional, and relational frameworks within which they are embedded.

In the face of this dynamic, the task is not merely to demand more public services but to imagine a different model of care: a health-care system that does not simply deliver services but instead sustains and strengthens the circuits of the procommons. This means recognizing health as a participatory process that involves communities, territories, and subjectivities in the shared construction of well-being. Proposals such as community medicine, participatory health systems, mutualist networks, and cooperative forms of care move in this direction: They do not deny the need for public resources but propose a model of management oriented toward relationality, dignity, and the coproduction of use value.

In both cases of health and education, "there is a circularity, a recursivity, in a spiral. And a balance" (Alquati 2021: 29). That balance is between the social costs of producing living human capacities—of reproducing the labor force as a commodity—and the use value this reproduction offers to the upper levels of the pyramid. For capital, the equation must always resolve in its favor: by minimizing these costs through austerity, informalization, and the externalization of reproductive labor onto the procommons. The struggle over health and education is therefore a struggle over reproduction itself—over whether it will be governed by profitability or by the relational logic of shared life. The same is true of other terrains at the meso-level. Artifact production, agriculture, and even, to a much lesser extent, destructive/realizing consumption are all meso-level fields marked by the same ambiguity. They can either serve the reproduction of life and relational value—or be captured by the meta-level's imperative to extract, accumulate, and command. The procommons, then, is a horizon of reorientation, always at risk of co-optation yet constantly asserting itself wherever people reclaim the right to shape what is useful, meaningful, and shared. It is our ground.

The political–institutional sphere

The final area that Alquati identifies at the meso-level—therefore subject to the attractors of both the higher and lower levels—is the political–institutional sphere. This is the expansive domain "in which almost half of the total income of this social system is spent . . . and largely precisely to make our reproduction work" (Alquati 2021: 31–2). But it does more than that. Politics, in this sphere, takes on a dual function.

Horizontally, it refers to the regulation of social reproduction at the level of reproductive final consumption: laws, norms, and policies that shape health, education, working conditions, subsidies, and the composition of social spending. It also includes regulatory interventions that emerge from or affect subjectivities rooted in the procommons. This encompasses a wide range of issues such as abortion rights, gender identity, migrant and LGBTQIA+ rights, the status of mutual aid or solidarity associations, self-production (e.g., hemp cultivation), and the legal framing—or criminalization—of grassroots organizing. These forms of regulation often act as boundary-setting mechanisms, delimiting what kinds of social cooperation are permitted and under what terms—frequently within legal architectures shaped to favor multinational capital.

Vertically, the political–institutional sphere refers to "the overall form of the system" (Alquati 2021: 31)—its macro-architecture and territorial organization—but also to its embeddedness in larger scales of capitalist command. This includes the relationship of the nation-state to the mega-level of the pyramid and its integration into broader geopolitical and geoeconomic configurations (to be analyzed in Chapter 14). It thus mediates between local processes of social reproduction and transnational circuits of capital, finance, and strategic control.

Taken together, these horizontal and vertical dimensions make the political–institutional sphere a key site for managing the tensions between social reproduction and capital reproduction. It is where conflicts over life, value, and legitimacy are codified, contested, and enforced—shaping not only what is reproduced but how, for whom, and under what conditions.

The political management of the meso-level has often followed a pattern of alternation between center-left and center-right formations, each articulating different responses to the recurring crises of social reproduction under capitalism. This oscillation has not been symmetrical or universally applicable, but in many contexts, it has provided a mode of governance calibrated to the demands of capital. Under neoliberalism, this alternation was stabilized through a selective politics of inclusion; civil rights, anti-discrimination protections, and symbolic recognition functioned not as transformative tools but as mechanisms to recalibrate legitimacy. These concessions offered partial recognition without disrupting the underlying architecture of accumulation.

This calibration, however, was always conditional. Rights were extended insofar as they remained compatible with profitability and institutional reproduction. Recognition expanded when social legitimacy faltered, and repression was never off the table—only offset or delayed. As economic growth slowed in the Global North, the material, symbolic, and fiscal costs of inclusion—anti-discrimination laws, welfare provisions, labor protections, and environmental standards—came under scrutiny. For capital, these were increasingly seen not as achievements but as constraints.

We are now living through a recalibration. The symbolic dial has turned: Inclusion is eroded while exclusion becomes central to legitimacy. Governance is no longer premised on diversity and opportunity but on order, tradition, and hierarchy. This is not a rupture but a mutation—what we may call authoritarian neoliberalism. The political center has not vanished;

it has been reoriented toward the gravitational pull of reaction. As Beuret (2024) observes, this new configuration does not reject liberalism outright but hollows it out from within, reconfiguring its crisis into a platform for moralized and exclusionary statecraft.

This shift manifests not only in discourse but in institutional rhythm. Where neoliberal meritocracy once offered conditional access through productivity and credentialism, merit is now fused with moral identity. The "deserving" citizen is defined not only by market value but by adherence to dominant norms—nationality, gender, race, and conformity. Merit becomes a gatekeeping device, repurposed to justify exclusion, consolidate resentment, and weaponize difference. Platform governance and algorithmic regulation now increasingly shape the political–institutional sphere. From welfare platforms that rank and exclude users based on risk scores to predictive tools used in criminal justice, immigration, and benefit systems, AI is operationalized to manage populations through automated discretion. This governance through code obscures political decisions behind technical parameters, reducing conflictual social questions to computational problems. In this way, platform governance acts as a relay of meta-level command—translating accumulation and control imperatives into everyday administrative routines. Yet it also produces new visibility, resistance, and critique. Movements challenging algorithmic injustice, fighting for data sovereignty, or designing democratic alternatives to platform infrastructures are reclaiming the political core of digital mediation. In doing so, they reopen the question: Who defines the rules by which we reproduce our lives?

The institutions once tasked with buffering systemic contradictions are increasingly instrumentalized for coercion and containment. This is not the end of neoliberalism's logic but its authoritarian intensification under strain—market primacy remains, now fused with affective governance through culture war, surveillance, securitization, and the abandonment of universal claims.

Authoritarian neoliberalism is not a coherent new system; it is a metastasis. It retains the DNA of neoliberalism—its disdain for solidarity and public goods—but sheds the residual universalist veneer. It manages contradiction not through alternation but through scapegoating. As electoral options narrow and abstention rises—not from apathy but from disillusionment—the meso-level becomes a key battleground. It is here, in the rhythms of education, health care, infrastructure, artefacture, and daily social cooperation, that competing visions of value collide.

Whether this field tips toward repression or regeneration depends on our capacity to build transversal alliances—coalitions that defend care, autonomy, and shared life beyond the violence of capital.

13

The meta-level

A central vector of systemic command

As we move to the meta-level of the capitalist system, we are not entering a separate sector or an external domain. We remain within the same terrain of social cooperation that defines the meso-level—the field of useful production and reproduction. But we enact and prioritize a distinct operational logic that organizes this terrain. At the meso-level, use value is in the foreground, while relational values linger in the background; at the meta-level, it is exchange value that dominates over use value. Use value does not disappear; it persists, but it becomes functional to the logic of accumulation. The systems of useful production and the corresponding praxes are thus not external to capital but embedded in its circuits, reconfigured in such a way as to serve its ends through what Karl Marx called real subsumption—the transformation not only of what is produced but of how, by whom, where, and according to which norms and temporalities. In short, this is the transformation of the measure of things within social cooperation. This is where the logic of exchange value consolidates its dominance—not as an autonomous sphere but as an organizing code that rewrites the norms of usefulness, the rhythms of life, and the distribution of means across the entire pyramid.

From this perspective, the meta-level must be understood not as a separate layer floating above social life but as immanent to it. As Alquati suggested, the levels of the capitalist pyramid are not spatially distinct but systemically co-constitutive, with the higher levels exerting a strategic function of command and domination over the articulation of the lower ones. The meta-level operates through the structuring of prices, investment flows, financial logics, and inter-capitalist competition, which in turn reshape what is produced, how it is produced, and for whom. In doing so, it reorganizes the institutions, infrastructures, and norms of the meso-level, bending them to the priorities of valorization. In this sense, the meso-level becomes increasingly functional to the operations of the meta-level, not only through market mechanisms but also through the transformation of its internal rationalities: What is considered useful, effective, or desirable is increasingly determined by its contribution to capital's self-valorization.

What Alquati calls the meta-level is therefore a central vector of systemic command, operating alongside the level of domination above it—where the imperatives of valorization and accumulation assert themselves most directly. The meta-level does not command through decree but through structuring environments—shaping what is seen as viable, rational, or desirable within the wider social field. As part of the autopoietic organization of capital, this level reproduces the systemic conditions for its own continuation: It continuously mobilizes, reorganizes, and disciplines social cooperation in ways functional to the accumulation of (exchange) value, ensuring that the reproduction of capital structures and reorients the reproduction of life. Following Alquati (1989: 118), the meta-level can be divided into two interdependent zones: the lower sublevel of valorization, and the upper sublevel of accumulation, which functions as both the goal and enabler of the system, channeling investments toward sectors that promise the highest returns.

The sublevel of valorization

Composed of interlocking M–C–M′ circuits, this sublevel constitutes the systemic, extractive, and transforming engine of what is conventionally referred to as "the economy." Its rhythms—expansion and recession, boom and bust—shape the conditions under which all other levels operate. But beyond these cycles, it generates the structural features of capitalist society: the polarization of income and wealth, the concentration and centralization of productive capacities, the consolidation of corporate power, the collusion between capital and state apparatuses, and the externalization of social and ecological costs onto the procommons and onto Gaia.

The meta-level thus functions as a strategic locus within the autopoietic organization of capital, where the energies of social cooperation emerging from the procommons and the meso-level are selectively oriented and channeled toward the logic of accumulation. Ownership over the means of production, control over investment flows, and dominance over the design of infrastructures and institutions endow this level with the capacity to exert a strategic force on subjectivity—not by directly determining behavior but by structuring the contexts in which desires, habits, and aspirations emerge and are made operable. These are contexts populated by markets to be created or conquered, competitive pressures, institutional metrics, and cultural codes, in which subjectivities are molded, seduced, and mobilized as partial figures: pliable consumers, disciplined workers, and self-optimizing individuals. The meta-level structures its environment primarily through what Marx called the capital circuit M–C–M′: the movement of capital in which money (M) is invested to produce commodities (C) only in order to return as more money (M′).[1] These circuits form the backbone of capitalist markets, shaping the field in which production, consumption, and social cooperation unfold. The higher the degree of their pervasiveness in social cooperation, the stronger the force field shaped by profitability metrics, competitive pressures, and webs of market dependencies. In this configuration, the reproduction of life is increasingly mediated by the logic of exchange: What cannot generate capital is treated as irrational, inefficient, or obsolete.

The contradiction between social reproduction and the reproduction of capital is not visible from the observational standpoint of the meta-level; instead, it is actively dissimulated and operationalized. The meta-level does not merely obscure this contradiction—it transforms it into a technical problem to be managed within the coordinates of valorization. It organizes the very conditions under which the subordination of life to capital appears not as a violent imposition but as common sense: by directing infrastructures, metrics, and institutional constraints in such a way that only what aligns with accumulation appears rational, viable, or even conceivable—while everything else is dismissed as inefficiency, excess, or risk. From this vantage point, the social crises generated by capital are systematically reabsorbed into the repertoire of the meta-level itself: Inequalities are addressed through market-based "inclusion"; care deficits through financialized welfare schemes or gig-work platforms; environmental collapse through "green" technologies that sustain growth; and reproductive strain through productivity-enhancing solutions such as AI in education or robotics in eldercare. Every problem of social reproduction is treated as an opportunity for profitable intervention. This is how the contradiction is not merely concealed but retooled to serve the very dynamics that produced it.

Every capitalist subject—a firm, a bank, a platform—exists through a specific praxis: the restless movement of money becoming more money. This is the M–C–M′ circuit, in which accumulation is not an outcome but a mandate, and valorization its mode of life. Each individual M–C–M′ circuit seeks to survive and expand within a market composed of countless other M–C–M′ circuits. It is therefore embedded in a relational ecology of competition and collusion, in which profitability and market share are determined not only by strategic decisions but through struggles waged on the bodies of workers, on territories, and on the metabolic fabric of the planet. These circuits are now globally interconnected, forming a planetary system in which the reproduction of capital hinges on differential advantage—often secured through the intensification of exploitation and the externalization of costs.

This competitive dynamic is not only external; it penetrates the internal organization of each circuit, shaping the management of labor, the design of production, and the metrics of success. Work is not primarily valued for its social utility but for its capital functionality—its capacity to generate surplus value, secure market position, and ensure capital's self-reproduction. The aim is no longer to produce what is useful but what is profitable.

From this vantage point, capital's measure of things—productivity, profitability, return on investment—imposes itself on the measure of social reproduction, which takes as its reference the procommons and the meso-level: the vernacular, the useful, well-being, relational values, ecologies, and the satisfaction of needs. The two logics coexist but asymmetrically: Capital imposes its rationality, while social reproduction struggles to assert its own.

In this context, social reproduction—in both its relational character and its material access to the means of life—is increasingly subordinated to the "laws of the economy" imposed by the meta-level. The latter thus operates as the central engine of the capitalist macro-system, what Pentenero (2018: 23) calls, following Alquati, "the level of the great processes of reproduction of the capitalist whole." Here we find the interwoven systems of capitalist valorization: the mobilization of social labor in forms functional to accumulation. This accumulation is not merely an outcome—it is a systemic meta-purpose that determines where capital flows, which sectors are prioritized, and how labor is organized.

Unlike the meso-level—where the emphasis remains on the usefulness of things—the level of valorization establishes a direct interconnection between usefulness and the logic of capital (Alquati 1989: 195). At this level, the M–C–M′ circuit is mediated by the labor process and does not culminate merely in the production of a commodity but in the realization of surplus value, which must be reinvested to sustain accumulation and open new paths of growth.

Thus, the work performed in production cannot be understood solely as socially useful activity—it must also be understood as work functional to capital, oriented toward profit. What matters is not the concrete content of the labor but its abstract character—what Marx (1976: 128) described as "human labour-power expended without regard to the form of its expenditure." Labor here counts only insofar as it can be quantified, compared, and folded into circuits of accumulation.

It is from this perspective that capital mobilizes the discourse of efficiency—not as a neutral concern with doing more with less but as a way of measuring and disciplining labor in accordance with its own ends. These dynamics reveal a deeper ambiguity in categories such as *efficiency* and *productivity*: While they could serve the aims of social reproduction—enabling more time for care, rest, or creativity—they are redefined within the meta-level to serve accumulation. Their meaning is not intrinsic but shaped by the dominant value regime.

Efficiency

Efficiency, like all human constructs, is neither inherently good nor bad; its value depends entirely on the context in which it is pursued and the purposes it serves. Technically, efficiency is just a ratio between the output of a given form of social cooperation and the resources required to produce it—whether measured as labor productivity (output per hour worked) or energy efficiency (output per unit of energy consumed).

On the surface, improvements in efficiency seem universally desirable: A worker produces more in less time; a liter of fuel covers more distance. From the standpoint of material life and social usefulness—that is, from the perspective of the procommons and the meso-level—such gains could indeed enhance well-being: less time working for the same livelihood, fewer emissions for the same level of production.

But at the meta-level of capitalist valorization, this logic breaks down. Increases in efficiency are no longer oriented toward human flourishing but toward reducing production costs in order to gain competitive advantage in the market and expand profit margins. The goal is not to work less but to outcompete others. What might appear as a neutral or universally beneficial gain becomes something quite different when seen within the ecology of relationships established by capitalism. Within this ecology, the effects of increased efficiency are circular and coercive: Labor is "freed" not for care, creativity, or rest but for displacement, unemployment, and precaritization. What emerges as a gain obtained through technical means becomes a social loss distributed through the dominant logic of capitalist markets. The same ratio—output per input—can either deepen exploitation or lighten the burdens of life, depending on the social relations in which it is embedded.

This contradiction has nothing to do with the morality of individual capitalists. Even if a company wanted to fully redistribute the gains of efficiency—through shorter working hours or higher wages—it would forfeit its competitive edge. In a system governed by market rivalry, even if oligopolistic, such a firm would be punished by losing market share, profitability, and eventually viability. Efficiency thus becomes a mechanism of coercion, not liberation—advancing productivity while undermining the very conditions that would allow its benefits to be socially shared.

Historically, increases in social productivity have, at times, supported wage growth and reductions in working hours. But this was never automatic. These gains were the result of struggles by workers and social movements, which forced legal and institutional changes. However, when the relationship between productivity and the social wage came under pressure—most notably in the 1970s—it contributed to the unraveling of Keynesian capitalism, which had relied on a relatively stable link between rising productivity and rising standards of living (De Angelis 2000). If we are to reclaim efficiency as a socially and ecologically meaningful concept, it must be inserted into a different ecology of cooperation—one that is not governed by capital's imperatives but by the needs and values of social reproduction.

The sublevel of accumulation

The accumulation sublevel marks the financial apex of the meta-level: the point at which capital no longer merely organizes production but commands it. Here, the logic of profitability becomes self-referential, and finance operates as a structuring principle that reconfigures social cooperation according to the demands of accumulation. This section clarifies how finance functions as both infrastructure and command, shaping what is produced, how, and for whom—regardless of its relation to actual human or ecological needs.

The Logic of M–M′ and Financial Abstraction

At this upper sublevel, the circuit of capital closes: Profits extracted from production are not simply consumed but reinvested in areas considered strategically or financially attractive based on expected returns. This process amplifies the dynamics of market competition. Individual capitals increasingly operate not only to sell goods but to attract liquidity, especially through financial markets, where expectations, forecasts, and ratings determine the future viability of entire sectors.

This is the realm of the M–M′ circuit: a form of accumulation that no longer requires the direct mediation of production. Money generates more money not by producing and selling goods but by trading in symbols and claims on future value—stocks, derivatives, real estate speculation, and venture capital flows. These instruments orbit the world of material production, extracting from it, anticipating it, and steering it, while remaining structurally indifferent to its concrete outcomes. What matters is not what is produced, how, or for whom but whether it yields sufficient returns. This is how speculative bubbles emerge, as in the case of tech startups valued at billions before producing anything tangible, or real estate developments built not for habitation but as placeholders in investor portfolios.

Finance and the Subordination of Social Reproduction

Crucially, this level also absorbs and redirects the very resources meant to sustain social reproduction. Pension funds, university endowments, health insurance reserves, and household savings are increasingly funneled into financial markets, linking the survival of families and institutions to the performance of capital. What should safeguard future care and well-being becomes a lever for reinforcing the pressures of accumulation. Social reproduction is thus subordinated not only ideologically or materially but also financially—through the transformation of future-oriented care into speculative capital.

At the accumulation sublevel, the content of use value becomes irrelevant. What matters is how quickly capital can be multiplied. This logic cascades downward, compelling public institutions, households, and even care systems to conform to its metrics. The result is a regime in which profitability trumps social or ecological meaning—disembedding economic life from the very conditions that sustain it.

This mode of command is operationalized through finance: a set of activities—concentrated in banks, investment funds, and intermediaries—that manage the flow of capital through credit, debt, and leverage. A brief historical reconstruction of the rise of financial command over the last few decades and its evolving logics will be offered in Chapter 15. Here, my aim is not to reconstruct the history of finance but to clarify its systemic role within the architecture of accumulation and its effects on social reproduction. While finance can serve multiple purposes, its dominant role within capitalism is the valorization of capital: the multiplication of money and the enforcement of a normative profit standard across the system. At its core, the accumulation sublevel operates through four interlinked functions: investment allocation, funding strategies, profit distribution, and risk management. These may appear technical or neutral, but they are shaped by systemic automatisms—benchmarks, credit models, and algorithms—that channel decisions toward accumulation, regardless of social or ecological consequences.

Finance is a stratified field, operating across multiple scales and domains: public finance, which governs state budgets and spending priorities; corporate finance, which structures investment and competition within firms; and personal finance, which disciplines households through credit scores, savings plans, and debt obligations. Despite this diversity, all levels are increasingly governed by the same metric: expected profitability under conditions of risk.

From Structural Adjustment to Fiscal Militarization

Financial decisions thus play a decisive role in shaping the landscape of social cooperation. They channel resources toward certain sectors while depriving others, legitimize some use values while marginalizing others, and foster cooperation in specific places while undermining it elsewhere. These decisions are not based on social utility—a criterion central to the procommons or the meso-level—but on speculative assessments of profitability, conditioned by broader political and institutional constraints. In this sense, from the perspective of social reproduction, finance acts as a selector of use values. It does not merely fund what already exists; it actively filters, disciplines, and steers the productive capacities of society, determining what can be brought into existence and what is left behind.

Finance also imposes a series of constraints and conditions on how borrowed money—whether by companies or nation-states—can be used. For example, since the 1980s and 1990s, structural adjustment policies led by the International Monetary Fund (IMF) and the World Bank have linked sovereign lending to sweeping economic reforms (Stiglitz 2002; SAPRIN 2004). Governments seeking loans to repay public debt were required to implement policies that prioritized fiscal discipline, market liberalization, and privatization. These reforms systematically dismantled social rights and welfare infrastructures, directly impacting the procommons and the meso-level in order to enhance capital profitability. Today, these mechanisms have not disappeared but have evolved into more technocratic forms of fiscal surveillance and conditional lending, often embedded in global recovery frameworks and green transition packages. As recent analyses note, structural adjustment has effectively returned—reshaped to fit a post-pandemic world marked by new crises of debt, austerity, and geopolitical realignment (Lawrence 2022; Sullivan and Hickel 2025).

A similar logic underpins more recent arrangements, such as the European Recovery Plan, launched in 2020 as NextGenerationEU (NGEU), a temporary recovery instrument aimed at supporting member states in rebuilding their economies after the COVID-19 pandemic. While it promises large-scale funding to national governments, many of these resources are tied to old and new forms of conditionality—some explicit, others buried in technical and bureaucratic frameworks. In Italy, for example, one requirement for unlocking Recovery Plan funds was the approval of long-postponed competition legislation under the Draghi government. This reform, among other effects, undermined the capacity of civic administrations to manage public services according to criteria of social utility, paving the way for further privatizations and reinforcing the alignment of the meso-level with capitalist valorization (Bersani 2020; Forum Italiano dei Movimenti per l'Acqua 2021).

Financial Metrics and the Erosion of the Commons

A reorientation of finance is now accelerating under the combined pressure of geopolitical tensions and military conflict. In response to the war in Ukraine, the European Union (EU) has begun reshaping its fiscal architecture to prioritize defense and security. Plans such as the proposed "ReArm Europe" initiative (later renamed as Readiness 2030) aim to mobilize up to €800 billion for military investment over the next few years, including €150 billion in loans and the redirection of existing EU funds such as cohesion funding. The European Investment Bank is also being encouraged to lift its traditional restrictions on defense-related lending. Platforms such as the Strategic Technologies for Europe Platform (STEP) further consolidate this shift, funneling public resources toward defense and "strategic competitiveness" objectives (European Commission 2025; Höller 2024).

These choices are not the result of resource scarcity but of political prioritization. Finance here does not merely reflect neutral technical expertise—it acts as a mechanism to reallocate and repurpose public wealth. In doing so, it increasingly marginalizes funding for social reproduction, care, and ecological transition, which become subordinated to an agenda of securitization, militarization, and accumulation. This dynamic exemplifies how financial governance operates not only through investment but through the active redirection of collective futures.

This reconfiguration of fiscal priorities is not confined to defense or macroeconomic policy; it also reshapes the governance of public services and the everyday infrastructures of care. Indeed, the broader phenomenon of public sector privatization—in all its forms, from public–private partnerships to performance-based investment metrics—can be understood as a strategic mechanism for subordinating both the meso-level and the procommons to the logic of the meta-level. This includes the extension of corporate hierarchies and managerial rationalities into areas previously oriented toward social value. The proliferation of ranking systems and competitive funding mechanisms, such as the Research Assessment Framework for universities in the UK, forces service providers to compete rather than collaborate, eroding the very principles of solidarity and shared purpose that underlie socially meaningful cooperation.

This is how finance disciplines the horizon of possibility. A striking example is the wave of speculation and windfall profits in the oil and gas sector during the first phase of the war in Ukraine: Rather than accelerating a transition away from fossil fuels, financial markets rewarded extractive industries, pouring resources into sectors that actively undermine the conditions of life. Another example concerns how financial markets constrain public fiscal policy. Government spending is often evaluated not against the urgency of social needs but according to its compatibility with debt servicing, credit ratings, and capital market expectations. The consequence is a political economy in which the metrics of accumulation trump democratic deliberation, and the provision of care, equity, and sustainability is consistently deferred or denied.

The panopticon of capital

On a global scale, the whole of the meta-level functions as a systemic command apparatus that seeks to discipline the lower strata of the pyramid—both the meso-level and the procommons. It operates like a panopticon of capital. The term *panopticon* refers to a prison design by Jeremy Bentham, later developed by Michel Foucault (1977) as a metaphor for modern disciplinary power: a central watchtower that makes inmates behave as if they are always being observed, thus inducing self-discipline. The panopticon of capital is thus not a centralized authority issuing orders but a dispersed and multilayered architecture—a meta-disciplinary dispositif that governs through market signals, financial constraints, and structural dependencies. This disciplinary order promises to reward certain behaviors—working hard, efficiency, and conformity with market logics—while penalizing other forms of cooperation that prioritize non-capitalist values. This form of power is not always visible to its participants. Like Bentham's watchtower, it works through the internalization of surveillance: Subjectivities regulate themselves in accordance with norms diffused across the social body, embedded in metrics, credit ratings, creditworthiness algorithms, logistical standards, and the everyday imperative to "stay competitive." Crucially, the enactment of these rewarded behaviors does not merely conform to the dispositif—it helps reproduce and stabilize it, embedding its norms into the infrastructures, expectations, and rhythms of everyday life. Within this framework, social cooperation is governed by a continuous compulsion to perform—to generate value for capital, or risk marginalization and exclusion from access to basic means of life. Yet the paradox is that widespread conformity, by reinforcing the dispositif itself, narrows the chances of reward; success is not guaranteed by alignment but distributed through an intensified differential logic that thrives on comparison, competition, and selective inclusion. The system must always exclude some in order to motivate all. Indeed, the logic of selective inclusion is not neutral—it operates through escalating exclusions that intensify as capitalist reproduction deepens. The more individuals conform, the higher the bar is raised and the narrower the margin of inclusion becomes. Inequalities widen, entire regions are rendered disposable, and growing segments of the population—along with ecosystems—are cast out as collateral damage in the pursuit of ever-shrinking zones of profitability (De Angelis 2007).

This disciplinary logic is not abstract; it is anchored in concrete mechanisms that translate financial and political command into the everyday structures of social life. This process is materialized through several key modalities. First, *financialization* amplifies this disciplinary reach by subordinating social priorities—such as housing, education, and public services—to speculative logics and profitability benchmarks. It converts rights into assets and reconfigures institutions around investor expectations (Gabor 2020). Second, global value chains extend the reach of capitalist discipline across space, orchestrating transnational flows of labor and commodities through hierarchies of cost, speed, and flexibility. These chains link dispersed sites of production and reproduction to the investment strategies and accumulation imperatives of capital headquartered elsewhere. As Sandro Mezzadra and Brett Neilson (2019) argue, global value chains are not merely technical infrastructures of production but political operations that organize territory, mobility, and labor in ways that reinforce capitalist command over cooperation. Third, *informalization*—the proliferation of precarious, unprotected, and invisible forms of labor—ensures that the burden of adjustment falls on workers and communities, not on capital. It keeps vast swaths of social cooperation off the books, while still extracting value through dependence, insecurity, and fragmentation (Sassen 2014).

Together, these mechanisms compose the meta-level's disciplinary ecology. They ensure that capital's power is not confined to markets but permeates political decision-making, institutional design, and the very rhythms of life—shaping the imagination of what is possible, what is valuable, and who gets to belong.

The geography of social reproduction

The global architecture of capital does not operate on a flat plane; it exploits differences. The uneven geography of social reproduction is one of its most potent levers of control. Processes at the meta-level not only shape but actively exploit the differentiated conditions of social reproduction across geographically distributed *fields of social reproduction*, placing them in continuous competition with one another (De Angelis 2007). These fields are historically constituted, context-specific ecologies—defined by political, cultural, and economic structures—that determine how life is sustained, cared for, and made meaningful in a given place and time. A social reproduction field is a situated ecology of everyday life, where bodies, infrastructures, norms, and environments converge to shape how people sustain and reproduce themselves and others. This includes not only cultural expectations and social relations but also access to public services, income, markets, community spaces, and reproductive support networks. It is the situated terrain where the struggle between capital and life takes form, where care is practiced, needs are negotiated, and futures are made or foreclosed.

Each social reproduction field corresponds to an average social wage and a general standard of living, which includes not only income but also access to public goods, social protections, and environmental conditions.[2] These standards are the outcome of historically situated struggles between the forces of capital and those defending life. As a result, social reproduction fields are not distributed equally; they are hierarchically configured at the global level, reflecting both colonial legacies and contemporary structures of accumulation.

These fields are experienced and valued differently depending on one's position. From the perspective of people embedded in these fields, reproduction involves dense webs of culture, normativity, and relational life—the everyday substance of the procommons and the meso-level. *From the point of view of capital, however, these fields appear primarily as cost profiles*, differentiated by wages, taxation levels, regulatory burdens, and ecological constraints. In this abstraction, what matters is how cheaply life can be reproduced and how flexible labor and territory are in the face of capital's demands. This global hierarchy of reproduction fields is the product of a long history of unequal development, rooted in colonialism and sustained by neocolonial dynamics. Historically, imperial centers managed labor costs by containing the effects of workers' struggles, such as reduced working hours and incremental wage increases. Rather than allowing a full translation of productivity gains into improved living standards, these systems worked to keep labor costs in check. At the same time, agrarian societies in the Global South were systematically pressured to dismantle self-sufficient modes of production and reorient their economies toward export. This dual mechanism artificially suppressed the global price of food and raw materials, thereby lowering the cost of reproducing labor in the core and sustaining profitability for capital in the metropolitan centers.[3]

From the late 1970s onward, in response to a structural crisis of accumulation, global elites initiated a planetary reorganization of production that reshaped and deepened the hierarchies among reproduction fields. This was not a simple return to the older international division of labor typical of colonial empires, where peripheral regions were fixed in the role of raw material suppliers and core regions specialized in industrial goods. Instead, the configuration that emerged under neoliberal globalization is more flexible, dynamic, and disciplinary. The relationship between reproduction fields no longer merely reflects market structures; it actively constitutes global market discipline.

The transformation known as the "deep integration" of global production (UNCTAD 1993) captures this shift: Capital increasingly outsources production across territories with lower reproduction costs, integrates transnational commodity chains, and intensifies trade between asymmetrically positioned regions. In this system, reproduction fields are locked into permanent competition, their conditions leveraged against each other to extract ever more surplus from labor and life. The result is a planetary restructuring of social cooperation that penetrates every domain of human activity.

In the neoliberal period, the logic of exploiting differences between reproduction fields was not only extended—it was institutionalized and generalized. Early experiments, such as the maquiladora zones on the US–Mexico border and the Free Export Zones in Southeast Asia, became templates for a broader global strategy. Capital systematically shifted production to regions where the costs of labor and life were lower, creating regulatory and infrastructural enclaves tailored to the imperatives of accumulation. Enabled by advances in communication and transportation technologies, this shift facilitated the formation of global value chains that integrate diverse reproduction fields into a competitive and extractive planetary system. From the garment factories of Bangladesh to large-scale agribusiness in Brazil and Kenya, and electronics in China, these zones have multiplied and expanded, allowing capital to reduce production costs while externalizing social and ecological burdens onto subordinated populations and territories.[4]

Yet this process is never static. Struggles over wages, environmental protections, and living standards within each reproduction field remain powerful drivers of capitalist restructuring. When costs rise in one context—due to social mobilization, legal reform, or ecological regulation—capital responds by reorganizing production, shifting geographies, and inventing new mechanisms of control. The map of global accumulation is thus continually redrawn by the push and pull between social reproduction from below and capital accumulation from above. In this sense, the meta-level does not merely float above the rest of the pyramid: It reconfigures the lower levels to ensure that their reproductive functions become subordinate to accumulation, using global asymmetries in life's reproduction as instruments of control and sources of profit.

The establishment of neoliberal globalism rests on the structural disparity between fields of social reproduction and on the reconfiguration of the global factory as a web of transnational production chains designed to exploit these asymmetries. Since each reproduction field embodies an average configuration of social and environmental costs—wages, taxes, public services, and regulatory standards—it becomes a "benchmark" against which capital assesses the profitability of its investments. These differences are not accidental but strategically produced and maintained. Capital plays reproduction fields against one another—ecological niche against ecological niche, procommons against procommons, meso-level against meso-level—in order to minimize the cost of reproduction it has to pay and maximize surplus extraction.

But this strategy is not without consequences. Wherever struggles succeed in raising the standard of social reproduction—better living and working conditions, stronger labor protections, gender equality, and environmental safeguards—the relative cost of capital investment rises. These areas must then either generate compensatory efficiencies to remain competitive or attract external income streams, as the United States does through its role in the international monetary system. Failing that, capital simply relocates, shifting production, logistics, and investment flows to places where reproduction costs are lower. In this way, capital disciplines social reproduction through mobility, transforming life-making into a competitive liability.

This perpetual blackmail lies at the root of the frantic race that defines contemporary social cooperation. It drives a generalized degradation of living conditions, fractures solidarities, and accelerates environmental breakdown. People and their procommons are pushed to adapt, not on the basis of their own values, needs, or ecological rationalities but according to the volatile calculus of competitiveness embedded in the system of social cooperation that ties them together. The consequence is a planetary condition of anxious adjustment under the threat of relocation, in which the capacity to live with others and to sustain the Earth becomes hostage to the reproduction of capital.

This architecture has been maintained through three main strategies. First, the aggressive liberalization of world trade since the 1980s has amplified capital mobility and competitive pressure. Trade agreements, export-processing zones, and investment treaties have facilitated the vertical integration of transnational supply chains and undermined national capacities to protect local reproduction standards. Second, the deregulation of capital markets has allowed finance to act as a disciplinary apparatus, punishing governments that pursue expansionary social wage policies or protections for workers and the environment. Third, structural adjustment programs imposed by the IMF and the World Bank in response to sovereign debt crises—particularly across the Global South—have systematically dismantled public services, devalued local currencies, and redirected national priorities toward debt repayment and investor confidence. Across contexts, these policies have produced a widespread collapse in the infrastructures of social reproduction.

In parallel, reproduction itself has been globalized. Transnational migration, particularly of women, has created what Arlie Hochschild (2000), Rhacel Parreñas (2001), and Bridget Anderson (2000) have theorized as a global care chain: a gendered and racialized international division of reproductive labor. Migrant women—employed as nannies, domestic workers, and caregivers—reproduce others' households in wealthier regions while their own families rely on unpaid kin labor or suffer systemic neglect. These care chains are sustained by economic pressures rooted in uneven reproduction fields, turning solidarity into survival strategies stretched across borders. This phenomenon is not new: Maria Mies (1986) had already shown how the global capitalist system relies on a "housewifization" of women's labor, invisibilized and devalued, yet central to capital accumulation on a world scale. Migrant remittances—routinely celebrated as "development"—function, in practice, as a transfer of the costs of social reproduction. Wages earned in the centers are sent home to pay for schooling, food, health care, housing, and care for dependents—expenditures that capital and the state would otherwise fund through decent pay, public services, and welfare. In this way, costs are shifted from capital to households (private income replaces the social wage), from states to families (public provision is substituted by kin labor and out-of-pocket spending), and from center to periphery (peripheral communities subsidize the reproduction of labor in the core through exported care work and the emotional labor of separation). Remittances also stabilize peripheral balance-of-payments and fiscal accounts, masking deindustrialization and welfare retrenchment while normalizing low wages and precarious care regimes. The net effect is that the burden of sustaining life is pushed downward—disproportionately onto women and the least resourced communities—under the moral veneer of "development." These dynamics extend beyond formal labor. The globalization of reproductive labor forms an invisible infrastructure that sustains the visible economy. Even the purchase of cheap goods produced in regions with depressed reproduction costs reflects this transnationalization: Consumer access in one context is effectively subsidized by precarious lives in another. Reproduction circuits, like production chains, have been stretched across the globe, linking disparate territories through asymmetrical exchanges of labor, time, care, and ecological burden. In this way, the geography of reproduction is not just a backdrop to capital's operations—it is an active terrain of contestation, reorganization, and dispossession.

The ambivalent common in us

While the preceding sections analyzed the macro-logics of the meta-level, we now turn to their inscription in subjectivity—how systemic pressures shape agency, belonging, and the emotional registers of life under competition. The transformations described above have not only restructured production and reproduction across the globe; they have also profoundly reshaped how people perceive themselves, relate to others, and orient their actions. Here, the individual appears not as an isolated unit but as a *subject-holon* (Chapter 6): a living node in the wider circuitry of social cooperation, simultaneously part and whole, shaped by and shaping the systemic fields in which it acts. The meta-level thus inscribes itself in everyday consciousness, emotions, and relations, configuring the ways subjects experience worth, obligation, and possibility within the competitive architectures of value.

The marketization and financialization processes at the core of neoliberal globalization culminated in the 2007–8 financial crisis, a systemic rupture that exposed the fragility of the global capitalist order. At the same time, the growing urgency of ecological breakdown, amplified by climate justice movements, and the shock of the COVID-19 pandemic have further intensified the sense that something fundamental is breaking down in the promises of neoliberal modernity. What once appeared as inevitable progress is increasingly perceived as unsustainable, unjust, and disorienting—and yet, from the perspective of the subject, life must go on. People must still navigate their everyday obligations, search for meaning, secure their livelihoods, and make sense of a world that feels increasingly out of joint. This tension often breeds not only disenchantment but also a strange form of critical hypnotization: an awareness that something is wrong, paired with an inability to act outside the parameters of the very system that produces the malaise. The subject drifts between cynicism and compliance, irony and resignation—pulled by the gravitational field of a world that has lost credibility but not yet lost its grip.

Neoliberal globalization has not merely globalized production—it has globalized the competition between life-worlds. It is in this context that subjectivity today is being shaped by a deep contradiction: on one side, a shared condition of interdependence and exposure—the ontological common—a fundamental embeddedness in shared life processes, ecological limits, and social interdependence that we discussed in Chapter 1; on the other, the imperative to compete across every domain of life—work, education, care, and even social identity. This contradiction structures how people come to understand their agency, their responsibilities, and their solidarities. It is this double bind—being bound to the common and the interdependence it sustains, while simultaneously being bound to compete within and against it—that defines the core drama of subjectivity in the current phase of capitalist development.

This tension—between the pull of mutual interdependence and the compulsion to outcompete others within it—does not generate a unified response. Rather, it produces a fracture within the procommons: the emergence of two attractors that bifurcate the affective and symbolic registers through which people relate to their shared condition. Some respond by seeking security in closure, turning the common into a bounded identity to defend and investing in a politics of resentment, control, and purity. This impulse is not purely ideological—it is affective and aesthetic. It expresses itself through nostalgia, symbolic borders, and a yearning for order in a world experienced as chaotic and humiliating. Reactionary populisms like those of Matteo Salvini, Donald Trump, Viktor Orbán, or Marine Le Pen resonate here because they offer emotionally compelling narratives of dignity and community, albeit distorted through hierarchy and exclusion. They provide *aesthetic coherence* and *affective relief* to those caught in a world that demands competitiveness while denying stability. To them, the plight of the world—climate breakdown, racial injustice, and gender inequality—is either invisibilized or stigmatized, recoded as distraction or threat. Climate activists, migrants, or so-called woke sensibilities (which originally emerged from African American vernacular English, meaning to be alert to racial injustice, social inequality, and oppression) are not merely seen as obstacles to be overcome but as nuisances to be contained—figures of disruption that must be silenced or criminalized through repressive laws. In this affective economy, repression becomes a form of moral hygiene: a way to restore the imagined purity of the social order and to defend one's place within the competitive race for survival.

Others, however, experience the same condition differently. They turn not to closure but to care, not to identity but to relation. Here, the aesthetic registers are softer and more experimental, oriented toward repair, listening, and collective composition. This emergent sensibility recognizes the common not only as a threatened inheritance but as a fragile coexistence—an ecological and social entanglement that demands responsibility, attention, and shared transformation. This, too, is a response grounded in sensibility and emotion, rooted in forms of joy, grief, attunement, and the desire for reciprocity. It is no coincidence that practices of commoning often involve not just material sharing but also music, ritual, storytelling, and food—a reweaving of meaning through embodied experience.

Both tendencies can be seen as responses to what Gregory Bateson (1987) called a *double bind*: a situation in which one is subjected to contradictory imperatives that cannot be resolved within the same communicative framework. The contemporary subject is told, in effect, "You must live in common but only by competing against everyone else in it, even if such competition undermines the common conditions of life." This contradiction cannot be resolved through rational choice—it creates paralysis, confusion, or desperate compensatory identifications.

For Bateson, escape from a double bind requires a meta-communicative shift: a change in the level at which meaning is processed. In our context, this means developing practices, languages, and institutions capable of naming the contradiction, inhabiting it consciously, and generating new patterns of social cooperation that no longer reproduce its antagonistic logic. It means staying "woke" to systemic oppression and discrimination.

Yet closure and care do not stand on equal footing. Closure reproduces the double bind by intensifying repression, scapegoating, and hierarchical exclusion; it resolves the contradiction only by hardening it. Care, by contrast, gestures beyond the bind. It interrupts the logic of competition and opens relational possibilities that do not rely on domination. But when confined to ethical disposition or local practice, it risks remaining politically and strategically insufficient—unable, on its own, to reorganize the structural conditions that reproduce the contradiction.

For Bateson, escape from a double bind requires a shift in the level at which meaning is processed. In our context, this implies that the aesthetic and affective registers of care must sediment into institutional and infrastructural form—becoming part of a shared meta-language embedded in praxis and capable of reconfiguring the material conditions of social cooperation. Only then can the procommons move beyond reactive defense and begin to constitute itself as a generative force, crafting horizons that loosen the grip of competition and control.

This is the political and cultural task of the procommons today: to turn itself from a site of affective capture into an affective space of emancipatory recomposition. Such a shift cannot remain only at the cultural or symbolic level. To break the double bind, it must be coupled with the construction of a new systemic coherence—an autopoietic organization on the terrain of social reproduction. This means weaving together, across scales and levels, the dispersed energies of the procommons and the meso-level, while progressively subordinating the latter's institutional and productive logics to the former's relational and socially reproductive values—redirecting its infrastructures, governance mechanisms, and productive capacities toward the coordinated reproduction of life through socially determined use value rather than accumulation.

Here, the meta-communicative shift becomes material, expressed in new institutional forms, infrastructural experiments, and modes of collective praxis that reorient social cooperation away from competition and extraction. It involves the cultivation of spaces where the care for the common is no longer peripheral or residual but structurally central—where solidarity is not simply a sentiment but an organizing principle. And this must happen in every node of social cooperation, even those today most captured by capitalist measures of things: schools, hospitals, logistics hubs, care networks, factories, platforms, bureaucracies, and cultural institutions.

This strategic horizon cannot remain aspirational. It must be enacted materially and institutionally—through infrastructures that anchor care and cooperation beyond the metrics of competition Such a counter-system does not emerge fully formed; it must be composed through transversal processes that link otherwise fragmented practices across scales and spheres of cooperation, weaving them into coordinated circuits of mutual reinforcement. Only through such transversal organization of constitution and struggle can the scattered practices of care, sustenance, and solidarity escape subordination to the capitalist meta-level and begin to form the backbone of a coherent and living counter-system—one in which social reproduction is not merely reactive but generative of its own autopoiesis, infrastructure, and future. An immense cultural and material task—but already underway wherever people name the contradiction, engage in struggle, and begin composing ways of living otherwise.

14

The mega-level

The mega-level of command and domination

Having analyzed the meso- and meta-levels as terrains of contested social cooperation and value capture, we now ascend to the mega-level: the apex of systemic command, the site where the architecture of the capitalist world is continually reproduced. It is not simply a summit of power but a complex field of systemic regulation—sometimes orderly, sometimes improvised and unstable—through which domination is coordinated and recalibrated. To understand this level is to understand how the system breathes, reacts, adapts, and survives.

In this chapter, I identify and unpack six macro-functions—what I call the throbs of command—through which this level organizes domination, displaces contradiction, and governs the reproduction of the system. An illustration of the historical transformations of these throbs will be examined in the next chapter.

We must read this level through its aims, its composition, and its processes. The mega-level is enacted by a network of powerful actors that seeks both to maintain its own domination—emerging from the underlying pyramidal configuration—and to preserve the pyramid itself as a hierarchy of ends, asymmetries, exploitation, and separations that structure social cooperation. The meta-purpose of this level is simple: to ensure that capital reproduces its domination over social cooperation—that is, in the face of all contradictions and conflicts within and between the underlying levels, social cooperation remains fundamentally hegemonized by capital, by its measure of things, and by its logic of value.

But such hegemony cannot exist without a corresponding regime of world governance and political command. The historical conditions that structure the power relations among the powerful and between them and the upheavals rising from below are precisely the conditions through which this regime of governance is continually configured and reconfigured. As Pentenero (2018: 22) notes, following Alquati, "at this level, all relations are relations of domination, political in the strong sense, relations of power; from this level descends, innervating the entire structure of the model, the political nature of everything that exists. This is where all inter-level dimensions are constituted and begin."

It is therefore at this level that we see the emergence of a fundamental macro-function of the collective capitalist—"that is, macro-domination"—which consists, Alquati (1989: 25) writes, "in managing macro-contradictions, making them function precisely in this way: as a macro-engine. On the one hand, letting them go in order to recover them dynamically through innovation; on the other hand, risking major disruptions: this is the risk for which the capitalist is remunerated! That is why it is a difficult job (if it still is)."

The fundamental function of this level is therefore to read and address the crises and dangers that this underlying turbulance can trigger for capitalist domination over social cooperation and its prospects and "to transfer the contradictions of and within the system forward, at all levels, starting from the highest; thus defusing them, even if only in the short term, but often in the shortest possible time" (Alquati 1989: 25).

In other words, the mega-level exists to regulate the turbulent complexity generated by social cooperation and to keep this complexity compatible with the system of capital accumulation as a whole. It does this by reading crises and dangers, redirecting or diluting them, and pushing contradictions forward in space and time so that they fuel, rather than interrupt, accumulation. In cybernetic terms, this level is the system's *regulator*: It monitors disturbances and seeks to restabilize the overall order by filtering out disruptive variety and amplifying compatible forms of social organization.

From this standpoint, the mega-level operates as the command interface between the total variety of human and nonhuman cooperation (Gaia, the procommons, and the meso- and meta-levels) and the narrower field of capital's regulatory apparatus. Yet, as Ashby's law of requisite variety reminds us, a regulator cannot control a system more complex than itself unless it finds ways to reduce or absorb that complexity. The mega-level thus functions through a rhythmic interplay of filters—which compress variety from below—and amplifiers—which project selected norms, incentives, and commands downward. These rhythmic regulatory operations are what I call the throbs of command. This is the same logic already outlined in Chapter 8 and Figure 8.1, now seen from the top of the pyramid: Command must *reduce* the variety coming from below and *amplify* the variety it wants to circulate.

Through these throbs, the mega-level transfers contradictions and disturbances throughout the pyramid—sometimes defusing them, sometimes intensifying them, but always pushing them forward as new engines of accumulation. Rationalization itself, as Alquati observed, moves within these macro-contradictions: The system stabilizes itself by accelerating its own instability.

Take, for example, the contradiction of environmental destruction and climate change. The command of capital cannot act coherently on this front without subordinating accumulation to ecological limits. Instead, it pushes the contradiction forward, inventing market instruments such as carbon-trading that attempt to solve the problem through the same mechanisms that produced it. At the Rio 1992 Earth Summit, states adopted the United Nations Framework Convention on Climate Change (UNFCCC), which opened the door to emissions-trading schemes—but no binding constraint on accumulation was established. Since then, two results have followed: on the one hand, the expropriation of land and loss of control by small farmers subjected to the acquisitive logic of carbon markets (Grain 2024); on the other hand, a continued rise in emissions—more than doubling since 1992. Command here filters ecological variety (reducing the planetary crisis to a market signal) and amplifies accumulation (through the creation of new asset classes). War functions in the same way: by suspending urgent demands in the field of social reproduction—justice, ecology, and equality—and reorienting social cooperation around the immediacy of destruction.

The throbs of command, then, are the configurations and reconfigurations through which this regulatory work is performed. Each throb expresses a historically specific way of filtering and amplifying variety—an institutional and policy configuration through which the mega-level seeks to restore coherence and maintain domination. Keynesianism, neoliberalism, and today's authoritarian neoliberalism can each be read as distinct throb formations: strategic arrangements that translate systemic disorder into governable order by modulating the relationship between accumulation, social reproduction, and command. The throbs thus constitute the living rhythm of macro-domination—periods of intensified regulatory invention and adjustment through which capital reorganizes its control. Yet every such configuration remains in tension with the counter-rhythms of resistance and commoning rising from below, which continually overflow and reconfigure the system's limits. Ultimately, throbs of commands are force field dimensions.

To map these operations, Figure 14.1 schematically represents the throbs of command as rhythmic force fields overlaying the pyramid of capital.

Systemic synchrony and Ashby's law

If the mega-level is the locus of regulation, then its viability depends on how it manages variety. In cybernetic terms, this means that command must continuously absorb, filter, and redirect the multiplicity of signals generated by the rest of the pyramid. Here, Ashby's (1956) law of requisite variety becomes central: A system can be effectively regulated only if its

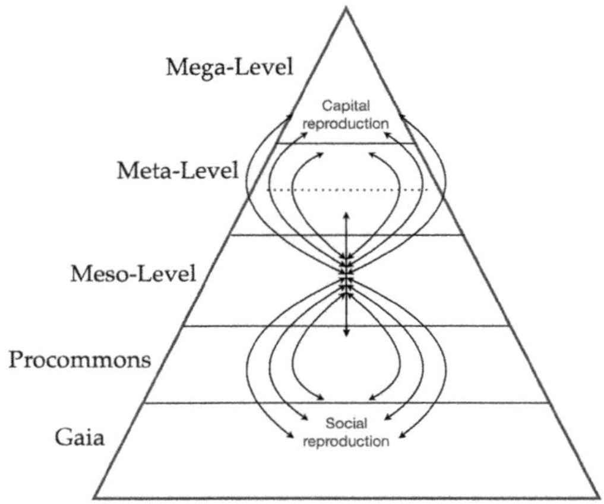

Figure 14.1 The pyramid and the throbs of command

regulating apparatus exhibits at least as much variety as the system it seeks to control. In capitalism, however, this law is satisfied not through democratic responsiveness or shared intelligence but through hierarchical differentiation. The higher we move in the pyramid, the lower the organic variety, yet the burden of regulation intensifies. The mega-level compensates for this imbalance through *filters* that suppress disruptive social and ecological variety and *amplifiers* that reinforce patterns of behavior, knowledge, and normativity aligned with accumulation.

As introduced in Chapter 8 (see Figure 8.1), Ashby's law of requisite variety can be visualized as a dynamic exchange between filters and amplifiers across the pyramid. The regulator at the apex must continually modulate these two functions, filtering out forms of variety that threaten systemic coherence while amplifying those that reinforce the dominant order. At the mega-level, this becomes the strategic function of command itself: a dynamic filter–amplifier system that translates the diversity of social cooperation into governable categories and projects selected responses—security, growth, and productivity—back down through institutions, media, policy, and infrastructure.

Regulation here is not equilibrium but oscillatory adjustment: a continuous effort to match, absorb, or preempt the turbulence generated by the lower levels. Yet oscillation does not exhaust the dynamics of command. At certain thresholds, regulatory oscillation gives way to phase transition—moments in which the very parameters of synchronization are redefined. The throbs of command emerge from this need for dynamic synchronization, but they may also be strategically intensified or redirected to precipitate such shifts.

They are not arbitrary metaphors but distinct modes of variety management: historically specific regulatory configurations through which the mega-level seeks not only to maintain coherence across the pyramid but, at times, to reorganize it. This sixfold differentiation—orienting purpose, coordinating macro-agency, crisiscraft, displacement, instrumentality, and threshold recalibration—corresponds to what Ashby called the "requisite variety" of viable systems: Too few regulatory functions would conflate irreducible roles, such as between direction and coordination or between displacement and crisis, while too many would generate incoherence. Historically, these throbs have materialized as concrete regulatory regimes—Keynesianism, neoliberalism, and authoritarian neoliberalism—each embodying a different calibration of filtering and amplification and of control and adaptation.

In this sense, the throbs are both functional abstractions and historical formations: patterned responses that capital deploys to metabolize contradiction, absorb turbulence, and reorganize domination. They resonate with the recursive dynamics described in Stafford Beer's *Viable System Model* (1981), in which systemic viability depends on the differentiation and synchronization of functions such as purpose-setting, coordination, and adaptation.[1] Each throb acts semi-autonomously, but their interaction composes the deep grammar of command—the living rhythm of regulation through which capital survives its crises.

Their force comes not only from their internal logic but from how they interact, reinforce, and compensate for one another. In moments of crisis, for instance, when *crisiscraft* intensifies, *displacement* and *threshold recalibration* pulse in synchrony, modulating perception, absorbing turbulence, and directing systemic stress away from the core. By "the core," I refer to the central circuits of capitalist reproduction—those institutions, regions, and value logics that sustain the viability of command. This includes both the geopolitical core (dominant states and alliances) and the systemic core (the accumulation imperative, financial infrastructure, and macro-governance mechanisms of the meta- and mega-levels). Their synchrony is often aimed at preserving this core by externalizing turbulence onto more expendable territories, bodies, and futures.

From this perspective, each throb can be read as a selective interface between systemic instability and strategic response. The throb of *purpose* filters social energies through profitability metrics. Coordinating macro-*agency* amplifies financial and technocratic logics while marginalizing democratic or reproductive imperatives. *Crisis management* converts emergency into policy leverage. *Displacement* makes local suffering appear as global necessity. *Instrumentality* reconfigures ethics around calculability. *Threshold recalibration* redefines exhaustion as manageable risk.

All of these are operations of requisite variety: ways of ensuring that capital's limited internal complexity, in relation to the whole of social and nonhuman life processes, can nonetheless control a vastly more complex social field. The mega-level cannot genuinely increase its variety to match the richness of lived experience below; instead, it reshapes the field of social cooperation to match its own operational logics. It simplifies complexity through standardization, privatization, and technocratization. The throbs thus do not merely react to crisis—they preemptively structure the perceptual and institutional conditions under which crisis becomes intelligible, and hence governable. They condition a form of life in which only those turbulences legible to capital can be addressed, and only in terms compatible with accumulation.

Throbs of command: rhythmic filters and amplifiers of capitalist domination

Command at the mega-level is not a fixed apparatus but an emergent, adaptive process: a strategic field in which the dominant agencies of capital attempt—never fully achieve—to stabilize systemic reproduction amid contradiction and revolt. As Ashby's law reminds us, no regulator can control a system more complex than itself unless it filters the variety coming from below and amplifies the responses that maintain coherence above; *at the mega-level, command is exactly this operation.* This level seeks *to* translate the turbulence of social cooperation into governable order. The throbs of command are the historical configurations of these oscillations: patterned pulses through which capital periodically filters, amplifies, and redistributes the variety generated across the pyramid.

A throb is thus not a metaphorical heartbeat but a cybernetic pulse: a systemic operation that condenses contradiction, recodes it as information, and feeds it back into the architecture of domination. Each throb enacts a specific mode of filtering and amplifying variety, culturally, institutionally, and materially, through which capital seeks to reassert control over its own disequilibrium. Together, they form the *deep grammar* of command: the tacit code that keeps domination synchronized across levels and scales, allowing capital to survive by transforming disorder into signal.

Unlike the physiological body, however, capitalist command has no single pacemaker. Its pulse arises from a macro-agency field—states, central banks, corporations, financial institutions, and military alliances—that modulate one another through filters and amplifiers distributed across the world system. When their synchrony weakens—when filters fail to compress variety or amplifiers overextend—the system enters arrhythmia: wars, crises, and authoritarian turns.

Each throb marks a distinct field of enactment—a regulatory zone where the macro-agency of command interacts with social cooperation to recover rhythm and coherence.

Let us briefly consider these: Each of the six regulatory functions operates through two interlinked modes of command—filtering, which compresses and selects variety, and amplifying, which projects and reinforces systemic norms. These modes are never separate: Every throb both filters and amplifies, at once defensive and projective, shaping the rhythms through which social cooperation is organized and value praxis enacted. In this sense, each throb is a *regulatory function of command*—a specific filter–amplifier configuration through which the mega-level translates systemic turbulence into renewed order. What distinguishes the six throbs is not the existence of these modes, which are constant, but the domain through which each applies them and the purpose each serves in maintaining domination.

These regulatory functions are not mechanical abstractions: They are enacted through the living circuits of social cooperation. In thought, we identify them as functions, but in reality, they operate as *praxis*—as patterned selections, enactments, and reinforcements moving through bodies, institutions, infrastructures, circuits, and relations. Each throb is thus a real abstraction: It performs its filtering and amplifying work only by mobilizing human and nonhuman capacities in certain ways, contributing to shape everyday decisions, policies, and desires across the whole social field. Through these recursive operations, the throbs transform social cooperation into a medium of command, abstracting life from within life itself. Through these throbs, command enacts its own metabolism within the living metabolism of society; its rhythms are not outside life but *within* it, bending the flows of cooperation toward accumulation under given conditions.

These are the six regulatory functions of command, each condensing the dual operations of filtering and amplifying into a historically specific logic of control.

1. *Orienting Purpose—Regulating the Horizon of Accumulation*
   This throb filters the horizon of possibility itself, reducing the vast plurality of social aims to a single teleology of accumulation. It amplifies this orientation through developmental, competitive, or nationalist narratives that bind legitimacy to growth. From Keynesian welfare to green capitalism, war regimes and techno-industrial sovereignty, it defines what counts as a viable world project. It operates not as an abstract aim but through the everyday selection of priorities, investments, and desires

that orient social cooperation toward accumulation. Whether in the design of policy, the pursuit of education, or the framing of "progress," this throb directs praxis by making certain ends appear self-evident and others unthinkable. Purpose is thus not decreed from above but enacted through the patterned rhythms of work, consumption, and aspiration that sustain capital's telos.

2. *Coordinating Macro-agency—Synchronizing Command*

   Here, the system seek to define forms of coherence among heterogeneous power centers—hegemonic states, financial institutions, and multinationals—through summits, policy coordination, and shared doctrines. Simultaneously, it filters out deviant trajectories (nonaligned states, insurgent movements, and experiments in autonomy) by excluding them from circuits of credit, trade, or diplomacy. But this synchrony is not mechanical; it is enacted through intra-macro-agency conflict and the praxis of countless mediations—diplomatic routines, data exchanges, managerial decisions, and logistical alignments—where cooperation and coercion interlace. Coordination is therefore not only institutional but lived: a choreography of compliance and adjustment that translates social cooperation into the rhythms of global command.

3. *Crisiscraft—Converting Turbulence into Order*

   This throb filters chaos into policy leverage. It absorbs shocks—financial collapses, wars, and pandemics—by redefining them as opportunities for "recovery" or "reform." Through amplification, crisis narratives legitimate exceptional measures and new regimes of accumulation. It is the moment when breakdown becomes productive for command. Yet crisiscraft also depends on social enactment; it mobilizes fear, urgency, and sacrifice within the social body, transforming collective anxiety into disciplined action. In the name of survival, cooperation is redirected toward restoring systemic equilibrium, turning disruption itself into a resource for reorganization.

4. *Displacement—Redistributing Contradiction in the Space-Time*

   This throb exports turbulence by amplifying capital's geographical and temporal elasticity. Contradictions are displaced through debt, trade, and military infrastructures, filtering out unrest in the core by externalizing its costs to peripheries, future generations, or ecological frontiers. Displacement is enacted through labor migration regimes, outsourcing, land deals, war, and everyday logistical practices that reconfigure where and how value is produced. These are not abstract transfers but lived movements—people, materials, and ecosystems stretched across space and time to maintain the flow of accumulation.

5. *Instrumentality—Rendering Life Operable and Calculable*
   This throb concerns the organization and deployment of means. It selects, designs, and aligns technical systems, procedures, infrastructures, and metrics in order to render social cooperation operable in relation to systemic ends. In contemporary capitalism, this often takes the form of translating the complexity of social life into calculable indicators—GDP, risk ratings, ESG scores—filtering lived realities into data points. But the calculable is only one expression of a broader instrumental logic that reduces heterogeneous relations to manageable variables and functional roles. It amplifies those measurements through institutions, media, and moral vocabularies that present efficiency and competitiveness as common sense, turning metrics into ideology. Instrumentality is enacted wherever numbers stand in for judgment: in classrooms, hospitals, workplaces, and bureaucracies, where human cooperation is rendered legible through performance metrics. These acts of quantification are forms of praxis: they teach the social body to perceive itself through the language of control, enacting abstraction as a daily routine.

6. *Threshold Recalibration—Managing Systemic Limits*
   Here, command filters the signals of systemic stress—unrest, environmental tipping points, and fiscal strain—and amplifies selective responses that stretch the system's tolerance band. Security doctrines, surveillance, austerity, and even partial reforms all belong to this adaptive circuitry. Recalibration does not solve contradiction; it delays rupture by redefining what counts as normal. Yet this adaptive work, too, is enacted through cooperation: through experts, media, and everyday subjects who absorb crisis framings, internalize scarcity, and enact restraint. At the same time, in moments of collective resistance—strikes, uprisings, and care networks—this same social body can invert the throb, forcing command to absorb the entropy it once displaced.

At the mega-level, the six throbs rarely operate in isolation; they couple and intensify one another under conditions of turbulence. Crisiscraft, for instance, often activates displacement (export the shock), instrumentality (measure and justify the shock), and threshold recalibration (redefine acceptable loss), producing cascades of regulatory adjustment. These couplings become especially visible in moments of systemic transition.

Purpose and coordination pulse together during reconfigurations of world order—Bretton Woods, the neoliberal turn, or today's authoritarian neoliberal mutation. Each historical regime of capitalism can thus be read as a particular throb formation: a temporary synchrony of filters and amplifiers that converts systemic turbulence into renewed, though always provisional, coherence.

Placed back into the architecture of the pyramid, the throbs function as mediators. They read signals from below—the energies of social reproduction, resistance, and ecological feedback—but only to reemit them downward in forms compatible with accumulation. They are sensitive but not to care and reactive but only to preserve command. As planetary crises multiply, their synchrony falters.

Filters clog, amplifiers distort, and the system enters a phase of command arrhythmia—still beating but no longer in time with the reproduction of life itself. Read in this way, the six throbs are not merely descriptive categories but regulatory functions that enact the two modes of command—filtering and amplifying—across distinct strategic domains, composing together the rhythmic circuitry of capitalist regulation.

The following sections examine each throb in turn, briefly tracing their abstract cybernetic roles, their theoretical lineages, and their concrete institutional and historical articulations.

Anatomy of the throbs: functional dynamics and theoretical lineages

Orienting purpose establishes the system's overarching telos—accumulation—without which regulation lacks direction. While Luhmann (1995) does not refer to accumulation per se, his theory of self-referential systems underscores the need for an internal guiding orientation, without which a system cannot differentiate relevance, assign priorities, or organize feedback. In the capitalist system, this guiding orientation is structured by the imperative of accumulation. Yet, as we will explore in the next chapter, this meta-purpose has historically been articulated through shifting sub-purposes—such as developmentalism, global competitiveness, financial stability, or the green transition—each expressing the imperative of accumulation under different historical conditions and strategic priorities.

Coordinating agency refers to the macro-assemblage of actors—states, international institutions, transnational corporations, and financial entities—whose differential capacities are neither fixed nor equal but historically shifting. Their synchronization into temporary hegemonic alignments reflects changing balances of power within the system of command, as analyzed by Gramsci (1971) through the concept of historical blocs and by Cox (1987) through his theory of world order as a contested and evolving structure of forces. This process unfolds within what Wallerstein (1974) and Arrighi (2010) identify as successive systemic cycles of capitalist hegemony—periods in which coordination among dominant actors stabilizes accumulation and command on a world scale.

Crisiscraft captures the strategic appropriation of breakdown and disruption as opportunities for reorganization—a function that resonates with Schumpeter's (1950) notion of creative destruction but more critically with Naomi Klein's (2007) analysis of disaster capitalism. Within the autonomist Marxist tradition, crisis is not understood simply as a spontaneous failure of capital but as a response to class struggle, thus driving capitalist development, as Mario Tronti (2019) argued in the 1960s. Harry Cleaver's (2024) extensive analysis of Marx's circuits of capital discusses the spectrum of capitalist relative and absolute surplus value strategies deployed in response to the "refusal of work" and autonomous struggles that disrupt accumulation. Antonio Negri (1984) theorizes crisis as a moment of rupture in the social factory, signaling the limits of command over labor's creative capacities. George Caffentzis (2013) and the Midnight Notes Collective (1990) extend this reading to global circuits, analyzing how energy crises, debt, and enclosures are used to restructure the reproduction of life across territories. This view of crisiscraft at the mega-level must be broadened beyond being merely reactive; it is also an anticipatory strategy, continuously reconfiguring the architecture of command in the face of insurgent recomposition or its fear.

Displacement denotes the spatial and temporal redistribution of contradictions: capital survives by disembedding crises from one context and reembedding them into another—often along the differentiated fields of social reproduction we examined in the previous chapter (Harvey 1982, 2006; Mezzadra and Neilson 2013).

Instrumentality names the technocratic rationalization and organization of means through which social cooperation is rendered operable in alignment with systemic ends. In contemporary capitalism, this often takes the form of production metrics and performance indicators that make the social legible to accumulation (Foucault 2008; Rottenburg et al. 2015). Yet these metrics are only one layer of a broader instrumental architecture that includes technical systems, procedural protocols, and infrastructural designs. They do not operate in a political vacuum: They are embedded within and legitimated by narratives that naturalize the priorities of capital in given contexts. From discourses of "good governance" and "competitiveness" to appeals to "efficiency," "innovation," "resilience," or "MAGA," capitalist instrumentality is always discursively mediated. It frames particular forms of life and labor as valuable, governable, and investable, while rendering others invisible, risky, or unworthy. Metrics, in this sense, are not neutral tools but narrative and technical artifacts that translate ideological projects into operational logics..

Threshold recalibration, finally, expresses the system's recursive awareness of its own limits—ecological, social, or geopolitical—and the anticipatory adjustments that delay collapse (Morin 2008; Urry 2016). A threshold, from the perspective of capitalist command, marks the point at which systemic contradictions—whether in the form of social unrest, ecological degradation, debt overload, or geopolitical tension—risk becoming unmanageable within existing modes of accumulation and regulation. It is not simply a quantitative boundary but a qualitative tipping point: a level of dysfunction beyond which the legitimacy or functionality of command is endangered. Calibration, in this context, refers to the strategic modulation of responses aimed at preempting or postponing such tipping points. This throb often comes into play when the other five prove insufficient—when systemic stress threatens to overflow containment. This may involve the deployment of surveillance and securitization apparatuses, financial containment strategies, or partial concessions and co-optations designed to reabsorb social or ecological pressure. It also involves discursive shifts, for example, from "growth" to "resilience," as well as broader ideological reorientations—such as the shift from classical liberalism to Keynesian state planning, from Keynesianism to neoliberal governance, and from neoliberalism to the current wave of authoritarian neoliberalism. Each transition reframes the coordinates of legitimacy and intervention, redefining what counts as necessary, possible, or tolerable within the architecture of command. Crucially, the goal is not to resolve the contradiction but to stretch the system's tolerance band—to extend its capacity to absorb volatility without altering its fundamental orientation toward accumulation.

This recalibration throb, therefore, is not about ecological adaptation or democratic negotiation; it is about preserving governability. It constantly redefines what counts as tolerable risk or acceptable damage, repositioning the line between normality and emergency. In doing so, it maintains the appearance of stability while shifting costs downward and forward—onto marginalized populations, future generations, and nonhuman life. The "awareness" it expresses is thus strategic and asymmetrical: a reflex of command that monitors turbulence in order to defer systemic transformation. This is why it operates in close synergy with displacement: When thresholds are breached or approached, the system recalibrates not by resolving pressures but by relocating their consequences—spatially, socially, or temporally—onto more governable terrains.

Crisis, recomposition, and the pulse of collapse

Placed within the broader architecture of the pyramid, the throbs mediate between levels. They read and react to turbulence from below, but they do so in ways that reaffirm the overarching aim of accumulation. They are sensitive to disruption but only in order to rechannel it. They are responsive but only to the extent that such responsiveness can be leveraged to maintain the hierarchy of ends that defines the pyramid as a whole. In this sense, the throbs are both reactive and projective: They absorb crisis, but they also seek to preempt it; they respond to resistance, but they also anticipate future fault lines. Their rhythm is both retrospective and anticipatory.

Yet these rhythms are not ahistorical. They take shape within specific configurations of world order, shifting in intensity and function as crises unfold, resistances mount, and hegemonies waver. The next chapter will trace their historical tempos—moments when these pulses coalesced into regimes of domination, and moments when their syncopation signaled systemic transition. Command, after all, is never outside history. *It seeks to be its metronome.*

Having mapped the six throbs as regulatory pulses within the architecture of command, we now return to them in greater detail. What follows is a closer analytic anatomy of each throb—not simply as a functional description but as a contested systemic operation shaped by histories of struggle, theoretical insight, and structural evolution. These elaborations allow us to ground the abstract force fields previously described in concrete institutional and ideological arrangements.

The first throb, orienting purpose, pulses through the system by establishing accumulation as the unquestioned meta-purpose. It is not a policy or a plan but a teleological orientation that seeps into laws, expectations, dreams, and despair. From the procommons to the meta-level of valorization, this pulse shapes what appears as socially reasonable or desirable. But this pulse is not steady—it intensifies, adapts, and reverberates in response to alternative value formations that emerge across the social field. From mutual aid and care work to vernacular practices and commoning; from struggles for rights, wages, and democratic access to demands for ecological limits on mega-infrastructure, waste, and toxicity in affected territories, other logics of coordination and meaning-making enact rival orientations that threaten to displace capital from its normative center. The throb of purpose must therefore continuously reassert itself—it does not simply orient; it *sutures*, binding the very idea of planetary order (whatever that may be) to the unspoken presupposition that capital must expand. It functions as a force field, one in which capital seeks to neutralize or absorb counter-pulses by realigning what is seen as viable, valuable, or even thinkable within the architecture of command.

The second throb, *coordinating macro-agency*, does not merely enact this purpose; it distributes and strategically synchronizes it. At this level, coordination is no longer about managing discrete institutions but about organizing heterogeneous power centers—states, financial institutions, transnational corporations, rating agencies, and international bodies such as the IMF, WTO, and BIS—into a loosely coupled yet functionally convergent apparatus. This is a field of contested hegemony, where different capitalist powers and blocs jostle for the capacity to influence the system's navigational logics.

War and military alignment belong to this throb's coercive register: They are not external to coordination but its violent form—moments when consensual synchrony collapses and command must be reestablished by force. The differing stances of Trump, Biden, and European powers toward Russia, for instance, reveal competing strategies of coordination: rival attempts to recompose macro-agency around distinct projects of accumulation and world order. From the Cold War to NATO's expansions, from "multipolar" discourses to proxy conflicts, the pulse of coordination beats through both diplomacy and war. It oscillates between negotiation and coercion, consensus and confrontation—always seeking, however destructively, to restore a functional synchrony among dominant actors.

The "pulse" of this throb can thus be found in the summits of Davos and the G20, in shifts in central bank tone, as well as in arms treaties, sanctions, and military coalitions: not fixed commands but patterned calibrations of capitalist power, alternating between coordination and coercion as means of maintaining systemic coherence.

The third throb, *crisiscraft*, is the command-level modality of strategic disruption and reintegration. We have seen at the meta-level how crises are operationalized as opportunities for restructuring accumulation and labor regimes. But at the mega-level, crisiscraft is not about survival of this or that corporation; it is about the hegemonic preservation of the system—absorbing, redirecting, or amplifying crisis in ways that recalibrate the structural conditions of accumulation and systemic coherence.

It is the capacity to absorb systemic shocks—financial, ecological, military, political, and epidemiological—and reroute them into new modalities of planetary order. This includes wars that suspend social demands in the name of national security, pandemics that accelerate digital enclosures, and climate catastrophes recoded into green financial instruments. The mega-level does not simply manage crisis; it orchestrates the dispositive through which crisis is defined, measured, and made governable. It is where "climate transition" becomes a site for geopolitical positioning and where "global health" becomes a terrain for securitization and control. Crisiscraft here is always world-making.

The fourth throb, *regulating displacement*, is often visible at the meta-level in the operations of global value chains, but its logic is shaped at the mega-level. This is where displacement becomes strategy, not merely logistics. While the meta-level organizes the extraction of value across territories through cost arbitrage and flexible production, it is the mega-level that institutionalizes the conditions under which such displacements are possible. Trade agreements, WTO rulings, geopolitical alignments, debt regimes, militarized borders, and energy corridors—these are not only the logistics of accumulation but the geoeconomic and geopolitical architectures that make global extraction durable.

Migration governance belongs fully to this throb. Trump's policies of militarized borders, expanded Immigration and Customs Enforcement (ICE), and the criminalization of migrants exemplify displacement as command. They operate as *filters*—excluding unwanted social variety, expelling surplus populations, and disciplining labor across borders—and as *amplifiers*—reproducing nationalist legitimacy, fear, and obedience. In this way, migration control functions not as an exception to globalization but as one of its regulatory pillars: It stabilizes accumulation by managing mobility, externalizing social crisis, and transforming displacement itself into a mode of rule that institutionalizes deportability as a labor-management tool, leveraging fear to depress wages, weaken collective organization, and intensify the precarization of the lowest segments of the labor market. This logic also extends to carceral geographies, where surplus populations are contained and territorial crisis is reorganized through prisons and policing, as Gilmore's (2007) analysis of California powerfully shows.

The mega-level ensures that a crisis in one region can be offset by the mobilization of another; that resistance in one zone leads to the creation of new peripheries; and that capital never runs out of space—or bodies—to exploit. The throb of displacement is thus about maintaining the global elasticity of exploitation through both logistical coordination and coercive containment.

The fifth throb, *rationalizing instrumentality*, builds on processes visible at the meta-level—metrics, performance indicators, financial ratios—but at the mega-level these are embedded within a broader architecture of technical, legal, financial, and infrastructural means that organize planetary governance. The mega-level does not merely adopt metrics; it designs and deploys regimes of legibility and operability, defining what counts as a good investment, a healthy economy, a secure border, or a sustainable city. The meta-level experiences these as constraints; the mega-level engineers them as instruments of command—through standards, treaties, monetary architectures, digital platforms, sanctions regimes, and regulatory frameworks as much as through indices and rankings. The Doing Business Index, ESG ratings, or sovereign credit scores are not simply reflections of underlying realities; they are technologies of abstraction embedded within this larger instrumental apparatus, shaping where capital flows and who governs. In this throb, the market is rendered moral and technical at once: efficiency becomes virtue, competitiveness becomes truth, and policy becomes calculation. Behind the numbers stands not neutrality but the organized command of capital, operationalized through infrastructures that present themselves as objectivity.

The sixth throb, *recalibrating thresholds*, governs the system's self-awareness. It is here that the system senses its own limits—not in a biological sense but in terms of tolerability: how much social unrest, ecological stress, debt, war or displacement can be absorbed without systemic fracture. This throb operates as both diagnostic and preemptive, guiding decisions on security, surveillance, and co-optation. It feeds into the others—justifying new instruments, displacements, and crises—while always scanning for signs that contradictions may spiral beyond control. At the command level, recalibration is not only reactive—it is also anticipatory. It is the throb of simulation, think tanks, scenario planning, quietly enacted emergency laws, attempted coups, and legal reforms—whether regressive or progressive—that seek to redraw the limits of the governable. While today it often takes the form of authoritarian reengineering—from Trump's attacks on voting rights to Meloni's plan to centralize power—threshold recalibration can also be seized from below through demands for expanded rights, climate justice, and radical structural transformation.

Such moments can generate openings, as the attempt to stabilize governability simultaneously exposes its limits and reshapes the terrain of struggle: moments when the system's own attempt to maintain governability inadvertently creates space for emancipatory reorientation and collective recomposition. It is a key battleground throb—one in which the direction of adjustment reflects the shifting correlations of force. It marks the moment when the reproduction of domination starts to encounter its own fragility and prepares for it not by retreating but by reinforcing command itself.

As previously recalled through Alquati's analysis, the mega-level operates by scanning the terrain of systemic reproduction for threats to capitalist domination, and by responding not through resolution but through strategic deferral. Its function is to read the turbulence emerging from below and to push contradictions forward—transferring them across levels and temporalities—so as to neutralize their destabilizing effects in the shortest possible time. Even the rationalization of command, as Alquati emphasizes, moves within and alongside these contradictions, treating them less as anomalies to fix than as levers through which the architecture of domination can be recalibrated.

Yet this process is anything but orderly. The pulsation of command unfolds through the friction of real history—through emergency summits and street uprisings, debt crises and military coups, speculative manias and sudden collapses. From Bretton Woods to the Chilean coup, from the fall of the Berlin Wall to the 2008 financial crash, from the Arab Spring to the wars of the present, the "coordination" of command has always been improvised amid disorder. Each attempt at regulation is at once a response and an experiment—crafted in boardrooms and backrooms, on battlefields and trading floors, in moments when the world seems to tremble.

In our time, this arrhythmic governance is everywhere visible. Trump's tariff wars, the planetary contest over rare-earths, the securitization of climate summits, the militarization of migration routes, the algorithmic steering of public discourse, and the paralysis of global institutions in the face of genocide and ecological collapse—all reveal a command structure improvising its coherence as it unravels. The mega-level still filters and amplifies, but its signals interfere, overlap, and distort; its rhythms break into competing beats. Capital's throbs now resound in a dissonant chorus of states, platforms, and militarized markets, each seeking to impose its own tempo on a world no longer synchronized.

The pulse is no longer steady. We live in a time of increasing arrhythmia. Planetary thresholds, intensifying contradictions, and recompositional energies rising from below are placing unprecedented stress on the architecture of command. These energies—rooted in the procommons, in emergent practices of commoning, in all sorts of social and environmental struggles, and in the defense and reorganization of life—are growing amid the converging crises of climate catastrophe, militarized governance, and creeping authoritarianism. The throbs still function—but they now do so in a climate of uncertainty, acceleration, and fragmentation. Their rhythms no longer align; their cycles no longer self-correct. They continue to regulate, but they also betray a system whose temporality is faltering—whose beat no longer reassures but alarms.

This, too, is part of the mega-level's reality: a regime compelled to command even as its own rhythms reveal exhaustion, asymmetry, and the incipient collapse of the very conditions of social cooperation in an age of ecological catastrophe. The throbs of command do not resolve contradiction. They seek to manage it—pulse by pulse, until the rhythm falters. In that faltering, a different beat may yet emerge.

15

A brief history of capitalist command since post-second world war

Mapping the pulse of capitalist command

The history of capitalist command is not a seamless continuity but a rhythmic succession of consolidations and ruptures. Periods in which the throbs of command operate in relative synchrony—stabilized through hegemonic institutions, geopolitical arrangements, and legitimizing narratives—are interrupted by moments of systemic turbulence, when contradictions can no longer be deferred. These transitions are not smooth adjustments but phases of reconfiguration triggered by social movements, crises of accumulation, ecological breakdown, or geopolitical contestation. Each throb—whether orienting accumulation (purpose), coordinating macro-agency, managing crises (crisiscraft), displacing contradictions, rationalizing through metrics (instrumentality), or recalibrating thresholds—responds to these pressures in different registers. But their interplay generates tensions that accumulate over time, straining the coherence of the command architecture until a new constellation emerges.

This dynamic echoes Giovanni Arrighi's (2010) theory of systemic cycles of accumulation and Wallerstein's (1974, 1980, 1989, 2011) world-systems analysis, in which phases of hegemonic coherence give way to periods of fragmentation and reordering. In this sense, the mega-level is not a fixed structure but a site of ongoing recalibration—a regulatory metabolism whose coherence depends on the ability to align the throbs of command across shifting terrain. Hegemony, here, is not imposed from above; it is metabolized through the recursive operation of these throbs. The system endures not by resolving its contradictions but by rhythmically managing and deferring them—projecting breakdown into new orders of control.

What follows is not a conventional chronology but a rhythmanalysis of capitalist command. I trace how each of the six throbs has evolved, recombined, or destabilized across three historical conjunctures of global capitalism: the postwar consolidation, neoliberal reconfiguration, and the current phase of planetary turbulence. Before turning to the historical periodization of these rhythms, however, we must first clarify certain general structural dynamics—particularly the central role of the dollar, fossil flows, and militarized infrastructures—in shaping the conditions through which the throbs of command operate.

From the end of the Second World War to the early twenty-first century, this rhythm was largely synchronized under US hegemony (Hudson 2003). The United States occupied the commanding heights of the global capitalist system not only through its overwhelming military and economic capacity but also through its role in organizing the institutional, monetary, and geopolitical architecture of postwar capitalism. Rooted in the outcome of the Second World War and institutionalized through the Bretton Woods framework and the creation of global governance institutions such as the IMF, the World Bank, other UN agencies, and later the WTO, this hegemony provided the gravitational center around which the throbs of command were coordinated.

At the heart of this configuration lay two interlocking pillars. First, military supremacy: The United States has maintained the largest military apparatus in the world, using interventions and a global architecture of strategic basing—hundreds of military installations and logistical hubs positioned across continents—to assert control over geopolitical chokepoints and the social reproduction fields that sustain global accumulation. Second, monetary command: Since Bretton Woods, and especially after the end of gold convertibility in 1971, the dollar has functioned as the world's principal reserve currency. This monetary hegemony has enabled the United States to finance its deficits, regulate capital flows, and discipline states through rate policy and volatility management.

Critically, this monetary command is anchored in fossil energy. The vast majority of global oil and gas transactions remain dollar-denominated, binding energy access—and thus the reproduction of capital—to dollar liquidity. This nexus underpins what we might call a system of imperial metabolic control, in which the flows of capital, energy, and legitimacy are regulated not only through finance and war but also through the material infrastructures of extraction and reproduction. Despite the mounting urgency of ecological breakdown, the system has doubled down: Fossil fuel investment and subsidies have more than doubled since 2020 (Black et al. 2023), reinforcing the extractive circuits that tie planetary reproduction to accumulation.

This metabolic order is policed by war. The 2003 invasion of Iraq and the 2011 intervention in Libya—both preceded by those regimes' efforts to de-dollarize their oil trade—illustrate the strategic defense of the dollar-oil nexus (Clark 2005). US global dominance is no longer based on territorial empire but on *monetary imperialism*—a regime of command executed through financial instruments, disciplinary flows, and the capacity to generate and withdraw liquidity (Vasudevan 2008; Desai 2013; Desai and Hudson 2021, Farrell and Newman 2023).

This system of control has enabled a particular form of globalization. Beginning in the 1970s, neoliberal restructuring accelerated the relocation of industrial production to Asia and the Global South. Enabled by the dollar's global reach, this strategy arbitraged labor costs, environmental regulation, and political repression—constructing a transnational architecture of accumulation that simultaneously weakened labor in the North and deepened dependency in the South. This was not just a search for efficiency but a strategic recomposition of command at the mega-level.

As Qiao Liang (2021: 68) observed, the genius of this system lies in its invisibility: "They did not openly plunder the resources and wealth of other countries, but exchanged them for a piece of green paper that costs them almost nothing." This "green paper" system—anchored in dollar liquidity, fossil flows, and militarized enforcement—became one of the central dispositifs through which the throbs of command circulated, regulated, and reproduced the architecture of domination across the capitalist pyramid. Taking my cue from Qiao Liang in his *Arch of Empire*, my general view is that dollar hegemony can be described as an imperfect breathing mechanism of the monstrous global capital machine. Inhalation: Capital and money flow back into the United States. Exhalation: Capital and money flow out. It goes without saying that this flow is associated with the unleashing of differentiated dynamics and pressures that restructure class relations around the world. Triffin's paradox (1960, 1968) describes the economic trap that occurs when the currency of one country—such as the US dollar—becomes the world's reference reserve currency.

For international trade to function even minimally smoothly, the world needs a reliable and universally accepted currency. This means that the country issuing that currency—currently the United States—has to inject sufficient dollars into the global system. The only way to do this is through persistent trade deficits: The United States buys more from the world than it sells. However, this constant flow of dollars leads to a problem: The more the United States imports and accumulates trade deficits, the more it increases its debt. Over time, this can undermine global confidence in the dollar itself. If countries begin to doubt its value, financial instability ensues. But there is a dead end: If the United States tries to compensate by reducing trade deficits—that is, by decreasing the amount of dollars in circulation—the world suddenly finds itself short of dollar liquidity. International trade slows, the global economy slows, and emerging currencies find more room to challenge the hegemonic role of the dollar. Thus, the United States finds itself trapped in a paradox: Either it continues to flood the world with dollars, increasing overindebtedness, or it tightens the supply of dollars, causing a global liquidity crisis. It is within these two poles that the space for US global strategic intervention operates, whether through war to assuage the risk of de-dollarization of the global economy, monetary diplomacy such as the Plaza Accord in 1985 to recalibrate trade imbalances, or the current Trump-era tariffs policies (De Angelis 2025a). From this perspective, Triffin's paradox is a paradox only in appearance: It expresses the systemic condition of dollar hegemony itself—too many dollars in circulation suffocate the system through debt, while too few starve it through liquidity shortages. It is, in other words, like the paradox of breathing: The danger lies both in excess and in deprivation, as well as in the fragile balance that keeps the global body alive under US hegemony.

But this system, long taken for granted, has for decades shown signs of fragmentation—periodic shocks, strategic overreach, and mounting contradictions that have steadily eroded its capacity to synchronize command. What once appeared as a coherent hegemonic architecture now reveals itself as a fragile assemblage, increasingly unable to reproduce the consent and coordination that sustained its dominance. Its claim to universality falters amid multiplying fractures, as the very throbs that once synchronized global command now struggle to contain the turbulence they helped generate. As we now turn to the periodization of capitalist command—from postwar consolidation through neoliberal reconfiguration to the current moment of planetary turbulence—I will briefly trace how each throb of command has evolved, adjusted, or faltered. This cannot offer an exhaustive history—each phase would merit a book of its own. Rather, what follows is an intuitive cartography of shifts in rhythm and coordination, an attempt to map not only the tempos of past hegemony but also the spasms of a command structure increasingly unable to synchronize its own pulse.

Postwar command: Bretton Woods and the Pax Americana

The period following the Second World War marks the consolidation of a hegemonic configuration at the mega-level of capitalist command, in which the United States emerges as the gravitational center of a new world order. This hegemony is anchored in two primary domains: internally, through a new model of national regulation founded on full employment, mass consumption, and class compromise—an expression of the "deal" we discussed in Chapter 2; externally, through the construction of a multilateral international order geared to stabilize capitalism globally while defending it from both socialist alternatives and internal disorder.

From the perspective of the throbs of command, this period is defined by the tight coupling of macro-functions. The meta-purpose of accumulation was embedded within the project of reconstruction and productivity-led growth. The devastation of war had cleared the ground for a new accumulation cycle, with the Marshall Plan funneling dollars into Europe to stimulate recovery, stabilize currencies, and rebuild markets for American goods. At the same time, the trauma of the Great Depression—and the systemic threat posed by organized labor and anti-capitalist uprisings—had left its mark: Economic management could no longer be left to the invisible hand alone. The state became a central actor in ensuring effective demand and social cohesion.

Yet this new social compromise was not simply granted from above. It emerged in reaction to the deep turbulence of the first half of the twentieth century, particularly the cycle of struggles that followed the First World War and the Russian Revolution. The specter of socialism haunted the capitalist world: mass strikes, factory occupations, and peasant revolts in Europe; uprisings in the colonial world; and a rapidly spreading discourse of revolution created an existential threat to the system. The rise of fascism and Nazism was, in part, a brutal response to this threat—offering order, nationalism, and capital-friendly repression where revolution loomed. The Second World War was thus not just a conflict between empires but a catastrophic outcome of unresolved contradictions within the capitalist pyramid, including the fear of recomposing class power from below. It is against this historical backdrop that the postwar social and political architecture must be read: the welfare state, the UN system, and Bretton Woods—all were forms of damage control and containment, *designed to save capitalism from its own unraveling*.

The *coordination of macro-agency* in this period was institutionalized through new international organizations—the IMF, the World Bank, the GATT, and the United Nations—which together constituted the scaffolding of an emerging global regime. The Bretton Woods system (created in 1944 and implemented in the postwar era) established fixed exchange rates and tied the dollar to gold, making the US currency the keystone of global liquidity. However, because the United States was unable to export sufficient capital to match its expanding global role, it effectively supplied the world with dollars through mounting current account deficits driven by military expenditures in Korea and Vietnam (Desai and Hudson 2021). These institutions also acted as stabilizing nodes in the global command system: They monitored, advised, and, where necessary, imposed rules on national economies to ensure their alignment with the overarching architecture of the capitalist order.

It was in this context that the discourse of development emerged as a key ideological and operational instrument of command (Escobar 1995). In the wake of decolonization and anti-imperialist struggles, the problem of global inequality could no longer be ignored. Rather than allowing it to become the basis for systemic critique, however, the development discourse reframed inequality as a technical and temporal gap—a lag in modernization that could be solved through planning, aid, and investment. The newly established World Bank took the lead in defining this agenda, presenting development as a linear path that the Global South could follow under the tutelage of the North. This depoliticized narrative masked structural dependencies, reinforced imperial hierarchies, and integrated postcolonial states into the circuits of global capital. It promised roads, dams, and schools—but delivered debt, export dependency, and new forms of elite capture. Development thus became one of the core mechanisms by which the mega-level extended its command into the formerly colonized world, domesticating aspirations of liberation within a grammar of growth. As a throb of command, development exemplified instrumentality—rationalizing inequality through metrics and models—while enacting a deep displacement of postcolonial autonomy into circuits of managed dependency.

This was also the era of *Keynesian crisiscraft:* Macroeconomic management by the state became the principal technique for absorbing shocks and avoiding the cyclical depressions that had marred earlier capitalist phases (De Angelis 2000). In the Global North, this meant full employment policies, legitimization of labor unions, wage-bargaining agreements, and the expansion of welfare states. This arrangement was deeply partial and exclusionary. It rested on racialized and gendered divisions. Above all, the expansion of postwar prosperity was premised on the devastation of the planetary commons, laying the groundwork for the ecological crises to come.

The throb of *displacement* during this period was shaped by the fact that capital had not yet been fully unbound from national territories, and production remained largely embedded in domestic economies. It thus operated through development projects funded by the World Bank and other institutions that restructured agrarian life, dispossessed communities, and redirected circuits of reproduction toward export dependency. Meanwhile, Cold War militarism—from the US interventions in Korea, Vietnam, Cambodia, and Laos to proxy conflicts across Africa and Latin America—served as both containment and dislocation, suspending local trajectories under the weight of geopolitical strategy. Informalized labor persisted in vast swaths of the Global South, and patterns of unequal exchange were maintained through price mechanisms, trade rules, and monetary asymmetries.

Instrumentality, meanwhile, was rationalized in the postwar period through technocratic planning and Fordist discipline. The dominant metrics were national GDP, industrial productivity, and labor-market integration. The World Bank's early development paradigms emphasized infrastructure, modernization, and growth, translating political questions into economic programming. Metrics were largely state-centric, and economists emerged as the new priests of policy—figures endowed with the authority to interpret social reality through the sacred languages of indicators and models. In practice, this meant that decisions about fiscal policy, social investment, and industrial expansion were increasingly framed in terms of the technical optimization of GDP output and efficiency. Robert McNamara, appointed World Bank president in 1968 after serving as US Secretary of Defense, became a paradigmatic figure of this technocratic shift (Caufield 1997). Under his leadership, the World Bank expanded its portfolio of development lending by deploying systems analysis and quantification, treating poverty as a logistical problem to be managed through metrics and targeted interventions. The economist-priest emerged not only as an adviser to governments but also as a governing subject in their own right—installing econometrics as a tool of both diagnosis and command.

In this configuration, instrumental reason became a language of command: a way to make domination appear rational, inevitable, and value neutral. Numbers replaced narratives, forecasts supplanted deliberation, and the complexity of reproduction was reduced to spreadsheets of control. This did not mark the disappearance of ideology but its reinvention in quantitative form.

The *threshold*, finally, was beginning to register its pulse. Not yet a planetary crisis but a growing sense of systemic unrest. From the late 1950s through the 1970s, a sequence of transversal struggles began to challenge the ideological and institutional fabric of the postwar order. Workers' militancy intensified, confronting the limits of the productivity compromise. The civil rights movement in the United States—culminating in landmark victories but also in widespread repression—exposed the racial foundations of liberal democracy. Feminist movements interrogated the patriarchal underpinnings of the family wage and reproductive labor. Anti-colonial and anti-imperialist struggles in Vietnam, Algeria, and beyond forced the capitalist core to confront its violent peripheries. Student uprisings from Berkeley to Paris to Tokyo challenged the bureaucratization of life and the moral legitimacy of imperial war. Environmental critiques emerged with force, culminating in the first Earth Day in 1970 and the early discourse on ecological limits.

These and many other movements did not merely seek redistribution; they demanded a transformation of the very grammar of social cooperation. They recomposed the energies of the procommons, opening new horizons of value, meaning, and resistance—often beyond the metrics and categories recognized by state and capital. They also carried a cost that capital had to bear: Materially, these struggles forced an expansion of the welfare state and public provisioning, and politically, they necessitated a costly apparatus of surveillance, policing, and repression. This double pressure—rising reproductive costs and intensified coercive expenditure—helped precipitate what James O'Connor (1973) famously termed the "fiscal crisis of the state": a structural contradiction between the legitimation and accumulation functions of postwar governance.

At the international level, the challenge to US command was compounded by shifting patterns of productivity and competitiveness. The economic recovery of Europe and Japan had matured, undermining America's postwar industrial dominance. Trade imbalances and capital outflows began to strain the Bretton Woods monetary system. By 1971, when President Nixon ended the dollar's convertibility into gold, the symbolic and institutional scaffolding of the postwar order was shaken. The first throb of systemic purpose began to pulse erratically, signaling that the period of institutional command was giving way to a more volatile, decentralized, and financialized phase of global capitalism.

Neoliberal reconfiguration: market sovereignty and financial command

If the postwar order stabilized capitalist command through institutional compromise and Keynesian regulation, the neoliberal era marked a radical reconfiguration of the pulsations of power. Born out of the long crisis of the 1970s—fueled by rising social unrest, stagflation, environmental limits, and the breakdown of the Bretton Woods monetary regime—this new phase did not simply dismantle the previous order. It reoriented its very metabolism.

The Chilean coup of 1973, in which the elected socialist government of Salvador Allende was violently overthrown and replaced by Augusto Pinochet's dictatorship, marked a symbolic and material threshold. Chile became the first laboratory for a new model of command: authoritarian in form, neoliberal in content. Guided by the Chicago Boys and advised by Milton Friedman, Pinochet's regime tested the architecture of market sovereignty under conditions of mass repression—a model that would be exported and adapted globally in the decades to come (Klein 2007).

This shift involved a recalibration of purpose. The *meta-purpose* of accumulation became both more abstract and more totalizing. Capital no longer needed to coordinate through fixed hierarchies or national industrial strategies; the market itself became the primary organizing dispositif, displacing the visible hand of the state with the invisible coercion of competition. Accumulation was no longer a goal among others—it became the organizing horizon of society.

Meanwhile, the locus of *macro-agency* did not shift away from states so much as it was rearticulated within a new transnational architecture of command. National governments remained central, but their functions were increasingly subordinated to the imperatives of market governance and financial discipline. States no longer coordinated capitalist accumulation through public planning or welfare expansion; instead, they were refashioned as facilitators of competitiveness, enforcers of austerity, and guarantors of financial credibility.

This reconfiguration took place within an expanding mesh of transnational institutions, financial markets, and corporate governance regimes. Central banks, credit rating agencies, and supranational bodies such as the IMF, the World Bank, and the WTO became nodal points in a new regime of "governance without government" (Rosenau and Czempiel 1992). Coordination no longer depended primarily on formal sovereignty; instead, it hinged on a state's creditworthiness, fiscal discipline, and attractiveness to capital.

Finance, which had already expanded in the postwar era under US monetary leadership, was no longer simply a lubricating mechanism for investment; it became the very medium of command. With capital controls dismantled and the Bretton Woods system abandoned, speculative flows, bond markets, and derivatives took center stage. Financial actors emerged as arbiters of national policy and transnational development, capable of disciplining states through interest rates, capital flight, and credit downgrades.

In this new regime, *crisis* was no longer a threat to be avoided; it became a strategic instrument of reorganization. From the Volcker shock of 1979, which aggressively raised interest rates to crush inflation and discipline labor, to the Latin American debt crisis of 1982, the collapse of the Soviet Union in 1991, and the Asian financial crisis of 1997–98, each moment of rupture served to restructure the political economy of entire regions. These crises were not simply economic shocks; they were leveraged to break labor union power, dismantle public provision, and reconfigure national economies to serve transnational capital.

Austerity, structural adjustment, and deregulation became enduring technologies of power. They enabled a redistribution of reproductive risk downward—onto households, communities, and feminized or racialized labor—and outward, across global territories. These transformations were foundational—not solely in a technological sense, as emphasized in mainstream accounts that foreground innovations in Information and Communication Technologies (ICT) and logistics (Gereffi et al. 2005)—but in a political-economic sense. It was this configuration that enabled the restructuring of the geography of accumulation through the arbitrage of social reproduction costs: Global value chains were not just technical networks but political infrastructures that exploited asymmetries in wages, environmental regulation, and reproductive provisioning. As analyzed in Chapter 13, neoliberalism's competitive logic did not merely relocate production; it decomposed the conditions of life, transforming reproductive fields into zones of extraction and experimentation.

This marked a new phase in the system's capacity for *displacement*. Deindustrialization in the Global North was not a retreat but a strategic reallocation of capital toward lower-cost and more governable social terrains. Global value chains were engineered to extract surplus by exploiting differences in wages, ecological regulation, gender norms, and state repression. This enabled capital to neutralize social conflict in one region by relocating exploitation to another, transforming economic competition into a planetary struggle between lifeworlds. Displacement, in this sense, was no longer a reactive mechanism triggered by disruption—it became a pervasive, anticipatory logic of command. While the relocation of crisis and contradiction has long been integral to capitalist expansion—through colonial extraction, forced migration, and imperial war—neoliberalism intensified and generalized this logic. The threat of displacement was no longer an episodic tool of restructuring; it became a permanent mechanism of global competition.

Even in the postwar period, export promotion and development planning tied peripheral economies to the needs of global capital. But these strategies were often mediated by state-led projects of national modernization. Neoliberalism dismantled this protective frame, embedding displacement into the everyday governance of competitiveness and transforming it from a developmental lever into a disciplinary threat. This reconfiguration not only restructured the geography of accumulation—it also deeply altered the temporality of social life. The continuous possibility of relocation, defunding, or abandonment introduced new forms of existential precarity, not only in the Global South but also within the core itself. Precarity here is not simply a condition of unstable employment—it is the ambient atmosphere of life under a regime in which reproduction is subordinated to the volatility of capital mobility. It is the permanent exposure to abandonment, a structural uncertainty that disciplines both waged and unwaged workers through the threat of displacement. This precarity has been especially gendered and racialized, intensifying the feminization of labor through the expansion of low-wage, care, and informal work; driving urban informalization as rural populations were expelled and absorbed into precarious urban economies; and normalizing platform labor as a fragmented, just-in-time response to unemployment and underemployment. Displacement is no longer the exception—it is the rule that governs the architecture of accumulation in a world increasingly stripped of buffers, protections, and alternatives. Precarity allows the redistribution of reproductive risk downward—onto households, communities, and feminized or racialized labor—and outward, across global territories (Standing 2011; Neilson 2015; Fraser 2016; Azmanova 2020).

Instrumentality in the neoliberal era took on an expansive and invasive form. As market sovereignty displaced state planning, instrumental rationality migrated from national bureaucracies to supranational institutions and corporate consultancies. The economist-priest returned as a structural adjuster, austerity architect, and central banker framed as a "neutral" technician, advancing a deep political restructuring of social life. Institutions like the IMF, shaped by the doctrines of Milton Friedman and the Chicago School, translated political choices into technical mandates—governance became a regime of quantification.

Planetary metrics such as credit ratings, debt-to-GDP ratios, ESG scores, and the Doing Business Index did not merely measure economic performance; they produced new standards of governability. Efficiency, flexibility, and competitiveness were recoded as moral imperatives—norms that penetrated policy frameworks and reshaped institutional routines in the capitalist world.

This logic extended deep into the social body. Universities were reorganized around metric-driven audits like the UK's Research Excellence Framework (REF), transforming academic labor into the pursuit of outputs, citations, and grants. Schools were restructured around standardized testing and league tables. Hospitals, museums, social housing, and NGOs became subject to key performance indicators, as managerialism displaced substantive judgment with benchmark compliance (De Angelis and Harvie 2009; Davis et al. 2012).

Even the language of sustainability was absorbed into this grammar. Environmental regulation was reframed through market-compatible instruments—carbon offset schemes, green bonds, and Environmental, Social, and Governance (ESG) frameworks—that served less to challenge extractive accumulation than to render it legible and investable. In this frame, sustainability is not the sustainability of ecosystems or lifeworlds but the sustainability of business models.

Crucially, this instrumental rationality is not neutral—it is political. It is legitimized by a culture that reframes crisis as opportunity and suffering as discipline. As Norman Lamont, Chancellor of the Exchequer under John Major, infamously declared in 1991 during the early 1990s recession, "Rising unemployment and the recession have been the price that we have had to pay to get inflation down. That price is well worth paying" (Parliament UK 1991). Such statements exemplify the moral calculus of neoliberal governance, where pain becomes proof of resolve. Stanford economist and Nobel laureate Paul Romer would later codify this ethos in technocratic terms at a venture-capitalist meeting in 2004: "A crisis is a terrible thing to waste" (Rosenthal 2009). These pronouncements distill the confluence of crisiscraft and instrumentality: the crisis is no longer an external shock to be absorbed but a vector of transformation, a chance to remake institutions, norms, and subjectivities to further propel capital accumulation.

And yet, pressure built within the system: a creeping sense that the limits of displacement had been reached. This was the threshold—the gathering contradictions of ecological degradation, debt saturation, and rising inequality. It emerged not only as material exhaustion but also as turbulence: protest, rebellion, and refusal. From the Zapatistas to the global justice movement, from anti-debt revolts in the Global South to the alter-globalization uprisings of Seattle and Genoa, new figures of resistance emerged, challenging the legitimacy of global command. These movements did not merely demand redistribution—they questioned the very grammar of globalization, denouncing the WTO, IMF, and G8 as engines of dispossession. Their critique cut across borders, linking struggles over land, labor, debt, and climate into a shared insurgent cartography (Midnight Notes Collective 2001; Kingsnorth 2004).

The state's response was swift and brutal. In July 2001, the massive and colorful alter-globalization movement in Genoa met police repression, the suspension of constitutional rights, the beating and torture of protesters, and the killing of Carlo Giuliani, a young activist. This signaled a turning point: a *threshold moment* in which dissent was reframed as a threat. Just two months later, the ISIS attacks on the Twin Towers became a crystallizing event, enabling a new strategic reorganization of command.

Under the banner of the "War on Terror," the United States sought to reassert its declining hegemony through a militarized, securitized extension of neoliberal logics. This was not merely a reaction—it was a deliberate strategy within the field of command, designed to compensate for growing geopolitical fragmentation and internal contradictions. War, surveillance, and the moral economy of punishment became tools to harden the existing architecture of control, to rechannel fear into legitimacy, and to reestablish thresholds of governability in the face of new turbulences. At its core, this was an orchestration of crisiscraft—capitalizing on rupture brought about by alter-globalization movements to reconfigure governance—yet it depended on a synchronized mobilization of other throbs: recalibrating thresholds of tolerance, displacing unrest through war and migration, and instrumentalizing security logics into new metrics of control. But this strategy emerged from fragility; it gestured toward a stable order even as that order fractured further. Its reverberations—across crisis management, global value chains, and political discourse—generated feedback across multiple throbs of command, all while displacement (through war and migration) restructured the social terrain from which new forms of resistance would soon emerge (Hardt and Negri 2004; Agamben 2005; Harvey 2005; Della Porta et al. 2006; Klein 2007; Sassen 2014).

Finally, the financial crisis of 2007–8 exposed the rot at the core of this regime. Throughout the neoliberal period, personal debt had been used to mask stagnating wages, with credit cards, subprime mortgages, and student loans propping up consumption. When the system collapsed, states rushed to rescue the banks, not the people. This revealed the deep entanglement of global command with financial speculation and the violent disciplining of everyday life.

Amid the wreckage, new uprisings emerged: the Arab Spring, the indignados, Occupy, Square movements, Black Lives Matter, and Ni Una Menos challenged both authoritarianism and market rule, calling for democracy not as a form of state power but as a collective reappropriation of life. The rise of ecological movements, especially among youth, signaled a growing refusal of capitalist temporality—its compulsive acceleration and disregard for planetary boundaries. These movements did not merely critique environmental degradation; they challenged the very rhythms through which capital organizes life—demanding a reorientation of time itself toward care, regeneration, and ecological reciprocity (Dean 2012; Butler 2015; Della Porta 2015; Malm 2020; Imperatore and Leonardi 2023).

Planetary turbulence: multipolarism, ecological breakdown, and the spasm of command

If the post-2008 period initially promised a rethinking of capitalist command—with talk of reform, Green New Deals, and "inclusive" recoveries—it quickly revealed itself as a time of intensifying contradictions and planetary disequilibrium. The throbs of command have not ceased to function, but they now operate in a field marked by instability, feedback overload, and fragmentation. Their rhythms are no longer smoothly integrated but increasingly spasmodic—sometimes reinforcing one another, sometimes short-circuiting. The result is not a new order but a condition of suspended reconfiguration: The old hegemony wanes, a new one has yet to take shape, and the system itself trembles under its own weight.

COVID-19 briefly interrupted the system—but in doing so, it also exposed its logic. As markets froze, states intervened in unprecedented ways: bailing out corporations, enforcing lockdowns, and publicly revalorizing care work—though not through wages or working conditions but through symbolic praise and temporary recognition. Amid this, grassroots networks mobilized mutual aid and solidarity, offering a glimpse of collective capacity beyond state and market. For a moment, capitalism appeared to pause. But this was not a reset. It was a rehearsal—a preview of the lengths to which command would go to preserve itself through digitized control, new forms of precarity, and the deepening of inequality (Sitrin 2020; Fassin and Fourcade 2021; Mezzadra and Neilson 2024).

Through all of this, the throbs of command adjusted, adapted, and recomposed—but their rhythm has grown arrhythmic, their pulse more fragile. The neoliberal era did not end with rupture but with a long, stuttering exhale—and in many ways, we are still caught within it. What comes next is not yet a new regime of command but the open struggle over whether such a regime can still be sustained at all.

At the level of *purpose*, the meta-goal of accumulation remains intact but the pathways to realize it have become contested and contradictory. Competing visions of capitalist futurity—green transitions, reindustrialization, techno-authoritarianism, and digital finance—proliferate, but none offers a stable horizon. Climate collapse has made the very idea of *a capitalist future* unstable, and the legitimation narratives of capitalist command—progress, growth, and freedom—ring increasingly hollow.

The throb of *agency* now shows multiple fractures. The United States no longer commands uncontested hegemony within the macro-agency; it remains powerful, but its ability to coordinate the global system has waned. Meanwhile, the geopolitical terrain continues to shift. The rise of China, along with the broader BRICS coalition, has challenged US hegemony both economically and strategically (Sciortino 2024). Their ascent is not a deviation from global capitalism but a product of it: an outcome of integration into neoliberal circuits of accumulation, with China's vast infrastructure projects, labor discipline, and increasingly high-tech innovation forming a new gravitational pole. The unipolar order has been cracking for a while and conflictual multipolarism is taking shape (Mezzadra and Neilson 2024). This is a world of competing centers, each advancing its own mode of accumulation and command: a global field in which rival centers of capital command compete for influence, resources, and symbolic power. Institutions once seen as authoritative—the UN, WTO, and even the World Bank—find themselves increasingly paralyzed or co-opted. The network of macro-agents has grown more polycentric but not more democratic. Their pulsations are out of phase, overlapping but discordant, each amplifying turbulence rather than stabilizing the whole. In this context, Trump's policies—from tariff wars and industrial reshoring to the weaponization of finance and migration control—become intelligible as attempts to defend US hegemony amid its chronic waning: efforts to reassert command not through renewed consensus but through coercion, protectionism, and polarization. These pulsations are out of phase, overlapping but discordant, each amplifying turbulence rather than stabilizing the whole.

But these actors do not escape the deep grammar of accumulation; they reproduce the throbs of command in their own registers. Dollar hegemony is countered by experiments in the digital yuan and BRICS currency platforms—yet the meta-purpose of accumulation remains untouched. NATO expansion is shadowed by new military alliances but the logic of militarized crisiscraft persists. Global governance itself falters under vetoes and institutional fatigue, revealing the decay of the coordinating capacities of macro-agency. Their pulsations are out of phase, overlapping but discordant, each amplifying turbulence rather than stabilizing the whole.

The throb of *crisiscraft*—once used to restructure and reintegrate the system—is now itself unstable. The *War on Terror* of the early 2000s offered a momentary reassertion of command through securitization and fear, but the invasions of Iraq and Afghanistan produced more disorder than control. In the current interregnum, command sheds its managerial mask and reverts to rawer modalities: war, borders, repression, and extraction. The war in Ukraine has become both a brutal conflict and a geopolitical hinge—testing the viability of US-led unipolar command while exposing the fragility of European sovereignty and energy infrastructure. The genocide in Palestine, unfolding in real time before a watching world, has torn away the last moral fig leaves of the post–Second World War human rights regime, revealing the deep instrumentalization of international law and diplomacy. At the time of writing, the US–Israel war on Iran further intensifies this expanding arc of regional war and systemic destabilization. These are not isolated crises; they are expressions of an order unraveling from its core.

In this fragmented horizon, the United States under Trump embodies a spasmodic mode of command—one that does not seek coherence but escalation, in view of a new coherence that seeks to reassert US hegemony. This strategy weaponized every available instrument: Trade tariffs become a form of displacement, redirecting crisis while destabilizing global value chains; international aid was cut and reconfigured to punish dissenting states and reward allies; environmental and social regulations were gutted to reinstate the primacy of profitability (De Angelis 2025a,c,d).

The rollback of Diversity, Equity, and Inclusion (DEI) policies, mass deportations, and the criminalization of protest mark a sharp recalibration of systemic thresholds—seeking to discipline not only institutions but subjectivities. DEI initiatives, often portrayed as gestures of inclusion, functioned in the neoliberal deal as techniques to manage social complexity: translating demands for justice, representation, and historical redress into bureaucratizable categories, measurable outputs, and administrable reforms. Their dismantling under Trump did not represent a retreat from control but rather a shift toward a cruder and more brutal form of simplification. This logic of simplification extends into the epistemic sphere: Trump's attacks on university programs—particularly those engaged in critical race theory, gender studies, or decolonial thought—aim not only to silence dissent but to flatten the plural knowledge systems through which social complexity is rendered intelligible. These interventions exemplify the throb of instrumentality in its most reactionary form: reducing education to compliance, culture to propaganda, and thought itself to a battlefield of ideological purification. They also engage the throb of threshold recalibration, shifting the boundaries of acceptable discourse and intellectual legitimacy. By purging critical voices from institutions of higher learning, the administration redefines what knowledge is allowed to count and who is authorized to speak it—filtering the horizon of possibility to align with authoritarian imperatives.

This trajectory of simplification and control has not remained at the level of discourse; it has manifested through escalating forms of coercion. It was sharply exemplified by the Immigration and Customs Enforcement (ICE) workplace raids in Los Angeles in June 2025—for example, at Home Depot and garment-wholesaler sites—in which predominantly Latino workers (as well as workers from other nationalities) were forcibly removed, sparking mass protests not only in Los Angeles but also rapidly resonating across other US cities, from Houston and San Francisco to Chicago and New York, and continuing into subsequent months. The deployment of federal troops without state authorization, under the pretext of immigration enforcement, added a militarized layer to this logic. These actions do more than enforce the law—they perform it, collapsing plural and intersecting struggles into binary antagonisms: patriotism versus lawlessness, order versus insurgency. Scapegoats are summoned—"woke ideology," "antifa," and "invasion"—to flatten a turbulent social field into a manageable spectacle. This is a compound operation of the throbs: Threshold recalibration seeks to push the boundaries of the tolerable; displacement renders targeted populations mobile and expendable; and instrumentality translates complexity into executable metrics—threat levels, clearance zones, and enforcement quotas. This logic also played out sharply in Minneapolis in January 2026, where the fatal shootings of Renee Good and Alex Pretti by federal immigration agents during protests against expanded ICE operations—incidents that federal officials initially described under the rhetoric of "domestic terrorism" casting those targeted or involved in the protests as such—sparked sustained mass demonstrations and solidarity actions across the United States, further revealing how such narratives are deployed to collapse complex social contestations into simplified dichotomies.

This volatile environment serves as a testing ground for authoritarian command. Each deportation, each arrest, each protest violently dispersed, and each court ruling on the legality of the president's executive orders becomes a data point in an experiment: How far can thresholds be pushed before fracture? The aim is not resolution but orchestration—of conflict, anxiety, and fear. Fear, in turn, becomes a tool of governance; undocumented migrants, rendered more precarious by the threat of expulsion, face worsened working conditions and downward pressure on wages. Their vulnerability is not incidental—it is instrumentalized to discipline broader labor markets and maintain hierarchies of disposability.

This strategy engages multiple throbs. Most explicitly, it enacts a recalibration of thresholds—shifting the bounds of what is politically and socially tolerable. But it also mobilizes instrumentality, distilling social complexity into simple metrics: "illegal equals threat," "protest equals instability." And it leverages displacement—removing people from workplaces, neighborhoods, and public space, and reframing communities not as holders of rights but as problems to be managed or expelled. The authoritarian directions of Trumpism are not aberrations. They are expressions of a broader systemic condition: a mode of capitalist command that can no longer match the complexity of the world it governs. Put simply, capitalist power can no longer cope with the complexity of society and the planet; and because adapting—particularly to ecological limits—would mean becoming something other than capitalism, it instead simplifies and hardens into more authoritarian forms. Rather than evolve richer modes of coordination or recognition—engaging ecological limits, reproductive demands, or plural justice claims—it doubles down on simplification and control. These moves deepen the very contradictions they claim to suppress. The result is a feedback loop of escalation without resolution: deportations trigger protest; protest invites repression; repression inflames unrest. This volatility is not incidental—it is structurally generative, as moments of turbulence become opportunities for authoritarian consolidation: Power feeds on disorder to justify its own intensification and to normalise the presence of the army in the streets. Yet turbulence itself is not the problem—historically, it is the condition of transformation. Turbulence is not the enemy—it is the moment when thresholds loosen and new forms can emerge. The danger for social reproduction lies in the asymmetry of capture: When crisiscraft outpaces commoning, instability is folded back into consolidation, and exceptional measures become ordinary.

This points to a deeper structural problem, already underscored through the lens of cybernetics. Every regulatory system must contend with the law of requisite variety: It can govern effectively only if its internal complexity matches that of the environment it seeks to control. Yet, in the capitalist pyramid, complexity increases as we move downward—toward the entangled realities of social cooperation, ecological interdependence, and reproductive life. Command from above is always insufficient. It copes not by confronting complexity but by simplifying it—filtering out what it cannot process and amplifying what reinforces its meta-purpose. These filtering mechanisms underpin the throbs of command and the dynamics they sustain.

Among these, the throb of displacement most directly embodies the logic of simplification and externalization. When the system's complexity cannot be governed internally, it is offloaded—across borders, institutions, or populations. Nowhere is the growing dysfunction of displacement more visible than in the contradiction animating today's poles of global social cooperation—nodes that are simultaneously sites of sovereign command and logistical conduits for capital circulation. As Mezzadra and Neilson (2024) argue—especially in Chapter 4 of their book—these poles are no longer merely state-centered; they are hybrid formations in which the regulatory authority of political sovereignty collides with the infrastructural imperatives of global supply chains. The pole as territorial regulator, concerned with borders, law, and legitimacy, now clashes with the pole as logistical node, governed by throughput, flexibility, and market speed. In other words, the pole must simultaneously secure territory and guarantee circulation—yet the measures required to reinforce one increasingly destabilize the other. This contradiction destabilizes both sides: Sovereignty is hollowed out by the demands of capital circulation, while logistical smoothness is disrupted by resurgent nationalist protectionisms and ecological limits.

This tension plays out differently across the global landscape but has become particularly volatile in the United States under Trump. Here, the throb of displacement has not only frayed under external pressures—such as COVID-19, geopolitical rivalry, and planetary thresholds—but has also been weaponized internally. Trump-era policies turn displacement into a domestic strategy of authoritarian simplification. Populations deemed surplus or threatening are filtered out not for logistical optimization but for symbolic consolidation. Reproductive risk is offloaded onto already precarious communities, while nationalist spectacle transforms systemic fragility into performative strength. In this way, the contradiction of the US pole of global capital is not resolved but politically instrumentalized.

This contradiction at the pole—between sovereign command and logistical subordination—illuminates a deeper fracture in the pyramid of capital. In its ideal functioning, the pyramid aligns the mega-level's strategic command with the meta-level's logistical and financial coordination. Poles—such as the United States or China—are supposed to stabilize this alignment: as sovereign centers that regulate territory and population and as logistical hubs that channel global flows of capital, labor, and goods. They are meant to translate strategic command into coordinated circulation without generating systemic friction.

But today, this dual role is cracking. The logistical imperatives of capital—speed, flexibility, and scalability—often collide with the sovereign imperatives of political authority—security, legitimacy, and territorial control. The result is systemic arrhythmia: Commands issued from above encounter blockages from below, while supply chains demand frictionless circulation that sovereignty cannot guarantee. Infrastructures seize, feedback loops misfire, and legitimacy frays. When coordination fails and integration proves insufficient, power shifts from managing complexity to compressing it. Authoritarianism emerges here not as an aberration but as a mode of crisis management. Faced with a world it can no longer govern through integration, capitalist command defaults to simplification. Rather than increase its internal complexity to match that of its environment through democratization across social cooperation—as cybernetic viability would require—it reduces the field by filtering, flattening, and repressing. The rollback of rights, mass deportations, and the criminalization of protest are not anomalies; they are techniques that seek to reassert control by shrinking the field of contestation. Displacement becomes spectacle. Sovereignty becomes siege. "Fake news" becomes an instrument for steering markets and justifying interventions.

In this sense, authoritarianism is fully aligned with the pyramid's logic: It stratifies, filters, and concentrates power to preserve the meta-purpose of accumulation. But this alignment is also its undoing. As the system clamps down, it reveals its own limits: It cannot regenerate legitimacy, it cannot manage planetary thresholds, and it cannot accommodate plural and relational forms of life. Its pulse persists—but it no longer seeks to harmonize. It spasms.

System in spasm: the throbs out of sync

Within today's conflictual multipolarism, capital's former capacity to disembed from crisis zones and reembed elsewhere is faltering. Sovereign resistance, geopolitical friction, infrastructural saturation, and breached ecological thresholds now block the smooth relocations that once defined systemic resilience. What once was framed as a flexible regulatory mechanism has become a zone of exploding contradiction. The poles of global capital—conceived as stable nodes where political sovereignty and capital logistics align—now fracture under the weight of this tension.

This fracture destabilizes the core coordination between orienting purpose (accumulation) and macro-agency (the distributed actors of command). As the system loses coherence, the throb of displacement—capitalism's classic way of externalizing crisis—begins to misfire. Supply chain breakdowns now ripple into inflation, interest rate spikes, and debt stress. States attempt to reassert control, but the networks they once built for capital's mobility now constrain their sovereignty.

Simultaneously, the throb of instrumentality, which rationalizes command through quantification, has grown hollow. Green deals, ESG metrics, and sustainability indexes promise transformation while doubling down on extractive growth. COVID-19 exposed these throbs in sharp relief. Both displacement and instrumentality were brutally illuminated: Survival was measured against supply chain continuity, while care was subordinated to profit logics. Mutual aid and calls for a just recovery briefly cracked the frame—but were rapidly absorbed, ignored, or repressed. Vaccine apartheid and wage suppression returned, reinstating accumulation through tightened control.

And now, the sixth throb—threshold recalibration—enters a state of permanent crisis. Planetary boundaries are not future risks but present ruptures. Yet rather than adapt, the system responds with delay, denial, and securitization. Wars are mobilized as instruments of recalibration, normalizing destruction, and raising the threshold of what is tolerable. Systemic breakdown is reframed as a strategic necessity. The pulse remains, but it is violently out of sync with planetary time.

This is not random turbulence; it is structural arrhythmia. The purpose of accumulation remains intact, but the coordination field of macro-agency—from central banks to military alliances—is fractured. The system no longer regulates itself through feedback and balance but through escalation and simplification. Crises do not invite rethinking; they become theaters of control.

In this context, *crisiscraft* does not resolve contradiction but manages it performatively—through orchestrated fear, emergency narratives, and spectacle. The denial of plural demands and relational complexity feeds into every throb, pushing the system deeper into volatility. Each throb misfires into the next: War produces displacement; displacement generates unrest; unrest invites instrumental control; control normalizes new thresholds; thresholds seek to preclude alternatives.[1]

But alternatives are all we need! Whether this systemic spasm will lead to a spiralling of the regime of war, authoritarian consolidation, fractured multipolarity, or emancipatory recomposition depends not only on how these throbs recalibrate but also on our capacity to enact counter-rhythms grounded in the generative logic of life.

16

The autopoiesis of the common

From affective capture to systemic recomposition

The order of things, that is, the hierarchical order of the rhythm of things

Complex autopoietic systems change not primarily by external force but through a reconfiguration of their meta-finalities. The orientation of the system—its purpose, its grammar, and its rhythm—shapes how its elements relate, adapt, and evolve. Capitalism is a mode of social cooperation whose orientation is hegemonized by capital reproduction rather than social reproduction. Radical transformation therefore requires reversing this hierarchy of value praxes.

The political and cultural task of those who see such a transformation as both desirable and necessary is to turn the procommons from a site of affective capture into an affective space of emancipatory recomposition. This shift cannot remain symbolic or merely ethical: It must build a new systemic coherence—an *autopoiesis of the common*—on the terrain of social reproduction. It means weaving together, across scales and levels, the dispersed energies of the procommons and the meso-level, while progressively subordinating the latter's institutional and productive logics to the former's relational and reproductive values. This weaving together is essentially what I call commoning. In this sense, the autopoietic reorganization of social reproduction resonates with Dinerstein's (2015) notion of "concrete utopia," where emancipatory practices emerge not as blueprints but as immanent negations of capitalist totality. The task is not only to connect the procommons and the meso-level but to reorient and limit the latter—to redirect its infrastructures, governance mechanisms, and productive capacities toward the coordinated reproduction of life, shifting the field of use value away from its subordination to accumulation and toward collectively determined priorities. This systemic recomposition is both political and affective: It changes not only what we do but also how we come to feel, perceive, and desire. It is the process through which social cooperation begins to enact new rhythms of life, transforming institutions, practices, and subjectivities alike.

The meso-level, however, is not a neutral layer awaiting reorientation. It is a field of tension where the forces of the procommons and the meta-level confront each other under the throbs of command. Production for use, which could sustain life, is continually reorganized by capital for valorization. Here, the infrastructures of everyday existence—energy, food, housing, transport, education, and so on—become the terrain on which two autopoietic logics struggle for dominance: one that reproduces life, and another that reproduces accumulation.

Commoning, therefore, unfolds not outside this conflict but within it. The systemic recomposition of life depends on how the procommons act within the meso-level—occupying its institutions and circuits, transforming its routines, and redirecting its technical and organizational capacities toward use value and social reproduction. To build a new systemic coherence is to make this terrain resonate with the rhythms of care and mutual sustenance rather than those of profit.

Every living system is rhythmic. Its continuity depends on the capacity to sustain patterns of recurrence amid variation—to maintain coherence without stillness. Rhythm, in this sense, is not merely temporal order; it is the *form of life's self-organization*, the pulse through which cooperation holds together difference. In social systems, rhythm is the way a society senses its own continuity amid change, how it attunes bodies, practices, and institutions to shared pulses of doing and being. It is how collective life becomes sensible to itself: how work, care, exchange, rest, and celebration compose the patterned temporality of existence.

Capitalism imposes its own rhythm upon this living multiplicity. The beat of accumulation—measured in ever more stringent deadlines, interest rates, and production cycles—forces the flows of social cooperation to conform to its tempo. Under its regime, the rhythms of social reproduction are subordinated to those of valorization; the temporalities of care, rest, and renewal are constantly compressed by the accelerations of profit. The throbs of command orchestrate this synchrony from above, aligning the multiple beats of everyday life into the pulse of accumulation.

Yet rhythm is never entirely captured. Within and beneath the imposed time of command, other pulsations persist—the slow rhythms of ecological cycles, the cooperative timing of mutual aid, and the irregular but resilient beats of revolt and solidarity. These are the *counter-rhythms* through which life resists abstraction, affirming its own temporality against the machinic acceleration of capital.

Systemic recomposition begins when these counter-rhythms find resonance across scales—when practices of sustenance, care, cooperation, and revolt begin to synchronize and amplify one another. In this resonance, rhythm becomes a mode of emancipation: a re-temporalization of society around the living needs of bodies and communities rather than the mechanical imperatives of capital.

To common, then, is to learn to feel and act rhythmically within contradiction—to attune cooperation to the temporalities of collective life as it struggles to reclaim control over the conditions of its own reproduction. It is to restore coherence not by imposing order but by composing relation. Rhythm is the experiential form of systemic recomposition—the way collective life re-coordinates its own reproduction without reproducing domination. To retime society in this way is to reorganize its architecture. The transformation of rhythm demands a transformation of structure: a reorientation of the pyramid itself, in which the rhythms of life become the measure of production, and not its residue. Rhythm becomes the sensitive form of this transformation: the way coherence is enacted and felt in collective life. To change the rhythm of society is to change its organization—to retime the flows of energy, care, and meaning that sustain it. It means *reversing the pyramid.*

The objective basis of hope lies precisely here: in the fact that the pyramid of capital's domination is never total. There is always a surplus of life, of care, of refusal—another rhythm beating within, and a value praxis bringing forth another world. Hope, as John Holloway (2022) reminds us, is not a sentimental anticipation of redemption but the living capacity for cooperation to generate variety beyond command. It is the pulse of life reproducing itself otherwise, even within the circuits of domination. From this excess, we can glimpse another systemic possibility: an *autopoietic intelligence of the common* that reorganizes the reproduction of life from within the very tensions that capital cannot contain.

Reversing the pyramid: from enclosure to enaction

We have now arrived at a systemic context in which the question of "*what is to be done?*" can no longer be posed in isolation from the architecture of the pyramid itself. If the pyramid has served as the organizational diagram of capitalist command—layering rhythm upon rhythm, subordinating all forms of life to the pulsation of accumulation—then transforming social cooperation requires more than opposition. It requires a profound reorientation: not merely a turning upside down but a shift in vantage point—a recomposition of value praxes, social relations, and rhythms of life that alters how hierarchy itself is conceived. What appeared as foundational but subordinated—Gaia, the procommons, and use value—must become

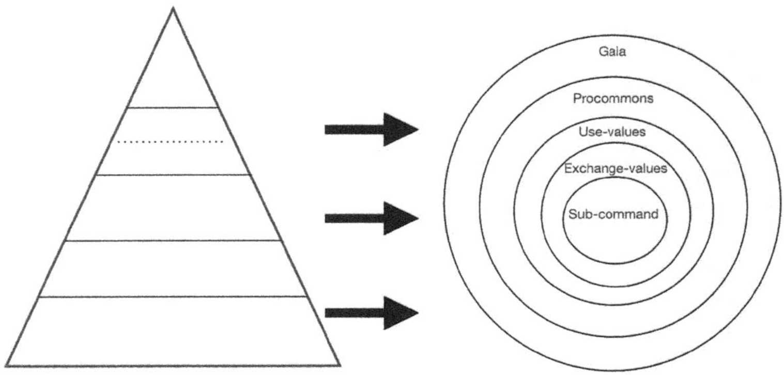

Figure 16.1 An imagined transformation to an alternative horizon of social cooperation

orienting conditions rather than exploited bases. Yet this inversion is not a simple reversal of hierarchy; it is a change of perspective—an alteration in how the system is seen and organized.

This reoriented pyramid is not an abstract utopia. It is a speculative cartography that begins from real alternative practices already unfolding in social cooperation. It is no longer a pyramid in the vertical sense but, seen from above, a series of concentric circles, in which the outer layers define the range of what is possible (Figure 16.1). What appears as hierarchy from the side becomes ecological embedding from above: outer layers do not dominate inner ones but condition and limit them. At the outer layer, we place Gaia—not as a resource but as the living limit, the biospheric intelligence whose rhythms must orient every other level. Within Gaia's limits operates the procommons: the relational fields that cultivate ecological equilibrium and, through shared care, vernacular knowledge, and mutual sustenance, define the horizon of social justice. Within this relational field unfolds the meso-level of use value—where social labor, infrastructural invention, and practical intelligence support the flourishing of all. Only then, subordinated to these, does exchange value find its role: not as the engine of accumulation but, bounded by the outer circles, as one vehicle among many (gift, administrative redistribution, and communal pots) for equitable distribution, for redirecting collective resources to regenerative ends, and for ensuring that the fruits of cooperation reach everyone. Finally, at the base, command: not as domination but as facilitation—what the Zapatistas call *mandar obedeciendo*, leading by obeying, a distributed process that seeks to harmonize pluralities of value practices rather than imposing singularity. In the concentric view, command no longer crowns the system but operates from within it, constrained and oriented by the outer conditions of life. Its legitimacy derives not from supremacy but from responsiveness. To lead by obeying is thus not a moral gesture but a systemic necessity: coordination remains indispensable, but it must emerge from and remain accountable to the reproductive fields that sustain it.

Seen in this light, the relation between procommons and meso-level becomes central: it is here that this reorientation must take institutional form. The procommons and the meso-level are not two separate worlds but two sides of the same living system. One generates meaning, belonging, and affective density; the other organizes and distributes energy, labor, and resources. Their relation is therefore regulatory: Each sets rhythms and thresholds for the other. Under capitalism, the meso-level is not autonomous: It is structured by the meta-level of accumulation and the command level of domination, which impose their rhythms of valorization and control upon the relational field of life. The task of commoning is to reverse this polarity—to make the rhythms of care, use, and relational value the measure of production, not its residue. This is what it means to build an autopoietic organization of social reproduction.

Under capitalist command, the *throbs* that regulate global coherence—purpose, agency, crisis management, displacement, instrumentality, and recalibration—act on the meso-level to align its production and governance with accumulation. Commoning gains systemic consistency only by interfering with these throbs: filtering their signals through other values, amplifying other forms of coordination, and inventing new rhythms of regulation. This is the passage from resonance to regulation, where affective and relational intensities begin to take organizational form, building the institutional capacities that sustain another systemic coherence.

But this imagined reordering confronts periods of disenchantment and a sense of powerlessness and impotence. The imagined reordering of the pyramid confronts not only structural inertia but also the affective paralysis that accompanies it. Paolo Virno (2021: 25) writes that "the impotent one is the person who remains transfixed by the spectacle offered by the coexistence of opposites. Or rather, the one who becomes hypnotised by such a spectacle."

To be hypnotized by such opposites—war and peace, or growth and destruction—is to surrender to the claustrophobic rhythm of the system itself, a rhythm that captures life by oscillating endlessly between poles that feed upon each other.

This spectacle of opposites is not merely ideological: It is the very engine of capitalist reproduction. Our subjectivities are entangled in its pulse—materially, emotionally, and culturally—so that the dynamic of enclosure reproduces itself through us. The challenge, then, is not simply to denounce this oscillation but to transform it: to enact counter-rhythms that dislocate its polarities and recompose life around another center.

Enter commoning, and its generative power, which transforms and regenerates by dislocating these polarities.

The binary of war and peace masks the continuity of militarized accumulation. War is presented as rupture, peace as restoration—but both are structured by the same logic: arms production, infrastructural destruction and reconstruction, and debt-financed security regimes. Peace becomes the name for a stabilized extraction zone, while war resets the field of dispossession. *Commoning intervenes here as the refusal of militarized life, cultivating nonviolent infrastructures of care, mutual aid, and solidarity economies that persist beneath and beyond conflict. It inhabits the space of peacebuilding not as state reconstruction but as a reweaving of life across fractures.*

Economic growth is lauded as progress, while ecological destruction is framed as unfortunate collateral damage. But the two are not opposed—they are entwined. Capitalist growth depends on destruction: of ecosystems, communities, and bodies. Each GDP uptick is paired with an unseen downtick in planetary habitability. *Commoning here reorients the purpose of activity, from accumulation to sustenance. It proposes forms of provisioning, producing, and dwelling that regenerate rather than deplete—measured not in growth curves but in the rhythms of renewal.*

Commoning, then, is not a fixed organizational form but a process in motion. It is a material, relational, and reflective collective praxis. It involves cultivating trust, reciprocity, belonging, and negotiation. It does not merely distribute resources—it institutes worlds. In the face of contemporary crises and their intensification, expanding commoning as a transformative horizon on the terrain of social reproduction has become not only a utopian horizon but a survival necessity.

What carries the transformative force of commoning is not ideology but a mode of enactment, grounded in valuing relations, bodies, rhythms, needs, and places. When critical ideas—forms of critical consciousness like the ones discussed in Chapter 5—walk alongside shared practices and situated inquiry, they can clarify direction, sharpen commitment, and illuminate the political conditions in which commoning operates. But it is through the expansion of commoning—through its experiments in open-ended organization, its rhythms of relational reproduction, and its weaving of the vernacular and the infrastructural, relational, and use values—that another logic of cooperation becomes real.

Consciousness draws from the resources of subjectivity to orient action. Hope is one such resource, a vital one—emerging not from rhetoric but from the resonances of our bodies, our relations, and our attunement to Gaia. In this sense, the political response to the command of the pyramid is to realign the political with the affective and relational—to invest our psychic, ecological, and social energies in the expansion of commoning as a living, material, and cultural force. In doing so, we prefigure another world while we enact the conditions for its emergence inside the pyramid-like shell of the old.

Autopoiesis, variety, and democratic recomposition of life

If resonance becomes regulation, then autopoiesis becomes the form of political life through which this regulation is sustained. In other words, what begins as shared resonance must become the ongoing work of collectively sustaining life—what resonates must learn to endure. The autopoiesis of the common is not a metaphor—it is the collective capacity to reproduce the conditions of existence through cooperation, reflexivity, and shared purpose. Every system, as Ashby reminds us, must generate sufficient variety to remain viable. The democratic challenge of commoning is precisely this: to distribute the capacity to respond, to sense, and to decide. To democratize variety is to make the intelligence of society coextensive with life itself.

This requires forms of organization that are open, plural, and recursive—structures that learn, adapt, and remain permeable to the environments they help create. Commoning, in this sense, is a distributed governance of variety; it expands the number of voices, rhythms, and relations through which society regulates itself, resisting and replacing the hierarchical control of command and domination with a networked, self-organizing coherence.

Under capitalism, this systemic intelligence is radically constrained. The filters of valorization and command narrow the range of what can be seen, said, and done. The system cannot process the immense diversity of needs, desires, relations, ecologies, and subjectivities that compose the social field. What cannot be instrumentalized is silenced or expelled. As crises deepen—climatic, demographic, and political—this regulatory deficit widens. The authoritarian turn in liberal democracies expresses precisely this incapacity: To manage contradiction, power reduces variety, shrinking the space of legitimate claims and participation. In cybernetic terms, it responds not by amplifying adaptive capacity but by suppressing the environment it cannot control.

The only viable response is not better management from above but a radical deepening of regulation from below. The democratic task of the common is to distribute regulatory intelligence—to extend the capacity for perception, decision-making, and coordination across the field of social cooperation. A democracy adequate to complexity is one that expands the internal variety of society, multiplying the ways the collective can know itself and act on itself. This implies rethinking spatial administration—local, national, and global—so that institutions become porous to this distributed intelligence, capable of listening, learning, and adjusting from below rather than insulating themselves from it. This is not a moral slogan but a systemic requirement for any viable future in the midst of deepening climatic and social crises.

To expand commoning is to build this autopoietic infrastructure of social reproduction: plural, transversal, distributed, situated, and coherent enough to confront the totalizing architecture of capitalist command. It means weaving new measures of things in place of the dominant ones and expanding the possibilities of access to the means of existence beyond the circuits inscribed in the pyramid. It is, in essence, the deepening of democracy within social cooperation—the extension of decision-making, creativity, and responsibility to all those who reproduce life.

Commoning expands not only across space but across subjectivities. It transforms those who take part in it, generating new capacities of perception and affection: the ability to sense interdependence, to coordinate without domination, and to inhabit time otherwise. In this sense, the expansion of commoning is both structural and subjective—it enlarges the field of cooperation while composing new ways of being within it.

Ultimately, the expansion of commoning is the process through which social cooperation regains control over its own reproduction. It is how the living variety of society becomes its own regulator, turning affect into organization, resonance into coherence, and resistance into systemic transformation.

The two terrains of commoning: counter- and alter-regulation

To expand commoning is also to articulate two complementary terrains of praxis: *alter-regulation* and *counter-regulation*. The first constructs new institutions and practices that operate by different metrics of value; the second resists and disrupts the regulatory apparatuses of capital that enclose and exploit life. The power of commoning lies in keeping these two dimensions articulated—creating spaces of autonomy while confronting the throbs of command that continue to shape the broader system. In this way, social cooperation learns to filter the logic of capital and amplify the rhythms of life.

Alter-regulation names the expansion and scaling of self-governing, participatory systems of social cooperation—commons that function as living institutions of a new order inside the old. They generate alternative modes of decision, rhythm, and value across all domains of reproduction: housing, food, education, care, territory, and technology. Against the cold rhythm of capital and the rigidities of bureaucracy, alter-regulation seeks to reweave life on cooperative terms. Its mode of scaling is ecological, not extractive: Commons resonate rather than replicate, forming distributed organizational ecologies through *boundary-commoning* (De Angelis 2017) and sympoietic cooperation (Chapter 3).

Yet alter-regulation depends on *counter-regulation*—the power of refusal, resistance, struggle, and voices from below. These are the vetoes, strikes, occupations, and mobilizations that block, contest, and open cracks in the architecture of enclosure and the throbs of command. Capital's pyramid never cedes ground willingly; it continuously reasserts its logic. Counter-regulation interrupts this advance, resetting the conditions in which alter-regulation can root and flourish.

In their reciprocal motion, the two form the double heartbeat of transformation. Counter-regulation resists and protects; alter-regulation builds and connects. Together, they compose the *cellular metabolism* of a society in movement, where survival practices coalesce into collective forms of life (Zibechi 2012). Commons—these hubs of commoning that generate systems—become infrastructures of hope. As they multiply and interweave, they raise thresholds of resistance and set material, relational, and normative limits to capital's violence: limits to extraction, to precarity, and to ecological devastation.

There is no guarantee of victory, no teleological closure. But there is orientation: a shared rhythm through which struggle and care, resistance and invention, can coexist and learn from one another. In this rhythmic coupling of counter- and alter-regulation, the autopoiesis of the common begins to take form as both refusal and creation, negation and composition—the living regulation of life by life itself.

Necessary and emergent commons

The dynamic of counter- and alter-regulation materializes concretely in the hubs, circuits, and systems we call *commons*: the living sites where struggle and creation take institutional form through processes of communalization. These movements are never merely abstract—they are embodied in the practices through which social cooperation reclaims or invents its own conditions of life. They unfold not linearly but cyclically, rhythmically condensed in what we call *social movements*: those periodic surges through which society reexpresses its capacity to resist, recompose, and reimagine itself.

Within these processes of communalization, two interdependent terrains of commoning take shape—what Micciarelli (2014) first distinguished as *necessary* and *emergent* commons, here reframed within my own framework of value praxis. *Necessary commons* reclaim what capital has enclosed: the infrastructures, services, and resources on which everyday life depends. They act within and upon the meso-level, seeking to subordinate its institutional logics to the priorities of social reproduction. *Emergent commons*, by contrast, create what capital has abandoned or cannot recognize: new forms of cooperation, care, and ecological interdependence that expand the horizon of social possibility.

Together, these two terrains compose the evolving ecology through which the autopoiesis of social reproduction begins to take organized form—the living metabolism of a society that learns to reproduce itself otherwise.

Necessary commons arise where social reproduction has been captured by capital yet remains indispensable to collective survival. Water, food, health, housing, education, energy, working conditions, communication, transport, and the climate—each represents an arena where the means of existence must be reclaimed from the logics of accumulation and reorganized around use value. These commons emerge through the slow work of counter- and alter-regulation: struggles for access and democratic governance, the redirection of public institutions toward participatory forms, the hacking of legal codes, and the reappropriation of infrastructures. What results is never a ready-made model but a hybrid and evolving form—shaped by the degree of collective organization and by the specific frictions between movements, institutions, and capital. In this sense, necessary commons are not designed but enacted; their contours are drawn through situated processes of negotiation, experimentation, and encroachment within existing systems. Their task is not merely redistribution but the democratic redefinition of necessity itself—turning what is "socially necessary" into a field of collective determination rather than a technocratic given.

Yet the expansion of the commons does not unfold solely through the encroachment and transformation of existing systems. Alongside these hybrid processes of institutional redirection, new forms of cooperation continually arise from below—often where capital retreats, abandons, or simply fails to sustain life. These are the emergent commons: collective experiments that do not reform inherited structures but create alternative ones from the ground up. Born in the interstices of crisis and neglect, they convert dispossession into invention and scarcity into cooperation.

Emergent commons arise from the creative energy of social cooperation itself. They are the laboratories where life reorganizes beyond the reach of existing institutions: community gardens, solidarity kitchens, fablabs, recuperated factories, social centers, mutual aid networks, and digital cooperatives. Often born from abandonment or collapse, they instantiate the autonomy of cooperation—the capacity to self-organize, self-govern, and generate value beyond the market and the state. They are prefigurative but not marginal: They train new capacities of coordination, cultivate relational intelligence, and rehearse the rhythms of a post-capitalist society.

Between the necessary and emergent commons flows a recursive dynamic. The struggles and institutional innovations of the necessary commons stabilize and amplify the reach of the emergent ones; the creativity and relational depth of the emergent commons revitalize and democratize the governance of the necessary. In this interdependence, an ecology of commoning takes shape—an evolving metabolism that connects the procommons and the meso-level, linking grassroots reproduction with systemic transformation.

The dynamics described above unfold through diverse organizational forms. Every process of communalization—the transformation of a use value and the relations surrounding it into a commons—emerges from situated struggles and desires. A commons is never simply a resource; it is a living system of relations that binds material or immaterial wealth to collective practice, to the rhythms of care and reproduction that sustain life (De Angelis 2017). This living system can take multiple organizational forms.

In every practice of commoning, there is an impulse to desert the logic of capital, to break from its imposed finalities and extractive relations. Desertion, however, takes distinct forms. One is *molecular*: Small groups or communities carve out spaces of refuge and partial autonomy, sustaining local circuits of care and reciprocity yet remaining fragile before capital's turbulence. The other is *cellular* or *constituent*: commoning that projects itself outward, weaving plural practices into assemblages able to scale, not by replication but by relational resonance. The cellular embeds the molecular, turning scattered refuges into an ecology of transformation. Autonomy, here, is never isolation but coordination—through the praxis of boundary commoning that connect struggles across difference and scale.

In this sense, communalization is never a purely local process but rather a systemic movement, an organizational ecology. It links the embodied and relational work of everyday commoning to broader institutional and political recomposition—extending the ecology of necessary and emergent commons across scales and struggles. To declare *this water, this school, this land, and this code* a common good is, above all, a reorientation of purpose and value praxis: a claim that the value of things lies in their shared use and in their capacity to nourish life in common.

From the standpoint of the autopoiesis of social reproduction, this ecology of communing is not limited to explicitly "commons-oriented" initiatives. It includes a vast diversity of organizations and movements that, across different arenas, enact life's defense and reorganization through counter- and alter-regulation. Workplace strikes contesting working conditions, struggles for public housing or clean water, feminist or queer networks reclaiming bodily autonomy, climate movements defending ecosystems, migrant solidarity campaigns, and unions of care workers—all contribute to this distributed process of reproduction. Each interrupts capital's filters and amplifiers while seeking to construct alternative rhythms of cooperation and value. From this wider view, the necessary commons are not confined to formal public goods or legally recognized entities; they are enacted wherever collective practices seek to redefine what society deems indispensable to life, even if this implies—as it often does—an increased cost of social reproduction borne by capital. They emerge within the very struggles through which people, institutions, and ecologies confront the throbs of command and begin to reorganize the terms of coexistence. Seen together, these initiatives compose the movement-ecology of the common—a living field of praxis in which counter-regulation (refusal, resistance, and defense) and alter-regulation (creation, institution, and innovation) intertwine as the two lungs of social autopoiesis.

These processes, however, are not free from risk. When commoning enters the institutional terrain, it faces the double-edged challenge of recognition and capture. Public-commons partnerships, community land trusts, municipal collaborations, and constitutional experiments (Micciarelli 2014, 2022; Bollier and Helfrich 2019; Russell et al. 2022; Brown and Milburn 2024) all represent attempts to reconfigure institutions toward life, yet they also expose commoning to bureaucratic instrumentalization, as happens—albeit in different forms—in many experiments in co-management or co-ownership between workers and employers within private enterprises. In these cases, cooperation is often reframed as a managerial technique, turning participation into a means of competitive efficiency rather than emancipation.

The challenge, therefore, is to maintain autonomy within interdependence—to ensure that institutional encounters amplify rather than neutralize the reproductive intelligence of the commons. This requires that the two movements of commoning, *counter-* and *alter-regulation*, remain in tension and mutually reinforcing. When they lose balance—when creation detaches from resistance or adaptation overtakes antagonism—hybrid forms risk being absorbed by the logic of valorization at the meta-level. Only through this rhythmic interplay between negation and construction can commoning sustain its autonomy while engaging the institutional terrain from within.

Despite these risks, the vitality of commoning lies precisely in its capacity to evolve across boundaries. Hybridization is not merely a symptom of capture but a field of experimentation—where necessary and emergent commons meet, adjust, and recompose their relations. It is through this ongoing movement between adaptation and resistance, institution and invention, that the commons remain living systems rather than fixed models. Ultimately, the distinction between necessary and emergent commons is not static. It expresses two temporal functions of the same living system: preservation and creation, defense and invention. Their interaction constitutes the autopoiesis of social reproduction itself—the capacity of society to sense, reflect, and reorganize the conditions of its own continuation. Within this ecology, subjects are neither isolated individuals nor dissolved collectivities; they are subject-holons (Chapter 6)—simultaneously part and whole, nodes of perception and coordination within the broader living system. Through their participation in the commons, people learn to act both locally and systemically, feeling the resonance between their embodied cooperation and the collective reproduction of life.

Commoning, in this light, is the praxis through which the subject-holon of the common takes shape in its emancipatory form. It is the enactment of autonomy as interdependence, of regulation as resonance, and of reproduction as creation. By sustaining and expanding the necessary and emergent commons, social reproduction begins to recompose itself—not only as a network of shared resources but as a living autopoietic order grounded in the rhythms, affections, and intelligences of the common.

Movement and the autopoiesis of the common

The autopoiesis of the common on the terrain of social reproduction requires social movements capable of sustaining coherence across diversity, as well as of sedimenting progress through their oscillations and defeats. Such a movement is not a singular organization but an ecology of organizations, what Rodrigo Nunes (2021) calls a political ecology: neither vertical nor horizontal but recursive—a field of differentiated nodes that coordinate through shared rhythms, resonances, and thresholds across the transversal field of social cooperation (Chapter 3).

As previously discussed, the dynamic of counter- and alter-regulation materializes concretely in the hubs, circuits, and systems we call commons: the living sites where struggle and creation take institutional form through processes of communalization. These dynamics are never merely abstract; they are embodied in the practices through which social cooperation reclaims or invents its own conditions of life. In this sense, counter- and alter-regulation are not external to social movements but *are* their rhythmic expressions, unfolding not linearly but cyclically and condensed in those periodic surges through which social reproduction reexpresses its capacity to resist, recompose, and reimagine itself.

Through these cyclical surges and interstitial practices, the movement gradually constructs an organizational metabolism—an evolving tissue of relations through which the capacities of diverse initiatives become mutually sustaining.

This ecology can be understood as sympoietic (Chapter 3), a living system of self-producing entities that co-generate their environment. Each node—a community initiative, a labor network, a feminist or ecological assembly, a cooperative, or a public-commons partnership—is autopoietic in itself, reproducing its own practices, relations, and meanings. Yet it also depends on the vitality of others and on exchanges of knowledge, care, and solidarity that make the movement more than the sum of its parts. The ecology becomes sympoietic when these nodes recognize one another as elements of a shared metabolism—when the question "what does my practice contribute to the flourishing of the whole?" becomes a criterion of political intelligence. Recognition, however, is only the first movement of autopoiesis; the ecology must evolve from awareness of interdependence toward the capacity to reproduce itself through it.

For such a movement to acquire autopoietic capacity, it must do more than connect—it must learn to reproduce itself. This means building recursive circuits of communication, reflection, and coordination that enable feedback between experience and strategy and between local experiments and systemic imagination. The movement's coherence does not derive from central command but from its ability to generate a shared *grammar of cooperation*: norms, narratives, and infrastructures across many areas of social reproduction that allow mutual intelligibility among heterogeneous struggles. This is how the movement begins to perceive itself—and to act—as a living system.

In this sense, the autopoiesis of the common is not limited to the reproduction of individual commons; it is the collective self-production of the *movement of commoning* as an ecosystem. Each node contributes to the system's variety—its capacity to respond to crisis and change—while also drawing stability from the shared rhythms of solidarity and reciprocity that circulate within it. The ecology thus becomes a counter-systemic intelligence, capable of sensing and responding to the autopoiesis of capital not with reactive mimicry but with autonomous creativity.

The challenge is formidable. The capitalist system reproduces itself by absorbing difference into the circuits of accumulation; it manages variety by commodifying or disciplining it. To oppose this, the movement must cultivate forms of recursive differentiation—remaining open and plural while maintaining a minimal coherence that prevents dispersion. This involves the creation of connective infrastructures—federations, assemblies, translocal networks, digital platforms, and learning processes—that enable flows of knowledge, trust, and resources. These infrastructures act as the *membranes* of the movement's autopoiesis—porous yet cohesive—enabling both the intake of external variety and the retention of internal coherence.

In this recursive interplay of autonomy and interdependence, the subject-holon reappears as the living operator of the movement's autopoiesis. Every participant, collective, or institution becomes at once a part and a whole—enacting care for its own reproduction while contributing to that of the wider ecology. The political intelligence of the movement lies in cultivating this dual awareness: that to sustain the whole, each must sustain its own openness; and that to sustain oneself, each must sustain the whole.

Through this process of sympoietic learning, the ecology of commoning begins to function as a self-organizing system, generating feedback loops between reflection and action, solidarity and innovation, the local and the planetary. It becomes capable of producing its own temporalities, its own rhythms of coordination and renewal—the living pulse of an alternative autopoiesis grounded in the reproduction of life.

At this point, the question of organization folds back into the question of relation. The autopoiesis of the common does not subsist on coordination alone; it endures through affective bonds, ethical commitments, and shared sensibilities that make cooperation desirable and meaningful. Its coherence depends as much on emotional attunement as on strategic articulation. Every recursive circuit of the movement—every feedback loop between bodies, institutions, and ecologies—carries a pulse of attachment, trust, and care. In this sense, love is not an ornament to political life but its connective tissue: the affective force through which the movement feels itself to be a living whole and regenerates the conditions of its becoming.

Commoning through love, schismogenesis, and hierarchy

Commoning is a stubborn, generative force of resistance and reconstruction. Neither nostalgia for lost commons nor an abstract utopia, it is a living praxis—an art of doing-with—rooted in territories, relationships, and the daily labor of social reproduction. Commoning is a way of inhabiting the world not to control it but to care for it together. Above all, it is an embodied love capable of transforming both subjects and worlds.

This is not the sentimental commodity of late capitalism. It is not a private feeling or romantic ideal; it is a relational force, a world-making gesture that enacts a cooperative, resistant subjectivity. In this sense, commoning is the plural enactment of love as a transformative relation between self and world.

Across religious lineages, love names distinct orientations to self, other, and world (Greenberg 2008): *agape* as unconditional grace in Christianity; *bhakti* as ecstatic devotion; Mahāyāna karuṇā as non-grasping compassion; Taoist ***ci*** as gentle alignment with the Tao; Sufi *ishq* as burning union; and neo-pagan love as immanent reverence for Earth and cosmos.

Contemporary ethical and philosophical currents deepen this plural grammar: Feminist care ethics reframes love as situated, political labor that sustains life (Gilligan 1982; Tronto 1993); Black radical thought understands love as practice of refusal and collective becoming (Baldwin 1963; Lorde 1984; hooks 2001); post-secular philosophy figures love as ethical asymmetry (Levinas 1969), fidelity to a truth-event (Badiou 2012), and *amor mundi* as the affective ground of political plurality (Arendt 1998). Taken together, love appears not as affective surplus but as a generative infrastructure of meaning and relation. A precursor to many of these threads, Spinoza (2018) anchors love in conatus—the joyful increase of our power to act with others and nature. God-or-nature (Deus sive Natura) grounds a eurhythmia (Lefebvre 2004) in which individual and collective rhythms align without domination. Here, love is not sentiment but an ontological and ethical labor of becoming-together.

These expressions do not flatten difference; they enact distinct modes of becoming—steward, devotee, witness, earth-kin, coauthor, world-lover, and a joyful participant in necessity. Rather than seeking a synthesis, commoning activates this plurality contextually, as situated practices that generate meaning, reorganize value, and sustain life amid fracture.

Read through enactivism (Chapter 4), subjectivity emerges from lived practices and situated relations. Commoning therefore weaves a polyphonic, polyrhythmic repertoire of cooperative styles that compose shared worlds. Social life unfolds through rhythms—bodily, spatial, and institutional—that can align or collide. Commoning cultivates a eurhythmic pulse (Lefebvre 2004): an adaptive synchrony between the rhythms of living and the rhythms of cooperation, capable of absorbing and transforming the arrhythmias imposed by the capitalist order.

This world is built on three interwoven planes—each a field where love gives rhythm to transformation:

- Gaia (Earth as coagent): ecological love as embodied reverence and regeneration—composting, conserving, and aligning with planetary cycles (ci, karuṇā).
- Procommons (relational sustenance): intimate, ritual, and embodied love—devotion that cooks and repairs; hospitality that embraces without condition (bhakti, agape).
- Meso-level (institutional imagination): love as justice and protection—responsibility to the Other (Levinas), joyful recognition of necessity (Spinoza), and love of the world as plural cohabitation.

Across all three planes, love is not the opposite of conflict but the force that renders conflict generative. It does not erase contradiction; it holds it open—offering form, rhythm, care, and time against fragmentation. Where capital accelerates, extracts, and abstracts, commoning composes eurhythmia.

The subject that emerges is not the entrepreneurial ego, consumer, or obedient functionary but a subject-holon capable of reflection: relational, affective, and situated—part and whole at once—whose agency is constituted through loving practice and rhythmic entanglement with others, systems, and ecologies. Not power-over but *powers-to-with*; not accumulation but social reproduction. *Homo communans* becomes itself through the loving-with of others and the world.

In an age of chaos and domination, commoning names another logic of life, organized not around exchange value but around the value of connection. It is a practice of love that tends as it builds and transforms as it tends. Drawing spiritual lineages and material practices into daily resistance, it joins the present to the not-yet.

Crucially, this plural, rhythmic enactment of love is not merely affective or symbolic—it is the enactive force that can build an autopoietic organization of social reproduction (Chapters 2–3): a living network that sustains life by reorienting practices, values, and relations around care rather than accumulation. Love here is the ontological principle of enactment through which subjects and systems co-emerge in praxis, composing not only a new way of feeling but a new way of organizing the world's reproduction.

Yet love confronts forces that fracture or capture it. To grasp this dynamic, consider Bateson's (1987) schismogenesis: social differentiation processes that, when unbalanced, spiral into rupture. Capital does not simply repress love; it selectively amplifies and disables it. It cultivates attachments through consumption, loyalty through identity, and dependency through hierarchy; it drives positive schismogenesis via competitive escalation and negative schismogenesis via homogenizing equivalence. Both stretch the connective tissue of love toward collapse, as seen most starkly in war, where differentiation is weaponized and relations are reorganized through destruction.

Commoning is not love in purity; it is love entangled with fracture. It is the labor of mending—resisting isolations that divide and assimilations that erase. Love becomes asymmetrical repair: generating relation without domination, divergence without disconnection. Another schismogenesis is possible: not a spiral into rupture but a plateau of resonant difference—polyphony rather than synthesis (Bateson 1987). Bateson observed in Bali that what appeared to be the absence of schismogenetic pressure was in fact the result of dense and rapid communicative feedback: Tensions were continuously modulated before they could escalate into polarity. In this sense, a plateau is not the absence of contradiction but the presence of frequent relational adjustment. Deleuze and Guattari (1988) describe such a plateau as a sustained region of intensity—a field in which heterogeneous elements coexist and interact without subordinating one another to a single organizing center. The plateau holds difference through rhythm, not resolution. This is reciprocity-in-tension: Conflict rendered generative through high-frequency feedback rather than allowed to harden into antagonism.

In this horizon, love acts as an antivirus against the recursive logics of division. It does not abolish conflict; it redirects it toward constructing shared life. The commons are not serene remnants but loving infrastructures of reinvention, forged amid unresolved fractures and sustained by the conviction that relation remains possible.

To love this way is to confront hierarchies structuring the present—centrally, the wage, which translates care, time, and knowledge into quantifiable units and disjoins action from relational depth. The wage stratifies life (productive/unproductive, formal/informal) and embeds equivalence at the heart of need. Commoning does not deny these hierarchies; it faces them as material realities that structure access to time, resources, and dignity. To subvert them, it must first recognize how deeply they organize social life, then challenge their imaginary, and finally struggle to transform the relations that sustain them. In this movement—from recognition to imagination to struggle—commoning reclaims the substance of value as socially reproductive and relational—grounded in the cooperative sustenance of life, reuniting labor and care, affirming that feeding a stranger, tending a garden, coordinating shifts in a hospital, sustaining a classroom, convivializing on the shop floor, holding space for shared joy and grief, making the rhythm of work less pressing, caring for bodies strained by labor, or restoring ecosystems exhausted by production are not "outside the economy" but integral to it. Their value is enacted in relation—through cooperation, care, and solidarity—not merely measured in outputs.

But wage hierarchies cannot be ignored; they mediate time, resources, security, and dignity. Displacing their centrality entails struggles for equity and redistribution, the building of counter-institutions, and a broader revaluation of what counts. Many forms of reproductive and caring labor are unpaid or underpaid; their collective revaluation within the commons is both resistance and redefinition. Similarly, epistemic hierarchies of expert authority exclude situated knowledges; love challenges them not only through critique but through accumulated trust, copresence, and shared learning, privileging accountability over certification.

Commoning does not merely invert hierarchy; it dissolves its premise. It proposes not a pyramid but a distributed ecology of care, where value flows by need, contribution, and relation—not rank. Authority becomes a capacity to respond—what the Zapatistas call *mandar obedeciendo*: facilitating through listening, accountability, and copresence. It is a sub-command enacted from within collective doing.

Thus, love's enactment disassembles hierarchy from below through everyday solidarity. It makes visible what was invisible, lifts what was made low, and hears what was silenced—not as charity but as relational justice.

This is the often-unspoken power of commoning: not merely to share resources but to recompose the social field—to reshape what matters, who counts, and how we become. Not through purity or abstract calls for unity but through the rhythmic tension of plural becoming. In this horizon, love is not a refuge or a reward—it is the infrastructure of a world becoming free.

By tying love to autopoiesis, we see why it is politically strategic: Love is the medium of system-wide enactment through which the autopoiesis of social reproduction can take hold—composing collectives (subject-holons), stabilizing rhythms, and coordinating across scales without reproducing capitalist domination.

Conclusion: the pulse of hope

This book began in a world in chaos and multiple crises of social reproduction—a world governed by a pyramidal logic that organizes life through command, accumulation, and control. We mapped its structure, traced its rhythms and ruptures, and followed its crises from mega-structures of domination to the molecular tensions of daily life. We saw how the pyramid functions as a spatiotemporal device: accelerating some rhythms, fragmenting others, and disarticulating conditions for collective flourishing.

Yet in every disrupted rhythm we found a pulse of refusal; in every fracture, a crack of emergence. The pyramid may dominate the present, but it is not the whole of reality. Beneath and beyond it pulses another life: the life of commons, reproductive insurgency, and subjects who—amid dispossession, exhaustion, and despair—still enact care, share time, create meaning, interconnect, converge transversally across diversity, and build new ground.

The power of this other logic lies not in vertical command but in poiesis—the capacity to make and remake forms. It is not a blueprint from above but a weaving from below: a rhythmic coordination of bodies, gestures, rituals, and systems that affirm life over profit, relation over abstraction, and love over domination. If the pyramid is an architecture of death, commoning is the choreography of life.

There is no promise of victory, no guarantee that this struggle will prevail. But there is movement, rhythm, pattern, and breath—the stubborn, collective beat of a world not yet exhausted by the logics that enclose it. In that beat begins another story: Subjectivities enacted through care, structures reorganized by use value, cooperation tuned to Gaia's limits, and politics remade by autopoiesis from below.

This is the poiesis of freedom: a quiet insurgency remaking the world through commoning, through love, through the rhythms of cooperation, yet to come—rhythms already pulsing in the here and now, resonant with those who came before us, whose unfinished gestures of care, refusal, and world-making reverberate in our doing.

Let the pulse continue. Bring to it our minds, muscles, and desires—organizing not only systems but the joy of living together even amidst the wreckage produced by the pyramid of capital. Let scattered beats of resistance become the vibrant rhythm of a world becoming free—free from the domination of the pyramid and attuned to the common: not only the condition we inherit but the project we enact. Let love itself become an organizational force of social cooperation—so that what we build together does not merely resist but composes, sustains, and transforms.

Notes

Chapter 1

1 My rendering of the fragment B89 (Diels–Kranz numbering): "The waking have one common world, but the sleeping turn aside each into a world of his own" (Burnet 1920: 140).

Chapter 2

1 Autopoiesis is the "self-asserting capacity of living systems to maintain their identity through active compensation of deformation" (Maturana and Varela 1980: 73).

Chapter 3

1 The framework developed here diverges from the paradigm of intersectionality while remaining in critical dialogue with it. Intersectionality, most notably articulated by Kimberlé Crenshaw (1989) and Patricia Hill Collins (2000), builds on Black feminist analyses of interlocking systems of domination (hooks 2000). It has been foundational in demonstrating how axes of oppression such as race, gender, class, sexuality, and ability intersect to shape subjectivity, vulnerability, and institutional power. It challenges single-axis frameworks and foregrounds the lived experiences of those who occupy multiple subordinated positions.

While intersectionality typically treats class as one axis among others, the approach presented here frames class not as an identity or positional trait but as the ontological antagonism that structures the force field itself: the conflict between the autopoietic reproduction of capital and the autopoietic reproduction of life. From this perspective, race, gender, and other identity formations are not separate layers added to class; rather, they are differently articulated within the force field, shaped by the gravitational pull of dominant attractors, and contested within specific reproductive arrangements.

Intersectionality offers a powerful grammar of positionality and lived experience and remains indispensable for analyzing how subjects navigate, endure, and resist the structured terrain of oppression. This framework, however, seeks to complement that grammar with a systemic ontology of antagonism, allowing positional complexity to be situated within the broader struggle over the organization of social reproduction.

Chapter 4

1 The origins of this enactivist perspective can be traced to the early work of Varela et al. (1974), especially to Varela et al. (1991). It has roots, affinities, and points of convergence with several other approaches. It is closely connected to the work of Humberto Maturana, with whom Varela collaborated (Maturana & Varela 1980; 1987), and who defined the living system in terms of autopoiesis. It also shares important resonances with the phenomenology of Husserl and Merleau-Ponty, as discussed in detail by Thompson (2007). Further intersections can be found in Piaget's (1971) genetic epistemology and in Searle's (1995; 2010) social constructionism. A critical and comparative engagement with these traditions lies well beyond the scope of the present work.

Chapter 5

1 *Conricerca* (co-research) is a method of inquiry developed within Italian *operaismo* (workerism) that rejects the separation between researcher and subject, instead emphasizing collective knowledge production from within social struggles. Unlike traditional sociology, *conricerca* does not merely study workers' conditions but actively engages them in analyzing their own experiences, with the aim of fostering political organization and autonomy. This approach parallels workers' inquiry, which also seeks to uncover class composition and struggles from the perspective of workers themselves, as well as militant research, which similarly embeds intellectual work within political movements. Participatory action research (PAR) and cooperative inquiry share *conricerca*'s emphasis on collaboration but often lack its explicitly antagonistic stance toward capitalist structures. Militant ethnography and embedded research align with *conricerca* in their commitment to activist engagement, though they often employ different methodological frameworks. All these approaches challenge the neutrality of traditional research, positioning knowledge production as an integral part of collective struggle.

Chapter 7

1 Contemporary critical theory builds on the insights of the original critical theory developed by the Frankfurt School, which acknowledged how working-class consciousness was divided and fragmented: "Global wars, waning revolutions, and waxing dictatorships had shown that many workers, rather than resisting war and dictatorship, embrace them, while others are ambivalent." To this division, traditional orthodox Marxists

remained "placidly untroubled" and "naïve." Instead, "critical theory broke from this tradition, acknowledging and problematising the antinomies of working-class consciousness." However, the early critical theorists' "rejection of blind optimism yielded to an equally blinkered pessimism, which vitiates most forms of 'critique' today. The task of critical inquiry into class and change, in a world of wage earners, remains ahead of us. The Frankfurt School led us to the brink of this theory and then turned away" Smith (2017: 369–70).

2 Phylogenesis refers to the evolutionary development of a species over time, tracing the changes in traits and structures across generations. Ontogenesis, in contrast, refers to the development of an individual organism from conception to maturity, focusing on the growth and changes within a single lifespan rather than across species. In the social realm, phylogenesis refers to the historically evolved, species-specific capacities for intentionality and relatedness—fundamental human abilities that have developed over time as part of our evolutionary inheritance. Ontogenesis, by contrast, refers to the ways in which these capacities are actualized, shaped, and transformed within an individual's lifetime through socialization, institutions, and lived experience. In this sense, calling intentionality and relatedness phylogenetic capacities highlights their evolutionary basis, while recognizing that their specific expressions and enactments are ontogenetically shaped by the diverse social structures and cultural contexts in which individuals are embedded.

3 If social relations are important for shaping and giving form to social cooperation, then it is crucial to ask ourselves whether there are fundamental types of social relations that guide these processes. Relational model theory (RMT), for example, posits that despite the infinite cultural and historical variations in human relationships, all social coordination relies on four universal relational models: communal sharing (CS), authority ranking (AR), equality matching (EM), and market pricing (MP). These models, and their different orderings, influence decision-making, task organization, and moral judgment, shaping norms, purposes, and practices across contexts (Fiske and Haslam 2005).

4 This aligns with autopoietic (Maturana and Varela 1980) and cybernetic (Wiener 1948; Bateson 1987) perspectives, in which systems organize and maintain the conditions necessary for their own reproduction. Niklas Luhmann (1995) also describes systems as self-referential entities that manage complexity by establishing internal order and regulating interactions with their environment. This fits with my claim that systems coordinate circuits, ensuring that transitions between steps internal to circuits occur. In economics and social reproduction theory, we can see this in how financial, logistical, or bureaucratic systems ensure the flow of capital circuits (e.g., banking, supply chains) or how welfare institutions sustain circuits of social reproduction.

Chapter 8

1 Emerging in the late nineteenth century as a response to classical political economy, neoclassical economics shifted its focus from production and labor to individual choice and market equilibrium. Thinkers like Jevons, Walras, Menger, and Marshall reframed economic activity as the outcome of rational agents maximizing utility, sidelining the structural distinctions between use value and exchange value that had been central to Smith, Ricardo, and Marx. By assuming that markets naturally allocate resources according to subjective preferences, neoclassical economics abstracts economic life from its historical and social conditions, masking power asymmetries, exploitation, and systemic inequalities. Today, it forms the dominant philosophical foundation of economic policy, shaping everything from labor regulations to welfare systems, and reinforcing a capitalist logic that prioritizes profit over social needs while presenting this order as natural and inevitable. This framework is not confined to elite policymaking but is widely disseminated through basic high school and university economics courses, where students are trained to see markets as neutral, efficient mechanisms. By collapsing use value into exchange value, neoclassical economics erases the distinction between producing for need and producing for profit. It presents markets as neutral mechanisms of efficient allocation, obscuring the historical and social conditions that structure production. This naturalizes capitalism by making profit-driven exchange appear as the only rational economic logic, masking the fact that markets do not just allocate resources but enforce power relations, shape social hierarchies, and subordinate human needs to capital accumulation.

Chapter 9

1 For an introduction to the evolution of Alquati's thought from operaismo to the 1990s, see Pittavino (2021). It is not easy to speak about Alquati's *Modellone*, which he developed in the context of the "ebb" following the long Italian "68"—a period marked in the 1980s by the shrinking of political spaces, the loss of political centrality of the industrial working class (partly as a result of restructuring and the precarization of labor), and the neoliberal and managerial mantra of becoming entrepreneurs of oneself. The key reference text for the *Modellone* is *Volume III of his Industrial Sociology Lecture Notes*, published in 1989 (Alquati 1989), although references to the *Modellone* can also be found in other writings. I have also used as a basis for my research the clear and intuitive illustration of Alquati's *Modellone* elaborated by Maurizio Pentenero (2018), which I have partially reworked in order to integrate it with other aspects of my analysis. What follows, I repeat, is a free engagement with Alquati's *Modellone*, seeking to interpolate

his insights with my own reflections, and to bridge those parts of his model that are less clear to me with considerations developed through my research on capitalism and the commons in recent years. Furthermore, Alquati often prefixed many concepts with "neo" to emphasize their new connotations in light of the major transformations of capitalism in the 1980s and 1990s. I avoid this not only because it weighs down the language, but also because my aim here is not to emphasize the novelty of contemporary capitalist transformations, but rather to map the reproduction of domination that takes place *through* these transformations in relation to the reproduction of society.

Chapter 10

1 See Cajete (2000), Kimmerer (2013), and de la Cadena (2015) for examples of Indigenous and relational cosmologies that offer rich alternatives to the modern separation of human and nonhuman, subject and object. These perspectives suggest that value, meaning, and responsibility can emerge not only from human praxis, but from reciprocal co-constitution with more-than-human life.
2 On the emergence and implications of the Anthropocene, see Steffen et al. (2015). For critical perspectives that question the homogenizing narrative of "Anthropos" and instead foreground historical and systemic drivers, see Moore (2016) and Haraway (2015). These critiques challenge the framing of planetary crisis as species-wide, calling attention instead to capitalism's ecological regime and the histories of colonialism, racialization, and extraction embedded within it.
3 While Marx's understanding of the labor-mediated transformation of nature already pointed in this direction, the first explicit articulation of the concept of the *production of nature* is found in Neil Smith's (2008) seminal 1984 essay.
4 The distinction between endosomatic and exosmomatic metabolism was introduced by Lotka (1956) and later taken up by Georgescu-Roegen (1971).

Chapter 13

1 See the appendix to Chapter 7 for an expanded formulation of M–C–M′ circuit that reveals the production process.
2 The "social wage" refers to the broader collective benefits (e.g., health care, education, and public infrastructure) that supplement direct wages. See De Angelis (2007) for its role in class struggle. On the concept of "unequal ecological exchange," see Hornborg (2009) and Patel and Moore (2017) for the ecological dimension of reproduction under capitalism.
3 For more detailed accounts, see Wallerstein (2004), Federici (2012), Rodney (1972), and Amin (1974).

4 For a broad analysis of how global value chains have reshaped economic development and industrial strategies in the twenty-first century, see Gereffi (2018). Mezzadra and Neilson (2019) rightly emphasize the political nature of their operations. For insights into spatial exploitation in specific cases, see, for example, Anner (2015) on the garment industry and Ghosh (2010) on the interconnections between finance and food that continue to generate food insecurity for a large part of the world's population, which not only deepen global food insecurity but also continuously reproduce the conditions of crisis upon which global value chain construction is predicated.

Chapter 14

1 The six throbs of command proposed here do not directly derive from existing cybernetic models, but they are informed by the logic of requisite variety (Ashby 1956) and engage critically with Stafford Beer's *Viable System Model* (1981). Beer identifies five interrelated functional systems necessary for any viable organization: System 1 (implementation), System 2 (stability and conflict resolution), System 3 (control and resource management), System 4 (intelligence and adaptation), and System 5 (policy and purpose).

While the throbs of command are not mapped onto these levels in a strict one-to-one correspondence, certain resonances can be observed. *Purpose* loosely echoes System 5 (policy/purpose-setting); *Agency* and *Instrumentality* correspond in part to Systems 3 and 2 (control and stabilization); *Threshold Recalibration* reflects the adaptive, future-oriented role of System 4.

However, *Crisiscraft* and *Displacement* fall outside Beer's scheme. They are historically specific to capitalist macro-domination, oriented not merely toward maintaining viability but toward the instrumentalization of crisis and the redistribution of systemic contradiction across time, space, and social strata. In this sense, the throbs extend Beer's organizational insight to a geopolitical and systemic register, one closer to world-systems analysis and autonomist critiques of command.

Chapter 15

1 A recent illustration of this performative logic was the October 2025 truce in Palestine, when massive global mobilizations forced the Trump administration to suspend the assault on Gaza (De Angelis 2025e). The ceasefire did not emerge from moral reconsideration but from instability—a counter-pulse of social cooperation that exceeded the regime's regulatory capacity. Despite the ceasefire, Israeli military operations continued, with hundreds of Palestinians reported killed in the months that followed. Yet the retreat was rapidly reframed as leadership: Trump's address to the Knesset

in the same month converted a forced pause into an act of sovereign resolve, restaging vulnerability as control. Parallel to this rhetorical maneuver, the creation of a "Board of Peace" institutionalized the management of the ceasefire within a securitized and technocratic framework, displacing political demands into administrative oversight. At the same time, reconstruction contracts, security provisioning, surveillance technologies, and logistics corridors revealed the vested commercial interests embedded in the management of destruction. Palestinian bodies appeared simultaneously as targets of military pacification, objects of humanitarian administration, and substrates of reconstruction markets—caught within circuits of extraction that monetize both devastation and repair. In this way, crisiscraft did not resolve contradiction but sought to absorb the counter-pulse, translating systemic fragility into a renewed performance of order.

References

Abraham, Y. (2023), "'A Mass Assassination Factory': Inside Israel's Calculated Bombing of Gaza," *+972 Magazine*. Available at: https://www.972mag.com/mass-assassination-factory-israel-calculated-bombing-gaza/ (accessed May 25, 2025).

Agamben, G. (1998), *Homo Sacer: Sovereign Power and Bare Life*, Stanford University Press.

Agamben, G. (2005), *State of Exception*, University of Chicago Press.

Alquati, R. (1975), *Sulla Fiat e altri scritti*, Feltrinelli.

Alquati, R. (1989), *Dispense di Sociologia Industriale*, Vol. III, Tomo 1 e 2, Il Segnalibro.

Alquati, R. (1993), *Per fare conricerca*, Calusca.

Alquati, R. (1994), *Camminando per realizzare un sogno comune*, Velleità Alternative.

Alquati, R. (2021), *Sulla Riproduzione della capacità umana vivente. L'industrializzazione della soggettività*, DeiveApprodi.

Althusser, L. (1971), *Lenin and Philosophy and Other Essays*, Monthly Review Press.

Altieri, M. A. (1995), *Agroecology: The Science of Sustainable Agriculture*, CRC Press.

Amante, A., and D. Lawder (2024), "G7 Leaders Agree to Deliver $50 bln in Loans to Ukraine as Soon as December," Reuters, October 25. Available at: https://www.reuters.com/world/g7-leaders-agree-how-deliver-around-50-billion-loans-ukraine-2024-10-25/

Amin, S. (1974), *Accumulation on a World Scale: A Critique of the Theory of Underdevelopment*, Monthly Review Press.

Anderson, B. (2000), *Doing the Dirty Work? The Global Politics of Domestic Labour*, Zed Books.

Anderson, B. (2006), *Imagined Communities: Reflections on the Origin and Spread of Nationalism*, Verso.

Andreucci, D., and S. Engel-Di Mauro (2019), "Capitalism, Socialism and the Challenge of Degrowth: Introduction to the Symposium," *Capitalism Nature Socialism* 30 (2): 176–88.

Anner, M. (2015), "Labor Control Regimes and Supplier Responses to Codes of Conduct: Insights from a Vietnamese Garment Export Factory," *Politics & Society* 43 (4): 503–27.

Arendt, H. (1998), *The Human Condition*, University of Chicago Press.

Aristotle (1985), *Nicomachean Ethics*, Hackett Publishing.

Armiero, M. (2021), *Wasteocene: Stories from the Global Dump*, Cambridge University Press.

Arrighi, G. (2010), *The Long Twentieth Century: Money, Power, and the Origins of Our Times*, Verso.

Ashby, W. R. (1956), *An Introduction to Cybernetics*, Chapman & Hall.
Atkinson, A. B. (2015), *Inequality: What Can Be Done?*, Harvard University Press.
Azmanova, A. (2020), *Capitalism on Edge: How Fighting Precarity Can Achieve Radical Change Without Crisis or Utopia*, Columbia University Press.
Azzellini, D., and M. Vieta (2025), *Commoning Labour and Democracy at Work: When Workers Take Over*, Routledge.
Badiou, A. (2012), *In Praise of Love*, Serpent's Tail.
Baldwin, J. (1963), *The Fire Next Time*, Michael Joseph.
Balibar, E. (1994), *Masses, Classes, Ideas: Studies on Politics and Philosophy Before and After Marx*, Routledge.
Balibar, E. (2001), *Spinoza and Politics*, Verso.
Barca, S. (2017), "The Labor(s) of Degrowth," *Capitalism Nature Socialism* 30 (2): 207–16.
Barca, S. (2020), *Forces of Reproduction: Notes for a Counter-Hegemonic Anthropocene*, Cambridge University Press.
Barca, S. (2022), *Workers of the Earth Labour: Ecology and Reproduction in the Age of Climate Change*, Pluto Press.
Bartolini, P., and S. Consigliere (2019), *Strumenti di cattura: Per una critica dell'immaginario tecno-capitalista*, Jaca Book.
Bataille, G. (1988), *The Accursed Share: An Essay on General Economy, Vol. I, Consumption*, Zone Books.
Bateson, G. (1987), *Steps to an Ecology of Mind*, Jason Aronson.
Battistutta, F. (2022), *Misticopolitica: Orizzonti della spiritualità post-religiosa*, Effigi.
Bauman, Z. (2000), *Liquid Modernity*, Polity.
Beer, S. (1981), *Brain of the Firm*, 2nd ed., Wiley.
Bender, E. M., T. Gebru, A. McMillan-Major, and S. Shmitchell (2021), "On the Dangers of Stochastic Parrots: Can Language Models Be Too Big?" In *Proceedings of the 2021 ACM Conference on Fairness, Accountability, and Transparency*, 610–23, ACM. Available at: https://dl.acm.org/doi/pdf/10.1145/3442188.3445922 (accessed May 25, 2025).
Bentham, J. (1988), *The Principles of Morals and Legislation*, Prometheus Books.
Bersani, M. (2020), "Recovery Fund: è tutto oro (o tutto loro) quello che luccica?" *DinamoPress*, Luglio 23. Available at: https://www.dinamopress.it/news/recovery-fund-oro-quello-luccica/ (accessed April 16, 2025).
Beuret, N. (2024), *Or Something Worse: Why We Need to Disrupt the Climate Transition*, Verso.
Bhattacharya, T. (2017), *Social Reproduction Theory: Remapping Class, Recentering Oppression*, Pluto Press.
Black, S., A. A. Liu, I. Parry, and N. Vernon (2023), "IMF Fossil Fuel Subsidies Data: 2023 Update," IMF working paper WP/23/169, Fiscal Affairs Department, August. Available at: https://www.imf.org/en/Publications/WP/Issues/2023/08/22/IMF-Fossil-Fuel-Subsidies-Data-2023-Update-537281 (accessed April 24, 2025).

Bland, W. L., and M. M. Bell (2007), "A Holon Approach to Agroecology," *International Journal of Agricultural Sustainability* 5 (4): 280–94.
Bollier, D., and S. Helfrich (2019), *Free, Fair and Alive: The Insurgent Power of the Commons*, New Society Publishers.
Borio, G., F. Pozzi, and G. Roggero (2002), *Futuro anteriore: Dai "Quaderni Rossi" ai movimenti globali*, Derive e Approdi.
Bourdieu, P. (1993), *The Field of Cultural Production: Essays on Art and Literature*, Columbia University Press.
Bourdieu, P. (1998), *Acts of Resistance: Against the New Myths of Our Time*, Polity.
Bratton, B. H. (2016), *The Stack: On Software and Sovereignty*, MIT Press.
Braudel, F. (1973), *Capitalism and Material Life 1400–1800*, Harper & Row.
Braudel, F. (1982), *Civilization and Capitalism 15th–18th Century, Vol. 2, The Wheels of Commerce*, Fontana.
Braungart, M., and W. McDonough (2002), *Cradle to Cradle: Remaking the Way We Make Things*, North Point Press.
Brenner, J., and B. Laslett (1991), "Gender, Social Reproduction, and Women's Self-Organization: Considering the U.S. Welfare State," *Gender & Society* 5 (3): 311–33.
Brown, G., and K. Milburn (2024), *Commoning the Public: Translating European New Municipalism to the UK Context*, Rosa Luxemburg Foundation. Available at: https://assets-global.website-files.com/647f122b84dd393f4681b0a5/65f1e8703ef823e1c4301531_Abundance_Commoning the Public _March 2024.pdf (accessed May 12, 2025).
Brown, W. (2015), *Undoing the Demos: Neoliberalism's Stealth Revolution*, Zone Books.
Burnet, J. (1920), "Herakleitos of Ephesos," in *Early Greek philosophy*, 3rd ed., A & C Black.
Butler, J. (1990), *Gender Trouble: Feminism and the Subversion of Identity*, Routledge.
Butler, J. (1997), *The Psychic Life of Power: Theories in Subjection*, Stanford University Press.
Butler, J. (2015), *Notes Toward a Performative Theory of Assembly*, Harvard University Press.
Caffentzis, G. (1992), "The Work/Energy Crisis and the Apocalypse," in Midnight Notes Collective (ed.), *Midnight Oil: Work, Energy, War, 1973–1992*, Autonomedia.
Caffentzis, G. (2005), "Immeasurable Value? An Essay on Marx's Legacy," *The Commoner* 10: 87–114. Available at: https://thecommoner.org/wp-content/uploads/2020/06/C-Caffentzis-Immeasurable-Value.pdf
Caffentzis, G. (2008), "From the Grundrisse to Capital and Beyond: Then and Now," *Workplace* 15: 59–74. Available at: https://ices.library.ubc.ca/index.php/workplace/article/view/182216 (accessed January 29, 2025).
Caffentzis, G. (2013), *In Letters of Blood and Fire: Work, Machines, and the Crisis of Capitalism*, PM Press.

Cajete, G. (2000), *Native Science: Natural Laws of Interdependence*, Clear Light Publishers.

Capra, F., & Luisi, P. L. (2014). *The Systems View of Life: A Unifying Vision*. Cambridge University Press.

Carrington, D. (1925), "More Than 150 'unprecedented' Climate Disasters Struck World in 2024, Says UN," *The Guardian*, 19 March. Available at: https://www.theguardian.com/environment/2025/mar/19/unprecedented-climate-disasters-extreme-weather-un-report

Castoriadis, C. (1987), *The Imaginary Institution of Society*, MIT Press.

Caufield, C. (1997), *Masters of Illusion: The World Bank and the Poverty of Nations*, Henry Holt.

Chan, K. M. A., R. K. Gould, and U. Pascual (2016), "Relational Values: What Are They, and What's the Fuss About?," *Current Opinion in Environmental Sustainability* 25: 87–91.

Ciesnik, S. (2025), "How Dependent Are Europe's Militaries on the US?," France24, March 10. Available at: https://www.france24.com/en/europe/20250310-how-dependent-are-europe-s-militaries-on-the-us

Citton, Y. (2017), *The Ecology of Attention*, Polity.

Clark, W. R. (2005), *Petrodollar Warfare*, New Society Publishers.

Cleaver, H. (2000), *Reading Capital Politically*, 2nd ed., AK Press/Anti-Thesis.

Cleaver, H. (2024), *The Fragile Juggernaut: Marx & Engels on Capitalism, Class Struggle and Crisis*, Brill.

Collins, P. H. (2000), *Black Feminist Thought: Knowledge, Consciousness, and the Politics of Empowerment*, 2nd ed., Routledge.

Cox, R. W. (1987), *Production, Power and World Order: Social Forces in the Making of History*, Columbia University Press.

Crawford, K. (2021), *Atlas of AI: Power, Politics, and the Planetary Costs of Artificial Intelligence*, Yale University Press.

Crenshaw, K. (1989), "Demarginalizing the Intersection of Race and Sex: A Black Feminist Critique of Antidiscrimination Doctrine, Feminist Theory and Antiracist Politics," *University of Chicago Legal Forum* 1989 (1): 139–67. Available at: https://chicagounbound.uchicago.edu/cgi/viewcontent.cgi?article=1052&context=uclf (accessed May 25, 2025).

D'Alisa, G., F. Demaria, and G. Kallis (eds) (2015), *Degrowth: A Vocabulary for a New Era*, Routledge.

Dalla Costa, M., and S. James (1975), *Wages Against Housework*, Falling Wall Press.

Damasio, A. R. (1994), *Descartes' Error: Emotion, Reason, and the Human Brain*, G.P. Putnam's Sons.

Damasio, A. R. (1999), *The Feeling of What Happens: Body, Emotion and the Making of Consciousness*, Harcourt.

Dardot, P., and C. Laval (2014), *The New Way of the World: On Neoliberal Society*, Verso.

Dardot, P., and C. Laval (2019), *Common: On Revolution in the 21st Century*, Bloomsbury.

Davis, K. E., A. Fisher, B. Kingsbury, and S. E. Merry (eds) (2012), *Governance by Indicators: Global Power Through Quantification and Rankings*, Oxford University Press.

Dean, J. (2012), *The Communist Horizon*, Verso.

De Angelis, M. (2000), *Keynesianism, Social Conflict and Political Economy*, Macmillan.

De Angelis, M. (2007), *The Beginning of History: Global Capital and Value Struggles*, Pluto Press.

De Angelis, M. (2017), *Omnia Sunt Communia: On the Commons and Transformation to Postcapitalism*, Zed Books.

De Angelis, M. (2021), "Commons," in B. Skeggs, S. Farris, A. Toscano, and S. Bromberg (eds), *The SAGE Handbook of Marxism*, vol. 2: 643–61, Sage.

De Angelis, M. (2025a), "Dollars, Duties and Domination," April 11. Available at: https://aworldincommon.substack.com/p/dollars-duties-and-domination?r=1to6pb (accessed May 2, 2025).

De Angelis, M. (2025b), "The Flotilla, the Demos, and Life Overflowing," *The Commoner*. https://thecommoner.org/the-flotilla-the-demos-and-life-overflowing/ (accessed October 20, 2025).

De Angelis, M. (2025c), "From Seattle to Trump and Beyond." Available at: https://aworldincommon.substack.com/p/from-seattle-to-trump-and-beyond?r=1to6pb (accessed May 2, 2025).

De Angelis, M. (2025d), "USAID Ambivalent no Longer," April 8. Available at: https://aworldincommon.substack.com/p/usaid-ambivalent-no-longer?r=1to6pb (accessed May 2, 2025).

De Angelis, M. (2025e), "Vital Resonance and Power Shaken by the Streets." Available at: https://aworldincommon.substack.com/p/vital-resonance-and-power-shaken (accessed October 20, 2025).

De Angelis, M., and D. Diesner (2020), "A Revolution Under Our Feet. Food Sovereignty and the Commons in the Case of Campi Aperti," in Derya Özkan and Güldem Baykal Büyüksaraç (eds), *Commoning the City: Empirical Perspectives on Urban Ecology, Economics and Ethics*, 69–85, Routledge.

De Angelis, M., and D. Harvie (2009), "'Cognitive Capitalism' and the Rat Race: How Capital Measures Immaterial Labour in British Universities," *Historical Materialism* 17 (3): 3–30.

de la Cadena, M. (2015), *Earth Beings: Ecologies of Practice Across Andean Worlds*, Duke University Press.

DeLanda, M. (2006), *A New Philosophy of Society : Assemblage Theory*, Continuum.

DeLanda, M. (2016), *Assemblage Theory*, Edinburgh University Press.

Deleuze, G., and F. Guattari (1984), *Anti-Oedipus: Capitalism and Schizophrenia*, Athlone Press.

Deleuze, G., and F. Guattari (1988), *A Thousand Plateaus: Capitalism and Schizophrenia*, Continuum.

De Molina, M. G., and V. M. Toledo (2014), *The Social Metabolism: A Socio-Ecological Theory of Historical Change*, Springer.

Della Porta, D. (2015), *Social Movements in Times of Austerity: Bringing Capitalism Back Into Protest Analysis*, Polity.
Della Porta, D., A. Peterson, and H. Reiter (eds) (2006), *The Policing of Transnational Protest*, Routledge.
Dempster, B. (1998), "A Self-Organizing Systems Perspective on Planning for Sustainability," Master's thesis, University of Waterloo, Ontario, Canada. Available at: https://citeseerx.ist.psu.edu/document?repid=rep1&type=pdf&doi=8207c73dfb568eae136c3ab9d8d549a3379f402a (accessed February 25, 2025).
Dempster, B. (2000), "Sympoietic and Autopoietic Systems: A New Distinction for Self-Organizing Systems," in J. K. Allen and J. Wilby (eds), *Proceedings of the World Congress of the Systems Sciences and ISSS*, presented at the International Society for Systems Studies Annual Conference, Toronto, Canada, July. Available at: https://citeseerx.ist.psu.edu/document?repid=rep1&type=pdf&doi=44299317a20afcd33b0a11d3b2bf4fc196088d45 (accessed February 25, 2025).
Desai, R. (2013), *Geopolitical Economy: After U.S. Hegemony, Globalization and Empire*, Pluto Press.
Desai, R., and M. Hudson (2021), "Beyond Dollar Creditocracy: A Geopolitical Economy," *Real-World Economics Review* (97): 20–39. Available at: https://www.paecon.net/PAEReview/issue97/DesaiHudson97.pdf
Dinerstein, A. C. (2015), *The Politics of Autonomy in Latin America: The Art of Organising Hope*, Palgrave Macmillan.
Dowling, E. (2021), *The Care Crisis: What Caused It and How Can We End It?*, Verso.
Dunlap, A. (2020a), "Bureaucratic Land Grabbing for Infrastructural Colonization: Renewable Energy, L'Amassada and Resistance in Southern France," *Human Geography* 13 (2): 93–115. https://doi.org/10.1177/1942778620918041.
Dunlap, A. (2020b), "Renewable Energy and Land Grabbing: Indigenous Resistance in Oaxaca, Mexico," *The Journal of Peasant Studies* 47 (3): 521–46.
Durkheim, E. (1982), *The Rules of Sociological Method and Selected Texts on Sociology and Its Methods*, Free Press.
Ellen MacArthur Foundation (2013), *Towards the Circular Economy: Economic and Business Rationale for an Accelerated Transition*, Ellen MacArthur Foundation.
England, P. (2010), "The Gender Revolution: Uneven and Stalled," *Gender & Society* 24 (2): 149–66.
Escobar, A. (1995), *Encountering Development: The Making and Unmaking of the Third World*, Princeton University Press.
Esposito, R. (2009), *Communitas: The Origin and Destiny of Community*, Stanford University Press.
EuroMed (2024), "200 Days of Military Attack on Gaza: A Horrific Death Toll Amid International Failure to Stop Israel's Genocide of Palestinians,"

April 24. Available at: https://euromedmonitor.org/en/article/6282/200-days-of-military-attack-on-Gaza:-A-horrific-death-toll-amid-intl.-failure-to-stop-Israel's-genocide-of-Palestinians (accessed April 25, 2025).
European Commission (2025), "Commission Unveils the White Paper for European Defence and the ReArm Europe Plan/Readiness 2030" [Press release], March 4. Available at: https://ec.europa.eu/commission/presscorner/detail/en/ip_25_793 (accessed April 16, 2025).
Fanon, F. (2004), *The Wretched of the Earth*, Grove Press.
FAO (2014), *The State of Food and Agriculture: Innovation in Family Farming*, Food and Agriculture Organization of the United Nations. Available at: https://www.fao.org/3/i4040e/i4040e.pdf (accessed May 25, 2025).
Farrell, H., and A. Newman (2023), *Underground Empire: How America Weaponized the World Economy*, Henry Holt.
Fassin, D., and M. Fourcade (eds) (2021), *Pandemic Exposures: Economy and Society in the Time of Coronavirus*, Hau Books.
Federici, S. (2004), *Caliban and the Witch: Women, the Body and Primitive Accumulation*, Autonomedia.
Federici, S. (2012), *Revolution at Point Zero: Housework, Reproduction, and Feminist Struggle*, PM Press.
Federici, S. (2020), *Beyond the Periphery of the Skin: Rethinking, Remaking, and Reclaiming the Body in Contemporary Capitalism*, PM Press.
Fisher, M. (2016), "All This Is Temporary," Rix Mix, London, February 23. Available at: https://www.youtube.com/watch?v=deZgzw0YHQI (accessed March 10, 2025).
Fisher, M. (2020), *Acid Communism*, Pattern Books.
Fiske, A. P., and N. Haslam (2005), "The Four Basic Social Bonds. Structures for Coordinating Interaction," in M. W. Baldwin (ed.), *Interpersonal Cognition*, 267–98, Guilford Press.
Folbre, N. (2001), *The Invisible Heart: Economics and Family Values*, New Press.
Forum Italiano dei Movimenti per l'Acqua (2021), "Il Recovery Plan di Draghi: più privatizzazioni, meno democrazia," *Il Manifesto*, April 10. Available at: https://ilmanifesto.it/il-recovery-plan-di-draghi-piu-privatizzazioni-meno-democrazia (accessed April 16, 2025).
Foster, J. B. (2000), *Marx's Ecology: Materialism and Nature*, Monthly Review Press.
Foucault, M. (1977), *Discipline and Punish: The Birth of the Prison*, Vintage Books.
Foucault, M. (1978), *The History of Sexuality, Vol. 1, The Will to Knowledge*, Random House.
Foucault, M. (1982), "The Subject and Power," *Critical Inquiry* 8 (4): 777–95.
Foucault, M. (2002), "Governmentality," in James D. Faubion (ed.), *Power: Essential Works of Foucault 1954–1984*, 201–22, Penguin.
Foucault, M. (2008), *The Birth of Biopolitics: Lectures at the Collège de France, 1978–1979*, Palgrave Macmillan.
Fraser, N. (2016), "Contradictions of Capital and Care," *New Left Review* 100: 99–117.

Freire, P. (1988), *Pedagogy of the Oppressed*, Continuum.
Fumagalli, A. (2018), "The Social Imperative of Universal Income: Rethinking Welfare in the Age of Precarious Work," *European Journal of Social Policy* 28 (3): 217–30.
Gabor, D. (2020), "The Wall Street Consensus: Why Financialisation Means the Poor Pay More," *Development and Change* 51 (3): 1–20.
Gambles, R., S. Lewis, and R. Rapoport (2006), *The Myth of Work–Life Balance: The Challenge of Our Time for Men, Women and Societies*, John Wiley & Sons.
Georgescu-Roegen, N. (1971), *The Entropy Law and the Economic Process*, Harvard University Press.
Gereffi, G. (2018), *Global Value Chains and Development: Redefining the Contours of 21st Century Capitalism*, Cambridge University Press.
Gereffi, G., J. Humphrey, and T. Sturgeon (2005), "The Governance of Global Value Chains," *Review of International Political Economy* 12 (1): 78–104.
Ghosh, A. (2021), *The Nutmeg's Curse: Parables for a Planet in Crisis*, University of Chicago Press.
Ghosh, J. (2010), "The Unnatural Coupling: Food and Global Finance," *Journal of Agrarian Change* 10 (1): 72–86.
Giampietro, M., K. Mayumi, and A. H. Sorman (2012), *The Metabolic Pattern of Societies*, Routledge.
Gilbert, S. F., J. Sapp, and A. I. Tauber (2012), "A Symbiotic View of Life: We Have Never Been Individuals," *Quarterly Review of Biology* 87 (4): 325–41.
Gilligan, C. (1982), *In a Different Voice: Psychological Theory and Women's Development*, Harvard University Press.
Gilmore, R. W. (2007), *Golden Gulag: Prisons, Surplus, Crisis, and Opposition in Globalizing California*, University of California Press.
Glenn, E. N. (1992), "From Servitude to Service Work: Historical Continuities in the Racial Division of Paid Reproductive Labor," *Signs: Journal of Women in Culture and Society* 18 (1): 1–43.
Gliessman, S. R. (2015), *Agroecology: The Ecology of Sustainable Food Systems*, CRC Press.
Godbout, J. (2000), *Le Don, la Dette et l'Identité: Homo Donator vs Homo Oeconomicus*, La Découverte.
Godwin, W. (2013), *An Enquiry Concerning Political Justice*, Oxford University Press.
Graeber, D. (2001), *Toward an Anthropological Theory of Value: The False Coin of Our Own Dreams*, Palgrave Macmillan.
Graeber, D. (2008), "Hope in Common." Available at: https://davidgraeber.org/wp-content/uploads/2008-Hope-in-common.pdf
Graeber, D. (2013), *The Democracy Project: A History, a Crisis, a Movement*, Spiegel & Grau.
Graeber, D., and D. Wengrow (2021), *The Dawn of Everything: A New History of Humanity*, Farrar, Straus and Giroux.

Grain (2024), "From Land Grabbers to Carbon Cowboys: A New Scramble for Community Lands Takes Off," February 17. Available at: https://grain.org/en/article/7190-from-land-grabbers-to-carbon-cowboys-a-new-scramble-for-community-lands-takes-off (accessed March 25, 2025).
Gramsci, A. (1971), *Selections from the Prison Notebooks*, Lawrence & Wishart.
Greenberg, Y. K. (2008), *Encyclopedia of Love in World Religions*, ABC-CLIO.
Guattari, F. (2000), *The Three Ecologies*, Athlone Press.
Haas, W., F. Krausmann, D. Wiedenhofer, and M. Heinz (2015), "How Circular Is the Global Economy? An Assessment of Material Flows, Waste Production, and Recycling in the European Union and the World in 2005," *Journal of Industrial Ecology* 19 (5): 765–77.
Haiven, M. (2014), *Crisis of Imagination, Crisis of Power: Capitalism, Creativity and the Commons*, Zed Books.
Hall, M., and E. Greenman (2015), "The Occupational Cost of Being Illegal in the United States: Legal Status, Job Hazards, and Compensating Differentials," *International Migration Review* 49 (2): 406–42.
Haraway, D. (2015), "Anthropocene, Capitalocene, Plantationocene, Chthulucene: Making Kin," *Environmental Humanities* 6: 159–65.
Haraway, D. (2016), *Staying with the Trouble: Making Kin in the Chthulucene*, Duke University Press.
Hardin, G. (1968), "The Tragedy of the Commons," *Science* 162 (3859): 1243–8.
Hardt, M., and A. Negri (2000), *Empire*, Harvard University Press.
Hardt, M., and A. Negri (2004), *Multitude: War and Democracy in the Age of Empire*, Penguin.
Harvey, D. (1982), *The Limits to Capital*, Basil Blackwell.
Harvey, D. (1989), *The Condition of Postmodernity: An Enquiry into the Origins of Cultural Change*, Blackwell.
Harvey, D. (2003), *The New Imperialism*, Oxford University Press.
Harvey, D. (2005), *A Brief History of Neoliberalism*, Oxford University Press.
Harvey, D. (2006), *Spaces of Global Capitalism: A Theory of Uneven Geographical Development*, Verso.
Harvey, D. (2010), *The Enigma of Capital: And the Crises of Capitalism*, Oxford University Press.
Hayek, F. A. (1945), "The Use of Knowledge in Society," *American Economic Review* 35 (4): 519–30.
Hayek, F. A. (1973), *Law, Legislation and Liberty, Vol. 1, Rules and Order*, University of Chicago Press.
Highmore, B. (2002), *Everyday Life and Cultural Theory: An Introduction*, Routledge.
Hochschild, A. R. (2000), "Global Care Chains and Emotional Surplus Value," in W. Hutton and A. Giddens (eds), *On the Edge: Living with Global Capitalism*, 130–46, Jonathan Cape.

Höller, L. (2024), "New Pact Boosts Defense-Industry Goals in EU Lending Scheme," Defence News, October 3. Available at: https://www.defensenews.com/global/europe/2024/10/03/new-pact-boosts-defense-industry-goals-in-eu-lending-scheme/ (accessed May 25, 2025).

Hollingsworth, J. R., and R. Boyer (eds) (1997), *Contemporary Capitalism: The Embeddedness of Institutions*, Cambridge University Press.

Holloway, J. (2022), *Hope in Hopeless Times*, Pluto Press.

hooks, b. (1984), *Feminist Theory: From Margin to Center*, South End Press.

hooks, b. (2000), *Feminism Is for Everybody: Passionate Politics*, South End Press.

hooks, b. (2001), *All About Love: New Visions*, William Morrow.

Hornborg, A. (2009), "Zero-Sum World: Challenges in Conceptualizing Environmental Load Displacement and Ecologically Unequal Exchange in the World-System," *International Journal of Comparative Sociology* 50 (3–4): 237–62.

HSE (Health and Safety Executive) (2023), *Work-Related Stress, Depression or Anxiety Statistics in Great Britain 2023*, HSE. Available at: https://www.hse.gov.uk/statistics/assets/docs/stress.pdf (accessed April 11, 2025).

Hudson, M. (2003), *Super Imperialism: The Origin and Fundamentals of U.S. World Dominance*, Pluto Press.

IEA (2021), "Security of Clean Energy Transitions." Available at: https://www.iea.org/reports/security-of-clean-energy-transitions (accessed October 20, 2025).

Illich, I. (1971), *Deschooling Society*, Harper & Row.

Illich, I. (1981), *Shadow Work*, Maryon Boyars.

Imperatore, P., and E. Leonardi (2023), *L'era della giustizia climatica*, Orthotes.

Jamaluddine, Z., H. Abukmail, A. Sarah, O. Campbell, and F. Checchi (2025), "Traumatic Injury Mortality in the Gaza Strip from Oct 7, 2023, to June 30, 2024: A Capture–Recapture Analysis," *Lancet* 405 (10477): 469–77. Available at: https://www.thelancet.com/journals/lancet/article/PIIS0140-6736(24)02678-3/fulltext#au10 (accessed March 25, 2025).

Jessop, B. (2016), *The State: Past, Present, Future*, Polity.

Kallis, G., S. Paulson, G. D'Alisa, and F. Demaria (2020), *The Case for Degrowth*, Polity.

Kimmerer, R. W. (2013), *Braiding Sweetgrass: Indigenous Wisdom, Scientific Knowledge, and the Teachings of Plants*, Milkweed Editions.

Kingsnorth, P. (2004), *One No, Many Yeses: A Journey to the Heart of the Global Resistance Movement*, Free Press.

Klain, S. C., P. Olmsted, K. M. A. Chan, and T. Satterfield (2017), "Relational Values Resonate Broadly and Differently than Intrinsic or Instrumental Values, or the New Ecological Paradigm," *PLOS One* 12 (8): 1–21.

Klein, N. (2007), *The Shock Doctrine: The Rise of Disaster Capitalism*, Metropolitan Books.

Kloppenburg, J. R. (2004), *First the Seed: The Political Economy of Plant Biotechnology*, University of Wisconsin Press.
Koestler, A. (1967), *The Ghost in the Machine*, Hutchinson.
Latour, B. (1999), *Pandora's Hope: Essays on the Reality of Science Studies*, Harvard University Press.
Latour, B. (2005), *Reassembling the Social: An Introduction to Actor-Network Theory*, Oxford University Press.
Latour, B. (2017), *Facing Gaia: Eight Lectures on the New Climatic Regime*, Polity.
Lawrence, P. (2022), "The Return of Recession, Debt and Structural Adjustment," *Review of African Political Economy* 49 (174): 523–30.
Lazzarato, M. (2011), *The Making of the Indebted Man: An Essay on the Neoliberal Condition*, Semiotext(e).
Lazzarato, M. (2014), *Signs and Machines*, Semiotext(e).
Lefebvre, H. (1991), *Critique of Everyday Life, Vol. I, Introduction*, Verso.
Lefebvre, H. (2004), *Rhythmanalysis: Space, Time and Everyday Life*, Continuum.
Leonardi, E. (2026), *Labour, Nature and Value: André Gorz Between Marxism and Degrowth*, Verso.
Levinas, E. (1969), *Totality and Infinity: An Essay on Exteriority*, Kluwer Academic Publishers.
Lewin, K. (1936), *Principles of Topological Psychology*, McGraw-Hill.
Liang, Q. (2021), *L'arco dell'impero con la Cina e gli Stati Uniti alle estremità*, Leg edizioni.
Linebaugh, P., and M. Rediker (2000), *The Many-Headed Hydra: Sailors, Slaves, Commoners, and the Hidden History of the Revolutionary Atlantic*, Verso.
Lorde, A. (1984), *Sister Outsider: Essays and Speeches*, Crossing Press.
Lotka, A. (1956), *Elements of Mathematical Biology*, Dover Publications.
Lovelock, J. (2000), *Gaia: A New Look at Life on Earth*, Oxford University Press.
Lowder, S. K., M. V. Sánchez, and R. Bertini (2021), "Which Farms Feed the World and Has Farmland Become More Concentrated?," *World Development* 142: 105455.
Lucha Indígena (2022), "A Cerrar el Congreso," 16 (189) Dicembre. Available at: https://ia601502.us.archive.org/25/items/lucha-indigena-dic-2022a-1/Lucha%20Indigena%20DIC%202022a1.pdf (accessed May 25, 2025).
Luhmann, N. (1977), *Power*, Columbia University Press.
Luhmann, N. (1995), *Social Systems*, Stanford University Press.
Lukács, G. (1972), *History and Class Consciousness: Studies in Marxist Dialectics*, MIT Press.
Malm, A. (2016), *Fossil Capital: The Rise of Steam Power and the Roots of Global Warming*, Verso.
Malm, A. (2020), *Corona, Climate, Chronic Emergency: War Communism in the Twenty-First Century*, Verso.
Marcuse, H. (1964), *One-Dimensional Man: Studies in the Ideology of Advanced Industrial Society*, Beacon Press.
Martinez-Alier, J. (2002), *The Environmentalism of the Poor: A Study of Ecological Conflicts and Valuation*, Edward Elgar.

Martínez-Faneca, L., C. Casafont-Bullich, and M. Olivé-Ferrer (2020), "Construction of Nursing Knowledge in Commodified Contexts: A Discussion Paper," *Nursing Inquiry* 27 (2): e12336.
Martínez-Faneca, L., and N. Fabrellas (2023), "Construction of Nursing Knowledge in Commodified Contexts: Views and Experiences of Nurses Regarding Primary Care," *Nursing Inquiry* 30 (4): e12579.
Marx, K. (1973), *Grundrisse: Foundations of the Critique of Political Economy (Rough Draft)*, Penguin.
Marx, K. (1975), "Theses on Feuerbach," in K. Marx and F. Engels (eds), *MECW, Vol. 5, Marx and Engels 1845–47*, 3–5, Lawrence & Wishart.
Marx, K. (1976), *Capital: A Critique of Political Economy, Vol. 1, A Critical Analysis of Capitalist Production*, Penguin.
Marx, K. (1977), *A Contribution to the Critique of Political Economy*, Progress Publishers.
Marx, K. (2010a), "The Eighteenth Brumaire of Louis Bonaparte," in K. Marx and F. Engels (eds), *MECW, Vol. 11, Marx and Engels 1851–53*, 99–197, Lawrence & Wishart.
Marx, K. (2010b), "The Poverty of Philosophy," in K. Marx and F. Engels (eds), *MECW, Vol. 6, Marx and Engels 1845–48*, 105–212, Lawrence & Wishart.
Maturana, H. R., and F. J. Varela (1980), *Autopoiesis and Cognition: The Realization of the Living*, D. Reidel Publishing.
Maturana, H. R., and F. J. Varela (1987), *The Tree of Knowledge*, Shambhala Publications.
Mauss, M. (1990), *The Gift: The Form and Reason of Exchange in Archaic Societies*, Routledge.
Mbembe, A. (2019), *Necropolitics*, Duke University Press.
McGann, M. (n.d.), "Enactive Cognition. A Cognition Briefing," in *euCognition: The European Network for the Advancement of Artificial Cognitive Systems.* Available at: http://www.vernon.eu/euCognition/cognition_briefing_enactive_cognition.htm (accessed March 3, 2025).
Meadows, D. H. (2008), *Thinking in Systems: A Primer*, Chelsea Green Publishing.
Mezzadra, S., and B. Neilson (2013), *Border as Method, or, the Multiplication of Labor*, Duke University Press.
Mezzadra, S., and B. Neilson (2019), *The Politics of Operations: Excavating Contemporary Capitalism*, Duke University Press.
Mezzadra, S., and B. Neilson (2024), *The Rest and the West: Capital and Power in a Multipolar World*, Verso.
Micciarelli, G. (2014), "I beni comuni e la partecipazione democratica. Da un 'altro modo di possedere' ad un 'altro modo di governare,'" *Jura Gentium: Journal of Philosophy of International Law and Global Politics* XI (1): 58–83. Available at: https://www.juragentium.eu/wp-content/uploads/2023/12/JG_2014_1_Micciarelli-1.pdf (accessed May 12, 2025).
Micciarelli, G. (2022), "Hacking the Legal: The Commons Between the Governance Paradigm and Inspirations Drawn from the 'Living History' of

Collective Land Use," in F. Savini, A. Ferreira, and K. C. von Schönfeld (eds), *Post-Growth Planning: Cities Beyond the Market Economy*, 112–26, Routledge.
Midnight Notes Collective (1990), "New Enclosures," in *Midnight Notes*, 10, https://libcom.org/article/midnight-notes-10-1990-new-enclosures (accessed March 3, 2026).
Midnight Notes Collective (2001), *Auroras of the Zapatistas: Local and Global Struggles of the Fourth World War*, Autonomedia.
Midnight Notes Collective and Friends (2009), *Promissory Notes: From Crisis to Commons*, Minor Compositions.
Mies, M. (1986), *Patriarchy and Accumulation on a World Scale: Women in the International Division of Labour*, Zed Books.
Mill, J. S. (2002), *Utilitarianism*, Hackett Publishing.
Miller, C., A. Russell, and G. Rachman (2025), "Ukraine Agrees Minerals Deal with US," *Financial Times*, February 25. Available at: https://www.ft.com/content/1890d104-1395-4393-a71d-d299aed448e6?syn-25a6b1a6=1
Milman, O., and D. Noor (2025), "Trump's EPA Aims to Cut Pollution Rules Projected to Save Nearly 200,000 Lives: 'People Will Be Hurt,'" *The Guardian*, December 19. Available at: https://www.theguardian.com/us-news/2025/mar/19/trump-epa-pollution-regulation-cuts
Mingers, J. (1995), *Self-Producing Systems: Implications and Applications of Autopoiesis, Contemporary Systems Thinking*, Springer.
Mollona, M. (2021), *Art/Commons: Imagining the Political Economy of the Art World*, Zed Books.
Moore, J. W. (2015), *Capitalism in the Web of Life: Ecology and the Accumulation of Capital*, Verso.
Moore, J. W. (2016), *Anthropocene or Capitalocene? Nature, History, and the Crisis of Capitalism*, PM Press.
Morin, E. (2008), *On Complexity*, Hampton Press.
Morini, C. (2022), *Vite lavorate: Corpi, valore, resistenza al disamore*, Manifestolibri.
Murray, W. (2025), "Ukraine War Briefing: Strengthen Kyiv's Hand Before Peace Talks, Says Nato Chief," *The Guardian*, January 14. Available at: https://www.theguardian.com/world/2025/jan/14/ukraine-war-briefing-strengthen-kyivs-hand-before-peace-talks-says-nato-chief
Negri, A. (1984), *Marx Beyond Marx: Lessons on the Grundrisse*, Bergin & Garvey.
Negri, A. (2000), *Kairòs, alma venus, multitudo. Nove lezioni impartite a me stesso*, Manifestolibri.
Negri, A. (2023), *The Common*, Polity.
Neilson, D. (2015), "Class, Precarity, and Anxiety Under Neoliberal Global Capitalism: From Denial to Resistance," *Theory & Psychology* 25 (2): 184–201.
Noble, D. F. (1984), *Forces of Production: A Social History of Industrial Automation*, Knopf.
Nunes, R. (2021), *Neither Vertical nor Horizontal: A Theory of Political Organization*, Verso.
O'Connor, J. (1973), *The Fiscal Crisis of the State*, St. Martin's Press.

Ostrom, E. (1990), *Governing the Commons: The Evolution of Institutions for Collective Action*, Cambridge University Press.
OXFAM (2023), "Climate Equality: A Planet for the 99%." Available at: https://policy-practice.oxfam.org/resources/climate-equality-a-planet-for-the-99-621551/ (accessed March 25, 2025).
Panzieri, R. (1976), *Lotte operaie nello sviluppo capitalistico*, Einaudi.
Parliament UK (1991), "Oral Answers to Questions," National Finance, Column 410, May 16. Available at: https://publications.parliament.uk/pa/cm199091/cmhansrd/1991-05-16/Orals-1.html (accessed May 2, 2025).
Parreñas, R. S. (2001), *Servants of Globalization: Women, Migration and Domestic Work*, Stanford University Press.
Patel, R., and J. W. Moore (2017), *A History of the World in Seven Cheap Things: A Guide to Capitalism, Nature, and the Future of the Planet*, University of California Press.
Pearce, F. (2025), "'Green Grab': Solar and Wind Boom Sparks Conflicts on Land Use," *Yale Environment 360*, February 20. Available at: https://e360.yale.edu/features/solar-land-grabs-agrovoltaics (accessed October 20, 2025).
Pentenero, M. (2018), *Modelizzazione e politicità intrinseca: Le dispense di sociologia industriale: uno sguardo sul nuovo millennio*. Unpublished manuscript.
Perelman, M. (2000), *The Invention of Capitalism: Classical Political Economy and the Secret History of Primitive Accumulation*, Duke University Press.
Piaget, J. (1971), *Biology and Knowledge: An Essay on the Relations Between Organic Regulations and Cognitive Processes*, University of Chicago Press.
Piketty, T. (2014), *Capital in the Twenty-First Century*, Harvard University Press.
Pittavino, G. L. (2021), "Romano Alquati: dall'operaismo agli scritti inediti degli anni Novanta," in M. Pentenero and L. Perrone (eds), *La riproduzione del futuro: Le ipotesi di Romano Alquati per una trasformazione radicale*, 6–18, Derive e Approdi.
Polanyi, K. (1944), *The Great Transformation: The Political and Economic Origins of Our Time*, Beacon Press.
Polanyi, K. (1968), *Primitive, Archaic, and Modern Economies: Essays of Karl Polanyi*, G. Dalton (ed.), Doubleday.
Prigogine, I. (1997), *The End of Certainty: Time, Chaos and the New Laws of Nature*, Free Press.
Princen, T. (2005), *The Logic of Sufficiency*, MIT Press.
Probst, T. M., and T. L. Brubaker (2001), "The Effects of Job Insecurity on Employee Safety Outcomes: Cross-Sectional and Longitudinal Explorations," *Journal of Occupational Health Psychology* 6 (2): 139–59.
Rancière, J. (1995), *On the Shores of Politics*, Verso.
Rancière, J. (2004), *The Politics of Aesthetics: The Distribution of the Sensible*, Continuum.
Read, J. (2022), "Two Great Tastes Part Two: The Introduction to Fischbach's La Production des Hommes," *Unemployed Negativity*, March 24. Available at: http://www.unemployednegativity.com/2022/03/two-great-tastes-part-two-introduction.html (accessed March 3, 2025).

Rödl, S. (2007), *Self-Consciousness*, Harvard University Press.
Rodney, W. (1972), *How Europe Underdeveloped Africa*, Bogle-L'Ouverture Publications.
Roggero, G. (2019), *L'operaismo politico italiano: genealogie, teoria, storia*, Derive e Approdi.
Roithmayr, D. (2014), *Reproducing Racism: How Everyday Choices Lock in White Advantage*, New York University Press.
Rosenau, J. N., and E.-O. Czempiel (eds) (1992), *Governance Without Government: Order and Change in World Politics*, Cambridge University Press.
Rosenthal, J. (2009), "A Terrible Thing to Waste," *New York Times*, July 31. Available at: https://www.nytimes.com/2009/08/02/magazine/02FOB-onlanguage-t.html# (accessed May 2, 2025).
Rottenburg, R., S. E. Merry, S.-J. Park, and J. Mugler (eds) (2015), *The World of Indicators: The Making of Governmental Knowledge Through Quantification*, Cambridge University Press.
Russell, B., K. Milburn, and K. Heron (2022), "Strategies for a New Municipalism: Public–Common Partnerships Against the New Enclosures," *Urban Studies* 60 (11): 2133–57.
SAPRIN (2004), *Structural Adjustment: The SAPRI Report: The Policy Roots of Economic Crisis, Poverty and Inequality*, Zed Books.
Sassen, S. (2014), *Expulsions: Brutality and Complexity in the Global Economy*, Harvard University Press.
Schmidt, A. (1971), *The Concept of Nature in Marx*, NLB.
Schor, J. (1991), *The Overworked American: The Unexpected Decline of Leisure*, Basic Books.
Schumpeter, J. A. (1950), *Capitalism, Socialism and Democracy*, Allen & Unwin.
Sciortino, R. (2024), *The US–China Rift and Its Impact on Globalisation: Crisis, Strategy, Transition*, Brill.
Searle, J. R. (1995), *The Construction of Social Reality*, Free Press.
Searle, J. R. (2010), *Making the Social World: The Structure of Human Civilization*, Oxford University Press.
Shiva, V. (1991), *The Violence of the Green Revolution: Third World Agriculture, Ecology and Politics*, Zed Books.
Shiva, V. (1997), *Biopiracy: The Plunder of Nature and Knowledge*, South End Press.
Singh, N. M. (2018), "Becoming a Commoner: The Commons as Sites for Affective Socio-Nature Encounters and Co-Becomings," *Ephemera Theory & Politics in Organization* 17 (4): 751–76.
SIPRI (Stockholm International Peace Research Institute) (2024), "Trends in World Military Expenditure, 2023," SIPRI Fact Sheet. Available at: https://www.sipri.org/publications/2024/sipri-fact-sheets/trends-world-military-expenditure-2023 (accessed April 11, 2025).
Sitrin, M. (2014), "Solidarity Health Clinics in Greece," December 19. Available at: https://zcomm.org/znetarticle/solidarity-health-clinics-in-greece/2014 (accessed May 25, 2025).

Sitrin, M., and Colectiva Sembrar (eds) (2020), *Pandemic Solidarity: Mutual Aid During the COVID-19 Crisis*, Pluto Press.
Smith, A. (1970), *The Wealth of Nations*, Penguin.
Smith, D. E. (2002), "A Feminist Methodology," in B. Highmore (eds), *The Everyday Life Reader*, 271–81, Routledge.
Smith, D. N. (2017), "Theory and Class Consciousness," in Michael J. Thompson (ed.), *The Palgrave Handbook of Critical Theory*, 369–423, Palgrave Macmillan.
Smith, N. (2008), *Uneven Development: Nature, Capital, and the Production of Space*, 3rd ed., University of Georgia Press.
Spinoza, B. (2018), *Ethics Proved in Geometrical Order*, Cambridge University Press.
Standing, G. (2011), *The Precariat: The New Dangerous Class*, Bloomsbury Academic.
Standing, G. (2017), *Basic Income: A Guide for the Open-Minded*, Yale University Press.
Stavrides, S. (2016), *Common Space: The City as Commons*, Zed Books.
Steffen, W., W. Broadgate, L. Deutsch, O. Gaffney, and C. Ludwig (2015), "The Trajectory of the Anthropocene: The Great Acceleration," *The Anthropocene Review* 2 (1): 81–98.
Stengers, I. (2015), *In Catastrophic Times: Resisting the Coming Barbarism*, Open Humanities Press.
Stiglitz, J. (2002), *Globalization and Its Discontents*, W. W. Norton.
Stiglitz, J. (2012), *The Price of Inequality: How Today's Divided Society Endangers Our Future*, W. W. Norton.
Sullivan, D., and J. Hickel (2025), "Plundering Africa—Income Deflation and Unequal Ecological Exchange Under Structural Adjustment Programmes," *Review of African Political Economy*, February 28. Available at: https://roape.net/2025/02/28/plundering-africa-income-deflation-and-unequal-ecological-exchange-under-structural-adjustment-programmes/ (accessed April 16, 2025).
Tamma, P. (2024), "EU Countries Back €35bn Loan to Ukraine," *Financial Times*, October 9. Available at: https://www.ft.com/content/c873dda6-23f5-4479-bf98-dfdebabffac7?syn-25a6b1a6=1
Terranova, T. (2004), *Network Culture: Politics for the Information Age*, Pluto Press.
The New Arab Staff (2025), "Israeli Deputy Knesset Speaker Calls for Killing of 'Subhuman' Palestinian men in Gaza," *The New Arab*. Available at: https://www .newarab.com/news/israeli-likud-mk-calls-killing-subhuman-palestinian-men (accessed March 25, 2025).
Thompson, E. (2007), *Mind in Life: Biology, Phenomenology, and the Sciences of Mind*, Harvard University Press.
Thompson, E. P. (1963), *The Making of the English Working Class*, Vintage Books.
Thompson, E. P. (1967), "Time, Work-Discipline, and Industrial Capitalism," *Past & Present* 38 (1): 56–97.

Thompson, E. P. (1971), "The Moral Economy of the English Crowd in the Eighteenth Century," *Past & Present* (50): 76–136. Available at: https://www.ias.edu/sites/default/files/sss/pdfs/Crisis-and-Critique-2018-19/thompson_moral_economy.pdf (accessed March 25, 2025).

Thompson, M. J. (2020), *The Specter of Babel: A Reconstruction of Political Judgment,* SUNY Press.

Thompson, M. J. (2023), "Toward a Critical Social Ontology," *Philosophical Forum* 54: 61–78. https://doi.org/10.1111/phil.12334.

Tisserant, A., S. Pauliuk, S. Merciai, J. Schmidt, J. Fry, R. Wood, and A. Tukker (2017), "Solid Waste and the Circular Economy: A Global Analysis of Waste Treatment and Waste Footprints," *Journal of Industrial Ecology* 21 (3): 628–40.

Torres, I. (2025), "Solar Power, Land Control, and Indigenous Resistance in Yucatán, Mexico," *Sustainability Science* 20: 1407–20. https://doi.org/10.1007/s11625-025-01718-3.

Triffin, R. (1960), *Gold and the Dollar Crisis: The Future of Convertibility*, Yale University Press.

Triffin, R. (1968), *Our International Monetary System: Yesterday, Today and Tomorrow*, Random House.

Tronti, M. (2019), *Workers and Capital*, Verso.

Tronto, J. C. (1993), *Moral Boundaries: A Political Argument for an Ethic of Care*, Routledge.

Tsing, A. L. (2015), *The Mushroom at the End of the World: On the Possibility of Life in Capitalist Ruins*, Princeton University Press.

Turkle, S. (2011), *Alone Together: Why We Expect More from Technology and Less from Each Other*, Basic Books.

UNCTAD (1993), *World Investment Report 1993: Transnational Corporations and Integrated International Production*, United Nations. Available at: https://unctad.org/system/files/official-document/wir1993_en.pdf (accessed April 17, 2026).

Urry, J. (2016), *What Is the Future?*, Polity.

Vaneigem, R. (1983), *The Revolution of Everyday Life*, Left Bank Books/Rebel Press.

Varela, F. J., H. R. Maturana, and R. Uribe (1974), "Autopoiesis: The Organization of Living Systems, Its Characterization and a Model," *Biosystems* 5 (4): 187–96.

Varela, F. J., E. Thompson, and E. Rosch (1991), *The Embodied Mind: Cognitive Science and Human Experience*, MIT Press.

Vasudevan, R. (2008), "Finance, Imperialism, and the Hegemony of the Dollar," *Monthly Review*, April 1. Available at: https://monthlyreview.org/2008/04/01/finance-imperialism-and-the-hegemony-of-the-dollar/ (accessed May 2, 2025).

Virno, P. (2021), *Dell'impotenza: La Vita nell'epoca della sua paralisi frenetica*, Bollati Boringhieri.

von Bertalanffy, L. (1968), *General System Theory: Foundations, Development, Applications,* George Braziller.

von Foerster, H. (2003a), "Cybernetics of Cybernetics," In *Understanding Understanding: Essays on Cybernetics and Cognition*, 283–6, Springer.

von Foerster, H. (2003b), "Ethics and Second-Order Cybernetics," In *Understanding Understanding: Essays on Cybernetics and Cognition*, 287–304, Springer.

Wallerstein, I. (1974), *The Modern World-System I: Capitalist Agriculture and the Origins of the European World-Economy in the Sixteenth Century*, Academic Press.

Wallerstein, I. (1980), *The Modern World-System II: Mercantilism and the Consolidation of the European World-Economy, 1600–1750*, Academic Press.

Wallerstein, I. (1989), *The Modern World-System III: The Second Era of Great Expansion of the Capitalist World-Economy, 1730–1840s*, Academic Press.

Wallerstein, I. (2004), *World-Systems Analysis: An Introduction*, Duke University Press.

Wallerstein, I. (2011), *The Modern World-System IV: Centrist Liberalism Triumphant, 1789–1914*, University of California Press.

Weber, M. (1978), *Economy and Society: An Outline of Interpretive Sociology*, University of California Press.

Wiener, N. (1948), *Cybernetics: Or Control and Communication in the Animal and the Machine*, MIT Press.

Wood, E. M. (2017), *The Origin of Capitalism: A Longer View*, Verso.

World Bank (2025), "Ukraine Fourth Rapid Damage and Needs Assessment (RDNA4), February 2022–December 2024," World Bank. Available at: https://documents1.worldbank.org/curated/en/099022025114040022/pdf/P1801741ca39ec0d81b5371ff73a675a0a8.pdf (accessed April 11, 2025).

Wright, S. (2002), *Storming Heaven: Class Composition and Struggle in Italian Autonomist Marxism*, Pluto Press.

Youvan, D. (2024), "A Comparative Analysis of the Explosive Impact on Gaza and Historical Bombings: Lessons from Hiroshima, Nagasaki, and Dresden." Available at: https://www.researchgate.net/publication/382394462_A_Comparative_Analysis_of_the_Explosive_Impact_on_Gaza_and_Historical_Bombings_Lessons_from_Hiroshima_Nagasaki_and_Dresden (accessed March 25, 2025).

Yuval-Davis, N. (2011), *The Politics of Belonging: Intersectional Contestations*, Sage.

Zibechi, R. (2012), *Territories in Resistance: A Cartography of Latin American Social Movements*, AK Press.

Zuboff, S. (2019), *The Age of Surveillance Capitalism: The Fight for a Human Future at the New Frontier of Power*, PublicAffairs.

Index

www.ingramcontent.com/pod-product-compliance
Ingram Content Group UK Ltd.
Pitfield, Milton Keynes, MK11 3LW, UK
UKHW020015230926
475877UK00001B/20

9 781350 541429